*The Syro-Anatolian City-States*

OXFORD STUDIES IN THE ARCHAEOLOGY OF ANCIENT STATES

*Series Editors*

Friederike Fless, Li Liu, Deborah L. Nichols, and D. T. Potts

*The Origins of Ancient Vietnam*

NAM KIM

*Urbanization and Religion in Ancient Central Mexico*

DAVID M. CARBALLO

*The Ancient Highlands of Southwest China: From the Bronze Age to the Han Empire*

ALICE YAO

*The Syro-Anatolian City-States: An Iron Age Culture*

JAMES F. OSBORNE

∴

OXFORD STUDIES IN THE ARCHAEOLOGY OF ANCIENT STATES

# The Syro-Anatolian City-States

## *An Iron Age Culture*

JAMES F. OSBORNE

OXFORD
UNIVERSITY PRESS

# OXFORD

UNIVERSITY PRESS

Oxford University Press is a department of the University of Oxford. It furthers
the University's objective of excellence in research, scholarship, and education
by publishing worldwide. Oxford is a registered trade mark of Oxford University
Press in the UK and certain other countries.

Published in the United States of America by Oxford University Press
198 Madison Avenue, New York, NY 10016, United States of America.

Library of Congress Cataloging-in-Publication Data
Names: Osborne, James F. (Archaeologist), author.
Title: The Syro-Anatolian city-states : an Iron age culture /
James F. Osborne.
Other titles: Syro-Anatolian culture complex
Description: New York : Oxford University Press, [2021] |
Series: Oxford studies in the archaeology of ancient states |
Includes bibliographical references and index.
Identifiers: LCCN 2020025845 (print) | LCCN 2020025846 (ebook) |
ISBN 9780199315833 (hardback) | ISBN 9780197545782 (epub) |
Subjects: LCSH: Syria—Antiquities. | Turkey—Antiquities. |
Iron age—Syria. | Iron age—Turkey. | Syria—History—To 333 B.C. |
Turkey—History—To 1453. | Mediterranean Region—Antiquities.
Classification: LCC DS94.5 .O83 2021 (print) | LCC DS94.5 (ebook) |
DDC 939.4/202—dc23
LC record available at https://lccn.loc.gov/2020025845
LC ebook record available at https://lccn.loc.gov/2020025846

DOI: 10.1093/oso/9780199315833.001.0001

1 3 5 7 9 8 6 4 2

Printed by Sheridan Books, Inc., United States of America

*For my mother, Grace*

# CONTENTS

# ACKNOWLEDGMENTS

THIS BOOK ON WHAT I LIKE to call the "Syro-Anatolian Culture Complex" has its origins in a graduate seminar co-taught by Peter Machinist and the late Lawrence Stager, my doctoral advisor, in Harvard University's Department of Near Eastern Languages and Civilizations. The subject was the history and archaeology of the Aramaeans, which inevitably led to discussions of a host of issues, including the confusing appearance of non-Aramaic inscriptions in ostensibly Aramaean cities, the influence of the Neo-Assyrian Empire on Syro-Anatolian culture, and a host of other themes that are addressed here. My interest in the Iron Age of southeast Anatolia and northern Syria and its diverse populations was piqued and led me to do my doctoral dissertation based on fieldwork at the site of Tell Tayinat, ancient Kunulua. That research, and the publications that came out of it, convinced me that scholarship on this time and place would profit from a more synthetic treatment that characterizes the Syro-Anatolian world in broad strokes and offers a model to explain its diverse properties. This book attempts to be such a treatment.

In the process of writing this book, I have been the extremely fortunate recipient of help, encouragement, and financial support from a true host of people and institutions. The ideas presented here were germinating during the several years I spent as a postdoctoral fellow, first at SUNY Buffalo's Institute for European and Mediterranean Archaeology, directed by Peter Biehl; then as a Mellon Postdoctoral Fellow in the Humanities at Johns Hopkins University under Gabrielle Spiegel, and hosted by the Near Eastern Studies Department then chaired by Glenn Swartz; and finally at Brown University's Joukowsky Institute for Archaeology and the Ancient

World, then directed by Susan Alcock. I could not have asked for better places to sojourn as a junior scholar.

It has been a true pleasure to have been at the University of Chicago's Oriental Institute (OI) and Department of Near Eastern Languages and Civilizations since 2015. I am deeply grateful to OI directors Gil Stein and Christopher Woods for their constant support and interest in my work, as well as welcoming me to the extraordinary intellectual community of the OI. While I have benefited tremendously from discussions with all of my colleagues, I am particularly grateful to Petra Goedegebuure, Theo van den Hout, and David Schloen for their willingness to talk about the Syro-Anatolian world. The same applies to my colleague, friend, and fellow Iron Age aficionado Catherine Kearns in the Department of Classics.

Although this book is not based directly on the results of a single excavation project, the site of Tell Tayinat features prominently in its pages thanks to my participation in the Tayinat Archaeological Project from 2005 to 2016. I will forever be grateful to TAP director Timothy Harrison for his encouragement of my studies as an undergraduate at the University of Toronto and for the generous freedom he provided for my research at Tayinat while I was a graduate student and postdoc. I am an archaeologist today thanks to him more than any other person. Chapter 4 includes results generated by fieldwork I have begun only recently, the Türkmen-Karahöyük Intensive Survey Project, and I am extremely thankful to the co-directors of the Konya Regional Archaeological Survey Project, Michele Massa and Christoph Bachhuber, for inviting me to join their team and conduct this work under their survey permit.

The bulk of the manuscript for this volume was written while I was a fellow at the University of Chicago's Franke Institute for the Humanities, whose financial support not only permitted an entire year of research leave, but whose weekly gatherings provided a robust forum of intellectual exchange and critique with scholars across the Humanities Division. I thank the institute's interim director Françoise Meltzer for facilitating my most productive period of writing. Tony Lauricella, interim director of the OI's Center for Ancient Middle Eastern Landscapes, supervised helpfully a team that digitized a number of archaeological surveys discussed in Chapter 2. At Oxford University Press I have been blessed by the patience of my editor Stefan Vranka and by the entire OUP team who continued shepherding the manuscript through to production despite the upheavals of the 2020 pandemic. Two peer reviewers provided enormously helpful feedback that benefited the manuscript greatly. In addition to their efforts, I thank those who volunteered their own time to read parts of the book as a personal favor, including Lorenzo d'Alfonso, Marian Feldman, Carolina López-Ruiz, Mirko Novák, and Mark Weeden. Kathryn Morgan deserves special thanks for reading through an entire draft. I am indebted to all of these friends and colleagues.

None of this would have been possible at all were it not for the unwavering support of my family. My mother and father, Grace and Ron, have always done everything in their power to help me reach this point. My daughters Lucy and Anne have been a constant source of joy. And I will be eternally grateful for the love and counsel of my wife Jen, and for the sacrifices she has made on my behalf.

## CHAPTER 1

# INTRODUCTION

## *History and Historiography of the Syro-Anatolian Culture Complex*

LIKE OTHER SUBJECTS, ANCIENT CIVILIZATIONS have their trends, waxing and waning in attention and readership as custom or fashion dictates. The Assyrians of Nimrud, Khorsabad, and Nineveh were the blockbuster hit of the mid- to late nineteenth century (Larsen 1996). The closest Near Eastern parallel today might be the ancient Israelites, whose authorship of the Hebrew Bible assures them a modern relevance. Sandwiched geographically between these two Near Eastern titans of modern reception was a culture that has only rarely penetrated the popular imagination. Not powerful enough in ancient times to create the spectacular imperial art of the Neo-Assyrian Empire, and not favored by the whims of history to have preserved an influential religious text, this culture is largely ignored in the popular imagination and treated only sporadically by mainstream ancient Near Eastern scholarship. Indeed, there is not even consensus on what the most appropriate term is to label them. The goal of this book is to paint a picture of a society whose overall portrait has never been drawn, a society I refer to as the "Syro-Anatolian Culture Complex" (SACC).

This group consisted of roughly a dozen small kingdoms surrounding the northeast corner of the Mediterranean Sea from the start of the Iron Age (ca. 1200 BCE) until the conquests of the Neo-Assyrian Empire in the late eighth century. The Syro-Anatolian city-states received attention in the late nineteenth and early twentieth century as colonial field projects launched massive excavations at their capital cities, all of which will feature prominently in the pages that follow: the Americans at Tell Tayinat, the French at Arslantepe and Tell Ahmar, the English at Carchemish and Tell Rifa'at, the Germans at Tell Halaf and Zincirli, the Danish at Hamath.

*The Syro-Anatolian City-States*. James F. Osborne, Oxford University Press (2021). © Oxford University Press.
DOI: 10.1093/oso/9780199315833.003.0001.

Following several decades of archaeological neglect, the past twenty years or so have witnessed a renewed flurry of excavation projects not only at the capital cities, but occasionally secondary and tertiary towns and villages as well. SACC is waxing again, and, as this book aims to demonstrate, this development has the capacity to transform our understanding of the Near East during the Iron Age.

There remains no synthetic overview of the Syro-Anatolian city-states that integrates what is known from archaeological, art historical, and textual sources. Several monograph-length studies have begun appearing that deal directly with the time and place in question in novel theoretical ways, yet these have been concerned with specific themes such as urbanism and landscape (Harmanşah 2013), monumental art and architecture (Gilibert 2011; Pucci 2008a), and craft specialization (Feldman 2014). There are two principal reasons why a volume of this kind does not yet exist, the first being the phenomenon already mentioned: the historical coincidence of the Syro-Anatolian city-states having been contemporaries of ancient Israel and the Neo-Assyrian Empire, both juggernauts in their own way. Wedged between these two groups both geographically and intellectually, the Syro-Anatolian city-states are often treated as an academic afterthought, kingdoms whose archaeological and historical records are significant primarily with respect to how their remains illuminate the history and social structure of their neighbors.

The other reason lies in the social and political world order of modern scholarship. Archaeological remains of the Syro-Anatolian polities straddle inconveniently the political border that is today shared by Turkey and Syria. This divide has often had the effect of restricting archaeologists' research purviews to one country or the other, and it has also scattered archaeological material across multifarious museums and universities. The problem is illustrated well by the current authoritative archaeological textbooks of the two countries in question, *The Archaeology of Syria* (Akkermans and Schwartz 2003) and *Ancient Turkey* (Sagona and Zimansky 2009), both of which understandably give only passing mention to Syro-Anatolian remains of the neighboring country. The result is that SACC is given short shrift, or worse, the misleading impression that a large and dynamic cultural complex did not exist. In addition, research into the Syro-Anatolian city-states is characterized by an intellectual landscape that is balkanized into tightly focused specialties of political history (Bryce 2003, 2012; Dion 1997; Hawkins 1982; Lipiński 2000; Sader 1987), epigraphy (Abou Assaf et al. 1982; Çambel 1999; Donner and Röllig 1966; Gibson 1975, 1982; Hallo and Younger 2003; Hawkins 2000; Tropper 1993), iconographic analyses (Bonatz 2000; Genge 1979; Kohlmeyer 2008; van Loon 1991; Orthmann 1971, 2002; Özyar 1991, 2003; Winter 1973, 1976b, 1976a, 1979), site morphology and urban trajectory (Brown 2008b; Casana and Herrmann 2010; Mazzoni 1994, 1995, 2000a; Pucci 2008a), and specific material studies (Bunnens 2000b; Hausleiter and Reiche 1999).

*The Syro-Anatolian City-States* aims to provide the reader with a more complete picture of these polities. It is not a chronologically organized textbook of material culture, however, with chapters on diachronic patterns in burials, ceramics, architecture, and so on. Nor does the volume move through the various city-states one by one, presenting and summarizing the literary and archaeological evidence that exists pertinent to that kingdom, though all of them are mentioned at various points. Instead, this volume offers readers a fuller awareness of this time and place through a series of thematic essays, each using archaeological, historical, and iconographic lines of evidence from multiple sites. In a sense, this book represents an answer to Bryce's (2012: 5–6) call for a comprehensive account of Syro-Anatolian material and iconographic achievements "within the context of a more broadly based presentation of social and cultural developments." The topics to which I devote attention in the chapters that follow include identity formation that accompanied diasporic processes at the onset of the Iron Age; the politics of movement as a framework for recasting static notions of the city-state system; hybridity and interregional interaction with the Assyrian imperial superpower; and concepts of space and power in their buildings, cities, and landscapes. These themes are, I hope, diverse enough, and require broad enough evidentiary exposition, that by the end the reader is left with a relatively complete understanding of the composition of SACC, as well as our archaeological, historical, and iconographic evidential corpora.

The volume's thematic structure does not mean the book is without a unifying argument, however. One proposal that links all of the essays contained here is the notion that these kingdoms were very much at the center of the ancient Near East during the Iron Age—economically, politically, culturally—despite the impressions to the contrary given by the hegemony of the Neo-Assyrian Empire in ancient sources and the sheer volume of scholarship on ancient Israel and Judah in modern ones. The Syro-Anatolian city-states may have been a periphery to the Assyrian scribes and to the biblical writers, but they were nevertheless a primary driving force in the Near East, especially during their heyday of the early first millennium BCE. Imbalanced geopolitical relationships, especially in their dealings with the Assyrians, were of course an undeniable reality. But it was nevertheless a full two centuries from the reign of Ashur-dan II (r. 934–912) to Sargon II (r. 721–705) before most of SACC was completely conquered, and in the meantime they would have a profound impact on Assyrian life, as well as on other neighboring cultures.

The idea that these kingdoms were as important in their day as their neighbors leads directly to the book's second overarching argument: the Syro-Anatolian city-states can and should be considered a coherent and recognizable, if variegated and ever-changing, archaeological and historical culture, the many particular features and circumstances unique to each polity notwithstanding. *The Syro-Anatolian City-States* shows that a broad similarity in material culture and historical records across the region belies the assumption that differences in the parts are greater than similarities in the whole, and that despite real and undeniable differences between them, these polities constituted a relatively homogeneous cultural and political phenomenon that spanned linguistic and political borders.

A recurring theme throughout the volume is the notion that our tacitly accepted model for understanding these kingdoms—the contemporary nation-state—is empirically inappropriate. Although there are a number of exceptions that appear in the pages that follow, with little explicit modeling of sociopolitical dynamics in scholarly literature, the nation-state has been offered as the inevitable Iron Age social arrangement, so ordinary and expected that critical treatment rarely arises. Sociologists Andreas Wimmer and Nina Glick Schiller (2002) refer to this phenomenon as "methodological nationalism," or an intellectual orientation that sees the nation-state as the fundamental unit of analysis and assumes that the nation-state's association of polity, territory, and ethnicity is the natural sociopolitical order. Methodological nationalism pervades disciplines across the social sciences and humanities, and Iron Age Near Eastern studies is no exception. Yet with language communities that spanned multiple kingdoms, with individual city-states occupied by multiple cultural groups, and with concepts of political space that do not correspond to contemporary political sovereignty, SACC is not the right subject with which to apply associations of state and ethnolinguistic categories onto the past. Instead of the nation-state, therefore, we need to look to new intellectual inspirations for understanding the Syro-Anatolian kingdoms in ways that are flexible enough for us to identify their shared values and behaviors even while still recognizing their tremendous diversity. For this reason, the case studies that appear in the following chapters are in dialogue with social theory drawn primarily from postcolonial and related literature of the 1990s and early 2000s, including diaspora studies, hybridity, Middle Ground encounters, and cultural mobility. All of these concepts share an emphasis on cultural and political fluidity and are thus ideal vehicles with which to de-essentialize our reconstructions of Syro-Anatolian social dynamics.

Before launching into the geographical, historical, and chronological background with which this introductory chapter will close, let us unpack in greater detail some of the issues already raised in order to provide a better sense of the chapters to come.

::::

## The Syro-Anatolian Culture Complex: Key Terms
### Syro-Anatolian

Nowhere is terminology as vexing an issue in Near Eastern archaeology as it is with the terms scholars have used to describe the cluster of Iron Age city-states in south-central and southeastern Anatolia, the northern Levant, and northern Mesopotamia. The primary reason for the terminological proliferation has been the complicated linguistic scenario of the area during the Iron Age. The inhabitants of these kingdoms spoke (at least) three different languages—Luwian, Aramaean, and Phoenician—which were written with vastly differing hieroglyphic (Luwian) and alphabetic (Aramaean and Phoenician) scripts (Gzella 2014; Hawkins 2003; Huehnergard 1995). Indeed, the fact that Luwian and Aramaic/Phoenician languages belong to different language families (Indo-European and Semitic, respectively), combined with their radically different writing systems, has resulted in scholarly specialties that scarcely overlap. Instead, researchers have treated separately the speakers—or, more accurately, the writers—of Aramaic (Dion 1997; Lipiński 2000; Niehr 2014; Sader 1987; Younger 2016) and Luwian (Hawkins 2000; Melchert 2003; Yakubovich 2011). This disciplinary legacy is not inherently problematic, but the resulting intellectual landscape leaves one to assume a priori that Aramaean and Luwian speakers did not both belong to the same cultural system (Gilibert 2011: 9–10).

To take one representative example, the city-state of Bit-Adini, centered around the archaeological site of Tell Aḥmar on the Euphrates River, has long plagued scholars attempting to reconstruct its ethnic constitution and development due to apparently conflicting historical and archaeological evidence, including multiple names for the capital city, Luwian Masuwari and Aramaic Til Barsip (Bunnens 1995; Ussishkin 1971). As Lipiński states, "The basic problem of the history of Bēt-'Adini is the obvious discrepancy between the Neo-Assyrian annalistic sources of the 9th century B.C., referring to an Aramaean tribal state the main stronghold of which was Til-Barsip, and the excavated remains of the ancient town at Tell Aḥmar, which are definitely Neo-Hittite in the very same period" (2000: 183). But this is only a problem if one assumes that a "discrepancy" between historical and archaeological sources necessarily implies a need to reconcile the apparent existence of two social groups (cf. Dalley 2000). If instead we were to allow the possibility that a single social formation can contain multiple ethnolinguistic elements simultaneously, then the discrepancy dissolves. One of the main arguments of this book is that scholars could profit from seeing these two linguistic groups as participating in a common, if variable and fluctuating, cultural phenomenon, unlike Liverani, for example, who refers to the Aramaeans and Luwians as "very different languages *and cultures*" (2014: 434, emphasis added).

Scholars will frequently take the additional step of assigning the terms "Luwian" and "Aramaean" to the polities themselves, such that those kingdoms with a greater number of Aramaic inscriptions, or with an Aramaic title, become "Aramaean" kingdoms (Sader 2000; Younger 2016), while those with a greater number of Luwian inscriptions, or with a Luwian title, become "Luwian" or "Neo-Hittite" kingdoms (Bryce 2012; Giusfredi 2010; Hawkins 1982; Thuesen 2002), the latter on account of Luwian's linguistic and historical relationship with the Hittite language. A related version of this title is "Late Hittite," German *späthethitisch* (Akurgal 1949; Güterbock 1954: 114; Orthmann 1971), referring to the continuity of other Hittite cultural traits besides language. But the relationship between language and social identity is by no means clear, especially given the fact that the overwhelming majority of the inscriptions available to us were written by elite, usually even royal, actors, who in some instances may have identified themselves as belonging to different ethnic groups than the populace.

Archaeologists and art historians, who are traditionally sensitive to the material and cultural links between neighboring city-states and thus recognize the need to avoid essentializing ethnic labels, will occasionally use the term "North Syrian" as a neutral geographic expression (Brown 2008b; Winter 1982, 1988), which is not ideal given how many of the pertinent sites are not in Syria. The label that is most commonly used by such scholars, however, is "Syro-Hittite," by which is meant a combination of the Luwian-speaking Neo-Hittite city-states and the Aramaic-speaking Aramaean city-states, and especially the particular combination that arose when local urban dynasties in Syria adopted rhetorical and visual modes of expression borrowed from the preceding Hittite Empire in Anatolia (Bonatz 2000: 4; Gilibert 2011: 9–10; Harmanşah 2013; Herrmann 2017b: 238; 2017a: 286–87; Mazzoni 1997, 2001, 2010; Pucci 2008a; Ussishkin 1970). Perfectly illustrating the terminological predicament described here, in David Hawkins's (1982) historical overview for *The Cambridge Ancient History*, these polities are referred to as "Neo-Hittite," but in the accompanying plates that appeared two years later (1984) they are now titled "Syro-Hittite." The appeal of "Syro-Hittite" is its inclusivity, its recognition of the fact that all of these polities can legitimately be considered together for various reasons. Its principal drawbacks, however, are numerous. For one thing, not all of the kingdoms that one would typically consider to be members possess demonstrated affinities with the Hittites (Tell Halaf/Gozan, for example). For another, the two elements of the compound phrase are not analogous: the first is geographic, the second, cultural—and, of course, not all of these polities lie within modern Syria. There is also the inconvenient fact that "Syro-Hittite" is already used in other ancient Near Eastern contexts, such as certain Late Bronze Age cuneiform traditions and sealing practices at Emar (e.g., Beyer 2001: 19–164; Cohen 2009).[1] But the most fundamental issue is a methodological one: the phrase involves a tacit assumption that Iron Age cultural expressions are only emulations of predecessors or legitimizing claims underwritten by past glories, and not the product of genuinely felt identity. That identity is predetermined as a given by the phrase "Syro-Hittite," such that historical processes of identity formation are presented as already understood and beyond the need of further examination.[2]

More accurate, perhaps, is Novák's (e.g., 2018: 259) "Luwo-Aramaean," which sounds peculiar but, by making both elements cultural in nature, is internally consistent. More compelling still is "Syro-Anatolian," which is beginning to gain traction (Gilibert 2011: 1 and passim) and is also internally consistent by using geography in both cases. A geographically oriented expression is also preferable insofar as analysis does not begin with prior assumptions of cultural mechanisms (e.g., emulation) already present. Such an approach is adopted by Feldman (2014: 3–4), who refers to early first-millennium ivories as having been produced in the "greater Levant," a deliberately blurry category that encompasses Israel and Jordan north to Cilicia and east to the Euphrates. Although I agree with the principle that unambiguous boundaries between social groups will forever remain elusive, "Levant" is perhaps too inclusive of the distinct kingdoms of Israel and Judah and their Transjordan contemporaries to be considered part and parcel of the cultural unit to their north, parallels notwithstanding. At the same time, other kingdoms that *do* belong would then be excluded, such as Malatya, which lay on the north side of the Taurus Mountain range, and Tell Halaf/Gozan, which lay some 175 km east of the Euphrates, not to mention the Tabalian kingdoms in Cappadocia and the Konya Plain.

For all of these reasons, this book employs consistently the term "Syro-Anatolian" to refer to the Iron Age city-states of the northeast Mediterranean. From this expression follows the argument that language be considered only one of many variables of cultural expression, and that we would do well to consider the full gamut. Like Feldman, I recognize that no clear edge delimiting inclusion and exclusion can, or should, be identified by the researcher for both methodological and theoretical reasons. Indeed, it is in the numerous exceptions to geographically conceived cultural zones that problems of interpretations are raised—and when solved, are revealed to be not problems so much as signposts leading us toward a greater understanding of ancient social dynamics.

## Culture

As mentioned, one of the core arguments sustained throughout the following chapters is that these city-states do belong to a recognizably consistent cultural group. But what did this cultural identity consist of, and how was it created and maintained? Beginning with an awareness that identity is a process that is constantly being renegotiated in time and space (Barth 1969; Jones 1997), the book's thematic chapters explore some of the ways in which Syro-Anatolian cultural identity was expressed, while still leaving room to consider the significance of chronological and regional variance. In this way, we are able to isolate recurring patterns in Syro-Anatolian identity, but also to avoid the trap of artificially creating a bounded and reified monolithic entity that fails to incorporate the subtlety and complexity of the archaeological and historical record. Participation in the Syro-Anatolian cultural sphere is evaluated in terms of broadly shared involvement in historical events, similar ideational concepts, and a widely distributed assemblage of archaeological features, including architectural form, ceramics, statuary and other so-called major arts, the visual iconography of small decorated objects, site morphology, mortuary patterns, and religious monuments. No single site possesses all of these traits, but all of them do exist in various permutations and combinations at Iron Age sites from Cilicia to the Khabur, and from the Taurus Mountains to the upper Orontes River.

To a certain extent this is a normative approach to culture (Lyman and O'Brien 2004), seeing in our subjects a shared collections of ideas and behaviors, notwithstanding the heavy criticism this concept received during the heyday of the New Archaeology on account of its excessive descriptive emphasis at the expense of explanation (e.g., Binford 1965). A more substantial critique is the recognition that culture is never a single, homogenous field in which all members participate in the same way (Clifford and Marcus 1986). Without this realization it becomes easy to slip into assumptions equating spatial variation in material culture with ethnicity, and from there to marshal these putative ancient ethnic groups toward contemporary political legitimacy (Shennan 1989: 5–14). On the contrary, throughout the field of culture lie cracks and fissures in which one finds the exploitation of marginalized members of society, subaltern cultural expressions, gender and class dynamics, and a host of other potentially radical challenges to generalizing cultural norms. Nevertheless, as William H. Sewell Jr. (1999) has argued, even though cultures may be contradictory, loosely integrated, contested, subject to change, and weakly bounded, the dialectic between meaningful symbols and human practices in particular times and places creates a thin but real coherence that is discernible to the analyst. As Sewell puts it,

[I]n spite of conflicts and resistance these worlds of meaning somehow hang together. Whether we call these partially coherent landscapes of meaning "cultures" or something else—worlds of meaning, or ethnoscapes, or hegemonies—seems to me relatively unimportant so long as we know that their boundedness is only relative and constantly shifting. Our job as cultural analysts is to discern what the shapes and consistencies of local meanings actually are, and to determine how, why, and to what extent they hang together. (1999: 58)

It is therefore imperative that, in our urge to identify material and ideational patterns held in common across the Syro-Anatolian city-states, we also acknowledge differences and take seriously the cultural processes lying in those fissures, otherwise all too easy to ignore.

Here I propose that we refer to this time and place as the "Syro-Anatolian Culture Complex," or SACC. I borrow the idea from Americanist archaeology's Southeastern Ceremonial Complex, the suite of shared artifacts, iconography, and mythology of the mound-building Mississippian cultures in the United States (Waring and Holder 1945).[3] Today the Southeastern Ceremonial Complex is recognized not just for its broad commonalities, but also for its distinct regional manifestations and patterns, even while a transregional thematic unity undeniably exists (Knight et al. 2001). The expression is an apposite one for the northeastern Mediterranean during the early first millennium, and not just by virtue of the use of geography for its principle of delimitation, as mentioned earlier. Referring to these kingdoms as participants in a cultural complex recognizes their shared heritage and material expressions, while still allowing space for local variations and historical contingencies; their culture was, after all, *complex*. In short, SACC permits us the flexibility to identify patterns as well as acknowledge difference.

## *City-States*

Closely related to the problem of how to address the Syro-Anatolian kingdoms as a cultural phenomenon is the issue of how we categorize them in a political typology: just what type of political entity were they exactly and what term should be used to label that entity? Perhaps the simplest option would simply be to call them "states," by which is usually meant a discrete community of individuals—real or imagined (Anderson 1983)—that is possessed of an unbalanced distribution of power that is justified and protected by violence, or the threat of violence, wielded legitimately only by the state itself (Weber 1965). Without getting into the vast literature on the archaeology of the state (see Routledge 2014), we are able to be more precise in our terms. I consider the Syro-Anatolian kingdoms to be strong examples of "city-states." Unfortunately, this phrase involves its own terminological dispute, with several archaeologists questioning whether the term has any value in a cross-cultural perspective. The need to define one's usage of it is indicated, for example, by one Near Eastern archaeologist rejecting its application to the upper Euphrates in the Early Bronze Age because the region was organized "heterarchically" (Cooper 2006: 61), while another scholar uses heterarchical social structure as the primary feature indicating that her research area *did* consist of city-states (Stone 1997).

Many scholars agree that the city-state is a global phenomenon that, despite local variances in each particular case, has structural features consistent across many different areas (Hansen 2000a; Mann 1986; Trigger 2003). Indeed, several works now exist that demonstrate the cross-cultural utility of the concept in multifarious global contexts (Griffeth and Thomas 1981; Hansen 2000b; Nichols and Charlton 1997), including an entry on the Syro-Anatolian city-states (under "Neo-Hittite") in one of these wide-ranging comparisons (Thuesen 2002).

The city-state concept has its origin in the study of Classical antiquity, where it was first coined in the nineteenth century (Fowler 1893). The expression is particularly apt in classical Greece, where the term *polis* is used interchangeably to mean both "city" and "polity," depending on context (Finley 1981, 1987/89). Since that time the city-state concept has expanded in use geographically, and it has been defined more recently as

> small, territorially based, politically independent state systems, characterized by a capital city or town, with an economically and socially integrated adjacent hinterland. The whole unit, city plus hinterlands, is relatively self-sufficient economically and perceived as being ethnically distinct from other similar city-state systems. City-states frequently, but not inevitably, occur in groups of fairly evenly spaced units of approximately equivalent size. (Charlton and Nichols 1997: 1; see also Hansen 2000a)

Not all aspects of this definition are applicable in our case; the assumption that city-states are traditionally territorial entities, for example (see also Trigger 2003: 94), is not accurate for SACC if my model of SACC's "malleable territoriality" is correct (see Chapter 5). But for the most part it is a helpful term, particularly with regard to their relatively small scale, the significance of a single city center that dominates the rest of the settlement pattern within the city-state, and participation in a political system involving multiple neighboring polities of the same basic composition, that is, a system not dissimilar from Colin Renfrew's peer–polity interaction model (Renfrew and Cherry 1986).

The most vocal critic of the city-state has been Joyce Marcus, who has leveled several arguments against the concept. Initially her criticism was that the city-state as an archaeological construct was invalid because it originated in Classical scholarship, partially (it would seem) because nothing of anthropological value can originate in the Classics, and partially because "polities all over the world to which the term has been applied do not resemble the Greek polis" (Feinman and Marcus 1998: 8). Of course, one need not argue that for a given polity to be a city-state it must resemble the Greek *polis*; scholars today consider Classical Greece as but one example of a much broader phenomenon, not the measuring stick against which all other similarly structured cultures are to be compared.[4] More recently, Marcus argues that the concept is invalid because "There is growing evidence that many of the city-states were created by the breakup of earlier large states" (Marcus and

Sabloff 2008: 23). The collapse of the Hittite Empire, for example, is certainly one factor (of several) in the rise of SACC (see Chapter 2) (e.g., Denel 2006; Thuesen 2002). But even when this is the case it is unclear why this criticism does anything more to the city-state concept than provide us with the circumstances for under-standing its origins.

A more subtle argument has been raised by Mesoamerican archaeologist George Cowgill, who says that there is little difference between "city-state" and "little state," implying that the term therefore has little productive value (2004: 527). This is a valid point, but size is not all that matters. One of the crucial features of the city-state concept is its recognition that these polities generally occur in groups of neighboring, similarly structured polities. This is why the comparatively isolated Teotihuacan can be characterized as a "small state," but the numerous polities in the Basin of Mexico that were subsumed by the Aztec Empire should be considered "city-states," for example (Smith 2008). It is the dense concentration of several polities in a constricted geographical area that facilitates their high degree of peer-polity interaction that is not attested in isolated polities. Furthermore, the expres-sion emphasizes appropriately the capital city, whose political importance increases inversely with the smaller size of the polity's areal extent. As Herrmann (2017a: 287) has aptly described the urban situation in the Syro-Anatolian context, these capital cities "were not only the royal seat and stronghold, but also became the centre of the kingdom's population and economic life." SACC's capitals, in other words, were both the symbolic and economic center of the polity. For all of these reasons this book refers to the political entities that made up SACC as "city-states," occasionally using "kingdom" or "polity" in a more or less synonymous fashion.

## Synchrony and Diachrony

In his seminal work *Ancient Mesopotamia: Portrait of a Dead Civilization*, Assyriologist Leo Oppenheim began his preface evoking the metaphor of the painting by way of explaining his text's rhetorical format: "A portrait aims at presenting an individual, not completely but in his uniqueness, and not only at a fleeting moment of time but also at that juncture where past experience encounters future expectation," noting further that because a faithful portrait of an ancient subject can never be properly rendered, the notion is more of an incentive than an end (1964: 1–2). He carries the metaphor further, likening accumulating chapters to a single work of art with the superimposed layers of paint that are necessary to create a finished product (1964: 3). But since there is no single portrait whose exam-ination provides the viewer with a complete understanding of the subject, what this book offers are multiple different viewpoints on the same subject that, after sev-eral angles have been observed, give the viewer something approaching a holistic comprehension. The historian R. G. Collingwood captures the approach employed here, noting how these multiple viewpoints contribute cumulatively to establish an ancient reality in the contemporary imagination:

> The idea of philosophy as a complete whole, to be turned this way and that in order to contemplate it from different angles, is so far misleading that it never is complete; we turn it this way and that not in order to contemplate the perfections of a finished article, but in order to continue the work of bringing it into existence. (1946: 351)

And by virtue of a portrait's ability to be apprehended visually in an almost immediate manner, we are also led to consider how best to appreciate the temporal aspect of our subject matter. As the portrait presents its subject frozen in a single moment of time, so *The Syro-Anatolian City-States* provides the reader with a predominantly synchronic vision of these polities, though of course historical considerations are always present. Such an approach is uncommon in archaeology, a discipline that rightly prides itself on its ability to trace change over time. Indeed, works such as the one offered here are made possible only by the context provided by advancements made in diachronic research; one might say that in archaeology, "vertical" research is analytically prior to "horizontal" studies such as this. But despite archaeology's diachronic analytical priority, it is through synchronic analysis—not really a "snapshot" or "slice of time" so much as a collapsing of the flow of time into a uniform, coexisting moment (Sewell 1997: 40)—that we are best suited to understand a culture based on its own categories of representation.

There are a number of dangers inherent in emphasizing the synchronic, however, not least of which is that, even within the span of a few hundred years—a brief stretch by the standards of archaeology—there is ample time for cultural processes to change significantly. This is a problem of resolution. Archaeology is prone to miss the potentially meaningful distinctions between, say, two neighboring buildings that were built at the same time, and two built a year apart from one another, and is thus quite likely not to notice the real interpretive dissimilarities of the two scenarios. The result is an inevitable telescoping of multiple different times and events into a single moment, a collapsing that is not only interpretively misleading, but also empirically inaccurate. No matter how advanced our methods become this problem will never go away entirely; it will always be possible to better understand the archaeological sequence that comprises a site, and the excavations of earlier generations will forever be at an additional disadvantage. All that can be done is to assess the evidence at hand and make the best chronological and stratigraphic conclusions possible with the material available.

Another, perhaps more pernicious, danger of concentrating on synchrony is the removal of one's subject matter from its historical context. All events are at least partially determined by events that preceded them, and thus a historical awareness must always be maintained. For exactly that reason, this book outlines the environmental and historical background of the Syro-Anatolian city-states in the next section of this chapter, describing in detail both the nature of our historical sources as well as evaluating the various chronological reconstructions of the region scholars have deployed. Likewise, Chapter 2 spends considerable energy interpreting the origins of SACC over time through the lens of diaspora.

Ultimately, however, the primary emphasis here is on the faithful reconstruction of SACC in horizontal terms. Again I turn to William H. Sewell Jr. (1997: 42), who noted that historians operate under a tacit understanding that, although diachrony may be historians' bread and butter, good analysis of the past inevitably involves a certain amount of synchrony. To do anything else is merely to reconstruct "what actually happened"—a worthwhile and necessary step perhaps, but uninteresting as a research agenda. This is not to say that transformations are unimportant, but that the historian can only understand transformation through a dialectical tacking between both diachronic and synchronic approaches: "Unless we can represent to ourselves and our readers the *form* of life in one historical moment or era, unless we can describe systematically the interlocking meanings and practices that give it a particular character, how are we to explain its *trans*formation—or, for that matter, even to recognize when and how it has been transformed?" (Sewell 2005: 185, emphasis in original). This book can thus be considered a study of the "particular character" of Syro-Anatolian cultural life.

What, then, are the portraits presented in this book, the views of our subject intended to provide a holistic understanding of SACC? The next chapter examines SACC's origins during the Iron Age I (ca. 1200–950 BCE), a period characterized by a tumultuous historical context that involved, among other things, movement of people. During the Iron Age I, the northeast corner of the Mediterranean slowly recovered from the collapse of the large-scale regional powers that had dominated the area during the preceding Late Bronze Age. Most of what eventually became the Syro-Anatolian city-states had previously been provinces of the Hittite or Mittani Empires, and once those had disintegrated it took many decades for most of the kingdoms to establish themselves fully as independent polities, a process that was complicated by the influx of foreign populations. The process did not take place evenly across the region, however, and some kingdoms show greater evidence for Bronze–Iron Age continuity than others. Here is where diaspora studies provides a strong case for understanding the formation of new cultural identities that are wrought by movement, identities that do not overlap easily with political cartographies.

Chapter 3 extends a similar line of reasoning into the Iron Age II (ca. 950–700 BCE), the period during which the Syro-Anatolian city states were fully ensconced as independent participants in regional dynamics. I argue that one of the intellectual consequences of a tacit nation-state model has been an excessive emphasis on stability and stasis, and that Iron Age scholarship would benefit from considerations of movement and cultural mobility. Even if actual movements of populations were taking place at a smaller scale in this period, mobility still characterized the Iron Age state, sometimes in counterintuitive places. One example is the consistent discovery of monumental reliefs in archaeological contexts that are not where they were originally installed, leading us to conclude that mobility was a defining feature of architectural elaboration.

Chapter 4 considers the relationship between SACC and its imperial neighbor in northern Mesopotamia, for of course the two had close cultural and economic relationships long before the Neo-Assyrian Empire absorbed SACC into its provincial apparatus. In this chapter I argue that, far from being a straightforward relationship in which SACC played the underling role of passive recipient of cultural influence from the hegemonic metropole, SACC and the Neo-Assyrian Empire in fact existed on an even cultural playing field in which both had profound and lasting influences on the other. In part, this conclusion is illuminated by the concepts of hybridity and Middle Ground interaction, first set in motion in literary studies and history, respectively, but both also increasingly deployed by archaeologists studying processes of cultural contact and empire.

Chapter 5 considers the Syro-Anatolian built environment at multiple scales of analysis. I demonstrate that a study of Syro-Anatolian principles of space and place teaches us a great deal about the political constitution of SACC. Starting at the level of the landscape, historical and archaeological records indicate a principle of regional sovereignty that is best described as "malleable territoriality," in which sovereign power is not distributed evenly across space as per the modern nation-state. Syro-Anatolian urbanism followed a distinct three-tiered hierarchical pattern across the region, and broad similarities of planning and form within the capitals indicates a high degree of urban planning. But more than that, I show how a detailed description of cities' royal inscriptions, monumental architecture, and symbolic statuary reveals that the city was planned not just in formal terms, but as a cumulative meaning-rich symbol of the royal order that was emphasized across the urban fabric. Not representations of the cosmos (sensu Wheatley 1971), these capital cities were instead "strange loops" that emphasized political power at all levels of the spatial hierarchy, saturated with rich symbolic imagery. Few secondary and tertiary settlements from the Syro-Anatolian world have been excavated, but two sites in particular—Çatal Höyük (Haines 1971) and Tell Mastuma (Iwasaki et al. 2009)—serve as strong representatives for each of these settlement tiers, respectively. Although the same principles of urban symbology are not attested in these settlements, their wide horizontal exposures of nonelite architecture allow us to understand patterns of settlement planning and growth across large neighborhoods. In the end, one is left with the impression that SACC really did consist of *city*-states, in the sense that villages and especially towns were more or less autonomous players in the Syro-Anatolian political imaginary.

This thematic organization of *The Syro-Anatolian City-States* allows the reader to enter the book at any point and learn about specific Syro-Anatolian cultural phenomena—diasporic origins, interactions east and west, cultural mobility, and space and place—according to his or her interests. However, the goal is that should one choose to read it from start to end, the result will be something approaching a holistic understanding of this time and place, including the diverse sets of data— archaeological, historical, and iconographic—that we use to analyze it. By the time the reader arrives at the brief concluding Chapter 6, it will hopefully have become apparent that we are justified to speak of SACC as having constituted a real and meaningful social group, one characterized by diasporic origins, cultural mobility, close cultural interaction with its political rivals, and variegated notions of space and power.

But before the volume begins in earnest with these themes, it is necessary to first establish a contextual baseline for SACC, and it is to this task that the remainder of this introductory chapter is dedicated.

::::

# Geographical and Historical Background of the Syro-Anatolian City-States

## *The Geographical Setting*

Despite being relatively small in their geographical extent, the Syro-Anatolian city-states encompassed a diverse environmental setting (Figure 1.1). The northeast corner of the Mediterranean, where SACC was located, marks the meeting point of three tectonic plates—the Arabian, African, and Anatolian—at the Maraş Triple Junction (Chorowicz et al. 1994), resulting in a complicated geological scenario that includes both lowland alluvial valleys as well as upland terrain. These same tectonic forces render the area prone to earthquakes but also provide it with rich mineral wealth in copper, iron, lead, silver, and gold deposits (Sagona and Zimansky 2009: 3). Unlike a number of ancient Near Eastern cultures in the region, whose centers are typically located either in the northern Mesopotamian steppe or the Anatolian highlands, Syro-Anatolian kingdoms are found on both sides of the Taurus Mountain range. This intimidating mountain chain runs east to west between these two geological zones, yet SACC is arguably present on either side.

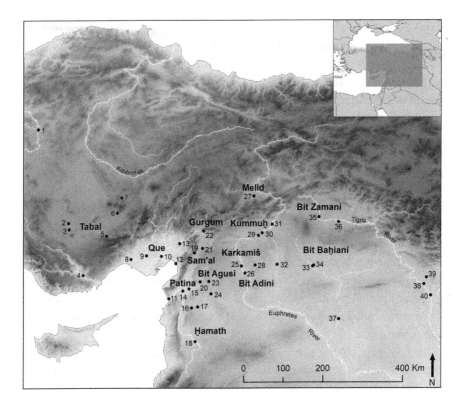

FIGURE 1.1

Map of sites and Syro-Anatolian city-states mentioned throughout the text: (1) Gordion;
(2) Türkmen-Karahöyük; (3) Kızıldağ; (4) Kilise Tepe; (5) Ivriz; (6) Kınık Höyük;
(7) Göllüdağ; (8) Tarsus-Gözlü Kule; (9) Adana-Tepebağ; (10) Sirkeli Höyük; (11) al-Mina;
(12) Kinet Höyük; (13) Karatepe-Aslantaş (Azatiwataya); (14) Tell Tayinat (Kunulua); (15)
Çatal Höyük; (16) Tell Mastuma; (17) Tell Afis (Hazrek); (18) Hama; (19) Zinciril (Sam'al);
(20) 'Ain Dara; (21) Sakçagözü; (22) Marash (Gurgum); (23) Tell Rifa'at (Arpad); (24) Aleppo
(Haleb); (25) Carchemish; (26) Tell Ahmar (Til-Barsip, Masuwari, Kar-Shalmaneser); (27)
Arslantepe (Melid); (28) Arslan Tash (Hadatu); (29) Samsat Höyük (Samsat); (30) Lidar
Höyük; (31) Tille Höyük; (32) Harran; (33) Tell Halaf (Gozan); (34) Tell Fakhariyah; (35)
Diyarbakır (Amedi); (36) Ziyaret Tepe (Tušhan); (37) Tell Sheikh Hamad (Dur-Katlimmu);
(38) Nineveh; (39) Khorsabad (Dur-Sharrukin); (40) Nimrud (Kalḫu).

Indeed, archaeological sites belonging to the Syro-Anatolian city-states have been
identified across at least four of the geographical regions described by Wilkinson
(2003: 17, Fig. 1.2) in his *Archaeological Landscapes of the Near East*, regions
that are supposed to have established the parameters of cultural expression: the
Mediterranean coast, Upper Mesopotamia, Levantine uplands and the adjacent
rift valley, and the Taurus/Amanus Mountains. In the system used by another
recent textbook, SACC would be found in four of Turkey's seven geographical

regions: Mediterranean, Central, Eastern, and Southeastern (Sagona and Zimansky 2009: Fig. 1.1), and at least five of the natural vegetation zones proposed by Van Zeist and Bottema (1991: Fig. 4). SACC, it would seem, defies easy geographical categorization.

As a result, we can only describe these kingdoms' geological context in broad strokes. Syro-Anatolian remains have been found along the Mediterranean littoral as well as the lowland alluvial valleys inland from the coast, the Amuq Valley and the Cilician Plain. Between these two large valley systems runs the north-south Amanus mountain range that serves as a natural barrier between Syria and Turkey, yet is traversed by the Belen and Bahçe passes, thus allowing for cultural continuity on either side of this divide. The Amuq Valley marks the northern extent of the Dead Sea Rift valley that parallels the eastern Mediterranean coast throughout the Levant (Wilkinson 2003: 16). The Orontes River runs through this valley system from Lebanon northward into the Amuq, where it abruptly turns southwest, past what would later become the Roman city of Antioch (modern Antakya) before debouching into the Mediterranean Sea by the ancient settlement of al Mina (Bridgland et al. 2003). The Orontes meets the sea in a small but rich delta wedged between the Amanus Mountains to the north and the Jebel al-Aqra—a tall mountain peak of long-standing mythological import in the region—to the south.

Traveling through a narrow opening in the southern edge of the Amuq, one can follow the Orontes south into the Ghab Valley, an archaeologically rich alluvial valley much like the Amuq, though here bordered on the west not by the Amanus Mountains but by the Lebanon and Nusariya chains whose northern terminus is the Jebel al-Aqra. The littoral in this region is extremely narrow and unable to support large-scale settlement systems, although small Iron Age sites do exist on the coast. Continuing south takes one into Lebanon's Beqaa Valley, roughly the southern extent of SACC with Damascus to the east, before one enters the kingdoms of Israel and Judah (Suriano 2014: 12–13).

The northern extent of the Amuq Valley is exited via the narrow north-south Islahiye Valley that sticks close to the eastern slopes of the Amanus. The valley terminates by the modern city of Kahramanmaraş, and from here, continuing north, one enters the foothills of the massive Taurus Mountains, characterized by a bewildering array of intermontane valleys and passes. Continuing through these narrow channels takes one eventually to the upper reaches of the Euphrates River, which, in its northern extent, marks another rough limit of SACC's geographical extent. Through the Bahçe pass one is able to move from the Islahiye Valley into the huge Cilician Plain, a highly fertile alluvial zone that, like the Amuq, had by the Iron Age already served as an interaction zone between Anatolia, the Levant, and the Aegean for centuries, a phenomenon that would continue in the early first millennium (Rutishauser 2017). Also like the Amuq, this geographical positioning contributed to a diverse cultural, linguistic, and material composition. The north edge of Cilicia is marked by the high slopes of the Taurus Mountains, and on their north face one faces the vast Konya plain and the Anatolian plateau. A wide variety of landscape monuments and hieroglyphic Luwian inscriptions have been found in this region, although archaeologically the region remains poorly understood in the Iron Age. The Kızıl Irmak provides an approximate north edge of SACC in this area.

The Amuq Valley's eastern access point, the small Afrin Valley, takes the traveler into what is today northern Syria. A number of Syro-Anatolian kingdoms were located in the rolling hills of this landscape all along the Turkey-Syria border as far east as the Khabur triangle at Ras al-Ain, the source of the Khabur River. The Euphrates River Valley cuts through this region from north to south, and served as the foundation for some of SACC's most significant political and cultural expressions such as the site of Carchemish, which literally straddles both sides of the modern border.

This complicated geological scenario is difficult to characterize as a whole, and of course that is precisely one of the reasons why the Syro-Anatolian kingdoms do not get treated as a combined entity. Several patterns do exist, however. The first is these polities' consistent location in areas of sufficient precipitation to preclude the need for water management beyond dry farming; the entirety of SACC's region is located north and west of the 200 mm/year isohyet (Wilkinson 1994). Indeed, the Mediterranean littoral and the mountains down its east coast receive upward of 1000 mm/year (Akkermans and Schwartz 2003: 4). A second is the city-states' dispersed nature across large geological transitional areas from the northern extent of lowland Mesopotamia's fertile crescent to highland Anatolia (in other words, from the Arabian plate to the Anatolian plate) and from the Near East to western Anatolia and the Aegean. On the one hand, as alluded to earlier, SACC thus serves as an ideal case for those who would like to defy environmental determinism. On the other, it helps explain some of the misconceptions of SACC in scholarship: a recipient of cultural influence instead of a provider; peripheral to cultural cores instead of a dynamic phenomenon unto itself; a hodgepodge of barely related characteristics instead of shared common traits.

Figure 1.1 shows how the specific Syro-Anatolian city-states lay across this diverse terrain. Though borders are not provided for reasons elaborated in Chapter 5, historical and archaeological evidence together indicates that the Orontes Valley system was where Hama and Patina/'Unqi were located, with the archaeologically unknown Aram-Damascus lying further south. East of the Amuq one found the kingdoms of Bit-Agusi, Bit-Adini, and Carchemish along the Euphrates, and Bit-Bahiani on the Khabur. The kingdom of Que occupied Cilicia. North of the Amuq into the Islahiye Valley one came across Sam'al followed by Gurgum further north, while in the intermontane valleys of the Taurus were situated Tabal (extending into Cappadocia and Konya to the north and west), Melid, and Kummuḫ, the latter again on the Euphrates.

## Sources of Information

The student of the Syro-Anatolian city-states has a wide variety of evidentiary material on which to draw. The most obvious of these, of course, is the archaeological record, and it is this corpus to which this book will most often turn. Within this category, the bulk of our information derives from excavations at the Syro-Anatolian capital cities that took place in the late nineteenth and early twentieth centuries, including associated features like nearby cemeteries. Not surprisingly, these excavations lacked the stratigraphic precision that archaeologists today have come to rely on. However, these same excavations' vast horizontal exposures have provided us with an ability to characterize these Iron Age cities spatially in a way that modern excavations' limited soundings are unable to achieve (Casana and Herrmann 2010: 56), such that they remain enormously helpful in reconstructing Syro-Anatolian culture.

As mentioned earlier, the excavation of these cities was very much part of the era's colonial project, with the excavators' nationalities reading like a "who's who" of European imperial ambitions: Germans excavated both Zincirli, capital of Sam'al (von Luschan 1893; von Luschan et al. 1898, 1902; von Luschan and Jacoby 1911; von Luschan and Andrae 1943) and Tell Halaf, ancient Gozan, capital of Bit Baḫiani (Hrouda 1962; Naumann 1950; Opitz and Moortgat 1955); French excavators worked at Arslantepe, ancient Melid (Delaporte 1934, 1940), Tell Ahmar, ancient Masuwari/Til-Barsip, capital of Bit-Adini (Thureau-Dangin and Dunand 1936) and Arslan Tash, ancient Hadatu (Thureau-Dangin et al. 1931); the English excavated Carchemish, capital of the city-state of the same name (Hogarth 1914; Woolley 1921, 1952) and Tell Rifa'at, ancient Arpad, capital of Bit-Agusi (Seton-Williams 1961, 1967); Danish excavators brought to light the remains of Hama, capital of ancient Ḥamath (Fugmann 1958; Riis 1948; Riis and Buhl 1990); and in the interwar period the Americans joined the group by excavating at Tell Tayinat, ancient Kunulua, capital of Patina/'Unqi (Haines 1971), and Gözlü Kule, ancient Tarsus (Goldman 1963). The remaining Syro-Anatolian capital cities have either not been explored archaeologically (Marash, capital of Gurgum) or received only limited salvage excavations or excavations pertaining to other periods (Adana/Tepebağ, capital of Que in Cilicia; Kummuḫ, modern Samsat Höyük; Tuwana, modern Kemerhisar). Many of these sites have latterly become the subjects of renewed archaeological expeditions, which has improved tremendously our understanding of specific archaeological sequences, as well as continued the unearthing of the monumental remains that played such a significant role in the city-states' political economy (Baghdo et al. 2009, 2012; Harrison *et al.*, Osborne et al. 2019; Marchetti 2012, 2014; Schloen and Fink 2009b, 2009a; Welton et al. 2011, 2019).

Although the archaeological record is undeniably biased toward elite social contexts, a small number of fortresses, villages, and towns have been excavated across the region, supplementing the view from the capitals. These include the fortresses of Karatepe in Que, famous for its lengthy bilingual Phoenician-Luwian inscription (Çambel 1999, 2014; Çambel and Özyar 2003), and Gerçin in Sam'al (von Luschan 1893; von Luschan and Jacoby 1911); isolated palaces such as Sam'al's Sakçe Gözü (Garstang 1908; Taylor et al. 1950); the large towns of Çatal Höyük (Haines 1971) and 'Ain Dara (Abu 'Assaf 1990; E. C. Stone and Zimansky 1999) likely in Patina, Tell Afis (Cecchini and Mazzoni 1998) and Tell Qarqur (Dornemann 2003) in Hamath, Sirkeli Höyük (Ahrens et al. 2010; Kozal and Novák 2013) and Tarsus, modern Gözlü Kule (Goldmann 1963) in Que, Göllüdağ (Schirmer 1993, 1999) and Kınık Höyük (Highcock et al. 2015) in Tabal, and likely the center of the storm god at Aleppo in Bit-Agusi (Kohlmeyer 2000, 2009); and the rural villages of Tell Mastuma in Hamath (Iwasaki et al. 2009), Kilise Tepe (Postgate and Thomas 2007b) and Kinet Höyük (Gates 2008; Hodos et al. 2005) in Que among several other projects in Cilicia (Novák et al. 2017), Tille Höyük in Kummuh (Blaylock 2009, 2016), and Porsuk in Tabal (Dupré 1983). Finally, all of these excavated remains can and should be combined with the regional settlement data provided by archaeological surveys in this area (e.g., Matthers 1981; M. V. Seton-Williams 1954; Yener 2005), which additionally expand our scholarly view to include settlements from every tier of the social hierarchy.

Although this vast corpus of information is on its own enough to supply the student of the Near Eastern Iron Age with a lifetime of work, it is complemented by another productive well of data from which we can draw: the historical record. I have already described briefly the nature of the indigenous texts. The languages are diverse: either Luwian (Hawkins 2000), Aramaic (or a dialect thereof, such as Sam'alian), or Phoenician (Hallo and Younger 2003)—or occasionally a combination of these, such as the Phoenician-Luwian bilingual inscriptions of Karatepe (Çambel 1999) and Çineköy (Tekoğlu et al. 2000), or the Aramaic-Akkadian bilingual of Tell Fakhariyah (Abou Assaf et al. 1982). The medium is almost exclusively the inscribed, stone, monumental inscription of the sort made to last for generations—hence their remarkable preservation today. Not surprisingly, therefore, the authors of the native sources are typically elite individuals, and most often a city-state's king, with the expected limited range of subject matter: military exploits, building projects, and divinely sanctioned legitimacy. This exclusivity is at least partially a consequence of transformation processes in the archaeological record, however: a small number of delicate lead strips recording economic transactions inscribed in Luwian hieroglyphs were found at Kululu in the territory of Tabal (Hawkins 1987) as well as several containing mundane correspondences at the Assyrian city of Assur (Hawkins 2000: 533–55), indicating the existence of a much larger corpus of such material in antiquity.

In terms of sheer volume, native Syro-Anatolian inscriptions are dramatically outnumbered by those written by their Neo-Assyrian contemporaries. In the course of their annual expansive military campaigns, the Assyrian kings had their scribes record the details of the multifarious lands and peoples they encountered, resulting in a veritable treasure trove of historical geography, including named landscape features, towns, polities, and political dynasties, many of which are unattested in the Syro-Anatolian sources themselves. Such information begins even in the Early Iron Age during the reign of Tiglath-pileser I (1114–1076 BCE) and extends into the time of Sennacherib (704–681 BCE), by whose reign the last of the Syro-Anatolian city-states had been conquered (Grayson 1991, 1996; Grayson and Novotny 2011; Tadmor and Yamada 2011). These texts have the same biases as the Syro-Anatolian ones—elite, royal, and disproportionately concerned with maintaining legitimacy—but now the historiographical challenges are compounded by the fact that the Assyrians were not native informants, but rather cultural observers whose understandings of local cultural phenomena were inevitably refracted through their own cultural lens (Bryce 2012: 4–5). This is not to say that Assyrian inscriptions are without value, however; on the contrary, they provide our single greatest source of Syro-Anatolian political history as well as precious information regarding the Syro-Anatolian economic structure, here indicated by the detailed booty taken in the course of their conquests.

## The Historical Sequence and Chronological Frameworks

In macroscopic terms, the historical trajectory of the Syro-Anatolian city-states follows the standard three-part narrative arc of the Western literary tradition: an introductory period in which, in a mysterious process only dimly discernible, inchoate powers gradually consolidate out of the turmoil of regional transformation; a climactic second stage in which the Syro-Anatolian city-states have become fully fledged political and cultural actors wielding their newly established power and influence on one another and on their neighbors in a strikingly visible manner; and a shocking dénouement that saw SACC's rapid and irreparable demise at the hands of forces beyond their control. In chronological terminology, these three narrative units are typically referred to as the Iron Age I, II, and III, respectively, or alternatively the Early, Middle, and Late Iron Age.

Microscopically, however, the grand account of SACC's rise, climax, and inevitable fall loses its sense of overwhelming homogeneity as one examines the details in greater resolution. For one thing, the Iron Age I period is hardly the historical "Dark Age" it was once thought to be, a period of political instability and incoherence indicated by a lack of inscriptions. The corpus of inscriptions belonging to this period grows every year, and each discovery provides additional support for robust political genealogies. This includes direct kinship relations with the Hittite dynasty whose collapse at the end of the Late Bronze Age was supposed to have been the transformative event that made history begin anew in the Iron Age (Hawkins 1988, 2009, 2011; Weeden 2013). To be sure, major historical processes were certainly taking place. However, the accumulating evidence for royal dynasties capable of making monumental inscriptions during the Iron Age I period suggests that the era was not as unstable and unformed as has been typically assumed.

And as the expanding historical record compromises the stability of the standard narrative, so too does the growing corpus of archaeological discoveries. The beautiful temple at 'Ain Dara in the Afrin Valley of northwestern Syria (Abu 'Assaf 1990), with its elaborate reliefs likely dating to the late second millennium (Orthmann 1993; Kohlmeyer 2008; Novák 2012), was an isolated anomaly until the discovery of the temple of the Storm God at Aleppo, which shows archaeological phases and iconographic continuities from the mid-second into the first millennium (Kohlmeyer 2009). Likewise, Tell Tayinat, ancient Kunulua, capital of Patina, once thought to have had no Iron Age occupation until the ninth century (Haines 1971: 66), is now recognized as having had a substantial Iron Age I phase (Welton et al. 2019). Indeed, what was once considered a region-wide period of dramatic change and instability (Ward and Joukowsky 1992) is now increasingly recognized for the growing evidence of continuity across the Bronze–Iron Age divide (Galil et al. 2012; Yener 2013).

In a similar vein, closer consideration of the historical record likewise exposes the weaknesses of SACC's traditional narrative arc. The fact that the conquest of the Neo-Assyrian Empire is often taken to mark the beginning of the Iron Age III period means that, in principle, individual Syro-Anatolian city-states should have different chronological schemas. This is especially apparent toward SACC's eastern extent, where the Neo-Assyrians were highly active even in the mid-ninth century BCE. Tell Ahmar, ancient Til-Barsip, capital of Bit-Adini, for example, was conquered by Shalmaneser III (r. 858–824) who converted the site into the major Assyrian fortress of Kar-Shalmaneser. Such dates are a full century prior to the conquest events of Tiglath-pileser III (745–727), Sargon II (721–705), and Sennacherib (704–681), who were responsible for the conquest of the western provinces and the quelling of intermittent revolts. It is thus overly simplistic to take the arrival of the Assyrians as a chronological benchmark.

In short, the standard account of the Syro-Anatolian city-states' rise involves more continuity and less "rising from the ashes" at their outset than has been assumed, and accounts of their fall require a good deal more city-state-specific particularism. This is partially a problem of new and inconsistent data, and partially a problem of the artificial nature of periodization (von Dassow 2012). Yet somehow a useable chronological framework needs to be superimposed on this uncooperative body of data in order to make sense of diachronic processes as well as for inter- and intraregional comparative purposes. This chapter opened by noting the high degree of scholarly specialization in Syro-Anatolian studies, with scholars divided not just into archaeologists, philologists, and art historians, but subcategories within these—Luwian and Aramaic philologists, for example. One consequence of this scholarly landscape is a diversity of chronological timelines, not all of which are compatible with one another. This introductory chapter will thus close with a consideration of how these disciplines have categorized and subdivided the Iron Age, concluding with the apparatus that will be used throughout this work.

Historical and philological studies are perhaps the most challenging to characterize in this regard by virtue of their tendency to focus exclusively on the Neo-Hittite or Aramaean kingdoms. According to Trevor Bryce, one of Anatolia's foremost historians and recent author of a military and political history of the Neo-Hittite kingdoms (2012: 195–289), the historical information falls into three periods of political evolution starting with the kingdom of Carchemish's rise in the void left by the Hittite Empire and eventually the rise of the other kingdoms during the Assyrian period of weakness following the death of Tiglath-pileser I (twelfth and eleventh centuries); a period of murky Neo-Hittite state formation, exemplified by the Suhi dynasty at Carchemish, that quickly became subject to Assyria as reflected in the dozens of Assyrian royal inscriptions (tenth and ninth centuries); and eventual absorption into the Assyrian Empire with kingdoms converted into Assyrian provinces ruled directly by Assyrian officials (eighth century). Each period's defining characteristic, in other words, is the city-states' political relationship with their more powerful neighbors.

This chronological timetable created in relation to outsiders is equally apparent in the historical summary offered by David Hawkins (1982). Hawkins's divisions lie in an "Early Period" characterized especially by the dominance of Tiglath-pileser I and a dearth of other Assyrian sources, "Ashurnasirpal II and Shalmaneser III" in the mid-ninth century, the "Successors of Shalmaneser III" until the mid-eighth century, "Tiglath-pileser III, Shalmaneser V, and Sargon II," and the reigns of "Sennacherib, Esarhaddon, and Ashurbanipal" (1982: 380–433). Hawkins's apparatus is high resolution in the sense that it takes seriously the real social changes that were occurring at a rapid pace largely as a result of forces beyond SACC's immediate control, and it does not create an artificial chronological formula for easy scholarly consumption. That said, although each of these five periods is provided a lengthy subsection treating "the native monuments," in each case this section *follows* consideration of the Assyrian sources and the Assyrian interferences with the west, again prioritizing Assyrian agency.

Discoveries since that publication have mostly rendered Hawkins's discussion of the Early Period sources moot—discoveries mostly analyzed and published by himself (e.g., 1988, 2011)—but the externally oriented temporal framework remains commonplace. For example, the same phenomenon is present in Giusfredi's socioeconomic history, for whom "archaeological sources themselves are actually of little help" (2010: 20), and who states that "of course, the reasons for such discontinuous behavior [in material styles] should be sought in the historical information we obtain from the sources" (2010: 22), the Assyrian expeditions in particular. Giusfredi's tripartite periodization is similar to, but slightly different from, Bryce: the Dark Age, the tenth century, and the ninth and eighth centuries (2010: 26). To the extent that Assyrian involvement is taken as one's chronological marker, this slight reformulation makes sense given the Assyrians' inward-looking posture during the tenth century, the period of Carchemish's Suhi dynasty, though it lacks Hawkins's historical subtlety and remains biased toward understanding the Syro-Anatolian city-states with respect to what other people had to say about them.

Scholars of Aramaic texts hold the same fundamental bias toward using non-native historical sources to create their chronological frameworks. Sader's (1987) useful synthesis of what is known about the kingdoms of Guzana, Bit-Adini, Bit-Agusi, Sam'al, Hamath, and Aram-Damascus, like Hawkins (1982), begins each city-state's historical sources with the Assyrian cuneiform material instead of the local Aramaic inscriptions, which appear second. Given that commentary and synthesis of the sources are not provided until both corpora are presented, it is perhaps revealing that the Assyrian sources are consistently given pride of place, and although it is true in one sense that "[l]'histoire de ces États araméens commence donc pour nous au moment où les annals assyriennes les mentionnent pour la première fois" (1987: 273), that sense is a strictly historic one, and one driven by the Assyrians at that. In a later synthesis of historical and archaeological data, Sader argues for a period of "peaceful settlement" in the eleventh–tenth century, an "urbanisation process" in the tenth–ninth century, and a final period of a "centralized monarchy" in the ninth–eighth century, a schema that interestingly divides the origin phase of the Aramaean kingdoms into two units (2000: 68–76). Dion's (1997) political history is highly similar in its reliance on the cuneiform sources to establish Aramaean narratives, though strictly speaking it does not provide a chronological timetable, much like Lipiński (2000), whose elaborate etymological reconstructions are founded primarily on his readings of Assyrian texts. A recent volume by K. Lawson Younger (2016: 23–28, Table 1.2), who follows the archaeological periodization of

Stefania Mazzoni (see later), is a significant exception to this pattern, signaling scholarship's increasing recognition of the need to incorporate data from neighboring disciplines.

The historical approach to the Syro-Anatolian city-states is thus characterized by its reliance on Akkadian sources and its variations on the chronological themes of rise, stasis, and fall. On the one hand, this use of external sources is understandable: Assyrian inscriptions are far more voluminous than Syro-Anatolian ones, and by their annalistic nature are much more prone to provide the genealogies and events that are the backbone of political history. On the other hand, it does provide the reader with a sense of SACC as having been devoid of cultural agency, a secondary historical phenomenon, whether such was the intent of the scholar or not. It has also typically (though not always entirely) excluded archaeological and iconographic corpora as sources of chronological information. Since this type of data derives directly from SACC itself, it follows that archaeology and art history need to be incorporated into our periodization at least as much as the texts.

Art historical timelines for the Syro-Anatolian city-states are founded on three major corpora: small and portable luxury goods, especially pieces of worked bronze and ivory; freestanding statuary, often accompanied by Luwian, Aramaic, or Phoenician inscriptions; and the reliefs carved on orthostats that lined the walls of monumental buildings. None of these sources is without its contextual problems, however. By virtue of their having been traded or looted from the Aegean to northern Mesopotamia, precious few of the luxury goods have been found in situ in the Syro-Anatolian region such that chronological reconstructions are necessarily the result of stylistic reasoning—not itself problematic, necessarily, but a less secure method than one using stratified deposits at the place of production. By far the majority of Syro-Anatolian ivories have been found at the Assyrian city of Nimrud, for example, where they were taken as part of the Assyrians' capture of booty (Herrmann 1986, 2009). Although less likely to have traveled afield from the Syro-Anatolian centers, large pieces of statuary are likewise plagued by less than certain contexts—found accidentally by farmers (Abou Assaf et al. 1982), for example, or discovered smashed to pieces by unknown individuals in antiquity (e.g., McEwan 1937: Fig. 11). In the end, these, too, have to be placed in time with the aid of stylistic comparanda.

The orthostats and their accompanying reliefs at first glance appear to lack this problem of unsecure context—they are found affixed to the walls of permanent buildings, after all—yet even here chronological reconstruction is less than straightforward (see Chapter 3). It is often unclear whether the reliefs as found were so arranged at the same time as the building to which they are attached (Aro 2003: 294). Indeed, the famous reliefs at Karatepe show two clear stylistic groupings on the same gateways (Winter 1979), a difference that likely has chronological implications for those groupings' dates, and that may relate to some of the orthostats having been taken from other buildings on site, or the nearby site of Domuztepe (Harrison 2009a). Likewise Tell Halaf, where the reliefs lining the wall of the palace of Kapara are possibly comprised of two different groups of reliefs based on size and iconography (Orthmann 1971: 119–23), one of which is possibly reused from an earlier building by virtue of iconographic and inscriptional elements along the abutting sides of the orthostats, and thus invisible to the viewer (Naumann 1950: 15 ff.). In addition, examples abound in which the reliefs themselves show clear signs of reworking as they got repurposed and redesigned, such as the slabs G/6 and G/7 (in Orthmann's labeling) from the Royal Buttress at Carchemish, which possess traces of earlier figures whose erasures in antiquity were not quite completed, and thus remain visible (Gilibert 2011: 47, n. 99; Özyar 1998).

Nevertheless, Syro-Anatolian orthostats and their associated scholarship usually provide the baseline for art historical chronological frameworks. The chronological foundation upon which everything that follows rests is Orthmann's *Untersuchungen zur späthethitischen Kunst* (1971), which developed the stylistic analysis of Akurgal (1949). Here Orthmann used the reliefs, especially those from Zincirli and Carchemish, to approximate three periods characterized by their stylistic evolution: Späthethitische (Late Hittite) I ca. 1000–950 BCE, Späthethitische II ca. 950–850 BCE, and Späthethitische III ca. 850–700 BCE, though he emphasized more their relative sequence than their absolute dating. This scheme has found widespread use (Aro 2003: 297; Novák 2019: 107), more so than the lower dates proposed by Genge (1979) on similar grounds. A revision of Orthmann's system has been proposed by Gilibert (2011), who includes a broader consideration of the reliefs' social and political context within SACC's elite circles to conclude that four distinct phases of monumental art are discernible: an "archaic transitional period" (ca. 1200–950 BCE) characterized by stylistic continuity with the Hittite Empire, an "age of civic ritual" (ca. 950–870 BCE) in which urban centers' ceremonial open spaces were decorated with monumental art and statuary, a "mature transitional period" (ca. 870–790 BCE) in which large-scale monumental art decreased while funerary stelae and luxury goods saw greater proliferation, and finally an "age of court ceremony" (ca. 790–690 BCE), when monumental art reappeared, this time with a focus on the inward-looking court (2011: 115–31). Though limited primarily to Carchemish and Zincirli, the broader contribution of Gilibert's framework is twofold: it incorporates factors beyond style in its categorization such as symbolic and social functions of art, and it considers a fuller range of artistic production like luxury goods and funerary stelae instead of limiting itself to reliefs alone.

If there is an archaeological equivalent to the efforts of Orthmann, it can be found in the many articles by Stefania Mazzoni, excavator of Tell Afis within the city-state of Hamath, and long the most prolific writer on all aspects of Syro-Anatolian material culture of the Iron Age (e.g., Mazzoni 1994, 1995, 1997, 2001, 2009, 2010). Mazzoni's effort to delineate a synthetic chronological archaeological sequence spanning the Iron Age (2000b, 2000a, 2014b) brings together a diverse array of data sets and is followed by a number of archaeologists, with minor variations (e.g., Lehmann 2008: 207). Deliberately avoiding the introduction of absolute dates, Mazzoni divides the Iron Age I period into three rough categories tethered first and foremost to the material sequence identified in her stratigraphic soundings at Tell Afis. The first phase, Iron IA, begins in the early twelfth century and ends somewhere around 1100 BCE; this period is characterized by its recovery from the instability of the Bronze Age political crisis. The Iron IB, roughly the eleventh century, sees the emergence of a new urbanization, especially with the beginnings of monumental art at Carchemish's Water Gate, a process continuing in the Iron IC, or tenth century, at which time Carchemish's public buildings were decorated, especially the Herald's Wall and the Long Wall of Sculpture (2000a: 31–41). The ceramic hallmark for this period is the painted pottery often associated with an Aegean origin.

The transition to the Iron II period is hardly unambiguous, but it is usually taken to be associated with the disappearance of the Iron I's painted pottery tradition and the widespread adoption of Red Slipped Burnished Ware in the northern Levant, plus a general trend toward greater urbanization and the new building of ceremonial centers, all of which seem to have begun around 900 BCE (Mazzoni 2014b: 685–87). Mazzoni refers to the ninth century BCE as the Iron IIA, beginning somewhere in the first half of that century (2000b: 128), and characterized especially by the development of SACC's most familiar temples and palaces, especially the famous porticoed *bīt-ḫilāni* palaces at Zincirli, Tell Halaf, and Tell Tayinat (Frankfort 1952; Osborne 2012), as well as other features common to urban citadels, such as the ubiquitous portal lion. This is also the time when bronze and ivory production in luxury goods became prominent (Winter 1976a, 1988) as indicated archaeologically, but also by the inscriptions of the Assyrian rulers Ashurnasirpal II and Shalmaneser III especially. Mazzoni's Iron IIB period then consists of the eighth century BCE until the Assyrian conquest and is manifested by additional major building activities at capital cities like Hazrek (Tell Afis), Zincirli, and Carchemish (2014: 692). The Iron III period is thus the period of Assyrian domination during the seventh and sixth centuries that halted SACC's urban and material expansion and absorbed the city-states into the apparatus of empire; as Mazzoni notes, "the process was not simultaneous, nor everywhere of the same intensity or effect (2014: 697).

Mazzoni's approach is commendable for its incorporation of multiple lines of evidence from urban planning to ceramic decoration. As she states (2014b: 685), it is an enormous challenge to organize and reconcile data from old excavations, decorated and inscribed monuments, ceramic sequences from newer excavations, and the historical sources. One outcome of marshaling such a diverse array of material culture into a common framework, however, is a highly atomized system in which every century from 1200 to 600 is assigned its own period; the opposite approach would be that of Harmanşah (2013: 2), for example, who refers to everything between 1200 and 850 BCE as the Early Iron Age, a span that for Mazzoni includes the Iron IA, IB, IC, and the start of the Iron IIA. In addition, so many of these subdivisions are characterized by rebuilding programs of monumental structures in the urban core that such building events lose periodizing value. Instead, it would appear that the act of monumental foundation was an event highly valued by SACC in cultural terms, and thus one that took place repeatedly throughout its existence (Harmanşah 2013). Nevertheless, the bulk of Mazzoni's rubric, especially her ceramic analysis of the tightly stratified deposits at Afis, is logical and convincing.

The great challenge, then, is coming to a reconciliation between the various approaches that have been advocated by philologists, art historians, and archaeologists. One could argue that no such compromise is necessary—after all, there is no inherent reason why linguistic, historical, iconographic, and material traditions ought to be expected to change at the same rate, in which case chronological approaches specific to the data set at hand might not just be inevitable, but actually desirable. Be that as it may, for SACC to be treated in a holistic manner, as is being done here, some kind of diachronic understanding must be adopted.

All of the scholarship outlined herein recognizes that the late second millennium starting around 1200 BCE or slightly later represents a genuine change in both the historical and archaeological records. As mentioned earlier, evidence for cultural and even political continuity is growing annually, but the Late Bronze political system is qualitatively and quantitatively distinct from the Syro-Anatolian city-states of the early first millennium, and the last centuries of the second millennium represent the transition between the two eras, however one wants to weigh evidence for continuity versus rupture. Likewise, there is broad agreement that the conquests of the Neo-Assyrian Empire represent a terminal point, after which not only the political makeup of the region changes irrevocably, but the material culture becomes more Assyrian in style. Although assigning an arbitrary date to what was in reality a piecemeal Assyrian takeover, the year 700 BCE appears to have found broad acceptance as a convenient scholarly shorthand to mark the transition to Assyrian hegemony, even if individual Syro-Anatolian city-states were in fact conquered earlier.

The real dispute, therefore, is where the transition lies from the Iron I to Iron II periods. As Mazzoni notes, the standard archaeological marker for this transition is the decline of the Iron I's painted pottery tradition and especially the widespread use of Red Slipped Burnished Ware (RSBW), despite the fact that RSBW likely did not originate at quite the same time everywhere it is found (2000b: 125–27). Recently presented Bayesian radiocarbon analysis from samples taken from the stratified Iron Age sequence at Tell Tayinat places that site's final Iron I phase in the third quarter of the tenth century (Manning et al. 2014); since the next phase involves the presence of RSBW, it follows that a date of approximately 950 or slightly later can serve as the turning point. What is appealing about this figure is its relationship to some of the other lines of evidence outlined earlier. Disregarding Assyrian inscriptions as a source for Syro-Anatolian periodization, and noting that urban renewal was a Syro-Anatolian phenomenon throughout the Iron Age, we are left primarily with the stylistic evolution of SACC's monumental art. Gilibert (2011: 119) notes that her "age of civic ritual" begins around 950 BCE, with its earliest constructions being the building efforts of Suhi II and Katuwa at Carchemish, whose orthostats set in motion the style of Syro-Anatolian art in the following centuries. Likewise, Mazzoni (2013: 480) notes that it is in the second half of the tenth century that the so-called minor arts like ivory production began to appear. It might be desirable to further subdivide both the Iron Age I and II into smaller units of time based on modest material changes or the different emphases in iconographic style, as Mazzoni does, but given the fact that both periods are ultimately characterized by slow and gradual material and artistic evolution, as well as by an artistic and ar-chaeological record that reflects the varied dynasties of the various Syro-Anatolian city-states, there is no compelling urgency for us to do so. This book, then, employs a simplistic two-part periodization of the Iron Age I, ca. 1200–950 BCE and Iron Age II, ca. 950–700 BCE, keeping in mind the many caveats that are necessarily in-volved with all of those dates. If some of SACC's features could be more finely fixed in time, others span the entire Iron Age. Among the latter is a fluctuating sense of mobility and migration, which is the subject of the following chapter.

## CHAPTER 2

# DIASPORA AND THE ORIGINS OF THE
# SYRO-ANATOLIAN CULTURE COMPLEX

IN A RECENT ARTICLE ON the Iron Age orthostats and Hieroglyphic Luwian inscriptions discovered in Aleppo's temple to the Storm God, Sanna Aro describes her original hesitation to include this material in a summary of Luwian art she was then writing (2003). She notes:

> I had to make a difficult decision whether or not to deal with Aleppo as Luwian. Despite the fact that a few Hieroglyphic Luwian inscriptions already long known were considered as having originated from Aleppo and some of the recently found orthostats from the temple of the Storm-God bear Hieroglyphic Luwian captions, I was well aware that to label Aleppo as Luwian would get a chequered reception. Traditionally, Bronze Age Aleppo is thought to have had mainly Semitic and Hurrian ruling classes and population, whereas only a few scholars have so far addressed the important issue of the physical presence of the Hittites in this city or elsewhere in north Syria. For the Early Iron Age and especially for the period from the 8th century BCE onwards, Aleppo is mostly considered to have been part of the Aramaic state of Bīt Agūsi/Arpad, thus emphasizing the Semitic element of the city. (2010: 1)

Aro's trepidation is understandable. As she points out, earlier known Luwian inscriptions had done nothing to prevent scholars from treating the city uncritically as an Aramaean center during the Iron Age. Nor is Aleppo unique in this regard. In fact, a tendency to essentialize the Syro-Anatolian city-states into tidy ethnic categories, often in the face of explicit evidence to the contrary, has characterized much of the scholarship on this time and place until recently. In this chapter I argue

*The Syro-Anatolian City-States*. James F. Osborne, Oxford University Press (2021). © Oxford University Press.
DOI: 10.1093/oso/9780199315833.003.0002.

that the diasporic processes that were involved in the origins of these polities render such characterizations misleading, and that models of shared cultural identity in the face of differences such as language are more accurate representations of the Syro-Anatolian Culture Complex (SACC)'s political composition.

One of the most enduring problems of Near Eastern archaeology has been explaining the dramatic and geographically widespread archaeological changes that are attested at the transition from the Late Bronze Age into the Iron Age around the year 1200 BCE. This issue has inspired an enormous amount of literature both popular (Cline 2014) and academic (Knapp and Manning 2016), and there does not appear to be an emerging consensus other than that the causes of the changes are both numerous and complicated. This book is not the place to intervene in these debates, but in the northeast corner of the Mediterranean Sea the changes that transpired led to the rise of SACC over the course of just a few generations. The goal of this chapter is to create an interpretive model for the rise of the Syro-Anatolian city-states and their hybrid cultural identity. Existing explanations for their formation during the Iron Age I have tended toward monocausality or have been restricted in scope to one of the two major ethnolinguistic groups of the region, that is, Aramaic and Luwian speakers.

In this chapter I use the framework of diaspora studies as an interpretive lens through which to view the development and expressions of SACC's cultural forms. Beginning as an exploration of the cultural ramifications of the Neo-Babylonian-caused Jewish exile of the sixth century BCE, diaspora as a cross-disciplinary domain of enquiry exploded in the 1990s and 2000s, as did its self-application by dozens of contemporary transnational migrant populations around the world (Tölölyan 2007: 648). Indeed, authors now argue justifiably that the term has been rendered meaningless by virtue of overextension to dispersals of any kind (Brubaker 2005). Although diaspora's explanatory power may have been adulterated by overapplication, it remains a helpful tool with which to explore the dynamics of cultural origins, and how the merging of cultural groups breathes new forms into life. And although it has become a recognized trope in a diverse array of modern cultural and literary contexts, archaeological studies of diaspora have been far more restricted, predominantly interested in identifying and interpreting the material evidence for the African diaspora to the New World that was wrought by the Atlantic slave trade (Orser 1998; Epperson 2004; Hayes 2015). It has also been applied toward identifying foreign populations using modern scientific methodologies (Eckardt 2010), or understanding the material manifestations of enclaves of long-distance economic traders in foreign milieus (Stein 1999). All of these studies explore what may be the most basic component of diaspora—the co-presence of cultural groups—yet, in light of the general disciplinary neglect of diasporic writers in archaeology, there remains a great deal of space for theoretical applications of diasporic insights in reconstructions of ancient life (Lilley 2004: 287–88; 2006).

Within the broad and diverse domain of diaspora studies one can identify two distinct intellectual trends. The first is the desire to classify particular historical and cultural contexts into a typology of diasporas, describing the various forms that diasporas can take, and isolating the features shared by those forms in order to articulate diaspora's essential characteristics. This approach is exemplified by Robin Cohen (2008: 18), who divided diasporas into five ideal types: victim (e.g., Jewish, African, Armenian), labor (e.g., Turkish, Indian), imperial (e.g., British), trade (e.g., Venetian, Chinese), and deterritorialized (e.g., Caribbean, Kurdish). With typologies like these in mind, scholars have attempted to delineate diasporas' shared traits, the elements that unify them as a common entity, usually landing on some or all of the following points: traumatic origins that shape collective memory and identity; geographical dispersal from an original homeland; a positive affiliation with the homeland manifested in an identity that preserves the homeland's cultural forms and that is maintained in the face of new cultural surroundings; and an explicit rhetoric that expresses a desire for return, even if that return is only an aspiration, one that serves to forge solidarity in hostile surroundings (Brubaker 2005: 5–7; Cohen 2008: 17; Dufoix 2008: 21–23; Safran 1991: 83–84).

It is certainly an important intellectual goal to establish a shared terminology that will facilitate cross-cultural and historical comparisons of particular cases. At the same time, however, the concern with establishing the precise boundaries of diaspora as an intellectual project has a tendency to be preoccupied with establishing whether specific instances of a movement of people should be labelled a diaspora or not, and thus to downplay the more exciting questions of the cultural consequences of migration and interaction in situation-specific circumstances. Even within widely accepted criteria there remains expansive room for debate that is not resolvable. Just how much does a cultural expression need to evoke the homeland before we consider it diasporic, for example, and what are the criteria by which we measure this? More broadly, the urge to determine the limits of diaspora as a universal cross-cultural category inevitably glosses over the nuances that make particular cases so fascinating. To take just one of Cohen's ideal types, the many and profound historical differences in the experience of Jews and Africans renders placing them both in a category of "victim diaspora" an unhelpful exercise, obvious parallels notwithstanding (Gilroy 1993: 207–12).

It is clear that SACC only loosely fits into the construct of diaspora as articulated by scholars like Cohen and Brubaker. Although the collapse of the Late Bronze Age may have been a traumatic experience on some level, and although at least some people migrated to the core region of SACC resulting in mixed cultural expressions in a single area (see later discussion), there is hardly a discernable rhetoric of longing for a geographical return.

Yet there is a second current within diaspora studies, one that is more applicable to the historical trajectory of SACC during the Iron Age. Scholars like Paul Gilroy, Stuart Hall, and James Clifford have been less interested in assigning their cases to typological categories and have instead focused on the cultural forms that take shape when one group of people is brought into contact with another, whether due to forced migration, market incentives, or any other kind of dispersal. Rather than emphasizing cultural boundary *maintenance* as an essential element of diasporic conditions, this body of work argues that population scattering and subsequent gathering, and the accompanying shuffling of polities' demographic composition it entails, leads inevitably to an *erosion* of boundaries, boundaries that are highly fluid, changes in their dividing lines over time, and continuous reconsideration of who can claim legitimate membership. This literature is part of an intellectual discourse that was situated explicitly counter to the homogenizing project of the nation-state (even though the nation-state itself may have been oversimplified by this work [Brubaker 2005: 10]). Arjun Appadurai (1996), for example, noticed how technological advancements allowed transnational communities of migrants to identify with one another in ways that cut across national boundaries, while Homi Bhabha (1990: 292) argued that nations' self-defining narrative strategies can only ever be ambivalent, producing "a continual slippage into analogous, even meto-nymic, categories, like the people, minorities, or 'cultural difference' that continu-ally overlap in the act of writing the nation." As we will see later, one's intellectual position vis-à-vis the nation-state greatly informs our understanding of the Syro-Anatolian city-states, since the modern political formation has been retrojected onto the Iron Age in contemporary scholarship.

More than simply offering an alternative approach to the contemporary nation-state, the literature on diaspora opens a new way of envisioning the cultural interactions wrought by population movements in the past as well as the present. In particular, this work illustrates how communities of diaspora maintain multiple attachments in networks that transcend political boundaries, and that they nego-tiate a complicated relationship with host cultures that are as often accommodating as they are resistant. As James Clifford (1994: 308) states, diasporas are "forms of community consciousness and solidarity that maintain identifications outside the national time/space in order to live inside, with a difference . . . the term *diaspora* is a signifier, not simply of transnationality and movement, but of political struggles to define the local, as distinctive community, in historical contexts of displacement." It is this sense of new communities being forged out of displacement that applies so aptly to the Iron Age context of SACC, for it is this process that leads to a recog-nizable cultural identity across the city-states, even while those city-states consist of heterogeneous populations. Now that we have moved away from essentialized ethnic categories whose identity depends on their relationship to a sacred homeland, we can understand diaspora "not by essence or purity, but by the recognition of a necessary heterogeneity and diversity; by a conception of 'identity' which lives with and through, not despite, difference; by *hybridity*. Diaspora identities are those which are constantly producing and reproducing themselves anew, through transformation and difference" (Hall 1990: 235). This sentiment of locally situated negotiations both between and within diasporic communities and their hosts is echoed in Avtar Brah's (1996: 183) insistence that the concept of diaspora is to be found specifically in the relationships among these various groups: "multiple journeys may configure into one journey via a *confluence of narratives* as it is lived and re-lived, produced, reproduced and transformed through individual as well as collective memory and re-memory." It is in these specificities that a unifying thread is found that ties disparate communities into a common entity, and this is why one finds that SACC has a distinguishable character even while it consists of multiple groups and histories. It does mean, however, that for the analyst SACC will forever consist of "complicated natives" (Clifford 1997: 4) whose slippery cultural identity we will never be fully able to grasp. The key to appreciating diaspora in the context of SACC will be not the understandable urge to separate cultural expressions into ethnopolitical typologies, but rather to appreciate their interpenetration (Gilroy 1993: 48).

This is especially true during the Iron Age I period and the gradual transition into the Iron Age II, when the kingdoms were slowly coalescing into what would become a coherent city-state system. These episodes involved social transformations that were determined at least in part by the movements of significant numbers of people. In the case of the Iron Age I, these movements came from multiple different sources: a possible migration of Luwian speakers from the Anatolian plateau into southeastern Anatolia and northern Syria, the rise of Aramaic as a spoken language associated with sedentarizing nomads, and the arrival of migrants from the Aegean as part of the so-called Sea Peoples phenomenon.

This chapter begins by outlining what might be called the standard model of the mechanisms behind SACC's origins, including new evidence that Aegean-derived migrants played a role, similar in some respects to the Philistines in the southern Levant. Unlike archaeology in the south, however, where theoretically nuanced works have treated the subject of the Philistines from a diverse range of anthropological perspectives on migration (see especially Yasur-Landau 2010), this body of literature has barely been tapped in the Syro-Anatolian region. In fact, the standard model of SACC is ultimately one that broadly equates language, ethnicity, and nation such that the Syro-Anatolian city-states end up resembling the nation-states of contemporary Western nationalism. I argue that a more accurate understanding of this time and place is one in which the nature of SACC is characterized not by the ethnically based differences between kingdoms, but by a broadly shared hybrid cultural tradition that was created by the mixing of many people in the population movements of the twelfth and eleventh centuries.

The first section describes the standard model that scholars have used to explain the rise of the Syro-Anatolian city-states, a model that is heavily influenced by assumptions of ethnolinguistic identity. After critiquing various aspects of this model, the chapter goes on to describe the contributions of migration and diaspora studies in fashioning a new understanding of how this process transpired. Most significantly, although there are a number of cleavage planes in its visual, material, and historical records, and although these differences arise in part as an outcome of a variety of different population movements and subsequent interaction, SACC consists of a basic unity that cannot be reduced or divided along ethnolinguistic lines.

::::

# The Standard Model
## *The Appearance of the "Aramaean" and "Luwian" City-States*

In scholarship on the rise of SACC, there is not just disagreement on how this process took place, but even a lack of consistency on what the subject is to be analyzed. In large part, this is due to the language-based ethnic assumptions that were outlined in the previous chapter, such that the rise of allegedly "Aramaean" city-states are considered separately from the emergence of "Luwian" or "Neo-Hittite" kingdoms, as if the two are not closely related manifestations of a larger, region-wide phenomenon. As a result, there does not exist a single model for the rise of the Syro-Anatolian city-states out of the transformations that followed the Late Bronze Age, with details being modified as new data are generated and incorporated into the model. That said, there are broad patterns present across a number of individual studies of the mechanisms that led to the formation of these city-states.

Foremost among these is a tacit reliance on the assumptions of neoevolutionary theory, especially with respect to scholarship on the Aramaeans. The principles of cultural evolution derive from the anthropologists and sociologists of the nineteenth century who developed a unified model for human development that moved in stages from savagery to barbarism and eventually ended in civilization (e.g., Engels 1902; Morgan 1877; Tylor 1881). To the modern ear these terms sound anachronistic at best, and ethnocentric and colonialist at worst, and the writing of late twentieth-century anthropologists has done much to discredit the problematic notions associated with this line of thought, such as the myth of the timeless, ahistorical native cultures existing in the ethnographic present in much the same way as they did before the invention of agriculture (Fabian 1983; Wolf 1982).

Yet mid-twentieth-century anthropologists and archaeologists picked up the linear cultural evolutionary approach to social change and adopted many of its fundamental tenets: that societies evolve in stages culminating in the state, and that each of these stages is characterized by a recognizable suite of social structures and norms (Fried 1967; Service 1962). To archaeologists, the most salient aspect of the model was the notion that these different stages, especially Service's band-tribe-chiefdom-state rubric, are expressed materially with a unique set of archaeologically identifiable features, such as V. Gordon Childe's (1950b) association of urbanism with the state.

A full discussion of evolutionary thinking in archaeology, especially its use of Marxian historical materialism to explain social change, its structural functionalist vision of social organization, and the positivist analytical methods it inspired, is not appropriate here. Largely inspired by recent social theoretical work that emphasizes historical particularism and relativism, the discipline has gravitated toward a general sense that ancient cultures need to be understood on their own terms, not merely as examples of cross-cultural universal stages, and that cultural behavior is as influenced by socially determined systems of meaning at least as much as it is by environmental conditions and demographic pressures (Smith 2011: 418–19; Yoffee 2005).

Explicit cultural evolutionary writing is not overly common in Near Eastern archaeology, but some of its fundamental assumptions do appear in particular contexts, one of which is the rise of the Aramaeans when they are envisioned as a distinct ethnolinguistic social group. This work was itself a corrective to an earlier generation of Near Eastern scholars who, with scant evidence, viewed the Aramaeans as a nomadic horde emerging out of the Syrian Desert to overwhelm the settled areas (Albright 1975: 532; Kraeling 1918; Malamat 1973). This vision of Aramaean origins filtered into sociological literature on the nation-state, as in Anthony Smith's *Ethnic Origins of Nations*, which opens by including maps of Aramaean nomadic tribes depicted as an arrow curving out of the desert and into the urban fertile crescent (1987: maps 2 and 3).

The response to this "invading horde" hypothesis was a turn to autochthonous developments in the cultural trajectory of already established communities. Sader (1992: 158–61) noted appropriately that internal processes need to be considered and that more-or-less fabricated migrations from the Syrian Desert are an unnecessary intellectual step. Instead, socioeconomic processes accompanying the Bronze Age collapse of the twelfth and eleventh centuries ought to be viewed as the "bedouinisation" of the formerly urban population (Sader 2000: 63). As evidence for this interpretation, Sader cites the historical inscriptions of Tiglath-pileser I

(r. 1114–1074 BCE) and the many regional surveys in the area that indicate an influx of small settlements in the twelfth and eleventh centuries representing the sedentarization of these seminomadic peoples.[1] In addition to the well-known surveys of the Khabur region, for example, recent survey work on the Euphrates south of Carchemish documents a dramatic increase in the number of sites from the Late Bronze into the Iron Age (Lawrence and Ricci 2016), as does survey in the Jabbul Plain west of the Euphrates River (Yukich 2013) (Figure 2.1). This interpretation of Late Bronze–Iron Age settlement pattern dynamics is followed closely

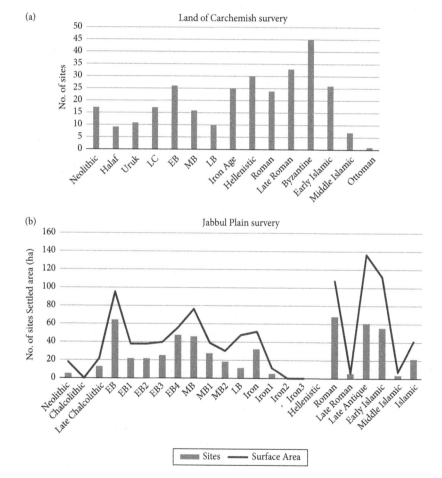

FIGURE 2.1

Histograms of the settlement patterns of (*a*) the Land of Carchemish survey showing number of sites by period (Lawrence and Ricci 2016), and (*b*) the Jabbul Plain survey showing number of sites and approximate settled area by period (Yukich 2013). (Anthony Lauricella and Siena Fite)

by several others (Joffe 2002; 434; Klengel 2000: 23–25). Schwartz likewise uses the historical record to see the earliest Aramaeans as seminomads who lived in a symbiotic relationship with adjacent sedentarists, eventually merging into one ethnic group (1989: 281–84). Though none of these scholars consciously deploy evolutionary thinking—the closest might be the title of Mazzoni's (1998) short book *The Italian Excavations of Tell Afis (Syria): From Chiefdom to an Aramaean State*, or Liverani's (2014: 434–37) description of an Aramaean evolution from tribalism to statehood—some of its assumptions are nevertheless present implicitly. These include a binary distinction between paired terms like urban/rural and tribe/state, with socioeconomic processes taking place in structurally different ways across the divide, and the belief that the state represents a qualitative shift away from traditional modes of social organization toward an impersonal, bureaucratic social structure.

There are a number of problematic points with this approach in the Aramaean context. At an empirical level, the survey data that are cited in support of an alleged sedentarization of a nomadic population (Morandi Bonacossi 2000; Sader 2000: 63; Wilkinson and Barbanes 2000) do not strictly require that interpretation. When one looks at the settlement pattern data for upper Mesopotamia—an unambiguous increase in the number of small sites during the Iron Age—a number of viable interpretations exist. One attractive alternative is a centrifugal ruralization process in which agriculturalists took advantage of the absence of political authority following the dissolution of the Late Bronze Age kingdoms and settled in areas that had not been under state control, an interpretation that has also been offered to explain similar settlement patterns in the Iron Age I southern Levant (Stager 1998).

Jeffrey Szuchman's (2007) reexamination of the survey data available from northeastern Syria and southeastern Anatolia for populations of sedentarizing nomads during the late second millennium found a regional pattern of small-scale settlements during the end of the Late Bronze Age as opposed to the Iron Age I, which in historical terms refers to a strong period for the Middle Assyrian kingdom, and not the subsequent political retraction prior to the Neo-Assyrian Empire. In other words, if sedentarization of Aramaean nomads took place at all, the evidence suggests that it was during the late thirteenth and twelfth centuries, not the late eleventh and tenth. In fact, the ethnographic and ethnoarchaeological records indicate that nomads are more likely to sedentarize during periods of strong, not weak, centralized authorities when the economic incentives for doing so are greater (Cribb 1991), and thus this finding is not as counterintuitive as it may appear. Furthermore, pushing the timeframe for Aramaean sedentarism back slightly allows more time for the development of the political complexity necessary for the urban project of the early first millennium BCE, whereas a late eleventh- and tenth-century sedentarization posits a transition from nomads to urban dwellers building orthostat-lined palaces at Tell Halaf, for example, in the span of just a couple of generations (Szuchman 2007: 204). In this revised scenario, the burgeoning of small sites during the late second and early first millennium in northeastern Syria reflects both a small number of newly sedentarized nomads and, more significantly, a new rural existence for previously urban dwellers. In both cases the settlement patterns reflect not quite a migration, but a demographic movement of peoples out into the countryside, part of a long-term process in the first millennium BCE that Tony Wilkinson (2003: 128–33) referred to as the "Great Dispersal."

The evidence for Aramaean nomads that does exist comes from the available textual references to the Aramaeans during their earliest years. These consist primarily of the records of the Assyrian king Tiglath-pileser I, who refers to his having moved to defeat the *aḫlamu* Aramaeans twenty-eight times. The oft-cited text reads:

I have crossed the Euphrates 28 times, twice in one year, in pursuit of the *aḫlamu* Aramaeans. I brought about their defeat from the city Tadmar of the land Amurru, Anat of the land Suhu, as far as Rapiqu of Karduniaš. (Grayson 1991: 36–38)

and another says that he

marched against the *aḫlamu* Aramaeans, enemies of the god Ashur, my lord. I plundered from the edge of the land of Suhu to the city Carchemish of the land Hatti in a single day. I massacred them (and) carried back their booty possessions, and goods without number. The rest of their troops, who fled from the weapons of the god Ashur, my lord, crossed the Euphrates. I crossed the Euphrates after them . . . I conquered six of their cities at the foot of Mount Bishri, burnt, razed, (and) destroyed (them). (Grayson 1991: 23)

Sader interprets these passages to indicate a nomadic Aramaean lifestyle primarily because of the term *aḫlamu*, which she notes was used in the second millennium to denote tribal peoples (2000: 64), an interpretation that is followed often. Although it may be true that *aḫlamu* generally means "nomad" or "barbarian" (Grayson 1976: 13n70), the author of these texts clearly seeks to represent the Aramaeans in a derogatory light via a long-standing Mesopotamian tradition of using transhumant subsistence strategies as a symbol of cultural inferiority (Glatz and Casana 2016).[2] In this case the use of the term *aḫlamu* likely had an ideological valence distinct from its literal translation. In addition, the explicit reference to Aramaean cities in both of these passages, while obviously overblown, should not be disregarded entirely, nor should their immense booty. Nothing in the passages of Tiglath-pileser I *requires* the reader to understand the Aramaeans as having strictly nomadic origins, however straightforward that interpretation appears at first glance, and despite the fact that the model of the originally nomadic Aramaeans has attained canonical status (Younger 2016: 35–107).

The same applies to the household terminology used in the Aramaic-language city-state names, such as Bit-Adini, Bit-Agusi, or Bit-Bahiani, where *bēt/bītu,* "house," is used in construct with the following personal name to denote the title of the kingdom. Some scholars have deduced from this *bēt* terminology that the Aramaeans were a tribal society (Joffe 2002: 434; Kühn 2014: 38–40; Postgate 1974: 234–36), and hence had nomadic origins. But although these titles may indeed indicate that the ruling dynasties of the city-states in question—or even Syro-Anatolian social structure writ large—were organized according to a patrimonial logic, it says little or nothing about the residency patterns paired with that logic. There is no need to presume that tribal social organization must originate necessarily from something other than the state, as contemporary anthropology and ethnohistory demonstrate (Khoury and Kostiner 1990), and indeed, a patrimonial, "tribal" mode of sociopolitical organization was the dominant paradigm of Near Eastern society throughout the preceding Bronze Age (Schloen 2001). It is more likely that Aramaean tribal terminology derives from this long-standing regional precedent than it does from an undocumented nomadism.

Perhaps the most problematic aspect of the nomadic origins of the Aramaeans is its assumed equivalence of the Aramaeans as a language-based ethnic group with Aramaean polities, akin to the traditional nation-state defined by Smith as "when a single ethnic and cultural population inhabits the boundaries of a state, and the boundaries of that state are coextensive with the boundaries of that ethnic and cultural population" (1995: 86). The Syro-Anatolian city-states as envisioned by much contemporary scholarship fit less easily with the second aspect of that definition, since of course there are multiple "Aramaean" kingdoms. But the first aspect—city-states being defined by their essential ethnic identity—is a critical component of how these Iron Age kingdoms have been envisioned.

Only rarely does the ethnic constitution of the Syro-Anatolian city-states appear as an explicit claim, as when Joffe (2002: 426; cf. Liverani 2014: 435) argues that the Levantine kingdoms that arose early in the first millennium BCE were "ethnic states," or "polities integrated by means of identity, especially ethnicity, and which are territorially based." Occasionally ethnic struggles are cited as the historical scenario explaining the presence of royal figures with Luwian and Aramaean names in a single polity, or a polity with names in both languages, as when Harrison (2001) invokes ethnic conflict to explain an alleged transition of the Neo-Hittite city-state of Patina into the Aramaean city-state of Unqi. Such transitions from one nation-state status to another is encapsulated by the title of Ussishkin's (1971) article, "Was Bit-Adini a Neo-Hittite or Aramaean State?"[3] Far more commonly, the fundamentally ethnic nature of the city-states is casually assumed and in need of no particular explanation or justification—hence the presence of monographs devoted to specific ethnic groups and their city-states, as we saw in the last chapter.

This issue raises the glaring deficiency in our long-standing assumption that Aramaean city-states represent the terminal point of an ethnic evolution that began with nomadism and ended with bureaucratic nation-states: to a greater or lesser degree, all of the putatively "Aramaean" kingdoms have evidence of other ethnic groups within their regions, both textual and material, and including the presence of non-Aramaean kings (or at least kings with non-Aramaic names). The most obvious of these groups, of course, is the Aramaeans' cultural neighbor, the Luwians. Such evidence for nonhomogeneous identity processes within the Syro-Anatolian city-states belies Sader's claim, for example, that "all state members consider themselves as such because they believe they are descendants of one eponymous ancestor, and this is the basis for the new state formation characteristic of the Iron Age: the National State" (1992: 161).

The appearance of the Luwians in the form of ethnically based polities during the Iron Age has garnered less explicit attention than the Aramaeans. In part, this is due to the Luwian language's existence spanning the Late Bronze Age and Iron Age, such that an explanation for their sudden "rise" is less obviously necessary. The origins of Luwian in pre–second millennium Anatolia is obscured by the lack of inscriptions in the region preceding the Old Assyrian trade colony period (ca. 1950–1720 BCE). Scholars debate precisely how the language evolved in relation to its Anatolian sister tongues (Melchert 2003) and the role of Luwian and other Anatolian languages in the ongoing debates surrounding the geographical location of the first Indo-European speakers (Mallory 1991; Renfrew 1987).

By the time of the Hittite Empire, Luwian speakers appear to be present in many parts of western and southern Anatolia, including the polities of Arzawa, Kizzuwatna, and Tarḫuntašša. The first arrival of Luwian speakers in southeastern Anatolia is thought to have taken place at least by the late fourteenth century, when Suppiluliuma I installed his son Piyassili/Šarri-Kušuḫ as viceroy in Carchemish. Epigraphic discoveries indicate that Šarri-Kušuḫ's descendants then ruled the city even beyond the fall of the Hittite Empire, demonstrated by a seal from the site of Lidar Höyük naming one Kuzi-Teshub as both the king of Carchemish and the son of Talmi-Teshub, previously the last known viceroy of the city under Suppiluliuma II, the last king of the Hittites (Hawkins 1988) (Figure 2.2). Such dynastic continuity would appear to be confirmed by the Luwian

FIGURE 2.2
Seal of Kuzi-Teshub, king of Carchemish, son of Talmi-Teshub and great-great-great-grandson of Suppiluliuma I, discovered at Lidar Höyük. (Adapted from Sürenhagen 1986: Abb. 3)

inscriptions and monumental art installed at the site in the Iron Age I and II periods, which shows clear affinities with Hittite stylistic conventions, even while incorporating local artistic practices such as lining the walls of public buildings with orthostats as had been done at Middle Bronze Age Ebla and Tilmen Höyük (Aro 2013; Harmanşah 2013: 168–80).

Yet despite this picture of autochthonous origins and long-term cultural continuity, migrations and movement are also described as being a defining aspect of Luwian-speaking communities throughout their existence. For example, Luwian populations in western Anatolia are described in Hittite annals as having been subjected to deportations and dispersed throughout the empire due to the policy of deportation and forced migration of citizens who lived in conquered regions (Bryce 2003: 62, 84; Košak 1981: 15), especially during the reigns of Suppiluliuma I and Mursili II. If the numbers of the deportees provided in the inscriptions are not overly exaggerated, then significant demographic shifts followed these forced migrations.

Large-scale movement of Luwian speakers has also been proposed in Iron Age contexts. A mid-twentieth-century view held, similar to an earlier vision of invading hordes of Aramaeans, that Luwian speakers arrived in the area as conquerors (Güterbock 1954: 114; Landsberger 1948: 23–35). Less dramatic positions are typically taken today. Bryce (2003: 87), for example, argues for an Iron Age Luwian migration of undetermined scale by making the argument that Luwians must have been among the Sea Peoples described by Merneptah in his Karnak temple inscription, which includes an invading group from Lukka, or western Anatolia. Leaving aside the question of whether Luwian speakers in western Anatolia were native to the region or were there due to Hittite displacement (Yakubovich 2010), Bryce argues that Luwians must have been a part of this group. A scenario that seems at least equally plausible, though without direct historical evidence, is Hawkins's proposal that "the main migration of Anatolian peoples to these territories followed the sack of their paramount capital Khattusha and the loss of central and western Anatolia," and that, given that the language of choice in Iron Age inscriptions was Luwian and not Hittite, these post–empire collapse Anatolian migrants must themselves have been Luwians (1982: 372–73). This assumption of a southeasterly migration from Hattusha and environs as a result of the empire's fall continues to be held (e.g., Yakubovich 2011: 537), and scholars cite the burial practice of cremation in Iron Age contexts at sites like Carchemish and Hama—a practice common in central Anatolia during the Late Bronze Age but introduced to southeastern Anatolia and northern Syria only during the Iron Age—as evidence (Singer 2005: 439). However, other than the proliferation of Hieroglyphic Luwian inscriptions in the region, direct historical evidence for this post–empire collapse migration is meagre, and it is possible that these inscriptions, burial practices, and Hittite iconographic continuity derive ultimately from Luwian settlers who arrived around the time that Suppiluliuma I established his viceroyalties in the region and who refashioned these ethnic markers in new configurations in the Iron Age (Bryce 2012: 52–60; Collins 2007: 214–15).

We will return to the question of migration shortly, proposing that diaspora is a productive theoretical lens through which to evaluate the various lines of evidence that do support reconstructions of population transfer from the plateau into the southeast. For now, the salient point is that, regardless of their origins in either a long-standing regional population or a recent population influx, the standard way that scholarly literature treats the Iron Age city-states is to describe them as "Luwian" or "Neo-Hittite" (Bryce 2012: 47–48; Giusfredi 2010; Hawkins 1982, 1995a; Thuesen 2002), the same casual equation of ethnicity and nation that we saw earlier with the Aramaeans.

## Messy Data: Continuity and Discontinuity in the Iron Age

The urge to portray the Iron Age city-states as having resembled the modern synthesis of state and ethnic group is understandable. After all, the archaeological record has furnished us with a number of royal inscriptions written in either Hieroglyphic Luwian or in Aramaic, two languages that do not even belong to the same language family. These inscriptions provide the names of rulers and related dynasts in these respective languages—in other words, they are explicitly concerned with the nature of political authority in the kingdom. If the primary historical texts we possess are royal figures discussing their lineage and associating that lineage with political order, it is only natural for a modern audience to slip into uncritical associations of ethnicity and statehood.

A closer look at the nature of the texts that are found within specific city-states, or that are written about them, makes clear that this association is no longer feasible. One city-state, ancient Sam'al and its capital city at Zincirli, illustrates well how the ongoing accumulation of evidence precludes tidy ethnic categorizations of the state. The kingdom is typically considered to be Aramaean due to the use of Samalian, possibly a local dialect of Aramaic (see Huehnergard 1995), or Aramaic itself in the majority of its inscriptions. These languages are used in royal texts such as the early eighth-century inscription of Panamuwa I on a monumental statue from the site of Gerçin and the late eighth-century inscription of Barrakib. However, the late ninth-century inscription of Kulamuwa, until recently the earliest monumental royal inscription from Sam'al, was composed in Phoenician (*KAI* 24; see discussion of Phoenician-language inscriptions in Chapter 3). In addition, a number of royal names presented in these inscriptions, including both Panamuwa and Kulamuwa, are Luwian names (Donner and Röllig 1966; Tropper 1993). The same is true of the recently discovered mortuary stele from Zincirli, composed in West Semitic Samalian by the Luwian-named KTMW (vocalization unclear) (Pardee 2009; Struble and Herrmann 2009). Indeed, according to the texts, individuals of the same family were being named in different languages, such as Panamuwa II, whose name is Luwian, but whose father and son were given West Semitic names (V. R. Herrmann et al. 2016: 67).[4] Already, then, the assocation of language with the ethnic nature of the city-state of Sam'al is challenged by the nature of the texts themselves: the language of the inscriptions and the language of the authors' names conflict. This one city-state's small corpus of inscriptions has alone generated a veritable cottage industry of scholarship attempting to slot this information into historical rubrics that would accord with contemporary assumptions surrounding language and the nation, especially at which times the city-state was Luwian and which Aramaean (see Niehr 2016: 306 for a list of the many relevant references)

A recently published inscription written in Hieroglyphic Luwian discovered in 2006 at Pancarlı Höyük, a site just 1 km southeast of Zincirli, has muddied the situation further (Herrmann et al. 2016). Until this time, the only Hieroglyphic Luwian texts found at or near the capital of Sam'al were a poorly preserved mortuary stele from Karaburçlu, 5 km north of Zincirli (Orthmann 1971: 76, 487), and a signet ring belonging to Barrakib (von Luschan and Andrae 1943: 95–96). Now we have an inscription fragment that the authors plausibly reconstruct as deriving from a monumental royal statue on the scale of the 2.85 m tall Hadad statue from Gerçin (Herrmann et al. 2016: 55, 65), demonstrating beyond doubt that Luwian was a major language of communication within Sam'al (Figure 2.3). In addition, although the inscribed statue fragment is dated on paleographic and linguistic grounds to the late tenth or early ninth century (2016: 56–60), the authors note the presence of an as-yet-unpublished lead strip inscribed in Hieroglyphic Luwian discovered at Zincirli itself in a late eighth-to-seventh-century context, further attesting to the continued use of the language throughout the city-state's existence (2016: n82). The earlier lack of Hieroglyphic Luwian inscriptions in Sam'al, therefore, would seem to be at least partially due to the accident of discovery.[5]

The authors of the Pancarlı Höyük inscription publication note two possible ways to interpret the presence of this monumental royal Hieroglyphic Luwian text in the midst of what is typically considered to have been an Aramaean city-state. Their first option is to consider the text as the first evidence for the use of Hieroglyphic Luwian by Aramaean kings, and the second is to reconstruct a pre-Aramaean Luwian regime, perhaps an offshoot of Carchemish or another Syro-Anatolian city-state, that was then replaced by the Aramaean dynasty, with the determining factor between these two choices being whether one dates the inscription to the early ninth or late tenth century, respectively (2016: 53, 68–70). For our purposes here the significant point is that, although the authors recognize the possibility that an Aramaean dynasty using Hieroglyphic Luwian in a royal inscription would both "soften our perception of the disruption of the initial 'Aramaean conquest,' and . . . further blur the lines between the so-called Neo-Hittite and Aramaean kingdoms" (2016: 70), it is nevertheless the case that the nation-state remains the tacit assumption in both interpretive options: Was Sam'al first a Neo-Hittite and then an Aramaean city-state, or was it an Aramaean city-state that occasionally used Hieroglyphic Luwian inscriptions?

Scholarship on Zincirli and the kingdom of Sam'al is not alone in this regard. Several city-states have produced inscriptions in more than one language, a problem that is usually resolved by means of earnest attempts to clarify and reconstruct city-states' histories as they pass from one ethnic identity to another, such as Patina/'Unqi (Harrison 2001) and Masuwari/Til-Barsip/Bit-Adini mentioned earlier (Bunnens 1995; Ussishkin 1971), or Hamath as it passed from the

FIGURE 2.3
Photograph and line drawing of the Hieroglyphic Luwian inscription discovered at Pancarlı
Höyük. (Photograph and drawing by Virginia R. Herrmann, courtesy of the Chicago-
Tübingen Expedition to Zincirli)

Luwian Urhilina-Uratamis dynasty to the Aramaean dynasty of Zakkur (Hawkins
2000: 400–401). The gradual accumulation of additional complicating evidence
like the Pancarlı Höyük inscription or the new readings of the Iron Age I name of
Patina as Walistin and Palistin, possibly connecting that city-state with the "PLST"
Sea Peoples group (see later), is never understood as a direct challenge to the association of ethnolinguistic identity and the state, but rather as further clues in solving
the puzzle of reconstructing the trajectory of national timelines. In a recent article,

for example, Sader (2014: 12–13) notes how new evidence increasingly demonstrates the close association of Neo-Hittite and Aramaean states, with the former even including ethnic communities of the latter, but remains committed to distinguishing their two political histories and attributing our difficulties in disentangling them to our "lack of sufficient documentation." Yet the more documentation appears, the messier our reconstructions are obliged to become, and the more these associations of ethnicity and polity are revealed to be strained attempts at foisting an inapplicable model onto an uncooperative subject.

This chapter proposes an alternative to this problem of multiple languages being located within a single city-state and jumbled across the region, one that is appealing by virtue of its simplicity: rather than represent an ethnohistorical puzzle that grows ever-harder to solve, the messiness of our textual data reflects what was, in fact, a messy ethnolinguistic landscape, and one that we do not need to connect directly to the political identities of the Syro-Anatolian city-states in which these groups lived. Note that this argument is not against the existence of Iron Age ethnic groups per se; it remains possible that the speakers of the primary languages spoken in this time and place considered themselves to be ethnically distinct from one another (Novák 2005). But two points follow from recognizing that our complicated linguistic data derive from a different mechanism than political affiliations. First, archaeological evidence for broad and consistent material and iconographic similarities across the region conflicts with the picture provided by our reliance on the language of elite texts for understanding the composition of SACC. Second, we need to look to a new theoretical source for identity formation if we are to understand how these various lines of evidence fit with one another, one that, to return to the inscriptions of Tiglath-pileser I, is able to accommodate, for example, *aḥlamu* Aramaeans living in cities, and in the district of Carchemish of the land of Hatti. One helpful avenue is to consider migration and diaspora theory, which lead us to recognize the fluidity and constant mobility of Syro-Anatolian people, objects, and concepts.

::::

# Diaspora, Migration, and the Rise of the Syro-Anatolian Culture Complex

## *Migration Theory and the Iron Age in Southeast Anatolia and North Syria*

As alluded to earlier, the changes in social structure that accompanied the transition from the Late Bronze Age into the Iron Age in the late second millennium have often been attributed to large-scale migrations of one kind or another. In the case of SACC, there are three major population movements to which scholars have pointed in order to set the stage for the eventual appearance of new city-states: Luwian speakers from central Anatolia, nomadic Aramaeans from the Syrian Desert, and, most recently, Sea People from the Aegean world. Earlier I critiqued the prevailing consensus that tribal terminology and dispersed rural settlement patterns necessarily indicate a large nomadic Aramaean population in the process of sedentarizing. Instead, this settlement pattern signature was the outcome of a small-scale sedentarizing event that took place slightly earlier than assumed (Szuchman 2007) combined with already-settled inhabitants of the region moving to a new rural way of life. Although the Aramaean case is not a migration per se, but rather a localized demographic movement, the other two are more traditional examples of migrations as typically conceived: long-distance movements of a group of people from a place of origin to a new land. But the body of anthropological literature on the topic of migration has never been brought to bear on either of these cases in the context of SACC, with the result that the region's relationship to migration is undertheorized. A full exposition of migration will not be possible here, and a study devoted to migration theory and the origins of SACC is much needed, much as Yasur-Landau (2010) has accomplished in the context of the southern Levant. Nevertheless, we can sketch the outlines of such a project, which already is enough to determine that although the evidence is hardly unambiguous or voluminous enough to make migration the sole driver of SACC's creation, it must have played a significant role.

Migration itself has waxed and waned in popularity as an explanation of culture change visible in the archaeological record (Dommelen 2014), and its reception among scholars maps closely onto larger theoretical trends of the last century. Culture historians like V. Gordon Childe considered it a logical account for the expansions and contractions through time of the culture groups that he mapped across prehistoric Europe based on their co-occurring assemblages of material attributes. This work developed and systematized similar approaches that had already appeared in the work of German archaeologist Gustaf Kossinna, whose writing would play a role in German nationalism. The theme of migration and the diffusion of culture that accompanied it (Kluckhohn 1936) was a consistent presence in Childe's writing from his first major works (1925) to later scholarship devoted to the subject (1950a). The processual archaeologists of the 1960s and 1970s, however, took exception to the deployment of migration as the inevitable mechanism offered to explain every change that appeared in the archaeological record. For one thing, archaeologists now seeking scientific rigor and the testing of hypotheses found the culture historians' lack of methodological clarity for the identification of migration—as opposed to any other process that might lead to cultural change—to be profoundly troubling (Myhre and Myhre 1972; Trigger 1968: 39–47). Even more fundamental than this methodological concern, however, was processualists' argument for a functionalist understanding of society according to which social groups are best understood as a system of related parts, with change in the system often deriving from within the system itself as individual components were obliged to adapt in the face of new circumstances such as environmental or demographic change (e.g., Binford 1965). This focus on inner mechanisms of change left little space for grand region-wide phenomena like migration that took place beyond the social system itself. While these theoretical and methodological debates unfolded, there likewise grew a suspicion of contemporary interest in migration as merely the result of societies ideologically tying their migratory origin myths with culture in a direct manner (Adams et al. 1978).

The gradual decline of the functionalist conception of society was accompanied by the slow resurgence of migration as a valid topic of archaeological interest, this time with a renewed focus on robust methodologies and the linkage of theoretical concerns with the practical considerations of identification. Recognizing that, although it does not explain many or even most changes visible in the archaeological record, migration is something that occurs in many social contexts past and present, archaeologists turned toward establishing responsible means of identifying and describing it. Anthony's (1990) article, in which he suggests that archaeologists need to stop being distracted by the often unidentifiable *causes* of migration in order to focus on their *structure*, argues that as structured behavior, long-distance migration can be distilled into a suite of characteristics (1990: 899–905): (1) conditions favoring migration will involve both "push" and "pull" factors; that is, some conditions will promote departing from the point of origin while others will promote arriving at the chosen destination specifically; (2) a "leapfrogging" pattern in which large expanses of territory are bypassed by the migrating group on the advice of scouts such as merchants, mercenaries, or craft specialists, who relay information about the physical and social landscape back to the group; (3) a "stream"-like dispersal (i.e., not a "wave"), in which largely kin-based groups depart from a constricted region and, based on preexisting knowledge, follow a tightly circumscribed route to their destination; and (4) return migration, or a counterstream of migrants returning to the point of origin based on the evaluation of opportunity costs for returning home versus remaining in the new territory.

These considerations, which Anthony draws from contemporary demographic studies, are a significant improvement on Childe's culture-historical approach, especially insofar as they recognize that migration is undertaken by defined, goal-oriented subgroups of larger cultural systems. Although it may be circular logic to assert the need for understanding the structure of a migration before identifying its signature (Anthony 1992: 174) when one needs an appreciation of its signature to identify that a migration has taken place at all, Anthony provides a basis on which to draw a series of archaeologically identifiable lines of evidence for migration.

One such line of evidence that archaeologists have advocated is the main-tenance of homeland cultural forms in private contexts with low visibility. Drawing on Bourdieu's notion of culturally ingrained bodily practices, or *habitus*, Burmeister (2000: 542) argues that migrants will practice "adaptation in the realm of the public sphere, the external domain, and invariability in the realm of the private sphere, the internal domain," with the external domain being more prone to change due to its visible presence in the society of the immigration area. It follows that material culture drawn from the internal domain, such as quotidian objects of domestic life, will be more informative for understanding migration. Similarly, archaeologists have begun to turn to isotope analysis to identify differences in the geographical sources of ancient dietary regimes between human populations, occasionally as small as neighborhoods within a single site, to demonstrate that migration took place at surprisingly small scales (Ezzo and Price 2002; Hakenbeck et al. 2010).

In a broader sense, all of these studies suggest that a more productive way for archaeologists to discuss migration might be to focus on what people *do* as opposed to the way they make themselves *look*, such that, for example, the technological style inherent in an object might be more indicative of identity than its appearance (Dietler and Herbich 1998). And the more high-resolution our analyses of migration become with the development of archaeometrical methods that can identify, for example, people consuming food and water from sources only a few dozen kilometers distant from one another, the more we will realize that small-scale and relatively short-distance movements of people were a constant feature of ancient life. Cameron (2013: 219–20), for example, has called for archaeologists to recognize that minor demographic or historical events lead to what she calls "population circulation" (Schachner 2010), or the continuous flow of people across landscapes both physical and social, challenging our associations of stasis and cultural identity in the process (see Chapter 3).

In addition to the late second–early first-millennium sedentarization and ruralization attested in northeastern Syria and southeastern Anatolia already discussed, the two primary migration events discussed in the context of SACC are those of Luwian speakers and, more recently, the Sea Peoples. As mentioned earlier, scholars argue that the surge of Luwian-language monumental inscriptions in southeastern Anatolia and northern Syria during the Iron Age is a direct result of Luwian migrants moving to the region in the wake of the collapse of the Hittite Empire (Hawkins 1982: 372; 1995a: 1297; Yakubovich 2011: 537). We may never know the structure (per Anthony 1990) of this migration event, and thus for now we are restricted primarily to looking for indicators that it even took place.

## *The Luwian Arrival*

The first and most obvious piece of evidence for a possible migration from the Anatolian plateau into southeastern Anatolia and north Syria is the existence of the Luwian inscriptions in this region. These represent a dramatic quantitative increase from the sporadic Late Bronze Age exemplars such as the hieroglyphs accompanying figures on the late fourteenth–early thirteenth-century orthostat found reused as a step in Temple Ib at Alalakh (Woolley 1955: pl. 48), now known to refer to the "Great Priest Prince" Tuthaliya and his wife Ašnu-Hepa (Yener et al. 2014). Although it seems reasonable to explain the surge in volume of Hieroglyphic Luwian inscriptions by means of an arrival of Luwian speakers, in fact this deduction conflates the *explanandum* and the *explanans*, such that the explanation for the presence of the inscriptions is a migration which we know to have taken place thanks to the presence of the inscriptions. There are, after all, other mechanisms that could account for the widespread use of Hieroglyphic Luwian in Iron Age monumental inscriptions. One proposal is that Carchemish acted as a cultural model to its neighbors and contemporaries, being a Hittite center that survived the Bronze Age collapse and that could therefore promulgate its own social norms (Bunnens 2000a: 17). In this case the use of Hieroglyphic Luwian in monumental displays across SACC becomes more of an ideological tactic than an attempt to communicate with an actual Luwian-speaking audience.

However, a small but growing corpus of nonmonumental Hieroglyphic Luwian inscriptions belies the argument that the language was only for display purposes. These texts include the mid- to late eighth-century Kululu lead strips (Hawkins 1987), the letters found at Assur (Andrae 1924), an inscribed lead strip dating to the late eighth–seventh century from Zincirli (Herrmann et al. 2016: 68n82), and several miscellaneous pieces from Hamath, including several bullae, a seal impression on a tablet, an inscribed shell, and an ostracon (Hawkins 2000: 420–23). The geographic range and relatively late chronological date of these inscriptions suggest that these texts were not simply the result of a powerful post–Hittite Empire Carchemish promulgating its cultural authority. More importantly, their mundane nature indicates the usage of the language itself as more than simply a medium for display, and it suggests the likelihood that issues of preservation, especially with thin lead strips, have conspired to prevent more of these documents from lasting to the present. Acknowledging the presence of nonmonumental Luwian inscriptions, few though they may be for now, obliges us to take more seriously the commonsense interpretation of the monumental inscriptions: they were composed in Hieroglyphic Luwian because they were intended to communicate with Luwian speakers in the region.

Another feature of Iron Age society that is mentioned in this context is the common practice of cremation burials (Singer 2005: 439) Unfortunately, Late Bronze Age burials from the Anatolian plateau are exceedingly rare, such that we know very little about the burial customs of that region in the period immediately preceding SACC (Seeher 2011: 388).[6] The same is true, in fact, for the Early Iron Age (Genz 2011: 343). Old Hittite cemeteries are more common, and while inhumations are present (e.g., Mellink 1956), there are also a large number of cremations. Seventy-one cremations were reported from Osmankayası (Boğazköy) (Bittel et al. 1958), for example, and 131 out of 135 burials from Ilıca were cremations placed in ceramic vessels (Orthmann 1967). This practice is difficult to assign to a specific ethnic group on the plateau, especially given the fact that cremations are occasionally found placed on top of inhumations inside of large vessels, as was the case at Demircihöyük-Sarıket grave 196 (Seeher 1993: 219, Taf. 21).

The lack of burials from the height of the Hittite Empire in the fourteenth and thirteenth century is puzzling, and the elite nature of the texts from this period, deriving predominantly from temple and palace archives, renders the historical record only partially helpful for reconstructing society-wide burial customs. Nevertheless, the texts informing us about the funerary rituals that accompanied the death of a king or royal family member describe a process that involved cremation on the night of the death (Singer 2009; van den Hout 1994: 59).

Cremation burials are found again in the Iron Age, now distributed across the Syro-Anatolian region. As Singer (2005: 439) noted, there are extensive extramural cremation cemeteries at the sites of Hamath (Riis 1948) and Carchemish's Yunus cemetery north of a small wadi that runs along the north side of the settlement (Woolley 1939–1940). In the latter, which dates to the late eighth and seventh century (some may be ninth century), or the Iron Age II and III periods, Woolley identified two principle types of cremation burial, "pot burial" and "bath burials," the former consisting of interments inside of bowls or kraters, and the latter in large bathtub-like vessels (Figure 2.4). Although Woolley does not provide counts, tallying up the burials in the publication provides totals of thirty-four pot burials and ninety-three bath burials (not individuals per se), all of which were for the exclusive use of cremations (1939–1940: 21–37). It appears that looting and Woolley's 1913 salvage excavations at the Deve Hüyük I cemetery located 26 km west of Carchemish likewise only produced cremations in these eighth-century burials (Moorey 1980: 5), although in this case no counts of any kind are available. If the Carchemish cremation burials so far date mostly late in the Iron Age sequence— and another cemetery of cremation burials recently found near Woolley's House A in the outer town is even later in the mid-first millennium (Bonomo and Zaina 2016)—the four periods of Hamath's cremation cemetery span the full Iron Age. These burials, which were excavated in opportunistic soundings underneath the

FIGURE 2.4
Photograph of cremation burials at Tell Sheikh Fawqani (Tenu 2009: Fig. 2, courtesy of Aline Tenu, Mission archéologique de Tell Shiukh Fawqâni). Cremated remains are contained within the two jars covered by inverted plates visible at left, and underneath the large inverted "bath tub" jar at right.

modern city that surrounds the acropolis, are exceedingly numerous (I: $n$ = 610; II: $n$ = 490; III: $n$ = 170; IV: $n$ = 400, plus several hundred more noted during modern construction), and date from the twelfth through the late eighth or early seventh century (Riis 1948: 192–93). With numbers as high as these, cremation was clearly a socially widespread burial custom.

Nor is the practice found in these two cemeteries alone, even if Hamath and Yunus are the two most famous examples. In addition to Deve Hüyük already mentioned, first-millennium cremation burials have been excavated at the coastal site of Ras el-Bassit, located just south of the Jebel al-'Aqra (Courbin 1993), and the site of Tell Shiukh Fawqani, 4 km south of Carchemish on the Euphrates River, where excavations in Area H north of the tell exposed almost 150 cremation burials in jars or krater urns dating to the twelfth through eighth centuries (al-Bahloul et al. 2005; Tenu 2009) (Figure 2.4). A small number of elite intramural cremation burials have also been found. These include one in a late phase of Carchemish's "North-West Fort" in whose urn was found gold, unspecified semiprecious stones, and ivory (Woolley 1921: 68), and two burial shafts on the acropolis of Tell Halaf that contained cremation urns and were topped by statues of seated women, the whole complex encased in a large mudbrick terrace (Naumann 1950: 159–67). Finds such as these suggest a distinction in who was permitted to be buried in intramural contexts, with such locations being reserved for wealthy or even royal individuals and extramural cemeteries being the common burial location (Struble and Herrmann 2009: 40). Otherwise, however, Struble and Herrmann (2009: 40) note that "fundamental similarities (across a range of elaboration) . . . suggest that beliefs and practices relating to death and the afterlife were otherwise shared broadly throughout this society." It is clear that the practice of cremation was chronologically durable and geographically ubiquitous across SACC, even into nearby cities controlled by the Assyrians, as demonstrated by cremation burials at Dūr-Katlimmu on the lower Khabur River (Kreppner 2008).[7]

The association of cremation burial practice with an Anatolian origin is not universally accepted, and one argument against it is the notion that any cultural practice is potentially variable and available for adoption toward a culturally strategic motive. Collins (2007: 89–90), for example, argues that "under certain social pressures, individuals or communities chose to practice cremation over inhumation. The choice was not ethnically driven, and the presence of cremation burials alone cannot be used to assume the presence of a large population of Luwians or other Anatolians in Syria." Instead, similar to the adoption and proliferation of Hieroglyphic Luwian, the practice is said to derive from the political stability of Malatya and Carchemish and concomitant appeal in generating a new cultural identity at the start of the Iron Age (Collins 2007: 90). And as proof that the practice was not brought to SACC's region as part of a post–Hittite Empire collapse migration, some note that there are Late Bronze Age cremation burials in the same region, especially a number of intramural cremation burials in the Late Bronze levels of Alalakh (Bienkowski 1982: 80–81; Woolley 1955: 202–23), and nine in the late thirteenth- to early twelfth-century levels at Tell Sabi Abyad (Düring et al. 2015), as well as contemporary cremation burials in adjacent regions like Phoenicia (see Chapter 3). Similarly, Bienkowski (1982: 83–84) points to the diversity in cremation practices, such as the cremation urns or kraters of the Yunus cemetery being placed in large "baths" which are not found in Hamath, or the two unique elite burial shafts at Tell Halaf.

But the difference in scale between the small number of such burials at Late Bronze Age Alalakh or Tell Sabi Abyad and SACC is so substantial that it still requires explanation, and there are many reasons why site-specific cemeteries might display slightly different burial customs from one another in the archaeological record, not least of which is the accident of discovery. The fact remains that cremation was suddenly adopted across the Syro-Anatolian region and then used throughout the Iron Age, and it appears to have been practiced at all levels of society. Therefore, although the lack of Late Bronze Age cremation burials on the plateau is problematic, the Middle Bronze cremation cemeteries from Anatolia combined with Empire-period texts are highly suggestive of the practice moving with its adherents at the Bronze–Iron Age transition. This is especially the case given the simultaneous use of Hieroglyphic Luwian across the region, which even Collins (2007: 87) is obliged to admit is only a logical practice for an audience of Luwian speakers regardless of how conveniently propagandistic the script itself may have been.

In addition to changes in burial practices, settlement pattern distributions can be informative for understanding demographic transformations interregionally. We have already seen how settlement pattern dynamics in this region were characterized by a dramatic surge in the number of small, rural sites. On the Anatolian plateau, however, the Late Bronze–Iron Age transition has quite a different settlement pattern signature. Surveys in central Anatolia are patchy in coverage, methodologically inconsistent from one another, and generally extensive in nature.[8] For these reasons, it is more difficult to draw generalizing conclusions than it was in northeastern Syria. Nevertheless, from their synthetic summary of this work, Altaweel and Squitieri (2018: 104) tentatively conclude that both the number of sites and total settled area across the plateau decreased at the end of the Late Bronze Age and start of the Iron Age, before increasing again in the centuries following. Looking more closely at settlement patterns in the Konya region, for example, a survey conducted by Sachihiro Omura (2000, 2001) revealed twenty-five Late Bronze Age sites west and south of the Tuz Gölü, but only eight in the Iron Age I period, before increasing again to thirty-seven in the following period (Figure 2.5).[9] Summarizing the many surveys in this region, Matessi and Tomassini Pieri (2018: 102) state that across the Late Bronze–Iron Age transition this region of south-central Anatolia "saw a drastic settlement drop of about 90%," even while they emphasize that indications of microregional continuity also exist. In short, the pattern in this region is not an influx of settlements in the late second millennium and early first millennium, as per the area south and east of the Taurus Mountains, but rather a marked decrease in the number of settlements. Trends such as these are indicative of significant changes to the regional settlement pattern, changes that are consistent with an increase of mobility and the late second-millennium depopulation of the area.

A full explication of material culture changes in the Anatolian plateau across the Late Bronze–Iron Age transition is not possible here. But it is worth noting that, despite evidence for continuity in certain locations such as the maintenance of the fortification walls at Kınık Höyük from the Late Bronze Age well into the Iron Age (Highcock et al. 2015: 123), the general picture is one of a marked decline in social complexity until the ninth century. Hermann Genz (2011: 359) describes the

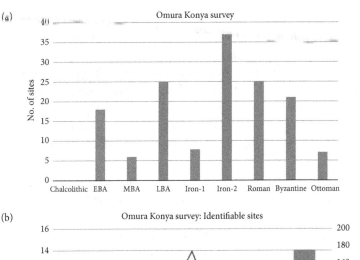

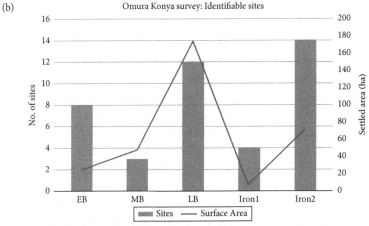

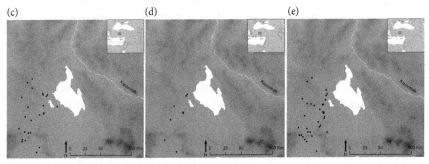

FIGURE 2.5

Results of survey work in northwestern Konya conducted by the Japanese Institute for Anatolian Archaeology as an example of settlement pattern changes across the late second to early first millennium BCE (Omura 2000; 2001): (*a*) total number of sites reported per period; (*b*) reported sites and settled area identifiable in satellite imagery; (*c*) identifiable Late Bronze Age settlements; (*d*) identifiable Iron I settlements; (*e*) identifiable Iron II settlements. (Maps aided by Siena Fite and Anthony Lauricella) evidence pertaining to settlements, burial patterns, metals and other crafts, seals, and economic organization to conclude that during the Iron Age I period there was "no evidence for a stratified society in most parts of Central Anatolia." Likewise, Geoffrey Summers (2017) finds very little evidence of technological continuity following the end of the Hittite Empire, noting, among other things, the end of cuneiform writing and an Iron Age lack of even Hieroglyphic Luwian within the Kızıl Irmak (as well as a curious delay before the resumption of Luwian inscriptions in Tabal several centuries later), and a steep decline in the production of monumental arts. With respect to settlement patterns in central Anatolia, significant central places in the form of major urban centers are lacking as the Iron Age begins. Iron Age I sites are present atop previously occupied sites, "although greatly reduced in size" (2011: 336), before recovering again in the early first millennium BCE. This necessarily brief overview of archaeological indicators for transformation in the Anatolian plateau at the end of the second millennium is consistent not just with political decentralization following the demise of the Hittite state, but also with regional depopulation and mobility.

In sum, the presence of cremation burials across SACC is, in and of itself, not sufficient and unambiguous evidence for a Luwian migration. On the contrary, other expressions of material cultural such as ceramics continued their gradual morphological evolution and interregional connections as one would expect in the absence of a massive demographic shift (e.g., Manuelli 2011; Pucci 2017). It does, however, combine with the adoption and spread of Hieroglyphic Luwian, changes hinted at in settlement pattern dynamics, the deployment of Hittite-style visual motifs and artistic programs, and marked demographic and material transformations on the Anatolian plateau to indicate that a group of people from the north and northwest of the Taurus and Amanus mountain ranges arrived in southeastern Anatolia and northern Syria at the start of the Iron Age for reasons that are complicated and still unclear—and, perhaps, impossible to identify fully.

What this fusion of an Anatolian burial practice and language with other local aspects of material culture indicates is a hybridized, diasporic cultural expression as outlined earlier in the chapter. Too complicated and multifaceted to be characterized as either "Neo-Hittite" or "Aramaean," the Syro-Anatolian city-states merged aspects of both into a cultural expression that, though complex and varied across the city-states, is identifiably consistent. As was the case with language, Zincirli is again the best case for making this point with respect to burial practices. The discovery of the mid-eighth-century KTMW stele in the lower town depicts a "mortuary repast" for the deceased individual, a common motif of Syro-Anatolian mortuary monuments (Bonatz 2000, 2014) (Figure 2.6). Furthermore, the accompanying inscription—written, as noted earlier, in Samalian despite the author's Luwian name—provides instructions for foods to be provisioned for

FIGURE 2.6
The KTMW funerary stele from Zincirli. (Photograph by Eudora Struble, courtesy of the Chicago-Tübingen Expedition to Zincirli)

various gods, including both Semitic deities (e.g., "Hadad of the Vineyard," itself possibly a Samalian rendition of a Luwian title) and Luwian deities (e.g., Kubaba the female tutelary deity of Carchemish) (Pardee 2014: 47). Some of this food is also to be partitioned for the "soul" of KTMW, which is said to reside in the stele itself (Herrmann in press).[10] Yet although the stele clearly belongs to the local mortuary cult, KTMW's remains were not found in the mortuary chapel along with the stele. This is as expected in light of the cemeteries described earlier, which are located outside of the cities (Herrmann 2014: 52). The inscription's explicit association of the KTMW's soul with the stele as opposed to with his mortal remains, which is typically the case with inhumations, is entirely consistent with both second- and first-millennium considerations of the body and soul in Hittite and Luwian texts (see Melchert 2010 and references therein; Hawkins 2015). Although we cannot say for certain, this separation of body and soul is highly suggestive of his body having been subjected to cremation.

This stele, then, exemplifies the complicated ethnic nature of SACC: a mixture of Luwian and Semitic deities, West Semitic language and script, Luwian onomastics, and Anatolian burial customs (Schloen 2014: 36–38). But rather than seeing it as evidence of "the ongoing vitality of inherited Luwian cultural traditions at Sam'al in the midst of an equally vital Semitic cultural milieu" (2014: 38), we can go further to recognize not simply the co-presence of two groups, or cultural borrowings from one to the other, but the existence of a single, hybridized cultural formation that fluctuates in its expression over time and between city-states in space.[11] This is the heart of the contribution that notions of diaspora offer for a model SACC, which is to be understood as consisting not of rival ethnicities whose associated city-states' ethnic historical sequences get clarified with the accumulation of evidence, but rather of a cultural expression that selectively and simultaneously fuses elements of both major ethnic groups to create something new.

## *Migrants from the Aegean*

Current migration theory's emphasis on people's actions, such as burial customs, instead of outward appearances, such as artistic styles, has brought us to a point of acknowledging the likelihood of at least a small-scale migration from the plateau into southeastern Anatolia at the start of the Iron Age. One of the most noteworthy developments in Near Eastern archaeology in recent years has been the growing re-alization that Luwian speakers were not the only possible migrant group into the region. New archaeological and textual evidence is combining to suggest that a group of people from Cyprus or the Aegean may also have arrived at the northeast coast of the Mediterranean as part of the famous Sea Peoples phenomenon so familiar to students of the southern Levant. In the latter case, the newcomers became the biblical Philistines and belonged to the Sea Peoples group the *plst*. Although a small number of scholars have proposed that Aegean-style material culture in Philistia is the result of trade or other mechanisms (e.g., Sherratt 1998), most archaeologists agree with the basic consensus that this new archaeological horizon represents an incoming population from the Aegean that formed a modest but significant com-ponent of the population of the cities in which they settled (Dothan 1981; Stager 1995; Yasur-Landau 2010).

Along the northeastern littoral, evidence pointing toward an Aegean presence in the Iron Age I period pertains to Cilicia and the Amuq Valley. In the case of the latter, a clear demographic shift was noted from the Late Bronze into the Iron Age I period in the settlement pattern data collected by Braidwood in the 1930s (Braidwood 1937) and confirmed by Yener's Amuq Valley Regional Project survey (Yener 2005). Of the forty-seven sites in the valley belonging to the Iron I, or Phase N in the Amuq Valley sequence, thirty, or 64 percent, represent new foundations. At the same time, thirty-five of these sites, or 75 percent, continued into the Iron II period, or Phase O. In addition, the mean site size decreases from 4.76 to 3.61 ha from the Late Bronze to the Iron I periods (Harrison 2001: 122–23). What this data indicate for the Amuq Valley, where the Syro-Anatolian city-state of Patina was located, is that the Late Bronze–Iron Age transition really was a significant demographic event, one that witnessed the creation of a large number of new, small settlements. Interestingly, settlement pattern data from the much larger region of Cilicia show significantly more evidence for continuity across the end of the second millennium. A number of surveys in this area—again of patchy quality and consistency precluding estimates of settled area—have recently been collated by Susanne Rutishauser (2016, 2017), whose data indicate approximately 149 sites across the region in the Late Bronze Age, and still 135 in the Iron Age I, followed by 156 in the Iron Age II.[12]

In the Amuq Valley, the primary diagnostic ceramic for surveyors to date the twelfth and eleventh centuries BCE appears to have been locally produced Late Helladic IIIC painted pottery (Braidwood 1937: 6; Casana and Wilkinson 2005: Fig. A.15; Yener et al. 2000: 188–89), a style of decorated pottery derived from Cypriot and Aegean ceramics of the Late Bronze Age and imitating contemporary Iron Age I forms from those regions (Figure 2.7). A similar phenomenon took place in Cilicia where, despite settlement continuity, surveyors and excavators have noted at least twenty-six sites that produced this new ware (Lehmann 2007: 498–500; Mee 1978; Seton-Williams 1954) and in western Syria south of the Amuq, especially at coastal sites such as Tell Kazel, and inland at Tell Afis, where stratified excavations have found the ware in abundance (Venturi 2000, 2007). Equally significant to the presence of the "Aegeanizing" LH IIIC pottery at these sites, where their identification on survey indicates that a high percentage would be found in excavation, is that they are found on sites of all sizes, including small rural villages. LH IIIC's spatial distribution is rather limited, being restricted to the Syrian coast, Cilicia, and the Amuq and its tributary valleys, not being found much further east than 'Ain Dara (Stone and Zimansky 1999: Fig. 27: 1, 3, Fig. 29) in the Afrin Valley (see Lehmann 2007: Map 3); LH IIIC pottery does not appear, for example, in the Iron Age I levels of Malatya (Manuelli 2011) nor in the renewed excavations at Carchemish to date (Giacosa 2016).

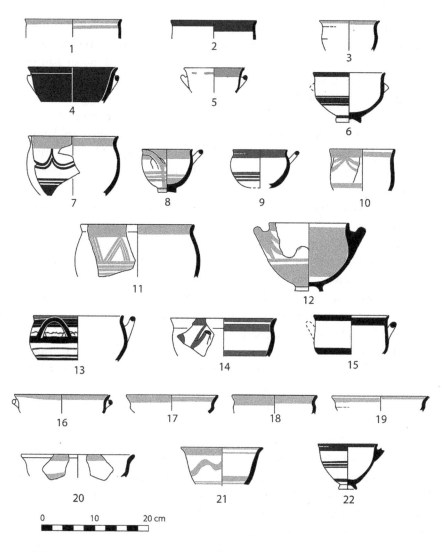

FIGURE 2.7
Locally produced Late Helladic IIIC pottery from Tell Tayinat during the Iron Age I,
Field Phases 6-3, or mid-twelfth century to early tenth century. (Welton et al. 2019: Fig. 15;
drawings by B. Janeway and L. Welton, courtesy of the Tayinat Archaeological Project)

This ceramic evidence raises the issue whether at least part of the new Iron Age
settlement system in the Amuq and Cilicia had its origins not just with arrivals
from the Anatolian plateau, but also in an arriving migrant population from the
Aegean world, in which case this population would likely be associated with the
Sea Peoples who are recognized as having migrated to the eastern Mediterranean

littoral further south. This is a tempting explanation, although as noted earlier the
Cilician settlement data at least are remarkably uniform between the Late Bronze
and Iron Age (Lehmann 2017: 247), and scholars have additionally noted that, given
LH IIIC's greater similarity with Cypriot ceramics than with the Aegean and the
limited range of LH IIIC forms, which seem restricted mostly to open vessels for
the consumption of liquids such as wine, economic interaction between the coastal
valleys and Cyprus is just as plausible (Lehmann 2007: 516–17). There are, however,
non-LH IIIC ceramic forms that are similarly Aegean or Cypriot in origin, such as
the steatite-tempered cooking pot, which is unlikely to have been an object of trade
(Birney 2008).

Recent developments in the history and archaeology of the city-state of Patina,
which was based in the Amuq, shed light on the issue. The 1930s excavations of
the University of Chicago's Oriental Institute focused primarily on the Iron Age II
period, exposing a series of monumental buildings in the acropolis, and not going
below these structures into the Iron Age except for a few small soundings (Haines
1971). Renewed excavations at the site have exposed a series of continuous Iron
Age I phases beneath a later temple (Building II) in an excavation area referred to
as Field 1. These levels, which span the mid-twelfth through mid-tenth centuries,
contain not just the locally made LH IIIC pottery recently described by Janeway
(2017), but also other indicators of Aegeanizing material culture such as a dietary
pattern that appears to be at least partially influenced by Late Helladic patterns
of meat consumption (Lipovitch 2006–2007: 158), hundreds of unperforated, cylindrical, unbaked clay loom weights, or "spool weights," which have also been
identified in Philistine contexts in the south (Harrison 2009b, 2009c; Janeway
2006–2007), and which are recognized as belonging to the warp-weighted loom
that was reintroduced to the region at this time (Cecchini 2000). Intriguingly,
however, the earliest Iron I phase in Field, Field Phase 6c, is characterized by continuity from the preceding Late Bronze Age both in ceramics and textile production.[13] It is not until the subsequent FP 6b, roughly the second half of the twelfth
century and into the early eleventh (Welton et al. 2019: 322), that locally made LH
IIIC pottery and cylindrical loom weights appear in significant quantities, which
may challenge the assumption that settlement pattern changes during the Iron Age
I necessarily took place entirely due to the arrival of Sea Peoples in the early twelfth
century. On the contrary, excavations in Tayinat's Field 1 demonstrate conclusively
that, although new Aegean/Cypriot connections are genuine, this was only one
of a diversity of cultural links that characterized the site in the Iron Age I period
(Welton et al. 2019: 325). Equally significant is the fact that although the nearby site
of Çatal Höyük did produce contemporary LH IIIC-style ceramics in great quantity, it completely lacked these other markers of foreign habits that are evident at
Tayinat (Pucci 2019: 290), which Marina Pucci (2019: 291–93) reasonably concludes

implies that migrants using this foreign assemblage of material culture arrived in a sufficiently small population that Tayinat is possibly the only place in the area that migrants actually settled, using pottery that would be emulated in nearby towns like Çatal Höyük.

At the same time as Aegeanizing Iron Age I material culture was being excavated from Tell Tayinat, new epigraphic discoveries were also shedding light on the site's Aegean connection during this period. The Iron Age II Luwian inscription TELL TAYINAT 1, discovered in the 1930s, has long provided the name of the local kingdom during the early first millennium in the form of an ethnicon, Walistinean, providing the place name Walistin.[14] The same name has been found on the early first-millennium inscriptions of MEHARDE and SHEIZAR, two stelae found upstream on the Orontes River in the kingdom of Hama (Hawkins 2000: 415–19), as well as the recently discovered ARSUZ 1 and 2 stelae found on the Mediterranean coast west of the Amanus Mountains and south of modern Iskenderun (Dinçol et al. 2015). At the same time, the discovery of the Bronze and Iron Age temple of the storm god at Aleppo (Gonnella et al. 2005; Kohlmeyer 2009) was accompanied by two eleventh-century inscriptions, ALEPPO 6 and 7, that write the name with an initial /P/, providing an alternate version of toponym as Palistin (Hawkins 2011). The two versions, Walistin and Palistin, may reflect different options of representing a fricative /f/ sound (Singer 2012: 463; Weeden 2013: 11).

The etymological association of Palistin in the Amuq with the *plst* Sea Peoples group of Iron Age I Philistia in the southern Levant is tempting, and indeed several scholars have argued on this basis for the presence of "a powerful Philistine kingdom in the Amuq Plain" (Hawkins 2009: 172), with the archaeological and textual evidence providing mutual support for the conclusion (Galil 2014). However, there is good reason to be cautious with this reconstruction on both archaeological and philological grounds. Archaeologically, it is important to remember that the name Walistin/Palistin only appears in Luwian-language inscriptions, not a language one would associate with incomers from the Aegean, and that these inscriptions only appear in contexts chronologically and culturally removed from the Aegeanizing material culture. At Tayinat, for example, Walistin is mentioned in the inscription TELL TAYINAT 1, which dates centuries after the appearance of LH IIIC pottery at the site in the mid- to late twelfth century (Weeden 2013: 15, Table 2). On the contrary, by this time the material culture of the site resembles the typical suite of Syro-Anatolian characteristics, including the *bīt-ḫilāni* palace and Red Slipped Burnished Ware pottery (Singer 2012: 466–68). ALEPPO 6 and 7 date late in the Iron I sequence, but here too there is nothing other than the name of Palistin itself that one would associate with Aegean immigrants. Nor is the name itself a perfect equation with *plst*. The final /n/ of the Luwian inscriptions is not found on any of the texts mentioning the *plst* of the southern Levant, which requires creative solutions such as Hawkins's proposal that "Palisiin" is a Luwian modification of the plural form *plstym*, "Philistines," "and Luwian being a language without final *-m* adapted the form to its own morphology" (2011: 52). Considerations such as these lead Younger (2016: 127–35) to argue tentatively that it is at least equally plausible that the gentilic Palistinean/Walistinean might have an Anatolian origin separate from the *plst* of the southern Levant.

These points are all important and pertain directly to whether it is appropriate to refer to the Walistin/Palistin in the time of Taita as a "powerful Philistine kingdom," but the fact of LH IIIC pottery in the Amuq, and especially in several phases of Tell Tayinat's Iron I levels beginning roughly 1150 BCE along with other aspects of Aegean material culture, cannot be disregarded regardless of whether one sees the similarity and near-contemporaneity of Luwian Palistin/Walistin and southern Levantine *plst* as a coincidence or as a meaningful etymological relationship. The Aegeanizing material culture alone, in other words, requires some form of explanation. Even while Lehmann (2007: 515) is correct to temper our scalar expectations for "clear evidence for a massive migration of Sea Peoples in the region," it remains likely that at least a small number of Aegean (or Cypriot) migrants did arrive in the Amuq during the twelfth century, apparently slightly later than in the southern Levant, settled at Tayinat and surrounding sites and mixed with the local population. Material evidence of their presence lasts roughly a century and a half before local cultural expressions are again completely predominant (Harrison 2009c: 187), at which time the only remaining evidence of the modest Aegean immigration may possibly be the echo of their name preserved in the name of the kingdom (Emanuel 2015: 24).

Developments in Cilicia have been only slightly less dramatic. For several decades, the city-state of Que that occupied this region has been famous for the highland fortress site of Karatepe. The site's complicated program of reliefs adorning its northern and southern gates has long been noted for the Aegean iconographic elements depicted on some of the orthostats, such as the parallel Özyar (2013: 128, Fig. 12) draws between Karatepe slab Nr. 0, with its representation of two antithetical shielded warriors, and Olympia B 1654, depicting a fight between two hoplites. Another famous example is the relief depicting a war galley in the right chamber of the North Gate: as Özyar (2014: 142, Fig. 6) notes, "in contrast to the round-hulled merchant ships of the Phoenicians, this type of long, shallow galley fitted with a ram is unmistakably of Aegean origins" (see also Çambel and Özyar 2003: 84–89) (Figure 2.8). Besides the reliefs, here was found a lengthy Phoenician-Luwian bilingual inscription that is dated to the late eighth century on the basis of its author, Azatiwada, naming his benefactor as one Awariku, king of Que, identified with the Urikki named in inscriptions by both Tiglath-pileser III and Sargon II (Çambel

FIGURE 2.8
Relief from Karatepe's North Gate, West chamber, depicting an Aegean-style galley. (Çambel and Özyar 2003: 84–89; photograph courtesy of Aslı Özyar, with permission)

1999; Hawkins 2000: 45–68; Röllig 1999). Another Phoenician-Luwian bilingual on a statue of the Storm God and base was discovered *ex situ* near the village of Çineköy (Tekoğlu et al. 2000), although this time authored by Warika.

Both of these inscriptions provide the name of the kingdom, and, as in the Amuq, the terms are highly suggestive. In the Karatepe inscription we see Awariku as king of DNNYM (Phoenician) and Adana(wa) (Luwian), while in Çineköy we have DNNYM (Phoenician) but now Hiyawa (Luwian). This term *Hiyawa* is clearly equivalent to Akkadian "Que" and forms the Luwian name of the kingdom alongside Adana, the Luwian name of the capital city (as it is today) (Hawkins 2009: 166). It is also likely that *Hiyawa* derives ultimately from Hittite "Ahhiyawa" as attested in the texts from Hattusha, texts referring to Mycenaean Greeks whom the Hittites encountered in their western Anatolian affairs, supported further by Herodotus's statement that Cilicians' original ethnicon was "Hypachaioi" (sub-Achaeans) (Bryce 2016; Tekoğlu et al. 2000).[15] As if this place name were not sug-gestive enough on its own right, both Çineköy and Karatepe cite the ancestor of Awariku/Warika as one Muksa (Luwian)—MPŠ (Phoenician), that is, Mopsos, the Greek hero who legendarily journeyed through Anatolia from west to east, founding a number of settlements in Cilicia. Regardless of this individual's histo-ricity, his name is another indirect association of the kingdom of Que with Aegean migrants. As Hawkins has summarized,

> The association of thirteenth-century B.C.E. *Ahhiyawa* of the Hittite Empire texts with the *Qawe/Que/Hiyawa* of the Assyrian and Hieroglyphic Luwian sources of the ninth to eighth centuries would postulate a movement of people termed *Ahhiyawa* in the twelfth century B.C.E. or later, from western Anatolia to Cilicia sufficient to establish *Hiyawa* as the country's name. The linking of such a migration to Greek traditions of Mopsos and the recognition of *Muksa/ Mpš* as the ancestor of the Cilician royal house lends further plausibility to the hypothesis. (2009: 166)

To be sure, the textual data from Çineköy and Karatepe derive from a late eighth-century context, several centuries after the Iron Age I period in which Aegean people are supposed to have arrived in Cilicia. Nevertheless, when these historical memories are viewed in light of the genuine dispersal of small sites with LH IIIC pottery across the Cilician plain during the Iron I as described earlier, it seems that here too there exists a robust case for at least a modest migration of individuals from the Aegean world at this time. Indeed, the sources converge in Que in an even more mutually reinforcing fashion than they do in Palistin.

::: 

## Conclusion

As described in Chapter 1, one of the advantages of referring to this cultural phe-nomenon as the "Syro-Anatolian Culture Complex" is that it enables us to recog-nize the fundamental cultural commonalities of the numerous city-states, while simultaneously permitting us to understand their incredible diversity and com-plexity not as a hurdle to be overcome, but as a defining characteristic of their nature. This principle is why diaspora is an appropriate lens through which to examine the origins of the Syro-Anatolian city-states and their variegated ethno-linguistic makeup across the Iron Age.

The vast literature on diasporas past and present typically emphasizes migration and dispersal, on the one hand, and a longing for return, on the other. In this chapter, we turned to literature on migration theory in anthropological archaeology to argue that, indeed, there is strong and still-accumulating evidence for a variety of migration events during the Iron Age I. Ironically, one migration scenario that needs to be recast in terms of demographic transformation is the sedentarization of Aramaic-speaking nomadic pastoralists and ruralization of former town dwellers. Equally convincing is the arrival of Luwian speakers from Anatolia, following which Hieroglyphic Luwian inscriptions and Hittite-style orthostat reliefs merged with local orthostat traditions and spread throughout SACC, outnumbering the Aramaic-language inscriptions even several centuries later by which time Aramaic had become the regional lingua franca. That such lines of evidence may pertain to incomers who were not strictly of the highest economic class might be indicated by a shared burial practice of cremation likely imported from central Anatolia, and the discovery of nonmonumental Hieroglyphic Luwian inscriptions. Still another likelihood is that a small population of migrants from the Aegean settled in Cilicia and the Amuq, leaving material traces, historical memories of Aegean origin, and possibly even linguistic clues preserved in subsequent place names in highly local contexts. None of these cases is fully unambiguous, but this cannot be taken as evidence that population movements did not take place. Instead, the ambiguity points to migrations that were small in scale and targeted in approach, as predicted by cross-cultural anthropological studies of migration patterns.

None of these migration events appear to have led directly to communities striving to return to their place of origin, or placing that memory on a cultural pedestal; at least, no such statements are preserved for us in the historical record. As we have seen, many scholars interpret the existence of Hieroglyphic Luwian inscriptions strictly as fabricated claims to a hoary historical legitimacy, which could, in its own way, be understood as an expression of longing for prior conditions. I prefer to understand the use of these texts not as an ideological strategy but as a genuine reflection of the Luwian-speaking nature of the authors. Similarly, the Aegean origin of a group of migrants did not become a central component of SACC's cultural identity; on the contrary, during the Iron Age II period, it is only reflected in a small number of etymologies. But the contribution of diaspora theory to our understanding of SACC is not its one-to-one equivalence with textbook case studies, but rather its illumination of how migration events are accompanied by cultural groups living side by side, groups whose cultural expressions eventually grow to resemble one another, and whose coexistence erodes our ability to speak of ancient polities in terms of ethnically oriented nation-states. As Stephen Greenblatt (2010: 2) states, "[t]here is no going back to the fantasy that once upon a time there were settled, coherent, and perfectly integrated national or ethnic communities." What will require further consideration is how these movements oblige us to reconsider the coalescing scholarly narrative of cultural continuity across the Late Bronze Age–Iron Age transition without reverting too far in favor of an earlier generation's predilection for complete transformations and "dark ages." By the start of the Iron Age II period, by which time the Syro-Anatolian city-states had reached the apogee of their socioeconomic complexity, Luwian speakers, Aramaic speakers, and Aegean descendants were living cheek by jowl in a shared cultural system. That shared sense of cultural identity cutting across political formations is where diaspora helps us understand the Iron Age, and, as we will see in the following chapter, mobility and culture were closely related even following the migrations of the Iron Age I.

# MOBILITY AND THE SYRO-ANATOLIAN CULTURE COMPLEX DURING THE EARLY FIRST MILLENNIUM

IN THE LAST CHAPTER I ARGUED that demographic transformations, including small-scale migration, sedentarization, and ruralization events that occurred during the late second millennium, led to an interaction of culture groups that combined over time to share a number of meaningful cultural expressions, a phenomenon that encapsulates aspects of diaspora as articulated by scholars such as Paul Gilroy and James Clifford. Because of the Syro-Anatolian Culture Complex (SACC)'s diasporic status, it is not possible to categorize the Syro-Anatolian city-states into convenient ethnolinguistic nation-states, and we are obliged to recognize a fundamental and trans-polity fluidity to SACC's cultural identity. Here I would like to extend a similar line of reasoning into the Iron Age II period, the early centuries of the first millennium BCE. Although the historical and archaeological evidence for migration is no longer present in this period, there is increasing evidence for a cultural mobility among the city-states that has long been underappreciated, likely as a consequence of our standard archaeological practice of excavating at single sites for multiple decades. The myopia that excavation inevitably produces does lead to spectacular thick descriptions of place-based practices, and indeed, there was a strong predilection for spatial stability, manifested most conspicuously in long-lived settlements on tells. Nevertheless, cultural mobility was a real and vibrant part of SACC's political landscape.

Perhaps, then, we need to reconsider the Syro-Anatolian city-states not necessarily as static political entities that constituted merely one episode in a long evolutionary cycle of Bronze and Iron Age state formation punctuated by periods of

*The Syro-Anatolian City-States*. James F. Osborne, Oxford University Press (2021). © Oxford University Press.
DOI: 10.1093/oso/9780199315833.003.0003

turmoil, collapse, and regeneration (Routledge 2014). This is, of course, the understanding presented to us by the terminology we use to describe complex political formations, the word "state" deriving from Latin's *status* (standing) and *stāre* (to stand). Instead, while never losing sight of the many cultural patterns that remained stable for centuries such as tell-based settlement, we need to supplement our traditional understanding of SACC with a recognition of its dynamic cultural character.

Recent work in political philosophy is challenging the appropriateness of the conventional model for complex polities. Rather than viewing the state as a static entity fixed in time and space, there is now a movement toward understanding political formations as continuous circulations of social flows. For example, Nail (2015) has proposed a radical rethinking of our theoretical approach to the state, arguing that it is in fact movement, and not stability, that constitutes the state by definition, a notion being picked up in related fields like human geography (e.g., Merriman 2012).[1] Although he attempts to reconstruct a historical sequence that defines the types of movements that characterized political formations across the ages, a sequence not unlike the stages of Marxian neoevolutionary theory, Nail's theoretical reorientation is clearly best suited for the twentieth and twenty-first centuries. It is in recent decades, after all, that we are witnessing unprecedentedly large and fast-paced migrations combining with new modes of communication that together foster a new sense of global social networks (sensu Appadurai 1996). Nevertheless, the point that we have for too long neglected the fundamental relationship between social movement and political authority is well taken. Nail refers to this relationship as *kinopolitics*, a helpful term that encapsulates the necessarily political character of movement and the mobile character of politics:

> Instead of analyzing societies as primarily static, spatial, or temporal, kinopolitics or social kinetics understands them primarily as "regimes of motion." Societies are always in motion: directing people and objects, reproducing their social conditions (periodicity), and striving to expand their territorial, political, juridical, and economic power through diverse forms of expulsion. (2015: 24)

Even if we decline to jettison completely our traditional notion of ancient states as being relatively stable political formations that existed in particular times and places, it is true that scholars studying SACC have not given sufficient attention to the social flows that comprised Syro-Anatolian political formations.

Like Nail, a growing number of sociologists and geographers are acknowledging what Urry (2007: 6) refers to as a mobility "structure of feeling," or a general recognition among scholars that intellectual emphases on sedentarism and stability have prevented us from seeing how much of human life is in fact facilitated and characterized by movement of many different kinds. Recent studies in a plethora of disciplines has stressed the importance of mobility and flows to numerous aspects of contemporary social life, including, among many others, communication networks, transportation and commuting, border crossings, migrants and refugees, travel and tourism, international trade and consumption, drug trafficking, environmental studies, and so on (Salazar and Smart 2011). Indeed, in the past decade scholars have begun labeling this growing transdisciplinary awareness a "mobility turn" (Urry 2007) or a "new mobilities paradigm" (Cresswell 2010; Merriman 2012: 13–14; Sheller and Urry 2006; Sheller 2017). Much of this literature is highly ambitious, seeking not just to correct the neglect of movement in the social sciences, but rather to transform the social sciences altogether: "a mobilities paradigm is not just substantively different, in that it remedies the neglect and omissions of various movements of people, ideas and so on. But it is transformative of social science, authorizing an alternative theoretical and methodological landscape" (Urry 2007: 18).

Archaeology is typically omitted from the excitement of this putative mobility turn, which has so far focused almost exclusively on the contemporary. This presentist bias is quite natural, given how the rapidly developing technologies of today's world have increased both the volume and speed of the movement of things, people, and ideas in unprecedented ways—as well as the state's ability to keep track of people in order to *prevent* movement. Compounded with the genuinely revolutionary aspects of modern mobility is the inherently immobile nature of the archaeological record. Archaeological sites are firmly rooted in place, and Near Eastern tells are particularly conspicuous in this regard. And the artifacts contained within them appear fixed in their matrix like the contents of a fruit cake, until exposed by the archaeologist's trowel. Although even these indicators of stability are ultimately misleading,[2] our interpretations of these features are inherently immobile in nature. But the cake metaphor so often invoked to explain the concept of archaeological stratigraphy, while certainly a useful methodological heuristic, precludes consideration of the ancient motion of things and people before they entered the archaeological record. It is this sense of mobility that archaeology historically neglects, although archaeological studies of mobility as an integral aspect of the past are now beginning to appear (e.g., Beaudry and Parno 2013b). To be sure, studies involving movement in some way have always been part and parcel of the archaeological project, whether the subject matter is migration, provenance analysis, ancient trade, and so on. But such studies are typically not about mobility per se, instead treating it as a property that facilitated whatever the actual subject is being considered (trade, migration, etc.), and not as a constitutive feature of ancient life itself.[3]

What, then, do we mean by mobility? Like historical archaeologists Beaudry and Parno (2013a), the present analysis is motivated by the scholarship described earlier, and especially by human geographer Tim Cresswell's approach to what he calls *constellations of mobility*, by which he means the interrelationships of movement, representation, and practice in historically and geographically specific situations (2010: 17–20). Respectively, these aspects of mobility refer to the fact of physical movement, culturally specific shared meanings of movement, and movement as it is experienced and embodied. To put it another way, all forms of mobility have "a physical reality, they are encoded culturally and socially, and they are experienced through practice" (2010: 20). In addition, these aspects of mobility are inherently and inevitably political in nature, "implicated in the production of power and relations of domination" (2010: 20), akin to Nail's concept of kinopolitics.

The forms of movement, the first aspect of Cresswell's constellations of mobility, take a variety of shapes. First and most obvious is the movement of culture groups, or portions thereof, with the concomitant cultural transformations that entails. This is, of course, closely related to migration and the strain of diaspora studies that was explored in the previous chapter, where it was argued that a number of demographic shifts resulted in a state of mixture that complicates the standard narrative of the Iron Age nation-state (Greenblatt 2010: 3), and diaspora studies has been explicitly connected to the new mobilities paradigm (Urry 2007: 35–36). But the movement of people is only one form that movement might take, with objects and ideas being other obvious candidates. The movement of objects is perhaps the most promising venue for the archaeological exploration of mobility, although the social and cultural significance of the phenomenon, its representational value, will be difficult to determine. The same is especially true for the practical experience of movement, which can be modeled in quantitative terms like least-cost path measurements, but which will forever be a challenge to reconstruct in the embodied, habitualized sense of practice advocated by scholars such as Bourdieu (1977).

None of this is to say that all aspects of human life, modern or past, are necessarily and inherently oriented around movement. Indeed, as advocates of the so-called mobility turn are careful to note, placing intellectual emphasis on mobility requires a focus not just on the importance of movement, but also on the significance of social situations characterized by more sedentary behaviors and especially by extensive immobile systems that render mobility possible (Urry 2007: 54). In this way the modern example of the explosion of air travel being facilitated by the stability of airport infrastructure perhaps has an ancient parallel in the daily back-and-forth of farmers moving from their houses to their fields along well-trodden hollow ways (Casana 2013; Ur 2003). The social significance of space and place in

SACC will be explored further in Chapter 5. In this chapter I focus our attention on the significant role played by the form, representation, and experience of mobility.

Although it is true that archaeology has paid insufficient attention to the social significance of mobility and may even benefit from a comprehensive reconsideration of its disciplinary focus on stasis and sedentarism, this chapter is not so aspiring as Nail's political philosophy or Urry et al.'s sociology; I do not seek to transform the discipline of archaeology into one that places mobility at the theoretical and methodological core of all of its practices. However, archaeologists of the Syro-Anatolian city-states would do well to recognize that cultural mobility was more important than is typically assumed, and that it is found in what appear to us to be a number of counterintuitive places, such that movement emerges not just as a coincidental feature of certain aspects of Iron Age life, but rather as one of SACC's defining characteristics. This chapter opens with a brief reconsideration of the Phoenician-language inscriptions that have been found surrounding the Gulf of Alexandretta at the northeastern corner of the Mediterranean Sea. Here I argue that, contrary to prevailing opinion, these inscriptions are a proxy indicator of the movement of Phoenician-speaking traders in and out of the region, likely for economic gain and resource extraction, and that this trade was likely in partnership with specific city-states, especially Sam'al and Que. I then consider the circulation of some of SACC's most famous contributions to the legacy of Near Eastern art and archaeology, the ivory luxury goods that moved around SACC along with their makers. In this case, the mobility of objects and traders weakens the bonds of the nation-state that scholarship has typically reconstructed, such that ivory good production is less implicated in the identity of particular polities than is usually assumed. Finally, in what may be the least obvious example of mobility, the chapter devotes the bulk of its attention to the orthostats and statues that adorned Syro-Anatolian monumental architecture, finding in almost every instance evidence for the movement of these ostensibly immobile objects, movement that, in many cases, was clearly done with a specific political agenda. In all of these cases, the political is never far from the surface.

::::

## The Phoenician Connection

Roughly coeval with SACC are the Phoenician city-states that rose to prominence along the central Levantine coast during the late second–early first millennium BCE, the cities of Tyre and Sidon in particular (Elayi 2018; Markoe 2000). These cities would quickly come to adopt their famous status as Mediterranean-wide traders, whether due to the need to supply goods and services to the neighboring Neo-Assyrian Empire (Frankenstein 1979) or, as seems more likely given new chronological discoveries that push these developments deeper into the ninth century, due to their own internal forces and pressures such as economic competition with Greek traders (Aubet 2008; Niemeyer 2004).

The Phoenicians' contemporaneity and close proximity make a connection with SACC logical. Surprisingly, however, often lost in the excitement over the apparent Aegean connection in the northeast corner of the Mediterranean during the Iron Age I is a thoughtful consideration of the presence of Phoenician inscriptions in the same region during the subsequent Iron Age II. There are three famous texts: the Karatepe and Çineköy bilingual inscriptions from late eighth-century Que, and the Kulamuwa inscription from ninth-century Sam'al, mentioned in the previous chapter. In the Phoenican case, also unlike the Aegean situation, there is no accompanying material culture that is unambiguously Phoenician in nature. Phoenicia's close proximity to Cilicia and the northern Levant renders such distinctions problematic, and either way it is likely that southeastern Anatolian and north Syrian Red Slipped and Burnished Ware pottery beginning in the late tenth century is derived from the slightly earlier red slipped Phoenician ceramics, a subject that needs further examination (Mazzoni 2000a: 41–42). Be that as it may, the existence of these texts requires an explanation, not least because none of the inscriptions were authored by an individual with a Phoenician name (Karatepe: Luwian "Azatiwada"; Çineköy: Luwian "Warika"; Karatepe: Luwian "Awariku"; Sam'al: Luwian "Kulamuwa"). The only interpretive issue that appears to be certain is that the geographical proximity of the texts cannot be coincidental, the intervening Amanus Mountain range notwithstanding. Whatever explanation one offers, this spatial clustering must be taken into account.

The solitary Phoenician inscription from Sam'al, the Kulamuwa inscription, has been explained in a number of different ways (Figure 3.1). Young (2002: 99) has proposed that Phoenician stood as a neutral language between the two primary ethnolinguistic groups of Samalian and Luwian, though selecting a language unknown to the city's populace hardly seems an effective neutral policy. It is possible that Sam'al had close political ties with, and thus received linguistic influence from, the city-state of Que in Cilicia, where the bilingual inscriptions were found (Lemaire 2001: 188). But Sam'al's political relationship with Que was often adversarial, as indicated in the Kulamuwa inscription itself, and in any event the Kulamuwa inscription predates the Que bilinguals, which would suggest that the linguistic influence went in the other direction. Finally, it has been argued that rulers drawn from the Aramaean tribes who had established themselves amid a Luwian population, but who had not yet developed writing for their native Samalian tongue, wrote in Phoenician in order to distance themselves from nearby Luwian kings (Yakubovich 2015: 48–49). This is possible, although Kulamuwa's own name is Luwian, not Aramaean, and it is further unclear why it would be more

(a)

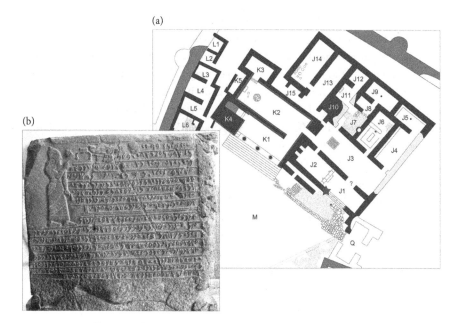

(b)

FIGURE 3.1

(*a*) Palaces J and K at Zincirli, with the location of the Kulamuwa stele in the western jamb of the portico into Palace J marked by a star (adapted from Kertai 2019: Fig. 2, with permission); (*b*) Kulamuwa's stele with Phoenician inscription. (Photograph © hittitemonuments.com)

straightforward to distance oneself from surrounding Luwian dynasties by re-course to a language spoken elsewhere rather than simply use the alphabet to write in Samalian, as happened within the kingdom shortly thereafter anyway, and as had already taken place with Aramaic as attested in a number of nearby ninth-century inscriptions such as the "little altar" from Tell Halaf (*KAI* 231) and the Melqart stele found near Aleppo (*KAI* 201) (Niehr 2016: 312). Most recently, Niehr (2016: 321) and Bryce (2012: 95) argue that Kulamuwa opted for Phoenician as a sign of prestige for his subjects in Sam'al and as a statement of his equal participation in the interna-tional affairs of the day. The prestige argument has been supported by attributions of non-Phoenician elements in the inscription itself, although problematically these have been explained by influence from Aramaic, in the form of the proper name construction "Kulamuwa bar Ḥayya" (Niehr 2016: 311), Samalian linguistic features (Tropper 1993: 31, 33, 35, 41–45), and Luwian, in the form of its tone, rhetor-ical structure, and relief script (Gilibert 2011: 82; Niehr 2016: 318).

An argument for an actual Phoenician-speaking audience for the Kulamuwa in-scription, as opposed to the language having merely a symbolic or prestige function, is suggested by evidence for the priority of Phoenician in the Karatepe and Çineköy bilinguals in Que, as has recently been proposed on linguistic and philological grounds. The prevailing view of these Phoenician-Luwian bilinguals has long been that the Luwian version of the text was composed first, and that the Phoenician thus represents a translation of the Luwian original (e.g., Lanfranchi 2007: 186; Payne 2006: 130). But this understanding is derived primarily from the assumption that the majority of the inhabitants of Que were Luwians, the descendants of the inhabitants of the Late Bronze Age kingdom of Kizzuwatna. The accumulating archaeological and textual evidence from Que pointing to the arrival of a small Aegean or Cypriot-derived non-Luwian population in Cilicia during the Iron Age I period that was presented in Chapter 2 prompted Yakubovich (2015: 44–46) to test this assumption, whereupon he identified a number of linguistic clues pointing toward Phoenician as the primary language of both inscriptions, including syntactical calquing in the Luwian, Luwian paraphrasing of the Phoenician original due to language-specific constraints, and mistaken or distorted meanings in the Luwian text. Cumulatively, these suggest that, contrary to the commonly held assumption for an original Luwian-language text, the primary language of both bilinguals was Phoenician, which was subsequently translated into Luwian.

Indeed, the visual properties of the inscriptions appear to confirm this finding. The Phoenician text of the Çineköy inscription, for example, is found on the front of the statue base tightly enclosed between the two animals, while the Luwian text sprawls around the base. The same applies at Karatepe, where the Luwian texts are almost haphazardly placed across a variety of orthostats, unlike the spatially unified Phoenician versions. Perhaps most indicative is the fact that at Karatepe the Phoenician language is provided with three versions of the text (Phu/A, Pho/B, and PhSt), while the Luwian is given only two (Hu and Ho). The additional third Phoenician inscription is found on the colossal statue, arguably the most important venue for a royal inscription at the site. Even without reading the inscriptions, therefore, let alone determining direction of translation on linguistic grounds, it is difficult to avoid the conclusion that the Phoenician exemplars were consciously prioritized.

Using ethnohistoric parallels, Yakubovich (2015: 48–49) interprets this Phoenician priority in Que as representing the desire of the earlier Greek settlers to distinguish themselves from the broader Luwian-speaking milieu; in a similar vein, Kulamuwa's use of Phoenician in Sam'al was to distance the new Aramaean arrivals from Luwian locals, at least until Aramaic became a written language. We have already seen how Aramaic was, in fact, used in written form by the time of Kulamuwa. A more significant problem to this interpretation of Greek settlers using Phoenician as a distinguishing marker is that the ethnohistoric parallels Yakubovich cites can only partially overcome the sociolinguistic awkwardness of the finding that Aegean settlers in Cilicia chose to write in Phoenician instead of Greek.

As problematic as all of these explanations are, the interpretive difficulty is compounded by the fact that there are several other Phoenician inscriptions in the region, whose cumulative social implications get downplayed in the debates surrounding Kulamuwa and Karatepe. These include (1) a fragmentary Luwian-Phoenician bilingual inscription on the bottom half of a limestone stele composed by Tuwana's famous king Warpalawas of the mid- to late eighth century. The object is currently on display in the museum at Ereğli, along with a destroyed colossal statue head reminiscent of the colossal statues from Zincirli, Tayinat, and Malatya. Both pieces were found during construction about 100 m from Warpalawas's famous rock relief at Ivriz. The inscription remains unpublished beyond a preliminary report (Dinçol 1994). (2) The Phoenician inscription of Hassan-Beyli, a poorly preserved orthostat discovered by F. von Luschan in the late nineteenth century just 13 km west of Zincirli, though on the west face of the Amanus Mountains. The inscription is fragmentary, and it possibly began on an adjacent orthostat. The barely discernable letters of line 3 may refer to the "king of Adana" (*mlk dn*), though this reading is hardly certain; line 5 clearly names Awariku ('*wrk*), the same name mentioned in Karatepe, incidentally dating the inscription to the mid- to late eighth century (Lemaire 1983). (3) The remarkable Phoenician/Luwian/Akkadian trilingual inscription found in 1993 in a private garden at Incirli, located approximately 10 km northeast of Sakçegözü, by Elizabeth Carter's survey in Kahramanmaraş. The Luwian and Akkadian inscriptions are unfortunately too worn to be read, but the Phoenician is just legible with enhanced lighting techniques, and it refers again to Awariku king of Adana, this time in the context of Matiel of Arpad's rebellion with Urartu against Assyria around 740 BCE, the outcome of which led Tiglath-pileser III to gift some of this land to Que (Kaufman 2007; Swartz Dodd 2012). (4) A late seventh-century inscription from Cebel Ires Dağı in rough Cilicia near Alanya. This text, too, mentions one Awariku, although since the text dates over a century later than the other examples, it must refer to a different individual (Mosca and Russell 1987).

Besides the Kulamuwa inscription, we thus have six major Phoenician texts clustered around the northeast corner of the Mediterranean. Of these six, two are composed by Awariku (Karatepe and Hassan Beyli), three are composed by Warika (Çineköy, Incirli, and Cebel Ires Dağı), and one by Warpalawas (Ivriz). The similarity of the names Awariku and Warika, previously thought to refer to the same individual, is seductive but deceptive; analysis of their variant etymologies suggests that, in fact, they derive from distinct Greek antecedents, leading to the possibility that these two names were used in alternating generations of rulers stretching from the mid- to late eighth century well into the seventh (Lipiński 2004: 119–23; Simon 2014). This fact, along with the roughly contemporary Ivriz inscription by Warpalawas in Tabal, west of the Taurus Mountains and as far west from Karatepe as

Samisat and Malatya are east of it, suggests that the use of Phoenician was geographically and temporally widespread in the region. Likewise, the use of Phoenician by the mid- to late ninth-century Samalian ruler Kulamuwa indicates that Phoenician was in use at least a century prior to Awariku. Such a geographical and chronological distribution implies a motivation for the use of the Phoenician language that goes beyond merely staking neutral linguistic ground, receiving influence from neighbors, or claiming an international prestige. The possibility must be raised that Phoenician was deployed in a modest number of monumental inscriptions because it was actually spoken by a modest number of the people who would have viewed them, that is, that genuine Phoenician speakers were another component of SACC's variegated ethnolinguistic makeup, at least in certain polities.[4]

This conclusion is supported by the presence of a significant number of nonmonumental inscriptions and other indicators of Phoenician presence across the ninth–eighth centuries (an admittedly broad time range) (see Lehmann 2008: 218–21) (Figure 3.2), including (1) a brief (and unprovenanced) inscription naming "(K?)rkdy, First of the Bodyguards" in late ninth-century script on a shield boss that Niehr (2016: 314), following the publishers, associates with Sam'al, and Kulamuwa's court specifically, on iconographic and paleographic grounds (Krebernik and Seidl 1997); (2) a Luwian-Phoenician bilingual seal, with the Phoenician text possibly reading "seal of the Tyrian" (Dupont-Sommer 1950); (3) a Phoenician seal from Aleppo; (4) an early Iron Age II spindle whorl from Area I excavations at Çatal Höyük in the Amuq plain, within the region of the city-state of Patina, inscribed with z rd nm' tw, translated by the publisher as "this produces spun(?) yarn" (Gevirtz 1967); (4) a late eighth-century Phoenician inscription on a storage jar from Kinet Höyük reading "to Sarmakaddinis" (Gates 2004: 408, Fig. 8); (5) the Melqart Stela, a stele with Aramaic inscription but Phoenician iconographic traits such as Egyptianizing cobras on the figure's skirt. The dedicatory genre and wording also indicate a Phoenician association (Peckham 2001: 31). The stele was found ex situ at Brayj near Aleppo dating to approximately 800 BCE. It is authored by Bar-Hadad, possibly a king of Bit-Agusi, and mentions the god Melqart, titular deity of the Phoenician city of Tyre, in which case it is even conceivable that a Phoenician shrine was present in the region (Pitard 1988); (6) a number of small bronze weights inscribed with "shekel of Hamath" in Phoenician script (Heltzer 1995); (7) the famous boast of Yariri, late ninth-century king of Carchemish, that he could read several different scripts, including Phoenician, prioritized at the top of his list following only Luwian itself (Hawkins 2000: 131);[5] and (8) the many stylistic and iconographic features of the Karatepe relief program (Winter 1979).[6]

Viewed cumulatively, this is a modest but nevertheless significant corpus of data, and one that dates consistently to the ninth and eighth centuries. Evidence

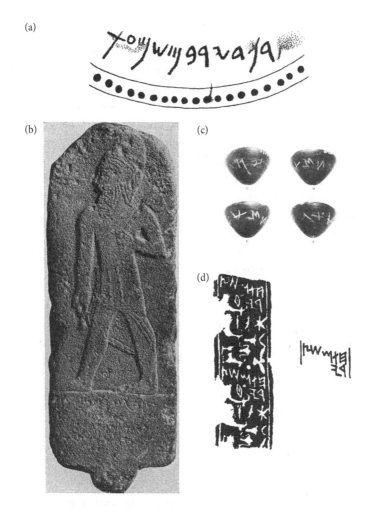

FIGURE 3.2
Indicators of Phoenician presence in SACC: (*a*) unprovenanced inscribed shield boss possibly from Zincirli (adapted from Krebernik and Seidl 1997: Abb. 1); (*b*) the Melqart Stele found at Brayj near Aleppo (Albright 1942: Fig. 1); (*c*) spindle whorl inscribed in Phoenician from Iron Age II Çatal Höyük, Area I (adapted form Gevirtz 1967: Pl. I); (*d*) Luwian-Phoenician bilingual seal, unprovenanced. (Adapted from Dupont-Summer 1950: Figs. 1–2)

for Phoenicians includes both linguistic and iconographic indicators, and the inscriptions range from the most monumental of venues to the most humble of objects, the spindle whorl. Finds such as these mitigate against the notion that all of these Phoenician objects and other indicators were simply a result of trade. It is difficult to intepret this body of evidence in any way other than that the Phoenician language was spoken in SACC, if only by a small number of people, even if other attributes of Phoenician material culture, especially pottery, are so far lacking (Lehmann 2008).[7]

It is remarkable that so few have seriously taken into consideration the possibility that Phoenician was used in ninth- and eighth-century inscriptions in SACC because there was at least a portion of the population there who were themselves Phoenician speakers, and who were intended as the primary audience of the texts. The archaeological contexts of the texts in question shed some light on this possibility. Kulamuwa's inscription was installed at the entrance to Zincirli's Palace J at the top of the steps into this *bit ḫilāni* (see Figure 3.1). The spatial layout of this building type was designed to encourage interaction between visitors and inhabitants even while tightly controlling visitors' movement through the space (see Chapter 5), implying that the text was intended to be widely seen by people who visited the palace. Indeed, according to David Kertai's visibility analysis of this space, an otherwise superfluous column was placed between the entrance into the palace area, Gate Q, and the Palace J portico precisely to block visibility of the Kulamuwa inscription from the gate itself, thereby drawing pedestrians in even closer for the visual unveiling of the monument (Kertai 2019: 92–93, Figs. 6–7). It seems most likely, therefore, that Phoenician speakers such as mercantile officials, even if not necessarily full-time residents of Sam'al, routinely conducted commercial affairs in the palace, and therefore with the ruling dynasty of Sam'al. A similar principle is even more apparent at Karatepe, where the Phoenician-Luwian bilinguals are located in the two gateways of the settlement, and thus were visible to anyone entering or exiting the town. It would again appear that the most felicitous interpretation of the presence of Phoenician text at Karatepe was to facilitate communication with actual Phoenician speakers within Karatepe, an interpretation that is supported by the presence of Phoenician motifs in the accompanying reliefs (Winter 1979: 137–38).[8]

What is the significance of all of this evidence for the existence of a Phoenician presence in SACC during the Iron Age II? One salient point is their very existence, certainly as a minority, but nonetheless at least semipermanent, presence within a number of the Syro-Anatolian city-states. This recognition complicates—as if additional complication were necessary—what we saw in the previous chapter to be an enormously complicated ethnolinguistic situation, and further erodes our confidence in the assumption that the Syro-Anatolian city-states comprised ethnically oriented nation-states. A more comprehensive account of the relationship between SACC and Phoenicia would also examine evidence for Syro-Anatolian influence in the central Levant, and although that will not be accomplished here, it is worth noting that the occupants of a number of settlements in the coastal Levantine region traditionally associated with Phoenicia began cremating their dead at the same time as SACC, that is, in the early first millennium BCE. Three hundred twenty Iron Age cremation urns were excavated in the Al-Bass district of Tyre (Aubet 2013: 145), for example, and cremations have also appeared at Tell er-Reqeish, Khaldé, Akhziv, Atlit, Tambourit, and Rachidiyeh (Aubet 2010: 78–79, with references). Although the notion is rejected by Aubet (2010: 80), it seems plausible that the practice of cremation appears in Phoenicia at the same time it becomes common in SACC precisely because the two regions were participating in a shared economic and cultural interaction zone.[9]

It is difficult to reconstruct the precise motivations for Phoenician speakers to spend time and energy in SACC. That they were present primarily for economic interests is suggested by the location of Karatepe itself, on the Ceyhan River in the foothills of the Taurus Mountains near its juncture with the Amanus range—a prime location for the extraction of resources necessary for Phoenicia's Mediterranean-wide trade.[10] The existence of Phoenician traders within the city-states of Que and Sam'al is supported further by the geographical proximity of the more monumental texts, implying strongly that Phoenician speakers were present in some number in this region specifically, and that the use of Phoenician here was not simply for "prestige" or "neutrality," both of which could in principle have happened anywhere in SACC. Rather, these texts were composed for the benefit of traders taking advantage of the region's rich sources of wood, precious stones, and metals found in the Amanus Mountains and surrounding areas (Çambel 1999: 1).

Mapping all of these isolated indicators of Phoenician presence, including not just the monumental inscriptions but also the objects listed earlier, indicates a clear spatial clustering at the northeast corner of the Mediterranean Sea (Figure 3.3). It therefore seems highly probable that Phoenicians maintained an economic interest in the Amanus Mountains and the nearby foothills of the Taurus Mountains from at least the mid- to late ninth century through the eighth century. The earlier date of the Kulamuwa inscription compared to the Karatepe and other nearby inscriptions a century or more later is perhaps indicative of the Phoenicians in this area finding a more willing partner in Que as their economic interests expanded or as Sam'al grew politically stronger and more economically independent. In this scenario it would make sense to associate the earlier Phoenician-inscribed spindle whorl in the Amuq Valley as a residue of traders sending goods south from Sam'al to enter the Mediterranean Sea via Patina and the Orontes Delta, and the later inscription at Kinet Höyük, as well as substantial Phoenician pottery reported at Tarsus (Goldmann 1963), as relating to the trade route south from Karatepe entering the Mediterranean via Cilicia.

The evidence that Phoenicians were involved in resource extraction from the mountains around the northeast corner of the Mediterranean is for now circumstantial. The growing evidence that Phoenician speakers were situated in this vicinity, however, is not, and the seal of the Tyrian combined with the Melqart Stela

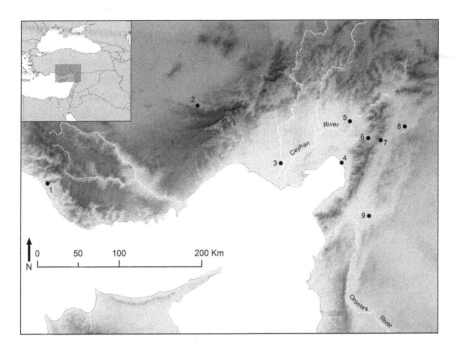

FIGURE 3.3
Findspots of Phoenician inscriptions and objects with known provenance in the Syro-Anatolian Culture Complex: (1) Cebel Ires Dağı, inscription of Warika; (2) Ivriz, inscription of Warpalawas; (3) Çineköy, Phoenician-Hieroglyphic bilingual inscription of Warika; (4) Kinet Höyük, inscribed storage jar; (5) Karatepe-Aslantaş, Phoenician-Hieroglyphic bilingual inscription of Awariku; (6) Hassan Beyli, inscription of Awariku; (7) Zincirli, inscription of Kulamuwa; (8) Incirli, Phoenician-Hieroglyphic Luwian-Akkadian trilingual inscription of Warika; (9) Çatal Höyük, inscribed spindle whorl. Not depicted are a number of seals of unknown provenance, the Melqart Stele, or the Arslan Tash amulets of uncertain authenticity.

mentioned earlier point toward Tyre as the specific origin of these individuals. The Phoenician phenomenon in this region thus becomes a strong case for the movement of people as outlined earlier. In this scenario, we see not a large-scale migration from one place to another, but a small-scale flow of people and (likely) things back and forth along proscribed routes and with a targeted economic agenda. It is also a form of mobility that is closely related to local political authority, and thus a good example of kinopolitics.

Whatever else the Kulamuwa stele may have been seeking to accomplish—boasting of his allegedly unprecedented accomplishments; apologizing for the involvement of Assyria in Sam'al's affairs; appeasing Assyrian viewers of the monument with Kulamuwa's Assyrian dress; mimicking Luwian monument production techniques with its raised relief inscription; and so on—the royal authorship of the inscription combined with its Phoenician language firmly implicates the proposed Phoenician involvement in this region in SACC's political sphere. It is not possible to be certain whether the stela represents Kulamuwa's command over the Phoenicians' commerce being conducted within his territory, or whether the choice to use Phoenician was an aspirational claim to economic control that did not actually exist. The former possibility is supported by the stela's location at the entrance to Kulamuwa's palace, as noted earlier; this context might even be taken to suggest that Phoenician-speaking traders regularly entered the palace to conduct their commerce. The latter possibility is bolstered by Kulamuwa's near-contemporary at Carchemish, Yariri, who claims to have been able to speak the Tyrian, that is, Phoenician, language (Luwian *sù+ra/i-*). Since this boast is more unambiguously aspirational—no Phoenician-language inscriptions are known from Carchemish, after all—it implies that SACC rulers vied to be considered the most influential local participant in the Phoenician trade. In either case, the relationship between power and movement represents a significant component of the representation, or social significance, of mobility with respect to the Phoenician involvement in SACC. Indeed, establishing control over movement as constitutive of legitimate rulership is indicated by the Karatepe inscription itself, which in both Luwian and Phoenician states that areas where men had previously been afraid to walk on roads had been so safe by Azatiwada's royal deeds that now even women could walk safely with their spindles (cf. Hawkins 2000: 53; and Röllig 1999). The early first-millennium rulers of Sam'al and Que considered mobility—of the Phoenicians and of their own subjects—to be part and parcel of their political domain.

::::

## Ivory Products and Ivory Production

Of all the things for which SACC is known today in Near Eastern scholarship, their highly specialized ivory products are perhaps their most famous. There has been an enormous amount of energy invested into cataloguing the corpus of material, and especially organizing the diverse corpus into meaningful categories. Paradoxically, most of the objects themselves were found outside of the Syro-Anatolian region. The bulk of our known ivory products, over 6,000 pieces in total, have been excavated at the Neo-Assyrian capital cities, and Nimrud in particular. These ivories have been published in a decades-long effort to present the ivory material that was found in all contexts from the palaces on the acropolis to Fort Shalmaneser in the southeast corner of the city, with the finds spanning the century and a half of exploration at the site (Barnett 1957; Herrmann 1986; Herrmann et al. 2004; Herrmann and Laidlaw 2009, 2013). The reason for this counterintuitive findspot is clear: the

Neo-Assyrian Empire prized these items and routinely took them from Syro-Anatolian cities as tribute and conquest booty, as described routinely in their royal annals. The ivories were then cached in palace storerooms, where they were pre served to be discovered by archaeologists. While we cannot be certain about the materials represented in the Neo-Assyrian palace reliefs, by virtue of their functional and formal parallels with physical ivory objects many of the items portrayed in the reliefs apparently depict ivories in use by the highest echelons of Assyrian society. The famous Garden Scene of Ashurbanipal, for example, shows inlays on the legs of Ashurbanipal's couch that functionally are very likely to have been made from ivory and that depict the well-known "woman-at-the-window" motif commonly attested in western ivories. Indeed, a number of objects in the feasting scene have known ivory parallels, including pyxides and fans.

That many of these objects were manufactured in the Syro-Anatolian region and not Assyria—a clearly discernible Assyrian tradition characterized by Assyrian motifs and incised, instead of relief, decoration is also attested among the ivories found at Nimrud (Herrmann 1997)—is documented by two primary lines of evidence. The first is the comparatively small corpus of ivories that were, in fact, excavated in the Syro-Anatolian sites themselves, having somehow managed to escape the hands of Assyrian plunderers. The corpus from cities within SACC is surprisingly robust, given that no one has yet presented a comprehensive catalogue of all ivories found in good contexts at Iron Age II cities in SACC: from published reports Marian Feldman (2015: 98) estimates approximately one hundred ivory pieces from each of Zincirli and Hamath, and another fifty from Tell Halaf. Other Syro-Anatolian sites have produced ivories that are either not in good contexts, such as Carchemish, or that were found in Assyrian-period contexts, such as Tell Tayinat (Harrison and Osborne 2012: 130), Arslan Tash (Thureau-Dangin et al. 1931), and Tell Ahmar (Bunnens 1997). This quantity of ivory is itself not sufficient to place the primary production zone within SACC compared with the much higher quantity that was discovered at Nimrud, but the second line of evidence is more suggestive: the relief decorations on the ivories possess a host of both iconographic and stylistic similarities to the scenes depicted on the stone reliefs that lined the monumental gates and palaces of Syro-Anatolian capitals (Orthmann 1971).

This ivory and stone material indigenous to SACC had begun to appear by the time the first Nimrud ivories were starting to be analyzed in greater detail than had been presented in Layard's original publications. Already in 1912 Poulsen (1912: 37–59) could create the fundamental typological subdivision that remains the basic framework for art historians today, assigning the Nimrud ivories into two major groups, one associated with Phoenicia, and one with Syria. The Phoenician group is identified especially by its Egyptian features such as lotus flowers, uraei, and Egyptian headdresses, while the Syrian pieces lacked these Egyptian motifs and instead resembled details from Syro-Anatolian reliefs, such as the motif of processing musicians. This was then developed further by Barnett (1935), who argued that most of the Phoenician group were found in the Northwest Palace excavated by Layard, while most of the Syrian group were located in the Burnt Palace excavated slightly later by William Kennet Loftus. In addition, Barnett listed a number of other Syrian traits, including specific motifs like scenes of animal combat and especially the physiognomy of high forehead, large eyes and nose, and small chin, all of which resembled figures found on the reliefs from sites like Zincirli, Tell Halaf, and Carchemish. Such lists were elaborated in even greater specificity by Winter (1976a), who was able to distinguish between, for example, the Syrian winged sun disc with suspended pendant volutes and the Phoenician winged sun disc with uraei (1976a: 4), or the Phoenician emphasis on symmetry within individual plaques as opposed to the Syrian trend toward symmetry in complete panels of plaques (1976a: 6). Winter goes on to argue that Syrian and Phoenician ivories have different geographical distributions, with the latter being concentrated more in the southern Levant and Cyprus, as well as a distinct chronological trend in which the Syrian group is found in ninth- and early eighth-century contexts, while Phoenician exemplars all date to the late eighth and seventh centuries (1976a: 11–20). This temporal distinction she interpreted in light of differential Assyrian treatment of their conquered subjects, the Syro-Anatolian city-states having been effectively eliminated as economically productive entities, and the seafaring Phoenician cities allowed to maintain their irreplaceable trade networks unmolested.

In all of these cases the Syrian nature of that group of the Nimrud ivories is confirmed through comparison with either actual ivories found in a Syro-Anatolian city-state or with the reliefs at a Syro-Anatolian site. The Phoenician group does not have the luxury of such comparisons with ivories or reliefs excavated in Phoenicia, that region having modern cities atop its ancient settlements, including both Tyre and Sidon. In this case, the consistently Egyptianizing motifs in the ivories are evocative of the area's long-standing relationship with Egypt, and other indirect lines of reasoning such as Phoenicia being noted for its ivories in roughly contemporary sources like the Hebrew Bible (e.g., Ezekial 27:6, I Kings 10:18).

With these broad categories of Iron Age ivories established, art historical scholarship moved forward toward greater specificity in identifications of specific schools or workshops of ivory production that could be associated with specific city-states. Winter (1981), for example, argued that the mixed stylistic qualities of the ivories from Arslan Tash, showing traits from both of the Phoenician and Syrian groups, represent a third "South Syrian" (subsequently known as Intermediate) category of ivories that she tentatively associated with Damascus, that city being geographically situated between the Phoenician and Syro-Anatolian core areas and thus expected to produce objects resembling aspects of both. Likewise, Wicke (2005) associates a particular subset of Syrian ivories portraying round faces and ringletted hair with the city-state of Sam'al.

Perhaps the most famous of these city-specific associations has been the isolation of a subcategory of the Syrian ivories known as the "flame and frond" school by virtue of its consistent co-occurrence of frond leaves with flame-like musculature on the hind legs of animals and mythical figures; other diagnostic elements include incised backbone and ribs and stomachs marked with a rectangle filled with cross-hatching (Herrmann 1989) (Figure 3.4). Herrmann identifies the geographical and political source of this school of ivory production at Tell Halaf

FIGURE 3.4
Ivories of the "flame and frond" tradition of Syro-Anatolian ivories (adapted from Herrmann 1989: Fig. 1). (*a*) Nimrud, Well AJ, IM 79514; (*b*) Nimrud, Well AJ, IM 79508; (*c*) Nimrud, Well AJ, IM 79508; (*d*) Nimrud SW 37, ND 10377.

by virtue of the ivories' undeniable parallels with reliefs along the exterior walls of Kapara's *bīt-ḫilāni* palace, many of which show animals with identical markings. The methodological reasoning of this association is clear: since large-scale reliefs cannot be expected to have traveled great distances, it is logical to associate the producers of similar-looking ivories to the city-state in which the reliefs are located regardless of whether the direction of artistic influence moved from so-called minor arts to major arts or vice versa. Others have challenged this methodological reconstruction, however, preferring to place their emphasis for determining place of origin on historical and sociopolitical context, which leads Winter (1989) to propose Carchemish as a likely origin for the flame and frond school, Mazzoni (2009) to suggest Hama, and Affani (2009) to argue for one subset that belongs to Tell Halaf, a second to Sam'al, and a third to an as-yet-undetermined city-state.

It is clear from these multifarious proposals for the origin of the flame and frond school of Iron Age ivories that there is widespread methodological disagreement on just what variables are to be used for determining place of origin, and how those variables are to be given ranked priority. For precisely these reasons Winter (2005) drew on the positivist impulse of the New Archaeology to argue forcefully for the need to create a consistent and agreed-upon ranked list of explicit and rigorous an-alytic processes to render attributions empirically verifiable. It is equally clear that identifying the geographical origins of identifiable groups of ivories is the primary concern of scholarship, whether as a prior condition to asking additional questions such as the determination of distribution mechanisms or as a goal in and of it-self. Furthermore, these geographical places of origin are then associated—tacitly or explicitly—with the city-state that existed in that region or that controlled the city to which the ivory group has been sourced, as summarized recently by one prominent ivory specialist: "one may wonder whether the specific stylistic rend-ering of a common imagery and typology is not related to the wish of expressing one's territorial and political identity" (Caubet 2013: 457). The inevitable outcome is a perpetuation of the nation-state model of the Syro-Anatolian city-states that I questioned in the previous chapter, a model that involves as its operating assump-tion the existence of discrete territorial political formations containing particular groups of people who produced monumental inscriptions and other products. This assumption that ivory groups derive from specific Syro-Anatolian (or Phoenician) city-states is then implicated in the circular reasoning that ivory production was a state-sponsored activity with specialists attached to, or otherwise determined by, the ruling elite, argued on the grounds that ivory products must have been made in specific city-states.

Before turning to deal with the organization of production, and especially how little about it is actually known, it should be noted that there are a number of interpretive issues associated with the mode of operation that divides the corpus into subgroups according to style and then associates those subgroups with particular political entities and associated specific historical reconstructions, assuming from the outset that periods and regions will necessarily be characterized by differences in style. Perhaps the clearest of these is the fact that all of the style groups that have been isolated show a great deal of variation within them, such that scholars struggle to agree on how groups are to be formed (Suter 2015). Indeed, group labels and contents have changed over time, even in publications by the same author, as scholars strain to identify consistent principles of membership. Likewise, it has recently been argued that the Intermediate tradition is essentially a collection of ivories which analysts cannot place in either the North Syrian or Phoenician groups (Wicke 2009). Individual publications will inevitably illustrate those pieces that show similarity, but the entire corpus of a group reveals a high degree of variability. The same applies to the orthostat reliefs from Syro-Anatolian cities that are often used as the anchor tying a stylistically determined class of ivories to a particular place: even at a single site the reliefs are hardly homogeneous, even while marked similarities are present in the reliefs between a number of sites (see further later). Although the subject matter of the ivories is more or less consistent, therefore, it is a precarious argument to tie what is in actuality a diverse and heterogeneous group of objects to workshops that existed in specific locations (Feldman 2014: 21–26, 31).

To these methodological concerns one should add the consideration that the significance of group-making is rarely considered on a theoretical level, although critiques of the connoisseurship mode of art historical analysis have certainly appeared in this context. Anthropological archaeology has long grappled with the significance of contemporary classification systems for understanding ancient patterns of behavior. The so-called Ford-Spaulding debate that took place in the 1950s, for example, raised the question of the extent to which typological classification schemes created by the analyst—precisely like the ones under consideration here—represent the original categories that were in place in the minds of the objects' makers, if at all (Ford and Steward 1954; Spaulding 1953). Such considerations are essential to research projects that use quantitative analyses in order to determine objectively valid groups of ivories (e.g., Cinquatti 2015). Absent any meaningful evidence for criteria from the craftspeople themselves, we are obliged to admit that our divisions of the ivory corpus are dependent on variables—for example, resemblance to reliefs, physiognomy, and so on—that are possibly significant to us alone (di Paolo 2009: 135–36). The Iron Age ivory carvers, meanwhile, may have formed groups based on other factors altogether, ones that we are not in a position to assess, and particularly so if the ivories' current appearance does not resemble their original applied colors, for example (di Paolo 2015). The subsequent interpretive step, associating our analytically derived ivory groups with Iron Age city-states, may thus be entirely erroneous if the groups themselves are historically inaccurate in an emic sense even if the ancient carvers *were* organized according to polity.

The aforementioned methodological considerations have led Feldman (2014: 39) to question even the most fundamental insight of twentieth-century scholarship on Iron Age ivories, the decades-long accepted division of the corpus into North Syrian and Phoenician traditions, with the latter distinguished especially by its Egyptianizing elements. Noting that for lack of excavation there are few ivories from the Phoenician cities themselves that would anchor that tradition geographically in the central Levantine littoral, Feldman wonders whether the chronological distinction between the two groups that was identified by Winter (1976a: 15–17)—North Syrian ivories dated to ninth- and eighth-century contexts, Phoenician ones to the eighth and seventh centuries—is not to be interpreted by the historical exigencies of the Syro-Anatolian and Phoenician city-states' interactions with the Neo-Assyrian Empire, as per Winter, but simply by chronology alone. If that is the case, then the possibility is raised that a single community of ivory carvers produced both traditions with a stylistic evolution across the roughly two and a half to three centuries the objects were being produced. This radical reinterpretation of the corpus is perhaps mitigated against by the reliefs at Karatepe, which show many stylistic parallels with allegedly Phoenician ivories (Winter 1979), and which are accompanied by a lengthy Phoenician-language inscription that appears to have been generated by and for a Phoenician audience (see earlier). Nevertheless, the fact that this proposal has been put forward at all, and seems to be gaining traction among art historians (Suter 2015: 42; for a contrasting opinion, see Fischer and Wicke 2016), is a testament to the paradigm shift currently taking place regarding the viability of associating stylistically determined ivory groups with geopolitical entities.

That the ivories were part of elite circles within SACC society has been less challenged. An elite-level organization of production has some support in the archaeological findspots of the few ivories that have been found in reliable and pre-Assyrian contexts, as well as in their function as determined from formal properties, which allows consideration of undecorated ivories that so often go unconsidered in stylistic analysis. Given a general paucity of information regarding ivory production within SACC, ivory consumption is here more directly informative about ivory's social significance. As Feldman (2015: 98) has recently shown in a recent survey of Syro-Anatolian ivories found in secure depositional contexts, "the consumption of ivory in the Iron Age Levant reveals the centrality of this material in almost all spheres of the highest social ranks." Ivory furniture pieces have been found in buildings J, K, and L, or the *Nordpalast*, of Zincirli, especially in those buildings' ceremonial reception suites (J and K) or their associated storerooms (L) (von

Luschan and Andrae 1943). Hamath Level E, likely destroyed in 720 BCE by Sargon II, produced ivories in its Building V on the southwest edge of the citadel, and smaller quantities in Buildings III and IV in the main excavated area at the citadel's southeast corner; these, too, are furniture decorations associated with reception, plus the odd independent object such as an ivory dagger sheath (Riis and Buhl 1990). Ivories from Tell Halaf are distributed across several contexts in and around the acropolis, but mostly concentrate within two burials: the first is an elite cremation burial accompanied by a statue of a seated woman, all encased within a large mudbrick terrace located outside the gate to the citadel; the second is a vaulted grave structure, the *ältere Gruft*, northwest of the Kapara's palace. These produced ivory containers, plaques, box inlays, and a pyxis (Hrouda 1962). In sum, ivory objects have been found at the very tip of the Syro-Anatolian social order and in contexts associated with reception and possibly also banqueting, including feasting associated with funerary ritual; furniture decoration is the largest functional class of these objects, complemented by an array of other items such as containers, sheaths, and handles (Feldman 2015: 107–9).

But the history of excavation at these sites has been overwhelmingly concerned with elite contexts at the expense of nonelite sectors. Our repertoire of ivories from SACC thus does not constitute a representative sample of Syro-Anatolian society, which may have been greater consumers of ivory products than has hitherto been assumed. The general lack of ivory in the extensive nonelite cemeteries at Hamath perhaps mitigates against this possibility, although it is equally possible that ivory was not considered an appropriate item for burial. Either way, although we cannot rule out the possibility that nonelite actors did not use ivory products, we can be certain that the highest echelons of Syro-Anatolian society *did*.

Does it necessarily follow from this consumption pattern that production was equally oriented in royal circles, and that the identification of subgroups of Syro-Anatolian ivories can be geographically and politically associated with specific city-states? It is perhaps a natural assumption from the findspots listed earlier that the makers of ivory products were specialists whose activities were in some way attached to the palace, making objects by royal demand and receiving subsistence goods in return for providing luxury ivory goods for royal use and elite-level exchange. However, it is by no means certain that this was the case, and in fact, there is good reason to suggest that ivory makers were not necessarily related directly to the city-state and its political apparatus.

As has long been noted, there is no direct archaeological evidence for ivory production in the form of excavated workshops in the Syro-Anatolian city-states, rendering any reconstruction tentative until new evidence is generated. Despite this problematic lack of direct evidence, however, there are tantalizing indirect details that can be used to generate a model for the organization of production, details that can be fitted into a series of expectations derived from cross-cultural anthropological research in craft specialization. This work is surprisingly underutilized in this context, a neglect which leads to misleading statements such as Di Paolo's (2009: 142) claim that there was no Iron Age ivory specialization, despite the fact that specialization is defined in terms of the degree of regular production of a commodity exchanged for others and the ratio of producers relative to consumers, both of which clearly apply in this case. Cathy Costin (1991: 3–18) outlined the four principal variables that characterize the organization of production in any given situation: *context*, or the degree to which production is affiliated with elite actors, which can vary from entirely independent craftspeople to those entirely attached to elite institutions like the palace; *concentration*, or the spatial signature of production, ranging from craftspeople distributed across the landscape to those nucleated in a single location; *scale*, or the size of the production unit, from small kin-based groups to labor-based factories; and *intensity*, or the amount of time producers devote to production activities. From various combinations of these variables that are attested in the ethnographic and archaeological record, Costin (1991: Table 1.1) creates a list of eight different types of production organization that occur repeatedly around the world.

Costin goes on to describe the specific archaeological evidence that correlates with the four parameters, and here is where indirect lines of reasoning become so important in the context of Iron Age ivories. Regarding context, direct evidence would consist of the actual workspaces of specialists, whose content and location could then be used to determine whether the specialists were independent or attached. In our case, Iron Age production activities have not been isolated; Riis and Buhl (1990: 254–56, 1033–36) argued on the basis of a small number of ivory chips that Building IV on the acropolis at Hamath was the location of an ivory workshop, although Mazzoni (2009: 109) argues persuasively that these items more likely consist of fragments from finished objects damaged at the time of the building's destruction. Indeed, given the modest material needs for producing an engraved ivory product, with no special rooms or permanent installations required and no tools more elaborate than a simple toolkit of chisels and awls necessary, it is conceivable that ivory workspaces will never be found archaeologically (Feldman 2014: 28).[11]

Indirect evidence for the context of production is slightly more illuminating, however. Unworked elephant tusks have been excavated in Rm J2 of Building K, part of Kulamuwa's palace, at Zincirli (Barnett 1982: 50),[12] and possibly at Tell Tayinat and Çatal Höyük in the Amuq Valley (Collon 1977: 222n25; Fischer 2007: Tab. 5a).[13] They have also been found at the second-millennium centers of Alalakh (Tell Atchana), where five elephant tusks, apparently from the Asian elephant (Collon 1977: 222),[14] were discovered in Rm 11 of the Level VII palace (Woolley 1955: 102, pl. XVIb), a small room that also contained frescoes and a number of tablets, while carefully deposited elephant bones (though not tusks) were excavated in rooms DD and DF of the Royal Palace at Qatna (Tell Mishrifeh) (Pfälzner 2013). All of this points to the clustering of the raw materials for ivory production in the Ghab and Amuq Valleys of the Orontes River, particularly since similar contexts were excavated in a number of other Iron Age cities that did *not* produce tusks in this fashion, even while other second-millennium remains and textual evidence suggest that the Balikh and Khabur Rivers were another core region at that time (Pfälzner 2013: 120–21). While royal figures in Iron Age capitals clearly obtained the ivory, less certain is whether the elephants themselves were native to the area, brought to the area from elsewhere and kept in a natural hunting reserve (as per Caubet 2013: 452; Collon 1977), or lived independently further afield. Environmental and archaeological evidence is accumulating that during the Middle and Late Bronze Ages Syrian elephants were a local presence in the Ghab and Amuq Valleys (Çakırlar and Ikram 2016; Pfälzner 2016). It is likely that holds true for the early first millennium until elephants disappeared from the area toward the end of the Iron Age II (Miller 1986), possibly the result of overhunting or an outcome of their interference with the agricultural production of first-millennium rural settlements that we have seen now dotted the landscape (Çakırlar and Ikram 2016: 178–79). Either way, the tusks seem to have made their way to palace storerooms before they were handled by carvers.[15]

We thus have a scenario in which the original raw ivory material was likely procured by the palace, a logical deduction from the difficulty and danger of elephant hunting alone. Likewise, the final ivory products themselves were used primarily, and possibly exclusively, by elite actors. Yet it is the critical time in between these two moments, during which the ivory is transferred to the carvers before being reacquired by the wealthiest citizens as carved products, which is so unclear. The simplest reconstruction would be to keep the ivory under the control of the palace at all times, leading to the conclusion that the carvers were economically attached to the palace. But this is precisely what other indirect considerations described earlier have challenged, especially the reconsideration of the traditional stylistic approach to determining group membership, given that the enormous variety of ivory products that cannot be tethered to specific locales would point toward ivory carvers that are not fixed in space or polity, and that instead formed a large community of practice that conducted their work across the region. In short, the parameter of concentration would appear to be highly dispersed, and not nucleated. For now, then, it seems prudent to propose that artisans procured their materials from the palace and then offered their final products as both commissions and as objects for purchase.

This tentative reconstruction of the context of production, which ultimately leaves the carvers as independent specialists even while the palace controlled procurement of materials, suggests that the scale of the production was relatively small, although this, too, is far from certain. We have no information about whether ivory specialists were organized by filial relations, nor do we have a sense of how new members were recruited to the craft. This variable is perhaps the least understood, although the rarity of the raw material already necessitates a relatively low scale threshold. The question of intensity, or whether ivory carvers were full-time or part-time specialists, can likewise only be determined through indirect means. For example, I have argued elsewhere that estimates of the agricultural catchments of settlements in the city-state of Patina during the Iron Age II period does not require anyone at any site, including the capital city, to have been devoted entirely to nonsubsistence activities, and that it is more likely for everyone to have been providing their own agricultural products (Osborne 2015: 13–14). Although full-time ivory production specialization (and other crafts) cannot be eliminated as a possibility, this finding reduces its likelihood by raising the prospect that all citizens were at least partially responsible for devoting time to generate their own subsistence.

In sum, it is likely that the highly specialized producers of these carved ivories were independent, dispersed, small scale, and part-time. Such a combination of these variables falls under what Costin (1991: 8) refers to as individual specialization, "autonomous individuals or households producing for unrestricted local consumption." This reconstruction differs from Suter's (2010: 996–97) "semi-dependent workshops" and conflicts with Herrmann and Laidlaw (2009: 69–70), who argue, albeit tentatively, that the ivories were carved under palace-controlled production. But their proposal is derived primarily from the fact that elites were the obvious consumers of the products, which in itself does not demonstrate how the craft specialists were organized. Likewise, their methodological assumption is that the corpus of ivories can be divided into discrete stylistic categories associated with specific city-states, which seems increasingly unlikely to have been the case. The suggestion put forward here, that the acquisition of raw material and the purchase of final products were both conducted by elites such as the palace, despite the independent status of the carvers, might seem unorthodox, but it is a better fit for the limited evidence available.

This proposal is tentative, to be sure, but it provides a working model for future research. It also accords well with current interest in the socially embedded nature of craft specialization (Hruby and Flad 2007), such as Feldman's alternative interpretation for how dispersed artists with no unambiguous political affiliations would nevertheless come to produce carved ivory products that resemble one another quite closely at the regional scale. In her argument, ivory craftspeople formed a fluid community of individuals bonded not by kinship or polity, but by practice and knowledge in the sense of Pierre Bourdieu's *habitus*, especially a practice and knowledge grounded in the collective memory of Late Bronze artists and their products (Feldman 2014: 43–78). Ivories and objects in other media belonging to the so-called flame and frond school, then, are not so much a coherent workshop whose political affiliation could be determined if only we could find the right variables to analyze with the proper methodology, so much as they are "the product of certain shared social relations that spanned this entire region . . . through their consumption, they contributed to shaping certain panregional community identities" (Feldman 2014: 57). This interpretation is supported by a large ivory plaque depicting two ibexes flanking a tree in the flame and frond tradition found in an early eighth-century context at Arslantepe (Manuelli and Pittman 2018), far north of the bulk of this tradition's findspots (cf. Herrmann 1989: Fig. 3) (Figure 3.5).

This, of course, is one of the central arguments of this volume: aspects of SACC demonstrate its reality as a genuine regional cultural phenomenon, documented in this case through one example of elite material culture. Yet one of the reasons the existence of SACC as a coherent cultural phenomenon has not yet been adequately argued by scholars is because its cultural expressions are, at a fundamental level, characterized by fluidity and movement. In the last chapter I noted how the linguistic data for SACC are inherently messy, and that we would be well served to consider this messiness not as a problem to be solved but rather as the key to understanding SACC's ethnolinguistic constitution. The same holds true with

FIGURE 3.5
Flame and frond ivory dating to ca. 800 BCE discovered at Arslantepe. (Manuelli and Pittman 2018: Fig. 4, courtesy of the Missione Archeologica Italiana nell'Anatolia Orientale, Sapienza University of Rome)

respect to the ivories under consideration here. Thematically consistent enough to be considered a legitimate region-wide category of material culture and artistic expression, but too stylistically diverse to be subdivided into meaningful political categories, the ivories are best understood as objects continuously in motion made by carvers who themselves were a fluid and interrelated community. The ivories found in an Assyrian administrative building at Arslan Tash (Thureau-Dangin et al. 1931) perhaps best exemplify this point (see Cecchini 2009 for a summary; Feldman 2014: 151–53, 167–68). With one piece inscribed with the name of Hazaʼel, ninth-century ruler of Damascus, the apparently mixed North Syrian-Phoenician style of the decoration was concluded to have derived from the Damascus region (Winter 1981). Whether or not this was the case—and it is entirely possible, given the presence of Hazaʼel's name on other objects known to have been taken by him from the city-state of Patina, that the ivories were not carved in Damascus at all—this inscription sheds light on the mobility of these ivories that would not otherwise have been identified. First they were carved in an unknown locale, then picked up by Hazaʼel, then at some later point acquired by the Assyrians (perhaps when they conquered Damascus), and only then made their way to the Assyrian center at Arslan Tash. The movement of these particular pieces would not have been appreciated were it not for the Hazaʼel inscription, and we thus have to be open to the likelihood that the findspots of the ivories found within SACC are in no way related to their place of production, all having had various lives in a number of places.

Although the current appreciation of the fluidity and mobility that characterized Iron Age ivory production is a significant step forward in our understanding of this material, we also cannot lose sight of the fact that these highly mobile objects and craftspeople were closely involved with political authority, even if not particular city-states per se. As described earlier, it is likely that the palace was responsible for obtaining the raw material in state-sponsored elephant hunts. We are also reasonably certain that elite actors, including the king himself, were the primary acquirers of the carvers' goods. The most vivid example of the ivories' kinopolitics is, of course, the Neo-Assyrian Empire's hoarding of the objects in their capital cities after taking them as conquest booty, but kinopolitics was clearly at play within SACC long before the city-states were reduced to Assyrian provinces. Mobility was clearly part and parcel of the ivories' existence, but it was forever tied with representations of elite authority both as a precious material that was inaccessible to most people (and that was often inlayed with additional precious materials) and as artistic items that displayed significant elements of cultural iconography. The mobility of the ivories and their lack of city-state assignations must not be taken as divorcing these objects from the political sphere, of which they were very much a part.

::::

## Monuments and Movement

If the mobility of ivory objects comes as small surprise, perhaps less intuitive is the fact that even SACC's ostensibly most immutable products—the carved orthostats that lined the walls of public buildings and the monumental statues that frequently accompanied them—were similarly implicated in kinopolitics. The reliefs are SACC's most famous legacy, their stone material preserving them to the present, and now lining the walls of museums in Syria, Turkey, western Europe, and North America.[16] Walls lined with reliefs have been excavated at some of SACC's most prominent sites, including Carchemish, Zincirli, Tell Halaf, Aleppo, and Karatepe. Furthermore, as Erhan Tamur (2017) has demonstrated, consideration of the full range of technological variables in these reliefs—stone materials, placement techniques, as well as visual content—renders it impossible to assign particular corpora to either "Aramaean" or "Luwian" ethnic groups. Similar to arguments presented in this volume, he states "the production and consumption of carved orthostats should be seen as part of shared social practices among the Syro-Anatolian city-states of the Iron Age" (2017: 46). That said, there are some cities whose monumental buildings were not lined with reliefs—or whose relief programs have not yet been discovered—such as Tell Tayinat,[17] Hamath, Tell Rifaʿat, and Tell Ahmar, but these centers have still produced monumental statuary of various kinds, including portal lions and royal and divine figures; these, too, were by no means fixed in place.

The use of undecorated orthostats in the Syro-Anatolian region has local precedents stretching back to the Middle Bronze Age at sites like Ebla (Tell Mardikh), Alalakh (Tell Atchana), and Tilmen Höyük. The innovation that took place during the Iron Age—engraving the orthostats with pictorial representations—merged that Late Bronze Age Anatolian custom, already attested in the region at the Hittite viceregency of Aleppo, with the Middle Assyrian tradition of wall painting (Harmanşah 2013: 153–88). As mentioned in Chapter 1, Winfried Orthmann's magisterial *Untersuchungen zur späthethitischen Kunst* (1971), which developed and systematized earlier pioneering efforts (e.g., Akurgal 1949), is the volume that has set the terms for the interpretation of Iron Age Syro-Anatolian reliefs in the decades since. Relying principally on stylistic criteria along with accompanying inscriptions when present, Orthmann (1971: 221) divided the extant corpus into what he called Späthethitische (Late Hittite) I ca. 1000–950 BCE, Späthethitische II ca. 950–850 BCE, and Späthethitische III ca. 850–700 BCE, although the reliefs' relative sequence was more significant than where they fell in absolute terms. Subsequent discoveries since the time of publication, especially the temples at ʿAin Dara and Aleppo and their associated relief programs, were then slotted into this framework. As is the case with ivories, reliefs displaying stylistic affinities are grouped together, although here the groups produced by the analyst are said to provide meaningful insight in chronological terms, with the basic principle being that details shared by multiple reliefs ought to demonstrate those reliefs' rough contemporaneity; Genge (1979: 47) goes so far as to apply this methodology to individual items, as opposed to Orthmann's groups. Either way, unlike the ivories, which were found mostly at Nimrud, the geographical and political associations of the reliefs are already provided by the city in which they were discovered. These stylistically derived groups are then used to establish relationships of shared workshops between sites, as Winter proposed for Sakçe Gözü and Zincirli (1976b: 52) and for Carchemish and Tell Ahmar (1983: 181).

As was the case in the previous section, there are a number of methodological difficulties associated with grouping the reliefs and placing those groups into chronological schemas. The presence of inscriptions can often be helpful, but it is not always clear whether the relief and accompanying inscription are contemporary. More problematically, there is so much diversity both within and between the groups established by Orthmann that it is difficult to relate them to meaningful chronological categories except in the broadest of terms. Such diversity has led even Orthmann to oscillate, for example, between considering the reliefs from Tell Halaf as "Neo-Hittite" or as a separate stylistic group altogether (2013: 525). Underlying the method is an evolutionary assumption in which allegedly cruder reliefs precede allegedly more sophisticated examples, when of course one region may retain stylistic traits long after a neighboring region has developed new ones, and individual artists will always have chosen from a range of available artistic styles. Such considerations render the relationship of style and chronology quite uncertain (Brown 2008b: 263–69, 277). To these considerations I would add the same point I raised earlier with respect to ivories: there has been little scholarly consideration of the degree to which, or even whether, stylistic groups determined by the analyst correspond to the groupings that would have been considered meaningful by the ancient carvers and viewers themselves. It is entirely plausible to speculate, for example, that some or all of the five subgroups Orthmann established for the reliefs from Carchemish would have been considered a single category by a craftsperson who worked there or, alternatively, that many more groupings were considered to exist, using variables entirely different from our modern stylistic considerations.

For my purposes here, what is remarkable about these orthostats and statues is the consistent challenges of provenance that they present to the researcher. In nearly every instance where they are found, the orthostats present what at first glance appear to be troubling spatial inconsistencies, with clear indicators that the context in which they were excavated was not the context in which they were originally installed. In much the same way as scholarship has approached Syro-Anatolian inscriptions or ivory production, these inconsistencies have tradition-ally been interpreted in functionalist terms, that is, to preserve stone (e.g., Ozyar 1998: 634). The discrepancy between original installation location and excavation is thus treated as a challenge to our interpretations of ancient art groups, one that increased data and refined methodologies will be able to resolve in the tradition of positivist analysis. Yet here, too, we need to account for the tremendous amount of inconsistently arranged orthostats by seeing this phenomenon not as a problem to be solved away, but as itself a meaningful social practice. These reliefs and statues were reshaped, reused, and repurposed by the architects and designers of Iron Age public buildings so often that we are obliged to recognize the practice as part and parcel of SACC's meaningful engagement with monumental art. Examining the reliefs from several sites, followed by an analysis of monumental statues, makes the practice of orthostat mobility clear.

## Carchemish

Carchemish is the necessary starting point, having served as SACC's type site for understanding Syro-Anatolian relief programs (Figure 3.6). Although Iron Age II monumental arts and inscriptions have begun to appear in the recently renewed Turco-Italian excavations directed by Nicolò Marchetti and Hasan Peker (Marchetti 2014), the majority of the reliefs were exposed in the early twentieth-century excavations led by Sir Leonard Woolley (Hogarth 1914; Woolley 1921, 1952).

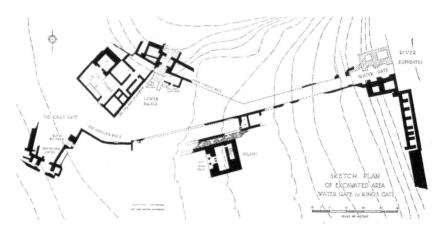

FIGURE 3.6
Plan of the relief-lined Inner Town plaza at Carchemish (Woolley 1952: Pl. 41a). The area in the corner east of the King's Gate and south of the Herald's Wall is the subject of renewed Turco-Italian excavations (see Chapter 4).

As noted earlier, Orthmann (1971: 30–37) divided the reliefs into five chronological groups. Since Carchemish is also the richest Syro-Anatolian site for monumental inscriptions that accompany the reliefs (Harmanşah 2013: Table 4; Hawkins 2000: 72–223), the dating of many of these programs is reasonably well secured, although stylistic extrapolations to independent or *ex situ* objects are less certain. Reliefs were found in several different architectural contexts in the city's inner town, whose combined effect was a large open plaza that was used for rituals and festivals (Gilibert 2011; Harmanşah 2013: 134–52).

Orthostats of the south tier of the Water Gate, so-named due to its location at the eastern edge of the city at the embankment that flanked the Euphrates River, were visible in situ above ground level at the time of Woolley's excavation; the superstructure of the north tier, however, had been completely removed by Roman-period activity (Woolley 1921: 104). Both carved and uncarved orthostats were found lining the buttresses of the gate's south tier, including examples that Orthmann places in the earliest Carchemish group, dating to the eleventh century (Woolley 1921: Plate B.28–31). But the reliefs are clearly not part of a single artistic program, and instead were cobbled together from multiple episodes of the gate's reconstruction. As Gilibert (2011: 29) has noted, "The carved orthostats . . . found in situ at the gate share a single common feature: they were all re-used from older phases of the gate." Of the four carved pieces that lined the buttresses of the south tier, none are consistent in size and all fit only poorly where they were installed. Even more conspicuous is the relief Woolley labels number 5 (what Gilibert refers to as number 6, and Orthmann as Aa/4), a scene depicting a libation being poured before the Storm God in a chariot pulled by two bulls, whose right side was not dressed to function as the corner stone it ended up being (Woolley 1921: 109). Stranger still is orthostat 6 (Gilibert's 7), a banquet scene, that was found upright but below street level inside of the foundation for the gate's north tier (Woolley 1921: Plate 17a). As Gilibert (2011: 30) rightly notes, this context strongly implies a symbolic motive to the burial, possibly as a ritual burial of the king's image. It also suggests that the other relief movements attested at the Water Gate were conducted for more than functional reasons.

The famous Long Wall of Sculpture installed by Suhi II does not appear to be the result of the any remodeling or orthostat transfer. However, the lengthy inscription that accompanies the reliefs seems to refer to a previous destruction event of the reliefs by a rival military leader, one Hatamanas, as the impetus for the installation. (The inscribed slab is apparently only one of several that would have joined it on either side, such that each line of the existing text is only part of an incomplete thought.) If that reading is correct, then we have another possible explanation for the movement of reliefs. Unlike the Long Wall of Sculpture, the reliefs of the Herald's Wall present what appears to us as a completely unorganized thematic otructure, Each relief is iconographically independent from its neighbors and depicts scenes of soldiers and animals attacking one another (hence the name of the wall, which struck Woolley as heraldic). Roman building activity compromised our understanding of the reliefs' layout, but the odd shape of the wall and the incoherent iconography of the reliefs have led Özyar (1991: 40) to follow the excavator's (Woolley 1952: 185–86) interpretation that the orthostats derive from an earlier structure and are deployed here in a repair project. The evidence for this reuse, however, is mostly circumstantial and derived from contemporary unease at the alleged lack of thematic consistency.[18]

The King's Gate, named after the royal palace that Woolley suspected lay to its south, and the associated Processional Way and Royal Buttress, is a complex architectural palimpsest of renovations and recycling (Gilibert 2011: 41–50; Marina Pucci 2008b: 217; Woolley 1952: 192–204). Four phases are present, the fourth of which is apparently following the Assyrian conquest, while the previous three can all be fairly securely dated to the tenth through early eighth centuries by means of associated inscriptions (Gilibert 2011: Table 10). Reliefs from the south face of the gate itself were either in situ or found in nearby Roman features with plausible original findspot reconstructions. Their iconography resembles the Herald's Wall and, like the Herald's Wall, their iconographic inconsistency leads one to assume that this was not their original arrangement. Gilibert (2011: 43) notes, for example, that a deer hunt scene is inverted, suggesting reuse. To explain why the reuse would not have maintained the correct order of slabs, Gilibert proposes an intriguing solution: "The new order, as in the case of the Herald's Wall and the Long Wall of Sculpture, appears to privilege the chromatic alternation basalt/limestone over thematic consistency" (2011: 43), which again has the effect of challenging the meaningfulness of our stylistic typologies.

While the early tenth-century date for the reliefs of the King's Gate's south face is based strictly on stylistic parallels to the Herald's Wall, the north face of the gate and the Processional Way is dated to the early ninth century by the lengthy door jamb inscription of Katuwas A11a. Ll. 4–5 of this inscription refers explicitly to the gate having been built by Katuwas's grandfathers—if intended literally, the gate was then first built by Astuwatamanzas—and Katuwas's insertion of the orthostats as a subsequent addition: "And these gates (of) my grandfathers passed down to me. While I built the holies of the temple, (or: the Holy (One)'s temple,) these orthostats 'came after' me, these gates I 'orthostated,' they were foremost in(?) cost(?)" (Hawkins 2000: 95). In the commentary on this passage, Hawkins (2000: 98) notes how context suggests that the curious phrase "came after" must imply something like "became available to," which, if correct, would indicate that Katuwas is stating outright that he transferred the orthostats from the temple he was then building to the gate—a royal declaration of orthostat transfer from one building to another.

The reliefs of the Processional Way appear to be mainly contemporary with one another, although Özyar (1998: 636) notes how the first of five reliefs of the processions, each depicting three women processing north (Woolley 1952: Plate B.19b; Orthmann's F/8, Gilibert's 73), is both thicker than the other four orthostats and also depicts the women's arms in a unique fashion, raising the possibility that this relief originates from a different program before being reused here. A monumental statue standing atop a double lion statue base was found badly damaged in the north portion of the Processional Way, where the procession consists of soldiers facing south. The statue base lay directly against the reliefs behind it, yet Woolley (1952: 194), followed by Gilibert (2011: 45), asserted emphatically that the statue was contemporary with the reliefs on the grounds that the soldiers' legs blocked by the statue base were left only roughly carved and thus did not receive the final touches reliefs typically underwent after installations. This reconstruction presents a curious scenario in which the reliefs were partially carved, installed but left incomplete, a statue base installed against them but left bare, the top portions of the reliefs then completed, followed by the statue installed on its base. More plausible is a scenario in which the statue and its base represent a later addition to the Processional Way.

The lengthy Processional Way is broken by the Royal Buttress, depicting Yararis's royal progeny, including his eldest son Kamanis, and thus dating to the late ninth or early eighth century (Figure 3.7). The reliefs and accompanying inscriptions appear remarkably unified as a coherent program. Yet even here there is clear evidence for orthostats' movement. The dimensions of each of the eight slabs are different (Özyar 1998: 637), and more significantly, two of them show clear evidence of reworking: one (Woolley's pl. B.8a, Orthmann's G/7, Gilibert's 77) depicts a paw and hindquarters of a lion in a fashion reminiscent of the Herald's Wall along its baseline, and another (Woolley's pl. B.7b, Orthmann's G/6, Gilibert's 78) also has traces of earlier carving on its own baseline; Orthmann (1971: 33n29) detects vestiges of a beard. Where these slabs had been placed originally is impossible to know, but clearly they were first used elsewhere. These faint hints of recycling raise the possibility that many or all of the reliefs as we now see them at any given site are simply the end point of a long chain of reuse events. Certainly every major venue for relief display at Carchemish—the Water Gate, the Herald's Wall, the Long Wall of Sculpture, the Processional Way, the King's Gate, and the Royal Buttress—has evidence for the movement of orthostats. Though some cases are more circumstantial than others (the Herald's Wall) or indicated by an accompanying text (the Long Wall of Sculpture), the fact remains that Carchemish's reliefs were in motion.

(a)

(b)

FIGURE 3.7

Reliefs from the Inner Town at Carchemish: (*a*) view of the Processional Entry and Royal
Buttress from the southwest. Note the alternating limestone-basalt colors of the Processional
Entry (Woolley 1921: Pl. B.17*a*); (*b*) western face of the Royal Buttress depicting the king
Yararis presenting his son Kamanis, followed by several royal children. Note evidence of
reworking, especially under the feet of the goat at far right (Orthmann's Karkemis G/7).
(Hogarth 1914: Pl. B.8*b*)

## *Tell Halaf*

The site of Tell Halaf, ancient Guzana, was the capital city of the city-state of Bit-Baḫiani. Its prodigious monumental remains have been famous since they were excavated by Max von Oppenheim early in the twentieth century. Tell Halaf was conquered by the Neo-Assyrian Empire early in their westward expansion efforts, though when precisely has been the subject of much debate, especially since the answer to that question affects how one dates the archaeological remains. The crux of the problem is that the ruler Kapara, builder of the site's famous *bīt-ḫilāni* (Gilibert 2013), is not mentioned in any of the Neo-Assyrian texts that discuss Guzana or Bit-Baḫiani. Most scholars now favor a late tenth-century date for Kapara, though it cannot yet be excluded conclusively that the site's so-called Kapara Period was a century or more later than this (see Younger 2016: 247–55, and Table 4.1).

The building was built on a terrace such that the rear wall loomed over a lower plaza with a massive 5.5 m foundation platform while the portico at the front looked out over a second, higher terrace (Baghdo et al. 2012). The original excavators identified an underlying building of identical plan as an earlier structure that they named the Altbau and assigned to a pre-Kapara phase (Langenegger 1950: 30–35). Subsequent excavations and reconsideration of the original findings have suggested that this structure is nothing other than the foundations for Kapara's *bīt-ḫilāni* (Cholidis and Martin 2010: 70; Pucci 2008a: 95) (Figure 3.8).

For our purposes, the significant issue is the carved orthostats that lined the walls of the building at its front façade, which were visible only to visitors who had entered the palace compound through the similarly decorated Scorpion Gate, and those along its rear wall that faced out overlooking the city, which alternated between red painted limestone and black basalt. These are precisely the reliefs that are so often discussed in the context of the flame and frond school due to their highly recognizable musculature and other features (see earlier). The reliefs are varied, showing animals, hunting scenes, soldiers, and composite beasts, among others images, even including one depiction of a man riding a camel, contributing to Albright's (1975: 536) hypothesis of a nomadic origin of the Aramaeans (see Chapter 2) (Figure 3.9).

Although explanations differ in precisely how and why it took place, it is accepted that the final deposition of these reliefs as they were excavated cannot have been their original layout, at least not entirely. The excavators proposed that, on account of their smaller size and cruder execution, the large group of small reliefs around the back of the building—182 were found, with space remaining for about 250 in total—must have preceded Kapara by a generation or two, and associated them with the Altbau, while the larger reliefs at the building's portico were dated to Kapara himself (Opitz and Moortgat 1955: 19). This division was fundamentally

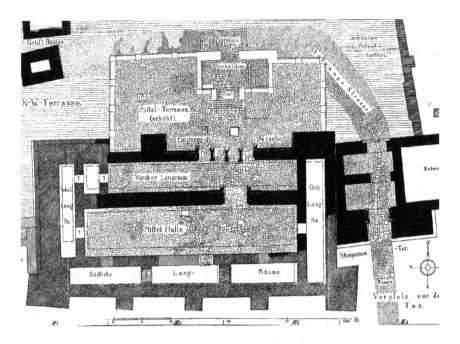

FIGURE 3.8
Plan of the bīt ḫilāni Palace of Kapara at Tell Halaf. (Langenegger 1950: Pl. 5)

FIGURE 3.9
Reconstruction of the south face of the Palace of Kapara, illustrating the row of small reliefs on the building's rear façade. (Langenegger 1950: 36, Abb. 8)

accepted, although scholars subsequently reduced the time between them to a matter of two decades by virtue of the two groups' stylistic similarity, if not final execution (Genge 1979: 130; Mellink 1958: 439). Most recently, accompanying the reevaluation of the Altbau, renewed consideration of the similarities between these two groups of reliefs has led to the proposal that they both, in fact, date to the reign of Kapara (Cholidis and Martin 2010: 145–46; followed by Gilibert 2013: 42).

It remains the case that there is evidence within the small group of reliefs on the building's rear face for secondary use and orthostat movement. For one thing, while several inscriptions on the front façade read "Palace of Kapara" (Akk. É.GAL-*lim* ^m*ka-pa-ra*), as do inscriptions on some of the small orthostats, other inscriptions on the small orthostats read "Temple[/Palace] of the Storm God" (Akk. É.GAL-*lim* U). For another, the red paint on the limestone blocks is inconsistently applied on the side strip, proving that in some cases those blocks had alternated between corner locations and spots in the middle of a row. Although it is possible that these alterations could have taken place mere moments before their final arrangement, and that the variant inscriptions refer to the multiple functions of the building for which being referred to as belonging to both Kapara and the Storm God was not inherently problematic, as Gilibert (2013: 43) suggests, the standard interpretation—that the Storm God small orthostats, and possibly others, were taken from a temple built during or slightly prior to Kapara's reign—remains more plausible. In this scenario, there are at least two, and possibly three (if one considers the façade reliefs separately), groups of reliefs on the *bīt-ḫilāni* palace, all close in date, but ultimately representing the end point of a series of orthostat movements. Most unambiguously of all, the recent reevaluation of the building's relief program has made it clear that not all of the orthostats on the building's south façade were found with images visible. Cholidis and Martin (2010: 137) list a dozen examples of reliefs that were unworked; whose reliefs were obscured by having been laid with the short side facing the wall exterior or by having been used as support for other orthostats (Figure 3.10); or that were damaged and reworked in antiquity. The *bīt-ḫilāni* façade as excavated, therefore, can only be taken as its final manifestation, not its original—or sole—appearance, since the orthostats used to decorate it were not fixed in position.

## Karatepe-Aslantaş

Karatepe, ancient Azatiwataya, was a fortress in the foothills of the Taurus Mountains north of Cilicia overlooking the Ceyhan River. Just 400 m south of the site, but on the opposite bank of the Ceyhan River, lies the site of Domuztepe, also occupied during the early first millennium BCE (among other periods). Although

FIGURE 3.10

"Small orthostat" reliefs from the south face of the Palace of Kapara: (*a*) Relief of a goose (A3,95) facing upward (with goose therefore not visible in this image), supporting an undecorated orthostat on the southwestern corner tower of the building (Cholidis and Martin 2010: Fig. V.123); (*b*) Reliefs along the building's second bastion from the west (Cholidis and Martin 2010: Fig. V.124). Note the second orthostat from the left (A3, 130) placed with its narrow side facing out and its decorated side, depicting a palm, within the matrix of the wall and thus not visible. (Photographs courtesy of the Max Freiherr von Oppenheim Foundation)

Karatepe is relatively small, and was not the capital of its city-state, it is neverthe-less one of the most important from SACC by virtue of the lengthy Phoenician-Luwian bilingual inscription that appears in each of the fortress's South and North Gates (see discussion earlier), but also because of the elaborate relief program that likewise was present in both of the excavated gates (Figure 3.11). The struc-tural remains within the fortifications were inconsistently preserved on the rocky

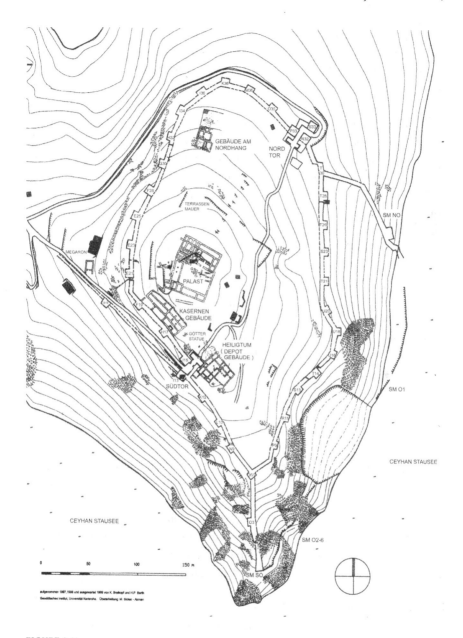

FIGURE 3.11

Plan of Karatepe-Aslantaş. (Çambel 2014: Beilage 1, prepared by K. Breitkopf, H. P. Barth, and M. Sicker-Akman, with permission)

outcrop, and the reliefs themselves were found smashed to pieces, leading to a multiyear conservation effort. Thanks to these remarkable efforts, we now have an understanding both of the relief programs that decorated the two gates (Çambel and Özyar 2003) and the available remains of the excavated architecture (Çambel

2014) As in Carchemish and Tell Halaf just examined, the reliefs consist of a number of different images whose relationships with one another are difficult to reconstruct. Scenes represented include hunting, banquets, ships at sea, animals, breastfeeding women, gods, and others (see Özyar 2003 and 2013 for a summary of the motifs).

The dating of the complex has been one of Iron Age archaeology's most notorious chronological problems, with estimates varying widely from the mid-ninth century (Ussishkin 1969) to the early seventh century (Frankfort 1996: 308) shortly after the discoveries were first made known, though still long before the final reports had appeared. Today a general placing of the site in the late eighth century or slightly later has found common acceptance. But scholarship has tended to elide the discussion of the chronology of the site itself with the chronology of the reliefs and the associated bilingual inscription, two datasets that are not necessarily equivalent. Certainly, the recently published nonrelief finds from the site reveal a site with a long history of settlement. Ceramics from the palace area have strong parallels with the destruction level of Tarsus (Bossert 2014: 149), possibly attributed to Sennacherib in 696 BCE, while earlier silos on the site contain ceramics stretching all the way back to the late eleventh century as attested by, for example, Cypro-Geometric I White Painted Ware (Bossert 2014: 134–35). Likewise, excavations in the palace area revealed four phases of the structure, indicating that it had undergone several stages of renovation (Sicker-Akman 2014: 76–80).

It should be no surprise, therefore, that the reliefs of the North and South Gates may not be the result of a single construction event. Nevertheless, the consistency of the relief program, or lack thereof, is at the heart of the chronological debates. What has always been clear is that the iconography of the reliefs reveals two distinct visual traditions. Such has always been maintained by the excavators (most recently Çambel and Özyar 2003), who referred to the two groups of reliefs as A and B, and has since been followed universally by archaeologists and art historians, including Orthmann, who referred to the two groups as Stilgruppe I and II (1971: 106–8). Among other distinguishing characteristics, most obvious are the different facial physiognomies of the two groups, especially A's pronounced noses and receding chins, and the squatter physical proportions of the figures in group B (Figure 3.12). Most scholars, regardless of when they date the reliefs, have followed the excavators' argument that although these two groups are clearly distinct stylistically, they represent not a chronological difference but rather the simultaneous presence of two workshops (Mazzoni 2008; Ussishkin 1969: 126).

This assessment was challenged by Irene Winter (1979), who noted enough clues in the archaeological record of the site and its neighbor Domuztepe to lead her to conclude that relief groups A and B must indeed have been carved at different times.

FIGURE 3.12
Adjacent reliefs from Karatepe's South Gate: *left*, SVl 2, attendants in the later style group B (Çambel and Özyar 2003: Taf. 142); *right*, SVl 3, feasting scene in the earlier style group A (cf. Winter 1979: Pl. 15*a*). (Drawings courtesy of Aslı Özyar, with permission)

First, the stylistic comparisons of the two groups with other Syro-Anatolian reliefs are to differently dated corpora, such as group A's physiognomic likenesses with the reliefs from Kapara's *bīt-ḫilāni*, which pushes group A at least into the ninth century BCE and likely earlier, and group B's shoes with turned-up toes and ankle thongs that are also present on the Ivriz rock relief of the late eighth-century ruler Warpalawa (1979: 117–18). These stylistic considerations do not render conclusive a chronological distinction between groups A and B, but contextual indications further support this line of reasoning. The slabs appear to have been installed somewhat haphazardly, or at least in such a way that remodeling was necessary. Most conspicuous in this regard is the join of the portal lion on the left side of the North Gate with the relief behind it (NVl 1 and 2) coupled with the Phoenician text on the next slab (NVl 3) spilling onto the relief of NVl 2; orthostat NVl 2, in other words, has been modified by the relief on either side of it (Çambel and Özyar 2003: Taf. 41, 45). The Hieroglyphic Luwian inscription of the North Gate is horrendously jumbled around the gate (Çambel 1999: Insert Plan). Also relevant is the fact that limestone is the dominant stone on the hill of Karatepe itself, whereas the source of the basalt for the orthostats is found on the hill of Domuztepe across the river—where another settlement was located, one with Syro-Anatolian stelae and statues of a style reminiscent of Karatepe group A found scattered across the hillside and reused in later occupation levels. Winter (1979: 125–32, esp. 131) thus makes the logical deduction that Karatepe's group A reliefs were taken from Domuztepe, and only group B was carved on site at Karatepe. In light of the multiple phases to Karatepe's palace noted earlier, Harrison's (2009a: 49) suggestion that the group A reliefs may have been recycled from the palace is also possible, as are other locations altogether.

The excavators have resisted this reinterpretation on several grounds: (1) damage from transportation (from Domuztepe or elsewhere) should be visible on the orthostats, but is not; (2) there is no structure yet found at Domuztepe that could serve as the original location of the orthostats' installation; (3) the orthostats were cut to fit with one another and with the bases beneath them; (4) basalt flakes and chunks were found in both gates, indicators of the final carving that took place after the roughly carved orthostats were installed (Çambel 1999: 10–11). Each of these points can be questioned in ways that allow for orthostat movement to have taken place. (The case of the portal line NVl 1 mentioned earlier is admitted to be the one case of a "drastic miscalculation" [Çambel 1999: 10]). First, the excavators note that there *was* damage to some reliefs, and that these orthostats were reused in other ways: "Orthostats that were damaged during the work process were discarded and used either as headers, with their carved face hidden in the wall behind, or else as stretchers behind doorjamb sculptures" (Çambel 1999: 10, with examples). There is no reason this damage could not have taken place during transportation, nor is there any particular reason to assume that these secondary pieces were not originally whole items that had been on display. Second, while the absence of an appropriate building on Domuztepe is problematic for Winter's reconstruction specifically, other original venues are possible, including other structures at Karatepe itself as mentioned earlier (and Domuztepe may yet produce buildings of this kind). Third, the cutting of the orthostats to fit one another may have happened after they were recycled. Finally, if such reshaping of the blocks had to take place due to their reuse, then this could just as easily be the origin of the flakes and chips found in their vicinity as their original carving.

It thus seems difficult to accept the excavators' long-standing assertion that the orthostats of Karatepe represent a single, coordinated construction event, with differences attributed to two contemporary workshops creating reliefs in two different styles. There is simply too much cause to accept the more plausible likelihood that, as attested at so many other Syro-Anatolian sites, the orthostats at Karatepe were not stable, but rather just as mobile as those found in neighboring cities. Whether they were borrowed from the nearby site of Domuztepe or simply taken from buildings at Karatepe (or elsewhere), the gateway orthostats from Karatepe were likely part of the common Syro-Anatolian phenomenon of orthostats and kinopolitics.

## Zincirli

Zincirli, ancient Sam'al, has long been famous for its monumental arts, including, among others, the Kulamuwa stele discussed earlier, the KTMW mortuary stele recently discovered in the lower city (Struble and Herrmann 2009), and a massive stele erected by Esarhaddon that parallels one from Til-Barsip (Porter 2000), found in the gateway to the acropolis known as the Citadel Gate. The Citadel Gate (Großes Burgthor) is one of two gates that was lined with orthostats carved with relief, the other being its counterpart in the fortifications of the lower city, the South Gate (Südliches Stadtthor) (see Herrmann 2017b: 239–45 for a detailed summary of the scholarship on these reliefs). The Citadel Gate produced forty reliefs still in situ at the time of discovery, while a further eight were discovered fallen in front of the walls on either side of the entrance niche of the South Gate (von Luschan et al. 1898; von Luschan 1902), with a likely ninth orthostat from this context found reused by villagers. The original excavator decided quickly that, on account of their slightly cruder style, the South Gate's orthostats were likely to have been produced earlier than those of the Citadel Gate (von Luschan 1902: 202), an assessment that has been accepted since. Orthmann (1971: 60–62, 133–36), for example, refers to the two corpora as Zincirli I (South Gate) and II (Citadel Gate), and dates them to the late tenth or early ninth century using parallels between Zincirli II and Carchemish's Long Wall of Sculpture and Processional Way, with Zincirli I then dating to the mid- to late tenth century. This assessment has been more or less accepted since (e.g., Gilibert 2011: 58–67; but cf. Pucci 2015: 55–56, who sees enough architectural and iconographic parallels between the two gates to call them a "single conceptual plan").

The Citadel Gate seems clearly the outcome of a well-coordinated building plan, with rows of orthostats securely fitted in the same dimensions as the building itself, large motifs spanning multiple orthostats, corner pieces being worked and displayed on two sides, and thematic consistency paralleled on both sides of the gate (Gilibert 2011: 61–67, Figs. 29–32). Even here, however, at least one orthostat (Orthmann B/1, Gilibert 72) appears to be a reworked stele, evidenced by its rounded bottom (Brown 2008b: 484).

Even while the Citadel Gate and its reliefs appear to have been a relatively stable construction until the Assyrian period, the South Gate is more complicated (Figure 3.13). In a comprehensive reexamination of the reliefs from both of these contexts, Virginia Herrmann (2017b) coupled an innovative seriation approach to stylistic comparanda with new evidence for the historical sequences at sites with which the Zincirli reliefs are often compared (such as the growing recognition of high dates for Kapara at Tell Halaf; see earlier) to demonstrate that the date of the Zincirli I reliefs needs to be raised to the first half of the tenth century, even earlier than the reliefs made by Suhi II and Katuwas at Carchemish (2017b: 260). This immediately raises a problem, since the earliest one can place the first ruler of Sam'al, Gabbar, is roughly 920 BCE, and neither of the major excavation projects at the site has found archaeological deposits belonging to this period.

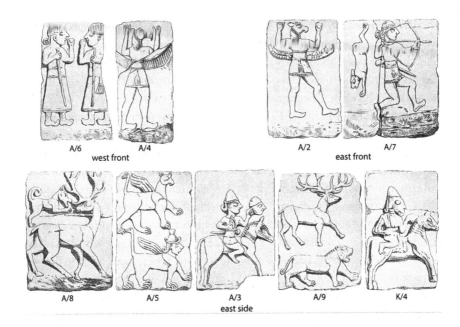

FIGURE 3.13
Reliefs from the South Gate at Zincirli, Orthmann's Zincirli I group. (Herrmann 2017: Fig. 5, after von Luschan 1902: Pl. 34 and Pucci 2015: Fig. 2; used with permission)

Herrmann's convincing solution to this conundrum is that the reliefs must have been imported to Zincirli from elsewhere, and very likely the site of Pancarlı specifically. It was at this site, just 1 km southeast of Zincirli, that a relief was shown to Henrik von der Osten in 1929, one which Orthmann (1971: 77) placed in his Zincirli I group by virtue of its similarities with the reliefs of the South Gate. It was also at this site that a recently published, and unfortunately only partially preserved, monumental statue with Hieroglyphic Luwian inscription was found reused in a modern field boundary wall (Herrmann et al. 2016). Herrmann's proposal thus seems correct, and even if one rejects Pancarlı as the source of the South Gate's orthostats, one is still required to find a different origin for them outside of Zincirli.

Herrmann proposes a specific historical scenario for this orthostat movement event, one involving a transition from a Luwian ruling dynasty at Pancarlı to a new Aramaean one at Sam'al (2017b: 262–63). Although such a transition may not be strictly necessary (see Chapter 2), the proposal that the transfer of reliefs from Pancarlı (or elsewhere) to Zincirli involved a complicated interplay of appropriation and emulation of earlier monumental legitimizations of authority with new statements of rulership (Herrmann 2017: 263–66) is highly compelling, and it serves as one of the strongest examples of kinopolitics in SACC.

## Arslantepe-Malatya

The site of Arslantepe, the Iron Age city of Malatya (Akk: Melid, Luw: Malizi), was capital of the Syro-Anatolian city-state of the same name, one that had a long history of interaction with its neighbors, including Carchemish and Urartu (see Hawkins 2000: 282–86). The tell of Arslantepe itself is quite small in area, just a few hectares in size, but its remains have had a large impact on our understanding of the upper Euphrates region. This is particularly true of the prehistoric periods, during which time Arslantepe was a critically important Chalcolithic and Early Bronze Age site (Frangipane 2018).

Surprisingly little is known about the Iron Age remains of the site, which until recently had produced only one substantial structure dating to SACC, the Lions Gate, so-called on account of the portal lions that lined its passage (Figure 3.14). The building was excavated during the early French excavations at the site, a project which unfortunately did not publish the associated material culture that would have been helpful to date it (Delaporte 1940). As a result, criteria for dating the building have been restricted to stylistic considerations of the orthostats and portal lions found in the gate and on the surface of the tell by earlier explorers (see Manuelli and Mori 2016: Fig. 7 for findspots). The inscriptions refer several times to PUGNUS-*mili*, a name we know to belong to two rulers of the twelfth- to eleventh-century Kuzi-Tešub dynasty (Hawkins 2000: 306; Mazzoni 1997: 310–11). This dating that would place these reliefs even earlier than Orthmann, who grouped the Lions Gate orthostats in his Malatya I and drew parallels with Carchemish reliefs from Suhis and Katuwas. Since the building was likely destroyed by Sargon II in 712 BCE, this reconstruction leaves the gate standing in its known configuration for four to five hundred years, an unrealistic configuration. Brief and almost entirely unpublished excavations by Claude Schaeffer found an earlier gate structure, but the lack of information precluded attempts to date its construction as well. Meanwhile, reevaluations of the reliefs published by Delaporte were finding indications that they might have been reused from an earlier context. These included their placement in the walls at inconsistent angles and their various sizes, plus the fact that the architecture of the gate, which seems like a standard early first-millennium gateway, appears later than the reliefs, which, besides being stylistically and thematically early, have rounded dowel holes common to the second millennium, in addition to their associated early Iron Age I genealogy (Özyar 1991: 123–33, 163)'.

The architectural sequence of the space adjacent to the Lions Gate has at last been clarified by recently renewed excavations in this area (Alvaro 2012: Fig. 2). This work made two discoveries critically important to the chronological reconstruction of the site: (1) two successive pillared-hall buildings connected stratigraphically to the

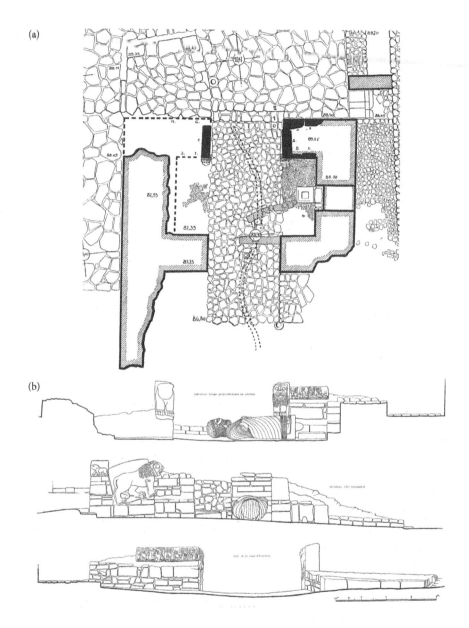

FIGURE 3.14
The Lion Gate at Arslantepe showing the location of the reliefs and their unorthodox elevation: (*a*) in plan (Delaporte 1940: Pl. XII); (*b*) in section. (Delaporte 1940: Pl. XV)

Lions Gate and sealing between their floor levels Urartian-style red polished pottery and painted Cypriot pottery dating to the early eighth century, demonstrating a late date for the final phase of the Lions Gate (Manuelli 2011: 71); and (2) a monumental fortification wall with an associated plaster floor on which were found two additional engraved orthostats in the same style as Orthmann's Malatya III group, that is, late in the Malatya sequence. Destruction debris of this wall has been dated by C14 to the late eleventh century, and thus it very likely related to the unpublished city gate found by Schaeffer (Manuelli and Mori 2016: 219–26). Given this new data, it would seem that the new excavations have found strong circumstantial evidence corroborating Özyar's interpretation of the Lions Gate reliefs as having been reused from an earlier gateway, one that itself probably went through several renovations and additions (e.g., the PUGNUS-*mili* reliefs likely predating the newly found orthostats).

In chronological terms, Malatya is thus one of the most dramatic examples of orthostat mobility, with reliefs dating as early as the twelfth century still finding use in a new building not destroyed until the end of the eighth. Clearly the rulers of Malatya felt that these reliefs were significant enough that they needed to be curated and left on display, no matter how anachronistic they might have appeared aesthetically.

## 'Ain Dara and Aleppo

The reliefs from these two sites are grouped together here since they derive from a similar date, context, and geographical area. Both sets of monumental arts are associated with large temples *in antis* ('Ain Dara) and *migdol*, or broadroom temples (Aleppo), common religious building types for the region since the Early Bronze Age, though taking a number of minor modifications in local manifestations during the Iron Age (Mazzoni 2010, 2014a). While the deity worshipped at 'Ain Dara is unknown, the Aleppo temple is the famous temple of the Storm God that had been known for decades from Bronze and Iron Age texts but not excavated until the 1990s and 2000s. Both buildings have engraved orthostats that derive from multiple periods of use.

'Ain Dara is a large, 24 ha site located in the Afrin Valley of northwestern Syria, an east-west valley that joins with the larger Amuq Valley to the west. Its ancient name and political affiliation are unknown, although from its location it is likely to have been a part of the city-state of Patina. Although the temple of 'Ain Dara is architecturally the descendant of a Syrian building type, the artwork that lined its walls is clearly related to the Hittite Empire in Anatolia and fragments of Hieroglyphic Luwian were found there (Abu 'Assaf 1990: 61, Taf. 51). The structure is thus emblematic of the hybrid cultural character that is SACC (Stone and Zimansky 1999: 4–5). It also cannot be excluded archaeologically that the building may have been built during the Late Bronze and only decorated with reliefs subse quently following a migration from Anatolia (Novák 2012: 51). Besides the temple itself (Abu 'Assaf 1990), survey and excavations in the broad lower city found continuous occupation stretching from the Late Bronze Age into the Iron Age II period (Stone and Zimansky 1999).

The temple consists of three primary spatial units: a columned portico, an antecella, and the cella, the latter having a raised platform in its rear half whose front façade was decorated with reliefs like the rest of the building (Figure 3.15). The rooms were paved with limestones, as were the thresholds between the rooms, which were decorated with the famous meter-long footprints of the presumed divine occupant. The excavator stated that the temple was built in three phases: the first a mostly hypothetical mudbrick structure decorated with a basalt guilloche pattern that was then covered by the second phase, consisting of the primary decorative program. The ambulatory surrounding every side of the building but its entrance is the third phase (Abu 'Assaf 1990: 20, Abb. 12–14).

Although it is true that the orthostats engraved with a guilloche pattern are covered in places (e.g., Abu 'Assaf 1990: Taf. 9b), the evidence for these divisions is minimal, nor are they demonstrated in the accompanying section drawing (1990: Abb. 15). It therefore has to remain as a possibility that the temple was a single construction event that simply had minor modifications made to its decoration. The same is likely true, in fact, of the reliefs themselves, which can only be approximately dated through stylistic means in the absence of intelligible inscriptions or associated material culture. The excavator (1990: 39–41) proposed three major periods of relief carving from 1300 to 740 BCE, consisting of (1) the mountain gods with raised arms along the façade of the cella's platform; (2) the lion and sphinx protomes along the front face of the building, the false windows in the antecella, and sculpture fragments of divine and other heads; and (3) all of the reliefs inside and around the exterior of the ambulatory, plus those on the front face of the pier between the antecella and the cella. However, these also likely belong to one primary phase of carving, despite minor differences between them, and close parallels with art from the Hittite Empire—such as the cella façade reliefs of the mountain gods with raised arms resembling those from Eflatun Pınar—suggest a date ranging from the thirteenth century to early in the Iron Age I (Mazzoni 2000c: 1043–48; Novák 2012: 50; Orthmann 1993), although the false windows are more reminiscent of the eleventh-century temple at Aleppo (Kohlmeyer 2008). As Stone and Zimansky (1999: 3) noted, some evidence of orthostat impermanence is present, such as fragments found buried in fill layers (Abu 'Assaf 1990: 61, Taf. 51), but even this indication of discard is not quite the same as mobility around the site. Beyond

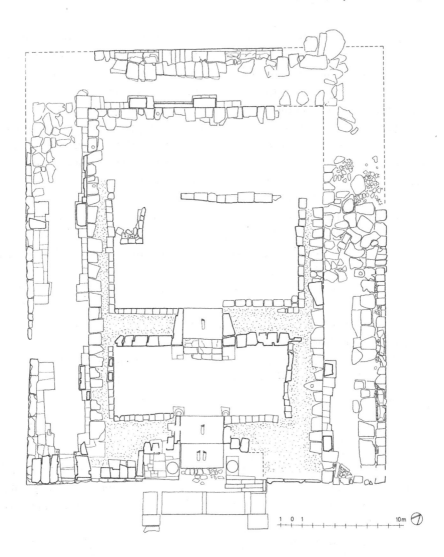

FIGURE 3.15
Plan of the temple from 'Ain Dara. (Adapted from 'Abu Assaf 1990: Abb. 18)

the specific chronological uncertainty that plagues the site, it seems that 'Ain Dara is a site whose reliefs do not provide significant evidence for movement.

Aleppo's Storm God temple is more complicated in this respect. As noted earlier, the site had been famous for its temple long before it was ever discovered, thanks to historical references to it stretching back to the late third-millennium texts from Ebla (Schwemer 2001). The Syro-German excavation of the temple was a much-anticipated discovery, and the reliefs that were found along its walls have generated much discussion (Gonnella et al. 2005; Kohlmeyer 2000, 2009). Excavations have shown that the temple of the Storm God was rebuilt on the same location near the center of the Aleppo citadel for over a millennium and a half starting in the mid-third millennium BCE. The huge Middle Bronze Age iteration of the temple had walls that were 10 m thick and a broadroom cella measuring 26.75 × 17.10 m (Gonnella et al. 2005: Abb. 117).[19] Although its walls were lined with orthostats, they were undecorated during this period. That changed during the subsequent Late Bronze and especially Iron Ages, when the walls were lined with some of the most elaborate mythological imagery from any Syro-Anatolian context.[20]

The architectural changes that took place in the late second and early first millennium are partially understood from stratigraphic evidence, and partially are logical deductions from the location of the reliefs. There are three interventions noticeable in the temple walls and reliefs at this time (Herrmann 2017b: 268–69). The first and most obvious change during the Late Bronze Age was a reduction in size of the broadroom by widening the north wall by 3.4 m. This wall was then decorated with plain orthostats well above ground level. A platform extended 1.8 m in front of this wall, and its front face, what the excavators refer to as the pedestal wall, was lined with engraved orthostats.[21] Only three LB reliefs, dated primarily on stylistic grounds by comparisons with Hittite imperial art, remain in this pedestal wall: one mountain god and two composite figures with the bodies of winged lions (Gonnella et al. 2005: Abb. 142, 148–49). The bulk of the east wall reliefs are also part of this group and consist of false windows resembling those from 'Ain Dara plus bull-men figures with their arms raised and, most conspicuously, a depiction of the Storm God of Aleppo, so labelled by an accompanying Hieroglyphic Luwian inscription (Gonnella et al. 2005: Abb. 124, 156). It is the presence of this depiction of the god in the east wall that led Kohlmeyer (2009: 195) to suppose that the orientation of the temple had changed, turning the structure into a bent-axis approach (Figure 3.16).

The second modification took place during the Iron Age and consisted of the insertion of a relief immediately adjacent to the Storm God in the east wall depicting a royal figure facing directly into the deity (Gonnella et al. 2005: Abb. 126). It is unknown what image this relief replaced. A lengthy incised Hieroglyphic Luwian inscription, historically and paleographically dated to the eleventh century, names him as one Taita—possibly Taita II based on the early use of the sign L.386 as a determinative as opposed to a word divider, as per the Meharde and Sheizar inscriptions that also refer to a king named Taita—and names his kingdom as the Land of Palistin (see discussion in Chapter 2) (Hawkins 2011). This new relief configuration of the east wall suggests to Kohlmeyer (2009: 199) that, by reducing the Storm God image to a dedicatory monument, the axis of the temple returned to its original direct approach.

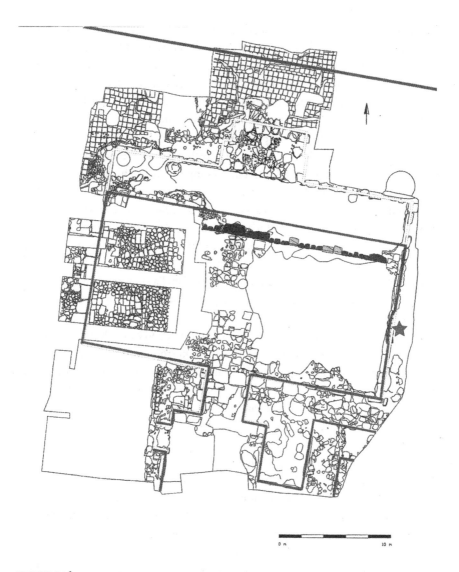

FIGURE 3.16

Plan of the Iron Age iteration of the Storm God temple at Aleppo (adapted from Kohlmeyer 2012: Abb. 4). The dark gray outline marks the plan of the Iron Age iteration of the temple. Shaded in black are the ca. late tenth–early ninth century reliefs of so-called Podestmauer, or pedestal wall, roughly 2 m in front of the inner face of the north wall; shaded in light gray are the reliefs of the late second millennium. The star marks the location of the Storm God and King Taita reliefs, as well as their accompanying inscriptions ALEPPO 5 and 6.

Finally, the reliefs of the north pedestal wall were replaced with a series of reliefs that, if Kohlmeyer's stylistic comparisons with the Suhis II and Katuwas reliefs from Carchemish are correct (and chronologically meaningful), date to around 900 BCE. The three Late Bronze Age reliefs mentioned earlier were left and not replaced for reasons that are unclear. These reliefs depict a number of animals, deities, demons, and hybrid beasts, with the Storm God and a bull-drawn chariot roughly in the center of the wall opposite the presumed direct axis entrance (Gonnella et al. 2005: Abb. 138). That the first-millennium orthostats of the pedestal wall were moved from elsewhere and not (or not only) simply recarved in place is shown first by the inconsistent sizes and shapes of their rear faces (Gonnella et al. 2005: Abb. 157). A number of their top surfaces have worked surfaces and edges that look like they were originally fitted into other installations. Most conspicuous of all is the large sixth block of the pedestal wall, whose front-facing relief of a combat scene and a mace-wielding deity is carved onto the underside of an incomplete lion turned onto its side and inserted into the wall (Gonnella et al. 2005: Abb. 115, 153).[22] With its rounded top, Relief 22, depicting a god holding a torch, looks like a reused stele (Kohlmeyer 2009: 201) (Figure 3.17).

The Temple of the Storm God at Aleppo is thus marked by not just a series of architectural modifications, but orthostats in motion from one place to another, visible most clearly with the insertion of the Taita's image opposite the Storm God in the east wall, the removal of (most) Late Bronze Age reliefs from the pedestal wall and the insertion of new ones that had been taken from other locations. The motive for these instances of movement are not all clear, although in the case of Taita it is an unambiguous case of kinopolitics, with royalty claiming the right to move and insert itself in strategic artistic locations. It is again tempting to conclude that properties of color were at play here, as we have seen elsewhere. The east wall shows a symmetrical alternation between limestone and basalt, and the basalt orthostats of the pedestal wall contrast distinctly with the limestone of the undecorated reliefs above and behind them on the north wall face proper.

* * *

What this review of the reliefs found across SACC demonstrates is the tremendous variability in their original locations, mostly difficult to determine with certainty, compared with their final destinations. In all cases, with the possible exception of only one ('Ain Dara), Syro-Anatolian reliefs have been shown to be surprisingly mobile in addition to being prone to reworking. Their size and weight apparently served no obstacle to their mobility, and one can only guess just how often they were transferred from one location to another. In this light it is significant to note that, unlike Neo-Assyrian reliefs with imagery spread across multiple orthostats, the imagery on Syro-Anatolian reliefs is typically restricted to individual orthostats. With a few important exceptions, such as Zincirli's outer Citadel Gate where several

FIGURE 3.17
Reliefs of the Storm God temple at Aleppo: (*a*) view of the rear face of the pedestal wall reliefs, with the Storm God and King Taita visible at left. Note the irregular shapes and sizes of the reliefs' back sides and their many worked faces. The unfinished crouching lion is boxed (Gonnella et al. 2005: Abb. 157); (*b*) the front facing reliefs on the underside of the overturned lion (Gonnella et al. 2005: Abb. 135 and 136); (*c*) close-up of the unfinished lion (Gonnella et al. 2005: Abb. 153). (Images courtesy of the Mission Archéologique d'Alep)

images are spread over two slabs (Gilibert 2011: Fig. 30), the ubiquity of scenes being contained to specific stones leaves the impression of the orthostats having been deliberately designed as such in order to facilitate this constant shuffling and rearrangement.

Scholars have often noted these intriguing discrepancies in individual instances, but only rarely is it recognized to have occurred in a number of different cities (such as Herrmann 2017b: 245). Explanations for its occurrence in each of these instances varies, if it is attempted at all.[23] Özyar (1998: 634) explains orthostat recycling at Carchemish in functionalist terms "because cut stone blocks—with or without reliefs—already available on any site were too precious simply to be discarded," while Harmanşah (2013: 151) interprets the same site in terms of social memory: "Through the use of architectural spolia in newly constructed structures or the appropriation of former monuments into new ones, a meaningful and material relationship with the past was established." Gilibert (2011: 43) proposes that the material properties of basalt and limestone and the contrasting color patterns that could be effected when the two stones were placed in contrast with one another was one of the main motivations to move orthostats from one place to another in the case of Carchemish's King's Gate and Herald's Wall, matching the Long Wall of Sculpture, Tell Halaf's small orthostats on the rear face of Kapara's palace and, as I noted earlier, possibly the contrast between the pedestal wall reliefs and the plain orthostats on the north wall of the temple of the Storm God at Aleppo. Herrmann (2017b: 265–66) interprets the practice in terms of newly ascendant authority figures appropriating and emulating earlier artistic strategies for their own ideological ends.

In all likelihood, more than one explanation is valid in each instance, even while none applies in every instance. It is difficult to deny the obvious economic benefit of recycling, since it nullifies the need to extract additional resources. However, the impressive color schemes that the shuffling of orthostats created is enough to demonstrate that it cannot have been done for economic considerations alone. It is also impossible to deny that the practice by definition involves an engagement with the past, one that has to be seen as self-consciously positive in nature and deliberately seeking to establish a sense of continuity, even though it is equally plausible that this was done in order to maintain genuinely felt identity rather than to create fictive ties to identities not one's own.

Regardless of specific motives in individual instances, it has to be acknowledged that the mobility of orthostats was a ubiquitous practice across SACC. If it is true that reliefs were a "material component of an architectonic culture" (Harmanşah 2013: 161), then it is also the case that this culture was constantly on the move. Examining the reliefs as archaeological objects, with only limited attention devoted to considerations of style, chronology, workshops, or even iconography reveals that, with the possible exception of 'Ain Dara, movement has taken place everywhere reliefs have been found: Tell Halaf, Malatya, Carchemish, Zincirli, Karatepe, and Aleppo. This practice thus needs to be recognized as an identifiable and meaningful attribute of SACC, something that took place across the region and in every city-state, and not simply a methodological challenge to understanding the "actual" nature of the reliefs as they existed at the time of their creation, one that will be overcome when the most appropriate analyses are brought to bear. The mobility of the orthostats is, itself, the way the orthostats need to be understood. Furthermore, this is a feature of monumental art across SACC, another justification for the term: importantly, for example, we see the practice of both mobility and alternating colors at Tell Halaf, ostensibly one of the most "Aramaean" of Syro-Anatolian cities, just as we do at Carchemish, the quintessential "Luwian" city.

There are significant interpretive implications for appreciating the primacy of orthostat mobility. For one thing, the recent emphasis on performance in Syro-Anatolian art and archaeology requires additional attention (Gilibert 2011; Harmanşah 2013). While state-sponsored spectacles surely took place, it is misleading to treat the excavated built environment as a stage fixed in place. Instead, the plazas and courtyards where performances occurred represent only the final appearance of a backdrop that was constantly changing; the significance of performative actions in these locales likewise shifted accordingly. It is also clear that orthostat movement was a practice conducted by authority figures. Indeed, in the case of Katuwas's manipulation of the King's Gate at Carchemish, he boasts of taking the orthostats from another context before installing them at the gate (see earlier). In itself this is as expected—the reliefs are clearly elite items found in elite contexts, so it is logical for their movement likewise to have been conducted by elites. It will be an important next step to continue geochemically sourcing the stones in order to learn more about the organization of production as has already been done at Tell Halaf, for example, demonstrating that the basalt was taken from a source far more distant than ones closer to hand (Drüppel et al. 2011). For now it is worth reiterating just how implicated royal authority was in the process, making orthostat movement a classic example of the relationship between politics and movement, or kinopolitics, one in which authority figures take seemingly stable objects and render them mobile in order to better communicate their message of legitimacy. In this way, regardless of the situational circumstances that acted as motives, the movement itself is as much a part of the message as the iconography.

::::

## Conclusion

An intellectual turn to mobility can do much to improve existing narratives on ancient states. Although it is unnecessary to replace entirely an existing paradigm of how best to conceptualize societies past and present, as some sociologists and geographers would have us do, a complementary stance that supplements existing understandings of particular aspects of ancient statehood can be highly beneficial. In this chapter, I have sought to accomplish this more modest ambition by advocating for the awareness of the importance of cultural mobility to certain aspects of SACC. Specifically, Nail's notion of kinopolitics, or the recognition that mobility and power are inextricably related, is a helpful way to understand what I see as accumulating evidence for mobility in some of SACC's most immobile places. If it is true, as Ando (2017: 7) argues, that "the legitimacy and stability of ancient states were secured discursively," then mobility is one of those discourses.

Mobility manifests differently, and in different degrees, across social life. While a full exposition of the multiple ways that mobility was a significant component of SACC is not feasible, in this chapter I selected three venues where a consideration of movement could benefit scholarly reconstructions of the Syro-Anatolian city-states. In each case, power and politics are involved, though in some cases more closely, and more obviously, than others. First, a collation of the evidence for Phoenician inscriptions within SACC, especially in Que and Sam'al but also their neighbors, is suggestive of an actual Phoenician-speaking presence in the region, one that was likely due to their economic interests in securing natural resources from the region to support their trading endeavors. Such is indicated above all by the Kulamuwa and Karatepe inscriptions, but also a number of other texts from the area. The elite contexts of these inscriptions, especially Kulamuwa's being situated at the entrance to his palace at Zincirli, require us to associate the movement of Phoenician people and their goods as part of Sam'al's political economy, just as Yariri's linguistic claim to be able to speak Phoenician, thereby seeking to participate in the Phoenician movement, is equally a political claim.

The most obvious case of movement, perhaps, is the finely carved ivories found scattered across SACC and especially in Assyria. The Neo-Assyrian hoarding of these items is one of the ancient Near East's most blatant examples of kinopolitics: an imperial power demonstrating and establishing its dominance by systematically forcing one of its subjects' most prestigious luxury goods into its own coffers and permanently removing them from social circuits. Even prior to the Assyrian booty taking, however, these ivories were highly mobile objects. This much has never been in doubt, but what a mobility perspective contributes is an additional reason to doubt the traditional association of ivory workshops with specific city-states that could be identified based on stylistic attributions alone. Regardless of whether one is prepared to jettison the long-established division of the corpus into North Syrian (i.e., Syro-Anatolian) and Phoenician works, as per Feldman, even within the former it is apparent that the objects' and crafters' mobility renders geopolitical attributions a suspect enterprise. At the same time, however, it is highly likely that political elites were both the suppliers of the raw materials and the most frequent consumers of the final product, such that kinopolitics is very much still at play.

Finally, this chapter surveyed the extant corpus of Iron Age reliefs not with an eye for stylistic categorization, chronological sequencing, or iconographic motifs, as has been performed by others already, but with the goal of tallying the evidence that these orthostats—ostensibly one of SACC's most physically stable features—were themselves subject to a great deal of movement. Archaeological context, accompanying inscriptions, plus indications on the stones themselves cumulatively reveal that these reliefs were on the move at nearly every site where they have been found. The practice is so frequent and so geographically ubiquitous that it has to be seen as a defining cultural component of SACC unlike, for example, contemporary Neo-Assyrian and Urartian reliefs which seem to be fixed in place once erected. Furthermore, it is inextricably linked with the political sphere, with at least one king (Katuwas) boasting openly of the practice. Orthostat movement was one means among many for Syro-Anatolian rulers to maintain legitimacy. Practices such as these contrast with SACC's geopolitical neighbors, and the following chapter outlines a number of ways that SACC acted as a cultural intermediary in the ancient Near East and eastern Mediterranean, receiving and offering cultural influences that would transform the region.

## CHAPTER 4

# ON THE EDGE OF EMPIRE
## *Middle-Ground Interactions with Assyria*

IN THE SUMMER OF 2009, Tayinat Archaeological Project excavators were in the final stages of unearthing a complete and well-preserved temple from the Neo-Assyrian occupation of the ancient city of Kunulua, capital of the Syro-Anatolian city-state Patina. This temple had more than one phase of use, including a construction phase that likely predates the Assyrian conquest, but its terminal phase and associated material culture belonged to the mid-seventh century. The finds that were concentrated on and around the podium in the inner sanctum clearly derived from the highest echelon of Assyrian culture, such as a glazed basin with a kneeling bull and rosette decorative pattern and a cache of Akkadian tablets, including a very large edition of the Esarhaddon succession treaty known already from Nimrud (Lauinger 2012; Osborne et al. 2019; cf. Wiseman 1958). Given this unambiguously Assyrian cultural context and date (the succession treaty provides a *terminus post quem* of 672 BCE for the temple's destruction), it was startling to discover a Syro-Anatolian pyxis lying upside down on the bottom step of the temple's podium—indeed, on the step adjacent to the glazed basin (Osborne et al. 2019: Fig. 19.2) (Figure 4.1).

This small, circular box, presumably used to contain material like incense or spices during ceremonial activities, is a relatively common product of elite Syro-Anatolian craftwork (Mazzoni 2001; Wicke 2008). The soft stone of their sides and lid (when present) are engraved in relief closely resembling the much larger orthostats, and art historians compare the two corpora to determine things like production center and place of origin (e.g., Winter 1983: pl. XLVI–XLIX in the case of Carchemish). The relief on the Tayinat pyxis depicts a bull being slaughtered in preparation for a feast being attended by two seated figures on either side of a table; behind the left-hand seated figure, who sits on a more elaborate chair than his

*The Syro-Anatolian City-States*. James F. Osborne, Oxford University Press (2021). © Oxford University Press.
DOI: 10.1093/oso/9780199315833.003.0004.

(a)

(b)

2

10 cm

FIGURE 4.1
(*a*) Photograph and (*b*) drawing of a Syro-Anatolian soft stone pyxis discovered in the mid-seventh century Neo-Assyrian destruction phase of temple Building XVI at Tell Tayinat. (Photograph by J. Jackson, drawing by F. Haughey, courtesy of the Tayinat Archaeological Project)

dining companion, is a fan-waving attendant. The ceremonial feasting scene shares many thematic similarities with those that appear on the freestanding funerary stelae found throughout the Syro-Anatolian Culture Complex (SACC) (Bonatz 2000), and it is reasonable to suppose that this pyxis was itself involved in a Syro-Anatolian funerary ritual. This interpretation is made even more likely by the fact that pyxides are represented on the tables of funerary feasting scenes known as such by inscriptions (e.g., Zincirli's KTMW stele: Struble and Herrmann 2009: 27–28, Fig. 8), or assumed to be so based on iconographic parallels (e.g., Karatepe's South Gate orthostat SVl 3: Çambel and Özyar 2003: Taf. 144–45).

The Karatepe relief just cited brings us directly to the question of dating, for it is with this relief especially that we find a number of similarities. Mazzoni (2001: 294–97) has noted that most archaeologically attested Syro-Anatolian pyxides belong to the tenth or ninth centuries, and this range is supported by the pyxis's shared motifs with the Karatepe orthostat: not just the seated figure beside a food-laden table, but the fan-waving attendants and, on the orthostat's lower register, a bull being led to the slaughter. Furthermore, the figures' large bulbous noses on both pieces indicate a shared physiognomy, one that led Winter (1979: 117) to conclude that this particular relief belonged to the earlier, ca. ninth century, of the two groups of Karatepe reliefs, group (A), based on parallels with reliefs found elsewhere in SACC (see discussion in Chapter 3). From archaeological and art historical parallels, therefore, we are presented with an extraordinary situation in which a Syro-Anatolian pyxis, found in a Neo-Assyrian phase of a building destroyed in the mid-seventh century, had likely been fashioned at least two hundred years earlier, and possibly up to a century more than that.

What was this centuries-old Syro-Anatolian pyxis doing among the cultic paraphernalia of the Neo-Assyrian temple? The cultural contrast could hardly be more stark, a local Syro-Anatolian antique amid the height of imported Assyrian fashion. One thing seems clear: the pyxis was no longer used for funerary rituals, as it likely had been before the conquest of Kunulua in 738 BCE. There is no evidence in the temple for funerary activity of any kind, nor have human burials yet been found in the building's vicinity. On the contrary, there are indications from the content and context of the Esarhaddon succession treaty, as well as its parallels with the Nimrud exemplars, that the temple, and thus its ritual contents, were used primarily for an annual *akītu* ceremony that involved the local province's delivery of tribute to Assyria (Lauinger 2013: 114). How the pyxis was involved in this rite is unclear. Pyxides could have been used to contain powdery items such as cosmetics, incense, or spices. Given their association with Syro-Anatolian feasts, the latter is more likely for the period of Kunulua's independence, but in view of the Assyrian rituals that took place in the temple, incense is more plausible at this time.

There are a number of interesting avenues one could follow with this one small object as guide. For the purpose of this chapter, what is significant is the Assyrian practice of partially incorporating—instead of entirely replacing—local ritual items into their own cultic practices, an incorporation that involved not a direct appropriation of the material object and its function, but a recommission of it to new ends. Whatever the specific nature of the pyxis's use before and after the Assyrians incorporated Kunulua into the apparatus of empire, details which will likely never be known completely, it was transformed from a vessel used in Syro-Anatolian funerary repasts to a container that facilitated Assyrian new year's rites and tribute giving. The pyxis, then, embodies the principle of SACC's interaction with Assyria as hybridized middle ground, using concepts and things in new ways to forge a new, mutually understandable, phenomenon.

In the last two chapters I have tried to show how the nation-state model so often deployed as the portrayal of the Syro-Anatolian city-states, a model so apparently natural that it does not require explicit justification or even naming as such, is not an accurate way for scholars to understand these polities. The nation-state as a concept is rooted in modern European political and intellectual history, yet even the classic nation-state formations of Europe have grown increasingly less homogeneous in their association of cultural identity and polity, as scholars of transnationalism and diaspora have argued since the late twentieth century. That the concept should be applied to past political formations is no surprise. But scrutinizing its application in the case of SACC is a productive enterprise, not only because it reveals the model to be inappropriate in the Iron Age context, but also because it helps us look to new sources of inspiration for how best to understand these city-states. The strain of diaspora theory advocated by the likes of James Clifford, Paul Gilroy, and Stuart Hall, among others, was valuable in this regard because it helped make the case that the Syro-Anatolian city-states, far from being "Aramaean" or "Luwian" in nature, were in fact hybrid formations wrought by demographic and cultural changes, constantly in flux, and always in a state of becoming. To assign these city-states to ethnolinguistic categories on the basis of the language of monumental inscriptions is a mischaracterization of the ancient reality. Where Chapter 2 evaluated the "nation" component of the nation-state, Chapter 3 took aim at the notion of stasis that implicitly accompanies the "state," finding evidence for cultural mobility in the form of foreign populations, luxury goods and their producers not being tied to particular political centers, and putatively permanent orthostats and their reliefs in a state of perpetual movement. Where diaspora showed us that SACC was a hybridized cultural phenomenon, cultural mobility highlighted its fundamental fluidity.

In this chapter I expand our scope beyond SACC to include some of its political and cultural neighbors. The central claim here is that SACC was not an insular entity, one that looked only to its own economic and political interests and developed culturally primarily thanks to the agency of its neighbors. I argue that although SACC may not have had the military heft to compete with the overwhelming force of the Neo-Assyrian Empire, it was nevertheless a major cultural influence on the empire's own material and visual arts. Studies of Assyrian cultural interaction with their western neighbors need to appreciate better the significance of Syro-Anatolian cultural production in Iron Age interaction. This chapter explores this theme via two major corpora, a selection of monuments whose authors and creators have deliberately fashioned as hybrid objects combining features of both culture groups, and the built environment of postconquest Syro-Anatolian cities, whose layouts are a mixture of Assyrian imposition and stubborn local continuity.

::::

## Models of Interaction
### *Middle Ground*

Recognizing SACC's role in the cultural expressions of its neighbors encourages us to see the region as a "middle ground," a place where cultural traditions are shared and exchanged, leading to innovative developments among all parties involved. The middle-ground concept has been deployed by historians in a number of different contexts since it was first introduced by Richard White (1991: 143–47), whose study of the interactions between European colonialists and native Algonquians in the Great Lakes region of North America during the seventeenth and eighteenth centuries transformed how scholars understand the highly complicated relationship between imperial hegemons and their less powerful, nonstate subjects. Whereas most historians had understood this interaction in terms of power imbalances and acculturation, or the process by which less powerful subjects gradually adopt the cultural norms of their conquerors via the dominant group's dictation of correct behavior, White argued for a more subtle interplay between the French and the Algonquians. Through creative misunderstandings, the expedient attempt to appeal to another culture's values in ways that were, in fact, misinterpreted and distorted, the French and the Algonquians inadvertently created a new cultural expression altogether, one that was mutually understood. None of this is to deny the continued existence of well-defined identities in both cultures, which remained distinct from the middle ground that grew between them. As White states,

> Although identifiable Frenchmen and identifiable Indians obviously continued to exist, whether a particular practice or way of doing things was French or Indian was, after a time, not so clear. This was not because individual Indians became "Frenchified" or because individual Frenchmen went native, although both might occur. Rather, it was because Algonquians who were perfectly comfortable with their status and practices as Indians and Frenchmen, confident in the rightness of French ways, nonetheless had to deal with people who shared neither their values nor their assumptions about the appropriate way of accomplishing tasks. They had to arrive at some common conception of suitable ways of acting. (1991: 50)

The critical historical conditions for a middle-ground scenario to arise include the collision of imperial and nonstate social formations, a balance in the power wielded between these formations such that neither is able to oblige the other to meet its demands through force alone, and a mutual desire to obtain something that only the other possesses (White 1991: xii).[1]

Since these conditions have existed in various configurations in multiple times and places, White's concept of the middle ground has been applied in historical contexts beyond North American colonial history. So far, however, it has appeared in ancient Near Eastern studies only in scholarship on the Middle Bronze Age Old Assyrian trade colonies in Anatolia, and Kültepe-Kanesh specifically. The 23,000 Akkadian-language tablets found in that city's lower town dating to roughly 1950 to 1720 BCE have long been a test case for theories of ancient cultural interaction and ethnicity by virtue of their providing a clear scenario of foreign (Assyrian) merchants living and working among a local (Anatolian) host society (e.g., Atici et al. 2014; Stein 2008). One of the most recent proposals is that the interaction between Assyrians and indigenous Anatolians constituted a middle ground as per White's formulation. Beyond the complex economic and political negotiations that this interaction involved, the daily contacts between them, manifested especially in the intermarriage between male Assyrian merchants and local women, must have contributed to the creation of strong social ties between the two groups and processes of cultural invention (Larsen and Lassen 2014; Lumsden 2008: 32–40). Detailed analysis of the specific terms used in the pertinent texts from Kanesh (*amtum*, second wife, and *aššatum*, first wife), even indicate this situation to be a classic middle-ground case of misunderstanding, deliberate misappropriation, and compromise leading to novel cultural practices (Heffron 2017).

Where a middle ground has been identified in an Iron Age context closer to the subject matter of the present work is in the early Greek colonial expansion of the eighth and seventh centuries BCE. Irad Malkin (1998, 2002) has argued that Euboean settlers at the sites of Pithekoussai and Cumae in the Bay of Naples during the mid-eighth century created a social dynamic between themselves, local Italic elites, and Etruscans that mirrored the situation of the Great Lakes in many ways. Rather than simply imposing their cultural practices on politically decentralized recipients, Greek presence on the west coast of Italy created new local cultural expressions that included modifications to the mythology of Odysseus, a variety of the alphabetic script, and feasting practices. The imbalances of Greek colonialism would become manifest in subsequent decades, at which point the middle ground ceased to exist, but at the outset of the process in the eighth century, colonists and local inhabitants were obliged to accommodate one another (Malkin 2002: 153–54). Even while it is clear that Etruscan and Italic cultures adapted Greek traits—instead of just adopting them as per acculturation—less apparent is the extent to which creative misunderstandings were at play in those adaptations. The sources are simply less explicit and less copious here than they are for French-native colonial history in North America (Antonaccio 2013: 241–42).

The same is true, of course, further to the east. Indeed, not all of White's conditions for the middle ground as so conceived apply in the Iron Age context of the ancient

Near East, meaning that the concept cannot be deployed whole cloth. There are two major differences between the social context of White's study and the one analyzed here. First, all participants in cross-cultural exchange in the eastern Mediterranean and ancient Near East during the late second and especially early first millennium belong to so-called complex societies in the sense that they are state-level sociopolitical formations. Assyria became a renewed aggressively expanding state in the tenth century. In the north, the Phrygians were building spectacular monumental architecture at Gordion, and even in the rugged highlands of eastern Anatolia the Urartian kingdom was formed. The engagement of the Syro-Anatolian city-states with any of these cultures is thus not strictly comparable with Algonquian–French interactions, although the much larger and more politically unified Neo-Assyrian Empire comes close to approximating the powerful political actor White envisioned. A related distinction is the fact that these cultures were not as foreign to one another as were Europeans and natives. Individuals from north Mesopotamia had long participated in economic trade with people as far as the Anatolian plateau, most dramatically attested in the Old Assyrian colony at Kültepe-Kanesh a millennium prior to the subject of this book. Likewise, they shared broad patterns of religious and other cultural beliefs and practices that would have been mutually intelligible. It is thus difficult to see how cultural differences could have been stark enough as to require the creation of productive misunderstandings. Indeed, enough similarities are present that Harmanşah (2013: 26) feels justified referring to SACC, Urartu, and the Neo-Assyrian Empire as participating in a broad cultural *koiné*, defined as "a shared network of ideas, practices, ideology, and material culture."

But enough of the historical criteria are present to make the middle ground a useful analytic. For over two centuries a regional balance of power existed between SACC and Assyria that was only really toppled in the mid- to late eighth century. Likewise, in the form of raw materials and precious luxury items SACC had goods that Assyria and others needed in order to make their statements of wealth and power, while SACC needed foreign markets to maintain the city-states' economies. The slow Assyrian conquest marked the end of the balance of power that characterizes middle-ground situations. Given the presence of some circumstances that parallel White's original formulation but not others, it is perhaps helpful to draw a distinction that White himself makes in later writing, reflecting on the various attempts historians had made to foist the model onto their subject matter since his book first appeared. The middle ground as a *process* involving cultural adaptations under conditions of culture contact, and in the manner described earlier—creatively modifying cultural resources to meet goals in ways for which those resources were not necessarily intended—is not always the same thing as the middle ground as an *object*, an actual construction of infrastructure made to serve as the basis of relations between groups (White 2006: 10). Although cross-cultural interactions were everywhere present in the Near Eastern Iron Age, an infrastructure established precisely to facilitate this interaction did not come to exist, as it did in the Great Lakes region three hundred years ago.

I argue in this chapter that middle-ground processes were nevertheless present in SACC's interactions with its neighbors, and the existence of these dynamics further erodes the nation-state's essentialist stance as argued in the previous chapters. As White states, there exists

> a culturalist disease of the late twentieth and early twenty-first centuries that amounts to a fascination with purity and otherness to which I intended *The Middle Ground* to be a partial antidote . . . contact situations created not only violence, xenophobia, and . . . a "failure to communicate," but also new cultural formations and new understandings. (2006: 13)

The shared network of similarities between Iron Age cultures described by others thus arises precisely because when two cultures are brought into economic or political contact with one another, changes are wrought to both, and in ways that might be divorced from power relations. Cultural influence does not flow in a single direction. In addition, the expression is inherently spatial in a way that is highly appropriate to the Syro-Anatolian city-states. SACC is indeed situated geographically between several major cultural formations: Cyprus and the Aegean world to the west, Phrygians and Urartians to the northwest and northeast respectively, Assyrians to the east, and the Israelites and their contemporaries to the south. Part of what makes SACC an influential partner in the ancient world is precisely this geographical context, which afforded it a number of cultural interlocutors. While much could be said about SACC's affairs with each of these entities, I focus here on Assyria.

### Imperialism, Culture Contact, and Hybridity

The literature on the archaeology of empires is as vast as the empires themselves. As political formations that covered large swaths of the globe, and whose shapes adumbrate dynamics of modern history, ancient empires have naturally attracted a great deal of scholarly attention. (For a recent review of the literature from an environmental perspective, see Rosenzweig and Marston 2018.) A review article by Carla Sinopoli (1994) summarizes what are still the primary models of imperial territorial and administrative control that archaeologists have applied onto their ancient case studies, most predominantly Eisenstadt's (1963) distinction between a weakly integrated patrimonially organized empire and highly integrated bureaucratic empires, and Luttwak's (1976) division of empires into weakly integrated hegemonic and highly integrated territorial examples (e.g., D'Altroy 1992). The Neo-Assyrian Empire has been examined under both of these rubrics, with major studies appearing using both the patrimonial (Rimmer Herrmann 2011) and territorial-hegemonic paradigms (Parker 2001).[2]

For this study, more important than Neo-Assyrian principles of social organization are the modes of cultural interaction and influence that these models assume. Whether explicit or implicit, the process underlying most treatments of Assyria's cultural engagement with its neighbors is acculturation, understood as the cultural changes that "take place when a people are exposed over a long period of time to a culture different from their own" (Herskovits 1938: 14), especially in contexts in which one of these interlocutors is significantly more powerful than the other. Over time, this exposure results in the smaller, less powerful culture becoming more and more similar to the larger, powerful one. This is the process that is implied in terms like "Hellenization," "Romanization," and, of course, "Assyrianization" (see, e.g., Bagg 2013: 122–29; Parpola 2004: 9–10). Since some polities within SACC and other political formations surrounding Assyria do indeed possess objects, or display traits, that appear Assyrian in nature, this is often the process that is assumed to have taken place, even while acknowledgment that the process was a complex one have become more commonplace (e.g., Gunter 2009: 34–40).[3] In today's postcolonial intellectual climate, the problems inherent with acculturation models of intercultural relations like "Hellenization" are now familiar (Dietler 2005: 55–58). As summarized neatly by Stein (2008: 28–29), they are threefold: the acculturation model simplistically equates political domination with cultural domination, treating domination as homogenous across all social spheres; it assumes that culture moves only in a single direction, with influence consistently radiating out from the core to the periphery; and it pays insufficient attention to the cultural agency of groups in the so-called periphery, who are always assumed to be passive cultural recipients rather than culture providers. These concerns reformulate White's formulation of the middle-ground concept for an explicitly imperial context.

If acculturation leaves too many possibilities for cross-cultural interaction out of our reconstructions of imperial dynamics, then another model must be sought. Morrison (2001: 4–5) encourages us to recast empires less as a political formation in a typological sense—that is, having a defined suite of characteristics that distinguish it from a nonempire—and more as a dynamic process that unfolds in highly particular ways in specific contexts. In ways that echo my treatment of the nation-state in previous chapters, Stoler and McGranahan (2007: 8–9) argue that we cannot treat empires as static, homogenous entities, but rather need to consider them as what they call imperial formations, "not steady states, but states of becoming, macropolities in states of solution and constant formation." The concept of empire as a process rather than a state or type opens space for us to appreciate the complicated and diverse ways in which empires like the Neo-Assyrians engaged with the cultures and polities they encountered. In this case we no longer need to assume that, because they constituted an "empire" as such, the Neo-Assyrians must have promulgated their cultural influences on their subordinates wherever they went in a relationship that was as imbalanced culturally as it was politically.

One way in which empires and their subjects engage with one another is cultural exchange, and here much work has been done allowing for the agency of political subordinates to come to the fore. In general terms strict imitation of cultural expressions from the metropole (and vice versa) are less common than adaptation, defined as "the transfer of . . . elements involving a debate with the original and a number of mostly deliberate changes of the model" (Wicke 2015: 564–65). For roughly the past two decades, one model that has gained currency in archaeology has been the concept of hybridity and closely related terms like creolization, mestizaje, and entanglement. Without getting into the subtleties of the distinctions between these terms and their theoretical underpinnings here (see Liebmann 2013; VanValkenburgh 2013), the basic principles in most cases are relatively consistent, and drawn especially from the postcolonial movement of the 1990s and 2000s. For most archaeologists, hybridity broadly refers to things or behaviors that possess traits characteristic of more than one culture and that are therefore indicative of the interaction between those groups. In the process, these new objects and behaviors are therefore fashioned in ways that derive, strictly speaking, from neither cultural formation, but rather exist as a new category of cultural expression. Drawing especially on the writing of Homi Bhabha (1994), for whom hybridity was a means to reclaim the voices of subaltern peoples whose perspectives had been distorted or silenced over the course of European imperialism, archaeologists value the concept of hybridity for several reasons. For one thing, it enables archaeologists working in regions conquered by imperial formations to emphasize the agency of conquered peoples whose material culture was for too long investigated strictly through imperial lenses. Even more fundamentally, hybridity recognizes that cultural influence everywhere travels in multiple directions simultaneously, and not only outward from political power centers. As Philipp Stockhammer (2013: 12–14) has pointed out, the great irony of hybridity is its hermeneutical trap: although it was designed to facilitate the erosion of essentialist cultural categories, recognizing hybridity necessarily involves the acceptance of originally pure cultural categories to begin with. Nevertheless, even while this book has proposed that the phrase "Syro-Anatolian Culture Complex" replace the array of unsatisfactory terms we have been using to date in part to avoid those terms' essentializing nature, it remains the case that the Syro-Anatolian city-states and the Neo-Assyrian Empire were distinct political formations. Hybridity remains a helpful heuristic in this case, as it allows us to read the historical and archaeological record of the region "contrapuntally," to

Vuike Said's (1993: 51) metaphor of postcolonial analysis, necessarily valuing all the constituent parts that make up classical music's counterpoint without privileging any one part. Similarly, we can overcome the essentialist assumptions of hybridity by keeping in mind that ultimately our focus is on processes of the social actors participating in cultural encounters as opposed to reified cultures per se (Dommelen 2005: 117–18).

::: 

# Syro-Anatolian and Assyrian Interactions
## Monumental Hybridity

One of the most intriguing examples of iconography closely resembling Assyrian style comes, surprisingly, from the westernmost part of SACC, as far from the Assyrian heartland as they ever traveled in that direction.[4] The relief and accompanying Luwian inscription from the west slope of Kızıldağ, a hill rising from the plains in southern Konya, the westernmost region of Iron Age Tabal, are found overlooking the broad valley floor on a prominent rock outcrop (Ramsay and Bell 1909: 505–12) (Figure 4.2). This outcrop, in fact, bears signs of much later activity, including Greek inscriptions accompanying footprints engraved on the rock's precipice, indicating much later ritual activity that took place in the monument's reuse (Rojas and Sergueenkova 2014). Such unambiguous reuse in an era undeniably later than the original period of use has inspired some scholars to consider the original monument itself as a palimpsest of monumental interventions. Though possible, such a scenario is far from certain, and it is equally probable that such reconstructions are missing the work's fundamentally hybrid nature by insisting that its contradictory features can only be the result of multiple temporal interventions.

The specific issue that has made the Kızıldağ monument so vexing is an apparent contradiction between the date of the Luwian inscription and the date of the relief. The inscription consists of three parts, of which only the first, KIZILDAĞ 1, remains in situ. This brief text is nothing other than the name and title of the individual, "Great King Hartapu."[5] Related text continues in the now-dislodged KIZILDAĞ 2 and 3 inscriptions adjacent to the first, "Beloved of the mighty Storm-God, the Sun, Great King Hartapu; Beloved of the Storm-God, the Sun, Great King Hartapu, son of Mursilis, Great King, Hero, built this city" (Hawkins 2000: 433–38). Archaic paleography, including similarities to the Hieroglyphic Luwian of the thirteenth-century Hittite Empire period inscriptions from Yalburt and Hattusha-Südburg suggest a twelfth-century date at the latest (see 2000: 429n60 for bibliography), especially if one accepts the (now unlikely; see later) argument that Hartapu's father Mursili is Mursili III/Urhi-Teshub, Great King of Tarḫuntašša and combatant with Suppiluliuma II (Hawkins 1992: 270; Singer 1996: 68–71). The relief that

(a)                                            (b)

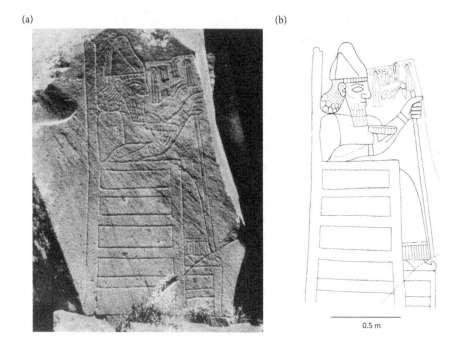

0.5 m

FIGURE 4.2

(a) Photograph and (b) drawing of KIZILDAĞ 1 inscription and accompanying relief on the rock outcrop at Kızıldağ (Tayfun Bilgen). (Photograph courtesy of Tayfun Bilgin, hittitemonuments.com; drawing adapted from Hawkins 2000: Pl. 236)

accompanies these inscriptions, however, does not resemble thirteenth- to twelfth-century reliefs from contemporary landscape monuments created during the Hittite Empire (such as Fıraktın or Yazılıkaya, for example). On the contrary, the seated figure on a high-backed chair, bearded, with his long hair curving out away from his neck, bearing a conical hat or helmet, holding a staff with his left hand and a gadrooned bowl in right, seems very similar in both structure and iconography to reliefs from SACC and Assyria during the ninth or eighth century, as has been noted since the mid-twentieth century (e.g., Bittel 1976: 238–39; Landsberger 1948: 20n39). This discrepancy between text and image is confusing, and no immediately apparent resolution presents itself (Orthmann 1971: 115n5; Akçay 2016).

The most straightforward interpretation would be that the two are not contemporaneous but rather represent two separate interventions in the monument separated by centuries. This has been proposed by several scholars (e.g., Hawkins 2000: 429, 434; d'Alfonso 2014: 228–29; Rojas and Sergueenkova 2014: 146–47).[6] Although the narrative of multiple episodes of activity does conveniently explain away the discrepancy, it is not entirely satisfactory. For one thing, it is difficult to avoid the impression that the text and image were conceived by the creator as a single enterprise. The initial Luwian sign MAGNUS.REX is aligned perfectly with the seated figure's staff, for example, and both align with the edge of the vertical rock face. The two appear as a single visual package, with the inscription providing a label—"Great King, Hartapu"—for the image. Nor is there any evident sign that the image is a reworked version of an earlier scene that was present (*pace* Sürenhagen 2008); both it and the text were cut from the same face of the rock without apparent modifications. If the image were not present at the time of the inscription's composition, then what was originally created would have been a king's aedicula with no accompanying image at all, a difficult (though not impossible) scenario to envision.

If, however, one assumes that the text and image are contemporary, then there are two solutions available: that the inscription is later than currently thought, or that the image of the seated ruler is earlier. The second of these two options does not appear to be possible. It is true that chronological associations of style groups in the Iron Age are less certain than is typically assumed, as argued in the previous chapter, in which case it is difficult to date the relief based on the seated figure's apparent early first-millennium iconography. But, among other features, the bowl held in the man's right hand is fluted in the manner of Syro-Anatolian bronze bowls attested archaeologically in the ninth and eighth centuries (cf. the KTMW stele, Figure 2.6), which means it cannot have been engraved several centuries earlier than that time.[7]

Is it possible, then, that the accompanying inscription is actually a later production than is currently thought? Based on the connections with known thirteenth-century products like Yalburt, the only way to draw this conclusion is if the Kızıldağ inscription appears older than it is. That this might, in fact, be the case, is indicated by the Kızıldağ inscriptions' parallels with the challenging TOPADA text, an inscription belonging to Wasusarmas, contemporary of Warpalawas (named in the text), and known to Tiglath-pileser III as Uassurme, king of Tabal (Weeden 2010; Woudhuizen 2007). TOPADA, therefore, can only date to the third quarter of the eighth century—yet its signary is so laden with old or unparalleled signs that it appears to be a deliberate attempt at producing an archaizing text (Hawkins 2000: 460–61).[8] Some of these archaisms are paralleled in the KIZILDAĞ texts, raising the possibility that these, too, are archaizing texts from the eighth century.[9] As noted earlier, Hawkins (1992) argues that the cumulative parallels between KIZILDAĞ and the Yalburt inscription necessitate raising the former to the Empire period or shortly thereafter. But to my knowledge, no one has considered KIZILDAĞ 1, the aedicula accompanying the relief of the seated figure, separately from the remainder of the brief Kızıldağ inscriptions. The cartouche of KIZILDAĞ 1 is unique among these four texts by not topping it with the winged sun disc, and by not adding the epithet "Hero": MAGNUS.REX $^1$há + ra/i-tá-pu-sa

MAGNUS.REX, "Great King Hartapu." This is the identical aedicula as begins TOPADA: [MAGNUS.]REX *wa/i*$_4$*-su-SARMA-ma sa* ⌜MAGNUS.⌝REX, "Great King Wasusarmas."[10] It is entirely possible, therefore, that while KIZILDAĞ 2–4 represent a conventional monumental text commemorating the founding of the settlement, KIZILDAĞ 1 is a later, archaizing text added to the site at the same time that the relief was inscribed.

Dramatic new archaeological and historical evidence that proves Hartapu was an eighth-century ruler was discovered in 2019, confirming that the relief and in-scription of KIZILDAĞ 1 belong together. The year 2019 saw the first field season of the Türkmen-Karahöyük Intensive Survey Project (TISP), a survey devoted to understanding the occupational history and nature of settlement at Türkmen-Karahöyük, a multiperiod site 14 km north of Kızıldağ (see Figure 1.1).[11] Even be-fore survey began, the site was clearly significant: at roughly 30 ha in areal extent, the höyük towers 35 m over the surrounding plain. Surface collections in the fields surrounding it, however, demonstrated that the höyük was merely the ancient settlement's upper city: in fact, from the Late Bronze through the Iron Age II pe-riod, Türkmen-Karahöyük was at least 125 ha in extent, and possibly larger (Figure 4.3) (Osborne et al. 2020). Accompanying the realization that Türkmen-Karahöyük was the largest site in south-central Anatolia from the Late Bronze through the Iron Age was the chance discovery of a Hieroglyphic Luwian stele, TÜRKMEN-KARAHÖYÜK 1, found in a canal running north-south along the ancient city's eastern limit; this text was composed by none other than "Great King Hartapu" himself (Goedegebuure et al. 2020).[12] The geopolitical implications of this new in-scription, which describes Hartapu's defeat of Phrygia (Luwian: Muška, written in the text as *mu-sà-ka* (REGIO)) and thirteen other kings in the area, are remark-able: for the first time, we know of a major Anatolian conflict between a Tabalian kingdom and Phrygia, pairing the two as opposing political poles in early first-millennium Anatolian political history (see Goedegebuure et al. 2020; Massa et al. 2020; Osborne et al. 2020 for further details).

For the purposes of the present argument, what is significant is how dras-tically our understanding of Kızıldağ has suddenly been transformed. First, the inscription's association with the massive site of Türkmen-Karahöyük renders the city Hartapu's hitherto unknown capital.[13] The Kızıldağ complex with its associated inscriptions thus comes to look less like a mysteriously decontextualized cluster of monuments, and more like a ritual center for Hartapu and his retine based at Türkmen-Karahöyük, who very likely undertook ritual processions from the city to the hilltop sanctuary and further south to the volcano of Karadağ and its own inscriptions of Hartapu (Massa and Osborne in prep.) (Figure 4.4). Second, on the basis of a number of paleographic parallels with sign forms in texts from Tabal and beyond, the inscription is securely dated to the eighth century BCE (Goedegebuure

FIGURE 4.3
(*a*) The upper mound of Türkmen-Karahöyük viewed from the northeast (photograph by James Osborne); (*b*) Iron Age II ceramic distribution on höyük and lower town, with dashed line indicating approximate extent of the 125 ha settlement. The star marks the findspot of the inscription; (*c*) photograph of inscription TÜRKMEN-KARAHÖYÜK 1 with Reflectance Transformation Imaging. (Photograph by Jennifer Jackson, courtesy of the Türkmen-Karahöyük Intensive Survey Project)

et al. 2020). For the first time, therefore, we now have an inscription by Hartapu that can be dated confidently—and that date is not early, in the Late Bronze–Iron Age transition, but late, toward the end of the Iron Age II.

The implication for scholarship on Kızıldağ is clear: the eighth-century Hartapu son of Mursili at Türkmen-Karahöyük must be the same Hartapu son of Mursili at Kızıldağ whose name is accompanied by a ninth- to eighth-century relief. The relief and the text of KIZILDAĞ 1 must therefore have been carved together in the eighth century. Any resemblances between KIZILDAĞ 1 and Late Bronze Age paleography can only be the result of deliberate archaizing on the part of the carvers. Indeed, taking this logic a step further, it has to be acknowledged that the *entire*

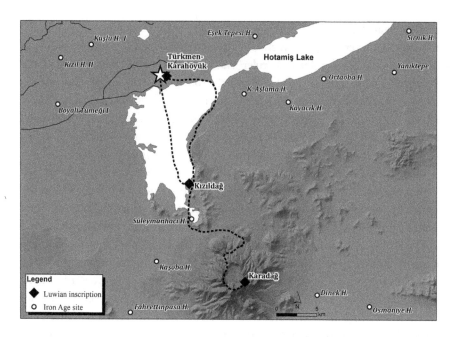

FIGURE 4.4
Map of possible procession routes from the site of Türkmen-Karahöyük to Kızıldağ and Karadağ. (map by Michele Massa, with permission)

suite of texts composed by Hartapu on the Kızıldağ outcrop is very likely eighth century in date.[14] Either way, it appears that KIZILDAĞ 1 and the accompanying relief belong together and date three to four centuries later than is generally thought.

According to this new reconstruction of the monument, we now have an eighth-century relief that would have looked highly modern at the time it was carved accompanied by an inscription that was deliberately made to look look antique. In addition, given the resemblance between the seated figure of Kızıldağ and rulers in Assyrian reliefs in details such as the bundled hair, it would seem to be a highly Assyrian-like image coupled with an archaic Hieroglyphic Luwian text that even contains the Hittite title "Great King." Visually, the monument is profoundly eastern; textually, it is markedly Hittite. But rather than understand this monument as an example of a Tabalian ruler's "Assyrian acculturation" due to "Assyrian influence" (Bryce 2012: 145), the two elements' contemporaneity obliges us to recognize a single, hybrid monument that can be called neither Assyrian nor Hittite but rather a new product that creatively fuses elements of both. In short, the Kızıldağ monument is a vivid example of a cultural product created in the middle ground: Hartapu consciously manipulated the popular visual tropes of the day even while laying claim to hoary local legitimacy, fashioning a previously unattested monumental style and demonstrating the ability of Syro-Anatolian agency to be foregrounded even while interaction with Assyria was taking place. According to Tiglath-pileser III, the Tabalian ruler Wasusarma—roughly contemporary with Hartapu—was deposed and replaced with the son of a nobody because he "acted as if he were the equal of Assyria" (Tadmor and Yamada 2011: RINAP 1, Tiglath-pileser III 49, ll. 27); what I am arguing here is that the Assyrian-like agency demonstrated by Syro-Anatolian rulers extended beyond military actions—which is how this passage is typically interpreted—and into matters of cultural production.

There are many more examples of visual culture from SACC being incorporated with Assyrian characteristics and merged to produce a new tradition, and it is not possible to survey them systematically here; among others, these include reliefs and statuary from Tell Tayinat (McEwan 1937: Fig. 10), Sakça Gözü (Garstang 1908), and Arslan Tash (Thureau-Dangin et al. 1931). I have highlighted Kızıldağ precisely because of its far western location relative to most of SACC, indicating that proximity to Assyria was not a necessary aspect of the hybrid processes being described here.

One object that does bear emphasizing in this context, however, if only because its sociolinguistic relevance featured so prominently in the last chapter, is the Kulamuwa stele from Zincirli (Orthmann's Zincirli E2; KAI 24) (see Figure 3.1). This object, which dates to the third quarter of the ninth century (Orthmann 1971: 201) and is thus slightly earlier than, the Kızıldağ monument as I have reconstructed it, has been analyzed from a variety of perspectives, including the translation (see especially Younger 2000c), rhetorical structure and grammar (Collins 1971; O'Connor 1977), and historical significance (e.g., Niehr 2016, and any major text on "Aramaean" history). Like the Kızıldağ monument, it too contains visual and textual attributes that point to Assyrian connections, among others, and its iconographic elements have likewise received significant attention (e.g., Brown 2008a). We have already discussed its significance to the role of the Phoenicians in SACC, but unmentioned in that context was the way in which the stele consciously produces a hybridized visual experience for the viewer.

Its slippery attributions are present not just in the tension between the Phoenician language of the text, the other Aramaic inscriptions from Zincirli, and the author's Luwian name (see Chapter 3). The script itself is allegedly Aramaic (Peckham 2001: 32), even while the high relief that characterizes the inscription and particularly the relief rulings separating the lines is evocative of Hieroglyphic Luwian monuments. In fact, the use of raised relief in alphabetic Semitic inscriptions is common only at Zincirli; elsewhere within SACC such inscriptions are consistently incised (Struble and Herrmann 2009: 20). Another similarity with Luwian texts is the presence of the introductory portrait figure with its similarity to the Luwian EGO "I am . . . " sign (Bunnens 2005: 22; Hawkins 1984: 78). Although not bearing a grammatical function, the figure occupies a similar structural location (see also Orthmann's Zincirli K/1 and K/11 stelae, 1971: Taf. 66–67). Hawkins (1984: 78) goes on to note that, counterintuitively, "the portrait figure itself and the divine symbols show not Hittite but Assyrian influence" in the form of Kulamuwa's tassled dress, pointed hat, hair and square beard form, lowered left arm, and raised right arm pointing to a winged sun disc (also Orthmann 1971: 66), all reminiscent of Ashurnasirpal II's only slightly earlier reliefs from Nimrud (e.g., Northwest Palace room B, relief 13).[15] Hawkins concludes that "the direct model for this would have been the Assyrian stela set up by Shalmaneser near Sam'al after his defeat of Khayanu [Kulamuwa's father] in 858 B.C." Regardless of the fact that this stele of Shalmaneser's is not attested archaeologically, this conclusion is a classic formulation of acculturation: the more powerful political formation enters an area, leaves behind a monument, whose visual tropes influence the cultural production of the passive locals.

More compelling are analyses that understand the Kulamuwa stele as representing a set of active decisions by its producers. Intriguingly, Brown (2008a: 344) notes that the very location of the stele—in the entrance to Palace J—is similar to Assyrian practice and a departure from SACC, whose cities' reliefs are typically consigned to gates and open areas. But while Brown is inclined to see the monument as the starting point in genuinely Aramaean visual representations, given the similar portrayals of individuals in subsequent reliefs at Zincirli that are accompanied by Aramaic or Samalian inscriptions (2008: 346–49), it seems more likely that its Assyrian visual qualities—given everything else we know about the stele, including its Luwian, Aramaic, and Phoenician properties—are the result of local artistic choices (Wicke 2015: 576). Such choices were logical in a social context characterized by fluid interconnections between ethnolinguistic groups and geopolitical interactions. In order to appeal to a diverse audience, the stele had to be made visually and textually intelligible and appealing in a variety of different ways, even while visual tropes stretching back to the Hittite Late Bronze Age continued to be used in other venues at the site (Herrmann 2017b). In short, the Kulamuwa stele is the epitome of a hybrid object, and we might think of Kulamuwa as the classic example of a king of the middle ground.

Kulamuwa is not unique in this regard. One other item that needs to be mentioned in this context is the statue of Hadd-yit'i found at the site of Tell Fakhariyah, located just 3 km northeast of Tell Halaf (Figure 4.5a). The identification of Tell Fakhariyah with the Mittanian capital city Waššukanni, first proposed by Opitz (1927), is based primarily on the etymology of the Iron Age toponym associated with the site, Sikan. Whether or not this holds true, as seems likely (see Younger 2016: 243–44 for a review), by the early first millennium the site had become primarily a cult center for the nearby city of Gozan, the archaeological site of Tell Halaf, capital of the Syro-Anatolian city-state of Bit-Baḫiani. The statue of Hadd-yit'i, found at the

FIGURE 4.5

(a) The statute of Hadd-yit'i from Tell Fakhariyah (modified from 'Abou Assaf et al. 1982: Pl. I); (b) the statue of Ashurnasirpal II from Nimrud, Temple of Ishtar Belit Mati (BM 118871, courtesy of the British Museum); (c) the statue found buried near Tor Q at Zincirli. (von Luschan and Jacoby 1911: Taf. 64)

site *ex situ* in 1979, records a bilingual inscription in Akkadian and Aramaic, and appears to date to the mid-ninth century on paleographic grounds and on the possible identification of Šamaš-nuri, Hadd-yit'i's father, with the Assyrian eponym of 866 BCE (Abou Assaf et al. 1982). The inscription has been analyzed many times, especially with regard to the Aramaic version's status as among the very earliest Aramaic inscriptions known, and the historical implications of the contrasting title of its author, Hadd-yit'i, and his father Šamaš-nuri, who in the Akkadian are referred to as "governor of the city of Guzana," GAR.KUR URU.*gu-za-ni*, but in the Aramaic are titled "king of Gozan," *mlk gwzn* (Greenfield and Shaffer 1983; Kaufman 1982; Lipiński 1994). There are enough discrepancies in the content of the two texts that determining the order of composition and translation is difficult on internal grounds alone. What does seem clear, however, is that the cuneiform version was inscribed first on the statue itself, as evidenced by its occupying prime of place on the front of the statue and by the fact that the Aramaic version appears to have run out of room, spilling onto space not intended for text (Abou Assaf et al. 1982: pl. VI–XIV).

While the political context of the governor-king titular alternation is interesting from a historical standpoint—we can only conclude that the author(s) of the inscription was content to provide subtly distinct messages about Hadd-yitʿiʾs political status to different readers—what has not been explored is how Hadd-yitʿiʾs dual role may be embodied in the properties of the statue itself. The basalt statue stands 1.65 m tall (about 2 m including its base) and is thus nearly exactly life size. The iconography of the individual's form and dress was analyzed by its initial publishers in terms of its similarity to Assyrian royal representations (Abou Assaf et al. 1982: 9–12), and these similarities are indeed striking: Hadd-yitʿiʾs curly hair bundles out to the side in the same way, his squared beard has the same proportions, and his gown is tassled in much the same way as the roughly contemporary statues of Ashurnasirpal II (Curtis 2014: 60–61; Layard 1853: 361–62) and Shalmaneser III from Nimrud (Figure 4.5b) (Kinnier Wilson 1962; Laessøe 1959). And yet from the waist down the gown is arranged horizontally, not diagonally; his cheeks and especially his upper lip are conspicuously clean shaven, unlike both Ashurnasirpal and Shalmaneser's mustachioed faces; his lips are pursed and slightly frowning; and his eyes are sockets for inlays that are no longer extant. All of these latter features are visually related to the monumental statues so commonly found throughout SACC at sites like Tell Halaf, Tell Tayinat, Malatya, Carchemish, and Zincirli. With this in mind, it is significant that Hadd-yitʿiʾs nose and ears have been hacked off, and indeed, his entire head seems to have been removed in antiquity, discovered 1 m away from its body (Abou Assaf et al. 1982: 4, pl. IV–V). Without archaeological context it is difficult to know more, but this effacement of the statue was itself a common practice in SACC, in which processes of countermonumentality were frequently levied against royal statuary, with damage to sensory receptors such as eyes, ears, and noses possibly intended to deprive the statue of its sensory efficacy (Osborne 2017a).

In both appearance and physical treatment, therefore, the Tell Fakhariyah statue is at least as much part of the Syro-Anatolian visual repertoire as it is the Assyrian. Perhaps the closest parallels come from the nearby site of Tell Halaf, where the statue of the seated couple from the lower city's "cult room" shows the male individual with a similar facial expression and the same vertical wavy lines down his beard, as well as the same hair part down the center of his head (Opitz and Moortgat 1955: 28–30, 120–21). Another roughly contemporary statue is the larger monument found at Zincirli adjacent to Tor Q, the gate leading to the entrance to Building J where Kulamuwa's relief was set in the portico (Figure 4.5c) (von Luschan and Jacoby 1911: 288–89, 362–68). Here we see again the horizontal alignment of the skirt, exposed feet and ankles (unlike the Ashurnasirpal II and Shalmaneser III statues), and the same beard shape, including the shaved upper lip. In this case, however, the individual's head is significantly larger and more rounded and set lower to the chest than any of Hadd-yit'i, Ashurnasirpal, or Shalmaneser, and likewise the upper and lower body are less naturalistic. It is difficult to escape the conclusion, therefore, that the Tell Fakhariyah statue was carved in such a way as to merge deliberately Assyrian and Syro-Anatolian visual tropes of royal monumentality into a single, hybrid entity that could communicate to both audiences with equal force. Visually situated exactly halfway between the iconographic traditions of Assyria and SACC, Hadd-yit'i resembles a ruler of both and neither at the same time. It is harder to discern whether the statue was carved by an Assyrian or Syro-Anatolian sculptor; the siting of the Akkadian inscription on the front might suggest the former, but of course the fact that the statue was found within the city-state of Gozan and depicts one of its own rulers implies the latter. In either case, searching for its pure cultural origins misses the point of the object, which was to avoid precisely these types of essentialized categorizations and preclude searches of exactly that kind.

When such hybrid works have been noted by scholars, as has long been the case for the Kulamuwa stele, for example, the typical explanation lies in the realm of political history: Kulamuwa must have presented himself as an Assyrian king in order to appeal to his newly allied Assyrians to help convince them to join his fight against Que. The accompanying inscription describes this conflict, stating that "Now the king of the Danunians was more powerful than I (or: too powerful for me), but I engaged against him the king of Assyria" (Younger 2000c).[16] In this line of interpretation, the Assyrian dress borne by Kulamuwa is the sartorial equivalent of bending the knee to the Assyrian ruler in grateful submission. A similar line of argument could in principle apply to the Tell Fakhariyah statue, interpreting its hybrid visual qualities strictly in light of Hadd-yit'i's alternating title, and seeking the precise historical moment when this particular political relationship would have been most likely. Yet even if this interpretive approach does help explain geopolitical forces at play between SACC and Assyria, it exaggerates the military might wielded by Assyria in the two centuries prior to the reign of Tiglath-pileser III, it allows the historical inscriptions written by Assyrian kings to carry excessive interpretive weight, and it ignores the impact wrought by SACC on Assyrian cultural productions (Harmanşah 2018).

That the Assyrians were a greater military force than SACC has been a staple of scholarship in the Syro-Anatolian world. In one sense this is indisputably true: the Neo-Assyrian Empire conquered each of the Syro-Anatolian polities, converting them to provinces in their imperial apparatus (Radner 2006.) Before this took place, many had been vassals of the empire, an intermediary status between independence and province. But we need to resist the tendency to telescope a process that took place over the course of many decades into a single interpretive statement and instead adopt a stance that allows for a fuller perspective. The Assyrian conquests occurred piecemeal, one polity at a time, and often with many years between them (Table 4.1). The conquest events took place in two major bursts: the mid-ninth century and over the course of thirty years in the second half of the eighth century. Shalmaneser III conquered Bit-Adini and Bit-Zamani in 856 BCE, as well as possibly Bit-Bahiani at or around the same time. The conquest of Bit-Adini in particular led to the reformulation of its capital city, Til-Barsip, as a major Assyrian outpost on the east bank of the Euphrates River, Kar-Shalmaneser. Just over a century later, Tiglath-pileser III resumed outright conquests in the west, a policy that was accelerated especially by Sargon II; the final conquest of a Syro-Anatolian city-state took place in 708 BCE. In other words, the majority of SACC enjoyed relative independence from the Neo-Assyrian Empire for approximately two centuries before being incorporated into the empire. Without pretending that

TABLE 4.1

*Dates and Rulers of the Neo-Assyrian Conquests of Syro-Anatolian City-States*

| Name | Conqueror | Date Conquered | Notes |
| --- | --- | --- | --- |
| Bit-Adini | Shalmaneser III | 856 BCE | |
| Bit-Agusi | Tiglath-pileser III | 740 BCE | |
| Bit-Bahiani | Ashurnasirpal II | mid-ninth century BCE | Precise date uncertain |
| Bit-Zamani | Ashurnasirpal II | 866 BCE(?) | Precise date uncertain |
| Carchemish | Sargon II | 717 BCE | |
| Gurgum | Sargon II | 711 BCE | |
| Hamath | Sargon II | 720 BCE | |
| Kummuh | Sargon II | 708 BCE | |
| Malatya | Sargon II | 712 BCE | Complicated history in final decades, reverting between independence, Urartian control, and Assyrian control |
| Patina | Tiglath-pileser III | 738 BCE | |
| Que | Sargon II | ca. 715 BCE | Precise date uncertain, Assyrian control established by the reign of Sargon II |
| Sam'al | Sargon II(?) | by 713 BCE | |
| Tabal | Sargon II | 713 BCE | Complicated history of the region of Tabal and its constituent city-states only partially known; Assyrian control fleeting |

*Note.* For historical details, consult Hawkins (2000), Bryce (2013), and Younger (2016).

individual polities were able to compete on an even footing with Assyria's military, or that SACC was able to provide a unified front against Assyrian aggression beyond the odd short-lived military alliance, we need to acknowledge that there were centuries-long stretches in which SACC and Assyria occupied positions that approximate parity.

Our tendency to look at the pre-conquest Syro-Anatolian past from the vantage point of the dates at which they were defeated by Assyria is compounded by the Assyro-centric nature of our historical sources. These texts, and the royal annals in particular, offer an overwhelmingly skewed portrayal of SACC's interaction with Assyria. That these texts are biased is obvious. But what typically goes unmentioned is the simple fact that we do not have in our possession an equivalent corpus of inscriptions from SACC that might serve as complementary historical sources. We know individual kingdoms must have been wealthy to have provided the quantities of materials listed by Assyrian kings as tribute and booty, yet enumerations of wealth are not offered in local inscriptions; we know Syro-Anatolian kingdoms got into conflict with one another and with Assyria, yet locally written accounts of these conflicts are scarce. For reasons that remain unclear, the undeniable military and economic significance of Syro-Anatolian city-states contrasted with their relative dearth of inscriptional remains suggests that the written word was not a prioritized rhetorical strategy. One of the few local inscriptions that *does* mention the Assyrians presents them as guns for hire: in the Kulamuwa inscription, Kulamuwa presents himself as able to deploy Assyrian forces as if at will, providing reinforcements to his attack on Que. As a principle, we cannot let the general absence of evidence of Syro-Anatolian inscriptions documenting military encounters with Assyria in which Assyria was the lesser of the two parties serve as evidence that this never occurred; indeed, it seems likely for the opposite to have been true on occasion. Likewise, we must keep foremost in our historical reconstructions the fact that Assyrian textual sources that describe interaction with the Syro-Anatolian world are overwhelmingly military in nature; there are few that describe the economic, cultural, religious, and other nonmilitary exchanges that must have occurred regularly (Harmanşah 2018: 259).

Furthermore, the lengthy passages in Assyrian royal inscriptions in which they boast of the great wealth they were able to harvest from their exploits in SACC have the unintended consequence of providing us with a picture of how wealthy Syro-Anatolian city-states must have been. Ashurnasirpal II's lavish description of goods he siphoned from Patina in 870 BCE, for example, is evocative of this phenomenon:

> I approached the city Kunulua, the royal city of Lubarna, the Patinu. He took fright in the face of my raging weapons (and) fierce battle and submitted to me to save his life. I received as his tribute 20 talents of silver, one talent of

gold, 100 talents of tin, 100 talents of iron, 1,000 oxen, 10,000 sheep, 1;000 linen garments with multi-coloured trim, decorated couches of boxwood with trimming, beds of boxwood, decorated beds with trimming, many dishes of ivory (and) boxwood, many ornaments from his palace the weight of which could not be determined, 10 female singers, his brother's daughter with her rich dowry, a large female monkey, (and) ducks. As for him, I showed him mercy. I took with me the chariots, cavalry, (and) infantry of the Patinu (and also) took hostages from him. (Grayson 1991: RIMA 2 A.0.101.1, iii, 71–84)

Reading this text strictly as an indication of Assyria's power—as Ashurnasirpal II presumably intended—simplifies the historical reality that the text indirectly points toward: that Patina was tremendously wealthy, with a diversified economy (textiles, metals, woodworking), and that it had a multifaceted military force comprised of at least three units (chariots, cavalry, infantry). A contrapuntal reading of this passage and others like it offers a different perspective on SACC's relative status vis-à-vis Assyria: more than serving as a vulnerable pool of wealth for Assyria to draw upon at will, kingdoms like Patina offered material goods Assyria could not produce, had access to raw materials that Assyria lacked, and had the means to put up a robust defense of those goods and materials should they be threatened. I do not intend to imply that each individual Syro-Anatolian city-state had the same critical mass of resources as the Neo-Assyrian Empire, but rather that we cannot take Assyrian royal texts at face value even if we accept that they are empirically accurate; on the contrary, by using superiority over Syro-Anatolian kingdoms as an indicator of Assyrian prosperity, these texts ironically index Syro-Anatolian wealth and power as well.

Finally, explaining cases of hybridity consistently in geopolitical terms pays insufficient attention to the impacts that SACC had on Assyria's own cultural production. This is a topic that would require much greater explication of Assyrian material and visual culture than is possible in this context, but a few salient examples are worth mentioning here. The first, and perhaps most obvious, point of similarity between the two regions is their shared use of orthostats decorated in relief to line the base of the walls of their monumental buildings—typically palace interiors in the case of the Assyrians and gateways and palace exteriors for SACC. While the narrative content developed by the Assyrians—not to mention scale, elaboration, and sophistication—was transformed to surpass the capacity of Syro-Anatolian craftspeople, whose products typically remained static stills even until the end of SACC, it appears highly likely that the idea of decorating their palaces this way in the first place was one borrowed from SACC. Winter (1982: 357) attributed this transferal to the western campaigns of Tukulti-Ninurta II (890–884 BCE) and Ashurnasirpal II (883–859 BCE), both of whom would have found reliefs on the course of their adventures before Nimrud's Northwest Palace and its elaborate relief program was built. More recently, it has been argued convincingly that relief orthostats of both SACC and Assyria represent the combination of north Syrian undecorated orthostats from the Middle Bronze Age with the Middle Assyrian tradition of wall painting (Harmanşah 2013: 157–62); however, primacy of inspiration is still attributed to SACC even by the Assyrians themselves, such as Tiglath-pileser I's (1115–1077 BCE) explicit acknowledgment that his reliefs derive from the region west of the Euphrates (Grayson 1991: RIMA 2, A.0.87.4, ll. 62–71), coinciding chronologically with, for example, the 'Ain Dara and Aleppo temple reliefs and the earliest programs at Carchemish and Malatya (Harmanşah 2007: 85–87).

Likewise, even if the content of Neo-Assyrian reliefs differed from their Syro-Anatolian counterparts in many ways, close similarities nevertheless appear in many places. For example, the famous banquet scene of Ashurbanipal from Room S of his North Palace at Nineveh (Barnett 1976: pl. LXIV) is visually structured the same way as a Syro-Anatolian mortuary feasting scene as seen on many funerary monuments found in SACC (Bonatz 2000). The KTMW stele for Zincirli, for instance, shows KTMW in an almost identical posture and chair as Ashurbanipal's wife, and they hold an identical gadrooned bowl (see Figure 2.6). Their table apparatus—three items, one of which is a pyxis—and the tables themselves are similar. The same and additional resemblances are attested in other Syro-Anatolian reliefs, such as fanning attendants in the feasting scene from the south gate at Karatepe, relief SVl 3 (Çambel and Özyar 2003: Taf. 144–45),[17] or the feasting scene engraved on the pyxis discovered in Tell Tayinat's Building XVI, described at the start of this chapter (Figure 4.1). Given that Ashurbanipal's feasting scene is, beyond its immediate function of portraying (Albenda 1977) or problematizing (Ataç 2012) royal power, also commemorating a death—that of Teumman, his defeated Elamite rival, whose head dangles from a nearby tree—it seems plausible that the Assyrians are deliberately modifying this Syro-Anatolian visual motif for their own ironic funerary monument, sending a not-too-subtle message to palace visitors.[18] In this case, no actual funerary rituals would have been performed for Teumman, and the scene is converted from one of reverence to one of mocking disrespect. As support for the notion that visual motifs in this scene are being borrowed and modified from SACC, one can note also that even Ashurbanipal's reclining pose on the couch, a unique depiction of the ruler in Assyrian art, is likewise attested elsewhere only in a depiction of a Syro-Anatolian ruler from Hamath in Band XIII from the (Assyrian produced) bronze decorated gates of Balawat (King 1915: pl. LXXVII; Schachner 2007: Taf. 13). Alessandra Gilibert (2004) provides a number of other parallels between Syro-Anatolian and Assyrian reliefs, arguing effectively that together they point toward an Assyrian borrowing of Syro-Anatolian communication strategies, as opposed to iconographic motifs per se, and similar rhetorical adaptations were made by the Assyrians to scenes depicted on small finds (Bonatz 2004: 391–93, Abb. 7–8).

Syro-Anatolian architectural elements that were incorporated by the Assyrians into their own buildings are another testament to nonmilitary interaction that spurred innovations in Assyrian cultural production. Pebbled courtyard surfaces arranged in checkerboard patterns of alternating black-and-white squares are one such item and have long been attested in Assyrian occupations of cities in the Syro-Anatolian region, such as Tell Ahmar/Kar-Shalmaneser and Arslantaş, as well as a small number of buildings in Assyria itself. However, Guy Bunnens (2016) has recently compiled evidence that in fact these floor patterns first appear in pre-Assyrian contexts, including from his own excavations in Area M at Tell Ahmar as well as possibly Tille Höyük[19] and the 'Bâtiment aux ivoires' from Arslan Tash, concluding that this floor pattern originiated in the Syro-Anatolian region before spreading to Assur and elsewhere in the Near East.[20]

Of course, the most well-known instance of Assyrian architectural borrowing from SACC comes not from comparatively minor architectural elements like floor design, but entire building suites or components thereof: the famous *bīt-ḫilāni* palace, the highly recognizable palace of SACC, with stairs leading to a columned portico that itself led into a long and broad throneroom. The *bīt-ḫilāni* has been an obsession of Near Eastern scholarship for generations, usually with respect to its etymology, geographical origins, and typological classification (for references see Osborne 2012). Much of Near Eastern scholarship's interest in the building has surrounded questions of Assyrian borrowing from the Syro-Anatolian region and identifying the buildings or features within Assyrian capitals that are most likely to represent the borrowed *bīt-ḫilāni* mentioned in Assyrian inscriptions and identified on the ground within SACC. Unfortunately, the reasoning is often circular and based on uncertain assumptions—not least of which is our lack of certitude that the palaces found in Syro-Anatolian capitals were, in fact, the buildings origi-nally called *bīt-ḫilāni*s (Lehmann and Killebrew 2010: 24–27). Most scholars have assumed that the texts' descriptions of column bases imply that the Assyrians' use of the term was associated with their own columned portico entryways identified in a small number of Assyrian complexes like Building F at Khorsabad (Loud and Altman 1938: 75–78), or the complex of accessibility offered by the combination of courtyards and broadrooms marked with a monumental façade (Winter 1982: 361). A new proposal sees the *bīt-ḫilāni* and it columns not in the entryways of Assyrian palaces, but in the interior room arrangements they developed in monumental buildings of the late eighth century and following (Kertai 2017), a suggestion that has the benefits of aligning with the dates of the texts that use the term, comporting with Assyrians' emphasis on decorating the inside of their palaces (unlike SACC), and generally providing a more plausible Assyrian *adaptation* of Syro-Anatolian architecture instead of direct borrowing.

For our purposes here, I wish to foreground that, wherever and however it became manifested in Assyrian royal architecture, the *bīt-ḫilāni* is a building which Assyrian rulers explicitly borrowed from their Syro-Anatolian neighbors (see Renger and Hrouda 1972–1975 for all references). In the words of Tiglath-pileser III, he built a *bīt-ḫilāni* "*tamšil ekal māt Hatti*," which Tadmor and Yamada translate as "a replica of a palace of the land of Hatti" (2011: RINAP 1, Tiglath-pileser III 47, Rev., l. 18). Sargon II is even more explicit, referring to the building under discussion as a *bīt-appāti*, "the exact copy of a palace from the land of Ḫatti, which is called *bīt-ḫilāni* in the language of the land of the Amorites" (Fuchs 1994: 239, 353, my translation). *Bīt-ḫilāni* is not, in fact, a term native to Akkadian, but rather, by virtue of being described as deriving from the "land of the Amorites," an expression that derives from Semitic speakers of Syro-Anatolia.

This passage from Sargon thus summarizes not only the specific point of this chapter—that SACC has been insufficiently recognized for its impacts on the Neo-Assyrian Empire, and was in fact a partner in something akin to a middle-ground phenomenon—but also the larger project of this book: the Assyrians apparently recognized a palace structure that was recognizable across north Syria and southeastern Anatolia, even while they struggled to label that region in cultural terms, alternating between "the land of Ḫatti" and "the land of the Amorites," more or less equivalent to our own terminological equivocation between Neo-Hittites/Luwians and Aramaeans. Meanwhile, the term *ḫilāni* appears to be derived etymologically from Hittite *ḫilammar*, "gate house" (Singer 1975), even while it made its way into a Semitic construct phrase. It would seem that the Assyrian ambivalent cultural associations are more accurate than our own essentializing impulse. As David Kertai has put it (2017: 88), "Assyrian inscriptions . . . do not seem to have made a strict distinction between these cultures and languages in the way modern scholarship has tended to do."

These large-scale iconographic and architectural interactions, in which visual and architectural motifs commonly deployed within SACC made their way into Assyria, find parallels in cases of portable material culture, whose full elaboration will not be possible here. But as evidence of the kind of interaction for which I have been arguing one can point briefly to ivory carving, in which Assyrian craftspeople apparently borrowed the idea of decorating ivories from SACC (Winter 1982: 356), but instead of carving them in relief engraved them with unmistakably Assyrian figures and patterns (Herrmann 1997); or the interplay between the production of Assyrian cylinder seals and Syro-Anatolian stamp seals of the frit "FSV" tradition (Flügelsonne, Skorpion, Vogel), in which motifs and carving technologies originate in Assyria, then are modified and expanded within SACC before being reintroduced and disseminated in Assyria, such that "the dichotomy between 'Assyrian cylinder seals' and 'Syrian stamp-seals' . . . seems to dissolve" (Wicke 2016: 89); or the mixed local and Assyrian ceramic repertoires of sites in the upper Tigris River Valley, in which Assyrian forms were imitated by local pottery producers and vice versa (Matney 2010).[21]

## *Syro-Anatolian Built Environments of the Neo-Assyrian Period*

If the aforementioned evidence for middle-ground-like interaction between SACC and Assyria during the tenth–eighth centuries discussed earlier shows the two regions as existing on a relatively equal cultural footing—contrary to the understanding of their relationship that is conveyed by Assyrian imperial texts, left mostly unchallenged by the comparative silence of Syro-Anatolian inscriptions on the matter, and therefore accepted uncritically today—it will be particularly interesting to see how the archaeological signature of their relationship developed in the eighth and seventh centuries. By this point the political and military strength of Assyria had become sufficiently great to have overwhelmed the Syro-Anatolian city-states, each of which eventually fell prey to the Assyrian expansion. As has been well documented, the incorporation of Syro-Anatolian cities into the apparatus of empire led to many changes in the built environments of these cities, especially in the form of new constructions of Assyrian-style monumental buildings, typically interpreted as governors' residencies. We will be looking in greater detail at the expressions of space and place that characterized SACC and its cities during the Iron Age II in Chapter 5; what I would like to do here is briefly survey the evidence for how these cities were modified after independence was lost. Contrary to what one may expect from historical records alone, looking closely at the Syro-Anatolian cities that are known to have been transformed from local capitals to provincial centers reveals that there was a great degree of continuity across this historical divide, usually considered the transition between the Iron Age II and III periods in archaeological terms (see Chapter 1). Although new structures certainly appear, the overall impression is one in which continuity of local building practices is at least as significant a component of Iron III cities as newly constructed buildings.

### CARCHEMISH

After accusing the local king Pisiri of disloyalty for his communications with Muški, Sargon II conquered the 90 ha city of Carchemish in 717 BCE, after which it became a provincial center in the Neo-Assyrian Empire. The site is perhaps best known for the monumental Iron Age II structures discovered in the Lower Palace area of the Inner Town, including features such as the Herald's Wall, Processional Entry, King's Gate, and the Long Wall of Sculpture (Woolley 1952). The renewed excavations in this part of the city, labeled Area C by the joint Turkish-Italian team excavating there, have uncovered the remains of a long suspected palace immediately east of the Processional Entry built by Katuwas around 900 BCE in Area C's Phase 10 (Pizzimenti and Zaina 2016: Table 1) (Figure 4.6). Crucially, they have also provided the first clear Assyrian-period structure in the Inner Town in the form of a reuse of this palace by Sargon in Phase 9, confirmed through inscriptions on baked bricks naming the building the "Palace of Sargon." Although detailed final reports are not yet available, preliminary descriptions and plans of the renovations made to Katuwas's palace—which apparently had the Processional Entry and the Herald's Wall as its western and northern boundaries, respectively—during the Iron Age III

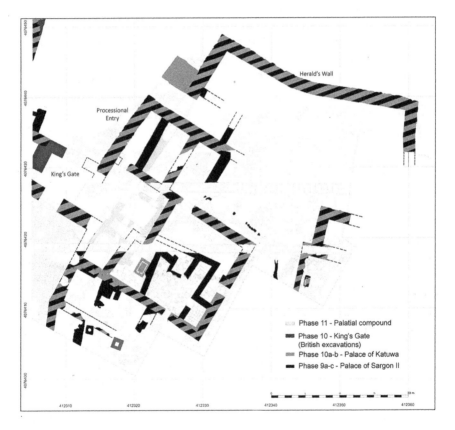

FIGURE 4.6
Plan of the Katuwas's palace reused by Sargon II in Area C of the renewed excavations at Carchemish. Note the extensive continuity between phases. The King's Gate and Processional Entry from Woolley's excavation are visible to the west, and the Herald's Wall to the north (cf. Figure 3.6). (Adapted from Pizzimenti and Zaina 2016: Fig. 3; Copyleft of the Turco-Italian Archaeological Expedition at Karkemish)

period (Phase 9) present a picture of the building's fundamental layout remaining intact even while its surfaces were replaced by a new checkerboard surface of black-and-white pebble mosaics, the sculpted orthostats that lined the Phase 10 walls were removed from view, and some interior spaces were further subdivided (Marchetti 2015: 367–69, Figs. 9–14; Pizzimenti and Zaina 2016: 364–66, Fig. 2). At the same time that the royal palace was being reused, five seventh-century buildings (Houses A, B, C, D, and G) that Woolley interpreted as elite houses were in use in the Outer Town (Woolley 1921). Indeed, according to the new excavations, the Outer Town's wall was constructed in the Assyrian period (Bonomo and Zaina 2016: 2), in which case the entire 55 ha Outer Town might have been first occupied at that time, although based on Woolley's discovery of an earlier fortification wall—his so-called Linear Anomaly—that enclosed a slightly smaller area of the Outer Town, it is possible that "[t]he 8th-century kings of Karkemish may have been the ones who first added an Outer Town to the old city, and this was later expanded under Assyrian rule" (Herrmann 2017a: 306).

## TELL AFIS

Tell Afis, located in northwestern Syria, was likely the ancient city of Hazrak, capital of Lu'ash, as identified by the Stele of Zakkur that was found at the site in the early twentieth century. The Iron Age III remains from the site's acropolis are badly preserved due to subsequent robbing of the building material, rendering its layout challenging to reconstruct during this period. The primary structure on the acropolis was an *in antis* temple that appears to have been in continuous use across the Iron II–III transition with only minor modifications (Temple A1–2; Mazzoni 2014a: 44-46) (Figure 4.7). East of the temple precinct was found the enigmatic Building G, a 20 × 20 m open-air structure sunk 5 m into the ground and extending above the ground a further 3 m with no apparent access at ground level (Cecchini 2014: Fig. 10). This building, whose function as "a site for ceremonial purposes linked to the central city power" (Cecchini 2014: 62) is determined only by its unique physical form, was built in the mid-eighth century. But unlike the nearby Temple A1-2, following its late eighth-century destruction—possibly at the hands of the Assyrians, although this is not clear—it was not rebuilt but was rather used as a waste dump in the seventh century. The acropolis of Tell Afis, therefore, presents two major Iron Age II structures with widely diverging trajectories into the Iron Age III period: one that was reused nearly exactly, and one that was destroyed and converted into a site for refuse.

## TELL AHMAR

Located just 20 km south of Carchemish on the Euphrates, Tell Ahmar—ancient Masuwari/Til-Barsip/Kar-Shalmaneser—experienced a dramatically different

FIGURE 4.7
Temple A1-2 at Tell Afis. (Adapted from Mazzoni 2014: Fig. 4)

historical and archaeological trajectory from its neighbor to the north: Til-Barsip was seized over a century earlier by Shalmaneser III in 856 BCE, providing the Assyrians with a permanent foothold on the Euphrates. The archaeological record reflects this geopolitical situation closely. The original palace of the early first millennium, Stratum 5 in the terminology of the renewed excavations (Bunnens 2009), was replaced with a large palace closely reminiscent of Assyrian palaces in their own capital cities, with elaborate wall paintings taking the place of sculpted orthostats (Thureau-Dangin and Dunand 1936). However, the precise date of this complex's construction is unclear. Shalmaneser III describes building a palace at Til-Barsip upon conquest (Grayson 1996: A.0.102.2, ii, lines 33–34), but findings on the acropolis by the recent excavations suggested to the excavators that the Stratum 5 buildings, including the monumental "Bâtiment est," remained in use for several decades after 856 BCE with the construction of the Assyrian palace taking place only in the eighth century (Bunnens 2009: 73, 78). If that is true, then even in Kar-Shalmaneser continuity of monumental architecture on the acropolis was attested, at least initially. In the city's lower town, excavations revealed several elite Assyrian-style residences in Areas C and E that date to the late eighth or seventh centuries BCE (Jamieson 2012), although there were indications in Area E for stratigraphically earlier structures that could not be fully excavated (Bunnens 2016: 62). It therefore remains unclear whether the lower town had an occupation prior to the late eighth century.

The gateway through the northeast segment of the outer city wall is also significant in this regard. Here were found two monumental portal lions, one in fragments but one well preserved, with a worn Akkadian inscription (Thureau-Dangin and Dunand 1936: 141–51, pl. XXXVII, Plan A, E). I have argued elsewhere that the practice of placing lion statues in city gates and signing them with the local ruler's name was a common practice throughout SACC, one that might even have been intended to imbue the lion statue itself with royal identity (Osborne 2014: 208–9). In this example, the portal lion's cuneiform inscription is composed by Shamshi-ilu, Shalmaneser III's field marshal, in the form of a royal dedicatory inscription. In the concluding passages, lines 19–24, rather than associate himself with the lion statues as per Syro-Anatolian tradition, Shamshi-ilu names the two lions "The lion who [ . . . ] , angry demon, unrivalled attack, who overwhelms the insubmissive, who brings success" and "Who charges through battle, who flattens the enemy land, who expels criminals and brings in good people" (Grayson 1996: A.0.104.2010). Here the Assyrians are deliberately playing on patterns of the Syro-Anatolian built environment, using the local trope of signing gateway lions in a recognizable way, but adapting it to their own propagandistic ends.

A similar case is attested in the nearby site of Arslan Tash where a number of reliefs were found in association with Assyrian-period monumental buildings (Albenda 1988). The site is so-named on account of lion orthostats that had long been visible on the site's surface, and that appear to be "essentially of Assyrian origin" (1988: 24). Excavations by Thureau-Dangin (Thureau-Dangin et al. 1931: 70–73, Fig. 22., pl. VI) demonstrated that these lions came from the eastern city gate. The southern lion was subsequently taken to Raqqa, whereupon it was discovered to have a trilingual Akkadian-Aramaic-Luwian inscription on its reverse; that is,

it was not visible after installation.[22] The Hieroglyphic Luwian inscription was
published by Hawkins (2000: 246–48), who refers to the brief text as a "building
inscription for [the] city Hatata." The first few signs of the Luwian are unfortunately not visible in the preserved squeeze, but likely identify the author. Here,
then, it seems like we have another creative adaptation of Syro-Anatolian practice: maintaining the short inscription that identified the author with the statue, but
placing that inscription on the reverse as per Assyrian practice with portal figures.

## TELL HALAF

Tell Halaf, the 75 ha Iron Age city of Gozan, was the capital of Bit-Baḫiani until it
became an Assyrian province by at least 808 BCE. The site's impressive architectural
and decorative programs were exposed by a German project prior to World War
I and in the late 1920s and, until the outbreak of the Syrian Civil War, by a joint
Syrian-German expedition. The architectural finds of the original project produced
a large bīt-ḫilāni palace on the west side of the acropolis—the Palace of Kapara, so-
called after the inscriptions naming him found on orthostats lining the walls and
the caryatid columns of the portico (see Chapter 3)—and the "Northeast Palace,"
interpreted as an Assyrian governor's residency, at the acropolis's northeast corner
(Naumann 1950: pl. 2). The recent work on the acropolis has resumed excavation in
both areas, with Sectors A and C referring to the bīt-ḫilāni and the governor's residence, respectively (Baghdo et al. 2009, 2012). In Sector A, the bīt-ḫilāni remained
in use following the end of the Kapara dynasty as demonstrated by glazed tiles and
fragments of Assyrian reliefs in its debris, and by the fact that no Assyrian-period
building was constructed above it. Elsewhere on the acropolis, however, substantial
changes seem to have occurred. One of these was the leveling of much of its southern
and eastern quadrants with massive mudbrick terraces to serve as foundations for
new monumental constructions, especially the large Assyrian governor's residence
in Sector C that is now known to extend across the acropolis's entire eastern side,
incorporating buildings that were thought to be separate entities by the original
excavators (Novák 2013: 273–74; Novák and Schmid 2019: Fig. 9) (Figure 4.8). This
remodeling of the acropolis following its incorporation into the Assyrian Empire
thus appears to be a more significant investment of energy, and a more dramatic
architectural transformation, than is attested in neighboring capital cities in the
Syro-Anatolian region. However, it is important to emphasize the continued use of
the Palace of Kapara, the locus of power for the independent city-state, even after
Bit-Baḫiani was incorporated into the empire.

Tell Halaf's lower town was modified significantly less than the acropolis,
with only some indicators of transformation in this part of the city (Herrmann
2017a: 306). Multiple phases of residential architecture span the Iron Age II–III
transition, and perhaps the most recognizable Iron Age structures are the local

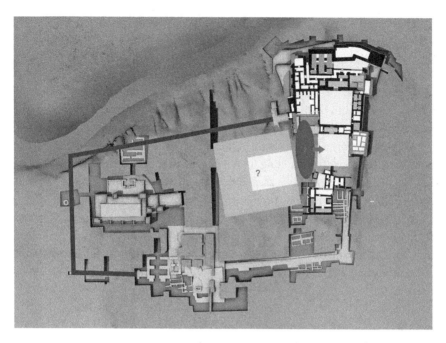

FIGURE 4.8
Revised plan of the upper mound and the Assyrian Governor's Palace at Tell Halaf. The palace entrance and likely additional rooms are marked as unexcavated areas on the plan by the excavators. Note the palace of Kapara still in use on the west side of the acropolis. (Novak and Schmid 2019: Fig. 10, with permission)

Kultraum building that produced the pair of seated statues discussed earlier and the Assyrian-built Stadttempel (Naumann 1950). With respect to the former, modern buildings in the lower town prevented the new excavations from being able to reconstruct clearly any stratigraphical relationships with features that may have postdated the building (Orthmann 2009), and similar problems challenged attempts to clarify the building sequence in the area of the Stadttempel (Orthmann et al. 2012: 112–21). For now, one can tentatively conclude that Halaf's lower town was occupied prior to the city's conquest, and that it continued mostly unchanged save for a small number of buildings that were added like the Stadttempel.

TELL TAYINAT

The Iron Age city of Kunulua, capital of Patina, was first excavated in the 1930s by the University of Chicago and since 2004 by an expedition out of the University of Toronto. The first excavators brought to light a sequence of monumental buildings in the upper city, especially a large *bīt-ḫilāni* palace, as well as several gateways. Unlike several other Syro-Anatolian cities, these buildings were devoid of decorated orthostato, although many pieces of Hieroglyphic Luwian inscriptions were discovered. Kunulua was conquered in 738 BCE by Tiglath-pileser III, at which time its upper city was altered in several significant ways. First, an Assyrian-style palace interpreted as an Assyrian governor's residency was constructed on the south edge of the tell (Haines 1971: 61–63, pl. 109), and the palace compound in the excavation area referred to by the 1930s excavators as the West Central Area was modified to include a large public platform, presumably for spectacles of performance (1971: 43–44, pl. 101). Other changes to the upper city included the likely construction of an elite courtyard building on the eastern edge of the tell, even while, as at Tell Halaf, the bīt-ḥilāni palace as well as two associated temples, Buildings II and XVI, continued in operation through the Assyrian period (Osborne et al. 2019). Tayinat's lower town is less well understood. An intensive surface survey discovered evidence that its first Iron Age occupation was in the ninth or early eighth century, such as fragments of Syro-Anatolian monumental statuary (Osborne 2017b; Osborne and Karacic 2017), although the bulk of the ceramics collected straddles the Iron Age II–III transition.

## ZINCIRLI

One hundred kilometers to the north of Tayinat lies Zincirli Höyük, the site of ancient Sam'al, incorporated into the Neo-Assyrian Empire late in the eighth century in an apparently peaceful transition. Turn of the century German excavations uncovered large portions of the city's Iron Age acropolis (von Luschan et al. 1898; von Luschan and Jacoby 1911), while an ongoing German-American excavation has exposed wide areas of the lower town as well as mapped a large percentage of it via remote sensing (Casana and Herrmann 2010). Zincirli's upper town has multiple bīt-ḥilāni structures, none of which seem to have gone out of use at any point. The first to be built were Buildings J and K in the mid-ninth century, including the Kulamuwa stele in the portico of Building J, followed by the Northwest Palace complex of the mid- to late eighth century, built by Barrakib to expand the already existing palaces by adding a large courtyard and two more bīt-ḥilānis to them (Hilanis II and III), followed by the seventh-century Palace G complex, a separate series of bīt-ḥilāni structures around a courtyard that presumably served as the Assyrian governor's residence (Herrmann 2017a: 294) (Figure 4.9). What the acropolis of Zincirli seems to show, therefore, is a gradual accumulation of monumental buildings until its final seventh-century plan was achieved, rather than an abrupt reordering of the upper city's spatial logic at any one point. The excavations in the lower town at Zincirli, meanwhile, have demonstrated a similar sequence of progressive monumentalization: agglutinated domestic buildings from early in Sam'al's independent existence were gradually replaced with larger-scale structures in the mid-eighth century before being replaced again with monumental

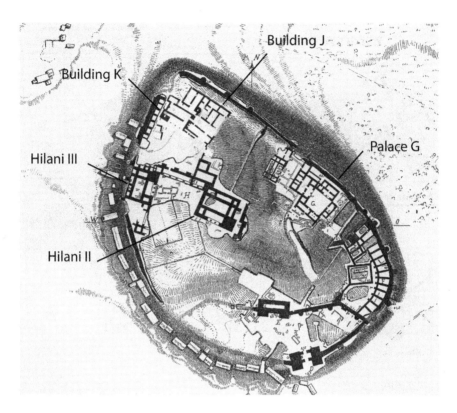

FIGURE 4.9
Plan of the upper city at Zincirli.

courtyard buildings in the seventh century, a process that Herrmann (2017a: 299–306) interprets as a gradual process of political centralization and social stratification (Figure 4.10). Ultimately, the city's formal incorporation into the Neo-Assyrian Empire appears to have had little immediate effect on its urban layout, which instead underwent gradual modification over the course of two centuries (Herrmann and Schloen 2016: 272).

There are several points to be gained from this survey of some of SACC's most important cities' architectural history following the permanent arrival of Assyrian administration. For one thing, it is difficult to discern a clearly articulated Assyrian policy of built environment modification that accompanied provincial incorporation; every city appears to have experienced its own urban trajectory across the Iron Age II–III transition. One pattern that is apparent is the continuity that characterizes urban built environments into the seventh century. Several sites (Carchemish, Tell Halaf, Tell Tayinat, Zincirli) saw their primary palaces continue in use, even while new buildings like governors' residences were constructed in

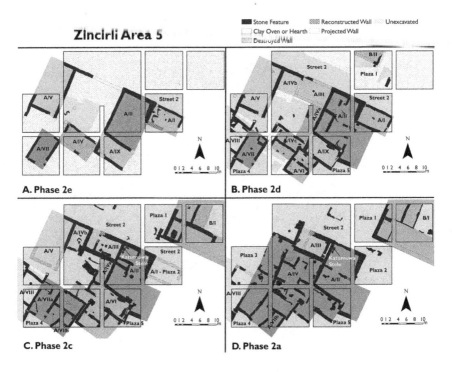

FIGURE 4.10
Progressive monumentalization of the lower town at Zincirli. (Herrmann 2017: Fig. 7; used with permission)

the upper cities, and the same seems to have been the case in the lower cities for those sites for which information is available. It follows, therefore, that it would be a mistake to accept the Assyrian records at face value with respect to the impact that their allegedly violent conquests had on local urban organization. On the contrary, local architectural expression was permitted to continue, and it seems likely that this was the case because Assyrian administrators were unwilling or unable to impose entirely new city plans on local inhabitants, choosing instead to allow existing architectural features to continue and to add their own additional structures where space was available; addition instead of replacement. More likely than not, the Assyrians recognized that adapting the built environment instead of completely reorganizing it was a necessary conflict-avoiding route to a pacific relationship with local forces. In a similar vein, the ninth- to eighth-century local urban practice of imbuing portal lions with royal symbolism was adapted at Tell Ahmar and Arslan Tash, not abandoned. Even after conquest, therefore, SACC remained a significant cultural force for Assyria, and as a result Syro-Anatolian cities became hybrid built environments incorporating both local and Assyrian features.[23]

: : :

# Conclusion

This chapter opened with the counterintuitive discovery of a Syro-Anatolian engraved pyxis in a securely Assyrian, seventh-century temple context at Tell Tayinat. Its local relief iconography contrasted starkly with the Assyrian kneeling bull on an adjacent glazed ceramic vessel, and even its color—black—marked the object as distinct from the beige and red tones of the other Assyrian objects in its vicinity. As described earlier, the object was likely used in local mortuary feasts and related rituals until it was brought into the temple, at which point it was incorporated into the Assyrian *akītu* ceremony. Upon reflection, however, the object's presence and reuse in a new social context should not occasion a great deal of surprise. Quite the opposite, in fact: there is such a large body of evidence for cultural exchange and influence between Assyria and SACC that to see the repurposing of local religious paraphernalia for Assyrian ends seems entirely appropriate. As we saw earlier, even the building in which it was found, Building XVI, was itself a repurposed local structure.

This is but one example of a larger phenomenon that this chapter has articulated. Rather than being a passive participant in regional cultural and geopolitical dynamics that were established by the Neo-Assyrian Empire alone, SACC was an active agent in these dynamics. On the one hand, our backward-facing temporal gaze collapses their final political interaction—conquest and subjectivity—onto previous interactions that took over two centuries to play out. Over the course of those decades, the two entities exchanged visual motifs and physical objects across a more-or-less even playing field. On the other, the different strategies of Assyrian and Syro-Anatolian rhetoric, in which the former boasted of military and political exploits abroad in voluminous detail while the latter preferred pithy inscriptions to commemorate building events, has created a profound historical imbalance in which the modern audience can all too easily accept as given the Assyrian tendency to present their statements of overwhelming superiority at face value.

This chapter has argued that, rather than understand the cultural dynamics between these two entities as having behaved along the lines of acculturation, or "Assyrianization," the standard (and usually tacit) interpretive framework with which scholars present interaction with Assyria, we would do better to view this interaction as a middle ground, one in which novel, hybridized cultural forms are fashioned by regular interaction at all levels. Some of this interaction, like trade patterns, can only be inferred from Assyrian records demonstrating their preference for western goods, even if only ever described as booty acquisition. Others are described explicitly as such in Assyrian texts, such as passages describing emulation of Syro-Anatolian palatial architecture "for their pleasure." But it is the material and visual records that prove the case for the existence of a hybrid middle ground in the early centuries of the first millennium BCE. Assyrian visual motifs getting incorporated into archaic Hieroglyphic Luwian inscriptions, as seems to have been the case at Kızıldağ, or Semitic inscriptions, as attested in the Kulamuwa stele; Assyrian and local expressions of monumental art merged in a single statue in a way that perfectly suited the individual's ambiguous titulary in the accompanying bilingual inscription, as took place with the statue of Hadd-yit'i from Tell Fakhariyeh; the adaptation of Syro-Anatolian artistic motifs like the funerary repast in Assyrian palace reliefs; the transformation and incorporation of Syro-Anatolian monumental architecture into Assyrian palace building; the creation of provincial urban centers that are a jumble of modified local buildings and new Assyrian constructions—all of this is more appropriately described as an example of middle-ground interaction than it is a unidirectional acculturation.[24]

Recognizing the hybrid nature of Assyrian–SACC interaction returns us to two of this volume's overarching principles: that SACC was an influential cultural force in the ancient Near East's Iron Age, one that has received insufficient acknowledgment from scholarship, and that it is inappropriate to consider the Near Eastern Iron Age, and SACC in particular, in essentializing ethnolinguistic terms given the tremendous amount of evidence for hybridity and interaction between these polities and the cultural groups that constituted them. As we shall see in the following chapter, similar considerations apply when one turns to the great deal of variability in the spatial principles operating within SACC's built environment.

## CHAPTER 5

# SPACE AND POWER IN THE SYRO-ANATOLIAN CULTURE COMPLEX

PREVIOUS CHAPTERS IN THIS BOOK have scrutinized aspects of cultural behavior in the Syro-Anatolian Culture Complex (SACC) and found that, in some
cases counterintuitively, many of these behaviors do not conform with expectations
derived from an ethnolinguistic nation-state model. Instead, the cultural practices
examined here have been characterized by mobility, both that of people and
things. This chapter shifts gears by looking at the phenomena of space and place as
manifested in the built environment of SACC, phenomena that are not necessarily
mobile in a physical sense, but that nevertheless occupied a fluid position in the
Syro-Anatolian cultural imagination in several respects. This chapter lifts our head
from the minutiae of portable artifacts or the biographies of individual orthostats
to look instead at the settlements those objects moved between, the layouts of the
cities in which they were found, and the structures against whose immobile walls
those orthostats were laid. In the last chapter we looked briefly at the built environment of SACC's major cities during the Iron Age III period to assess the evidence for urban continuity following the Neo-Assyrian conquest. Here, I examine
SACC's physical spaces and meaningful places during the preceding Iron Age II at
three scales of analysis: territory and landscape; cities, towns, and urban planning;
and architecture and the built environment. What emerges from this analysis is an
awareness that the relationship of space and power was highly variable depending
on scale and context, and also something that could be hotly contested. Spatial
analysis therefore offers an access point into both the strategies and tactics of political control and resistance.

In the past three decades, space has become a sufficiently influential subject
that scholarship now refers to this emphasis adopted by the humanities and social

*The Syro-Anatolian City-States.* James F. Osborne, Oxford University Press (2021). © Oxford University Press.
DOI: 10.1093/oso/9780199315833.003.0005

sciences beginning in the late 1980s and early 1990s as the "spatial turn" (Warf and Arias 2009). The essential argument of early efforts to theorize discussions of space was that space is not, or not only, an absolute property of human existence. It is also something that can be manipulated and experienced very differently across time and between cultures. If that is the case, then we are obliged not to abandon, but to think critically about, the use of absolutist quantitative methods that have been the staples of positivist geography and archaeology, and to complement them with the humanistic perspective offered by sensitive readings of landscapes and texts.

This more relativist spatial stance has its origins in French social theory. Michel Foucault is often cited as a historian who realized that the spatial property of life was worth subjecting to intellectual scrutiny, and his writing inspired humanist geographers to consider not just the spaces constructed by builders and authority figures, but the social relations that led to these projects as well as the nature of the built environment in lived human experience. Foucault (1984) notes that in every attempt at spatial control there remains the possibility for spatial resistance, or strategy and tactics respectively (a theme more fully developed by de Certeau [1984]). Even the most oppressive built spaces like concentration camps still, after all, have their resistance groups. For Foucault, the material built environment is an essential part of human relations, including power dynamics, which means that we have to understand something of those relations before drawing conclusions from the built environment alone.

The most impactful theorist on the humanities and the social sciences has been Henri Lefebvre, and especially his volume *The Production of Space* (1991), translated from the 1974 original. The book's thesis remains powerful today: "*(Social) space is a (social) product* . . . space thus produced also serves as a tool of thought and of action . . . in addition to being a means of production it is also a means of control, and hence of domination, of power" (1991: 26, emphasis in original). Although Lefebvre does not consider Foucault's and de Certeau's insistence on the capacity for individual tactics to resist strategies of domination, the consistency between Foucault and Lefebvre with regards to their claims for the historically contingent nature of space is clear. Lefebvre (1991: 27) is adamant that the particularities of social space are revealed to the extent that one recognizes its fundamental overlap with both mental and physical space. Concepts commonly ascribed to the mental component of human experience and those commonly attributed to the material, including the built environment, cannot be investigated separately because they constitute an irreducible and mutually reinforcing relationship. These notions had a powerful impact on humanistic geographers (Soja 1989; Tuan 1974, 1977), who cited such works to supplement geography's positivist methodologies with conceptions of spatial experience.

Such insights have similar implications for archaeologists and ancient historians. Acknowledging that space is neither a universal, objective category, nor merely a sensory faculty, anthropologist Adam Smith calls for a relational approach to space, bringing Lefebvre's dissolution of the material-mental dichotomy to archaeology. For Smith (2003: 69–70), "meaningful discussions of space center on relationships between subjects and objects rather than essential properties of either . . . To come to terms with space is to account for the relations between subjects and objects in terms of social practices." Bemoaning what he calls "the relentless temporocentrism of modernist political theory," Smith (2003: 13) argues that by overemphasizing the explanatory power of time we treat space as merely a problem of engineering, when in fact space has the capacity to reveal patterns of ancient social processes. And not only do we miss interpretive opportunities by ignoring the analytical power of space, we risk making empirical errors of judgment, since of course the practical social relations are always taking place some*where*. As we saw in Chapter 1, with several notable exceptions research in SACC has been preoccupied by questions of origins, ethnic histories, developments in site morphology over time, and the evolution of particular aspects of material and visual culture. One consequence of our traditional diachronic emphasis is that the spatial properties of Syro-Anatolian social life have not been sufficiently explored. The goal of this chapter, therefore, is to shift our focus from when Syro-Anatolian cultural developments took place, to where.

Our general lack of interest in the spatial properties of the creation and experience of SACC's built environment is again part and parcel of scholarship's tacit employment of the nation-state model as the appropriate means with which to understand the Syro-Anatolian city-states. This is so because according to the nation-state template of political sovereignty, authority is considered to be homogenously distributed across the polity, such that the same political principles apply consistently regardless of the venue of social action. This model has been challenged on theoretical and empirical grounds even in contemporary contexts, let alone ancient case studies. Part of the reason it has remained so persistent is that modern scholarship, and archaeological and Near Eastern scholarship specifically, arose at roughly the same time as the nation-state and its political processes. As many geographers have elaborated, the nation-state's approach to sovereignty and space has its historical origins in the Peace of Westphalia in 1648, a series of treaties signed between European powers that used the demarcation of clearly established borders as one of the mechanisms to secure the continuity of peace. Here began the principle of Westphalian sovereignty, according to which each nation-state was responsible for the exercise of sovereignty within its own territory. A corollary of this condition is that the state itself is held to be uniformly and evenly distributed across space, while crossing a border involves the transfer to an entirely different sovereign nation. Yet no commonsensical as this model may appear, it has proven to be at least as seductive as it is inaccurate. John Agnew (1994, 2009) calls the assumptions inherent in Westphalian sovereignty the "territorial trap," referring to our excessive reliance on the conceptual bundling of sovereignty and territory, and with it the expectation of political power that is evenly distributed across space within bounded containers. If Westphalian expectations can be challenged in a modern geopolitical context, as transnational scholarship has argued strongly in many contexts (e.g., Appadurai 1996), then so much more so in antiquity, where principles of space and power take on further dimensions of variability.

The archaeology of territoriality has received limited attention, with archaeologists for the most part operating under the tacit principles of spatially homogeneous sovereignty. Notable exceptions exist, especially archaeologists who advocate for a network-based model of territory (e.g., M. L. Smith 2005, 2007). For our purposes, the critical point is less the development of new conceptions of territory—which is, after all, an inherent aspect of social life—and more the recognition that territorial patterning is highly variable and dependent on social, historical, and spatial context (VanValkenburgh and Osborne 2013). One consequence of highlighting territorial variability is the recognition that conventional borders are only likely to have arisen in particular circumstances (Ristvet 2008). But particularism is a critical component of the spatial nature of social life at all scales. In the ancient Near East, such context- and region-based variability has been proposed by Bradley Parker (2001, 2013) with respect to the Neo-Assyrian Empire, as he attempted to break away from debates between the so-called inkblot model of evenly distributed territoriality (Postgate 1992) and alternative network proposals (Liverani 1988).

It is, in fact, SACC that has seen some of the most sophisticated archaeological work on space and place in the Near East, partially because of an earlier generation's archaeological practice of generating massive horizontal exposures that lend themselves more to spatial analysis than they do paleoethnobotany, for example. Building on the empirical summaries of urban histories established by Stefania Mazzoni (1994, 1995), Ömür Harmanşah (2013) has studied the highly dynamic landscapes and urban centers of this region, arguing for a place-based understanding of urban foundations that sees the creation of new cities as tightly enmeshed with kingship and social memory. And, as discussed in Chapter 3, Alessandra Gilibert (2011, 2013) and others (e.g., Pucci 2006) have argued for the stage-like role played by the built environment in urban festivals that were aimed at furthering the legitimacy of rulership.

But much of the existing scholarship on space and place in SACC has been either restricted to a single spatial scale (e.g., urbanism); has accepted the spatial narratives of power described in texts at close to face value, ignoring or downplaying evidence for resistance and contestation that is indeed attested in the archaeological record;

or has been limited primarily to one or the other side of the putative interpretivist/ positivist divide. The present chapter opens at the scale of landscapes and settlement patterns, transitions into cities and their monumental buildings, and closes with the modest layouts of towns and villages, all of which combine to demonstrate the extreme variability of space, place, and power that is manifest in the historical and archaeological records. This study furthermore emphasizes the cracks in the façade of homogenous power distribution that is conventionally implied by the historical and archaeological record, noting wherever possible the evidence, relatively rare though it might be, for radical challenges to spatial expressions of authority. This chapter celebrates both the built environment as quantified by the remote analyst using techniques developed in spatial analysis like space syntax, as well as the built environment as experienced and interpreted by those who dwelt within it using historical sources and contextual interpretation of the archaeological record, tacking dialectically between the two positions (Sewell 2005: 318–72).[1] In the end, this study demonstrates again, this time in the context of space and place, how the Syro-Anatolian city-states of the Iron Age II period are characterized more by models of fluidity and variability than they are by the stable, homogenizing vision of the nation-state.

::::

## Territory and Landscape
### *Settlement Patterns and Malleable Territoriality*

For all the landscape archaeology that has been conducted in the Syro-Anatolian region in the past several decades, it is surprisingly difficult to isolate settlement patterns within individual city-states during the Iron Age II when the polities were at their political apex, that is, from the mid- to late tenth century until the end of the eighth century. Partially this is due to patchy or partial regional coverage, and partially to unhelpful ceramic records that do not change over time in ways that are discernible at the low-resolution quality of surface collections. Whatever the cause, there are precious few analyses of the settlement patterns that characterized the landscapes of individual Syro-Anatolian polities. In Chapter 2 we looked macroscopically at the changes that characterized the settlement patterns of the Syro-Anatolian region across the Late Bronze-Iron Age transition, noting mostly that site distribution changes were evidence for demographic changes that likely included the movement of people. Here we will look briefly at some of the settlement patterns of the Iron Age II period—at least to the extent that chronological resolution is sufficient—when the Syro-Anatolian city-states were fully formed, and interpret them with an eye toward political authority and territorial control.

One regional survey that does meet the necessary conditions—having been conducted in a large and geographically contained valley, and having a clear ceramic marker for the start of the Iron Age II with Red Slipped Burnished Ware—is the Amuq Valley Regional Project (AVRP) that has taken place roughly within the Iron Age city-state of Patina. Analysis of the settlement data published by this survey (Yener 2005) provides a clear outline of which settlements were occupied during the early centuries of the first millennium BCE (although Red Slipped Burnished Ware continues into the Assyrian period, referred to ceramically as Amuq Phase Od; Swift 1958) (Osborne 2013). Figure 5.1 shows the distribution of sites identified by AVRP as having been occupied during this period. There are fifty in total, plus an additional five in the Orontes delta that was surveyed at the same time (Pamir 2005).[2] The primary complication with this dataset, as with many surveys, is the problem of estimating site size: since the sites were surveyed extensively, it is difficult to know how much of a site was occupied at any given time period. Similarly, and related, at even the relatively high chronological resolution offered by AVRP, the possibility that all fifty-five were not occupied contemporaneously is unavoidable (Kintigh 1994). Nevertheless, the AVRP survey is a strong one for understanding Iron Age II settlement pattern dynamics.

The data present clear evidence for a three-tiered settlement hierarchy. There is one large site at approximately 35 ha: Tell Tayinat, ancient Kunulua, the capital city of Patina. Below Tayinat is a handful of moderately sized settlements, including Çatal Höyük (10 ha), Tell Hasanuşağı (7 ha), Tell Mastepe (6.25 ha), and Tell Salihhiyeh (4.5 ha). Below these, then, are several dozen settlements that are 1–3 ha in size. What is so intriguing about this settlement pattern is its correspondence with the inscriptions composed by campaigning Neo-Assyrian rulers who described their interactions with local polities in detail. Here, too, the campaign accounts describe three types of settlements encountered by the Assyrian army, ranked in terms of size and significance. The first is the "royal city" (Akk: āl šarrūti), the residence of the ruler and capital city (Ikeda 1979: 76). Typical features of the royal city in these texts include a palace, treasury, harem, and officials. The second settlement category was the ālāni dannūti, or "fortified cities." These were often named and, like the royal city, were associated explicitly with a fortification system. Finally, there were the ālāni ša limēti, or "cities in the neighborhood." These settlements were never named. Instead, in order to provide a general impression of the extent of inflicted destruction, they were listed in counts of the total number of villages sacked by the Assyrian ruler (Liverani 1992: 125).[3] From his analysis of Assyria's annual military campaign accounts, Liverani concludes that there were, on average, slightly more than three fortified cities for every royal city, and approximately twenty villages for every fortified city (1992: 138). The archaeological-historical convergence evident here is bolstered even further by the fact that Çatal

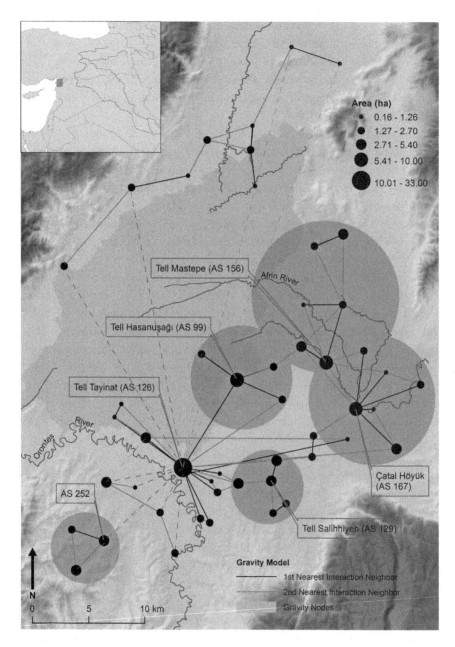

**Area (ha)**
- 0.16 - 1.26
- 1.27 - 2.70
- 2.71 - 5.40
- 5.41 - 10.00
- 10.01 - 33.00

Tell Mastepe (AS 156)

Afrin River

Tell Hasanuşağı (AS 99)

Tell Tayinat (AS 126)

Orontes River

Çatal Höyük (AS 167)

AS 252

Tell Salihhiyeh (AS 129)

**Gravity Model**
——— 1st Nearest Interaction Neighbor
——— 2nd Nearest Interaction Neighbor
Gravity Nodes

N
0     5     10 km

FIGURE 5.1
Settlement pattern of the Syro-Anatolian city-state of Patina during the Iron Age II period, also illustrating first and second degrees of interaction predicted by gravity modeling. Sites' first nearest interaction neighbors connected with a black line; second nearest interaction neighbors connected with a gray line. Dashed line indicates the presence of the reconstructed marsh between two sites.

Höyük, one of Patina's second-tier settlements, was indeed found to be surrounded by a substantial fortification wall (Haines 1971: 4–5), while CORONA satellite imagery of another, Tell Hasanuşağı, shows the site to be surrounded by the dark shaded ring that is the signature of denser vegetation caused by a topographic dip (and thus disproportionately high water retention), indicating the likelihood of an ancient moat around the town.[4]

Gravity modeling further confirms this three-tiered hierarchy indicated by site sizes and Assyrian royal inscriptions (Osborne 2013: 783–86). Gravity modeling is a reductive quantitative procedure that is used to predict the degree of economic interaction between two settlements. It is predicated on the assumptions that inter-action between two sites decreases with distance, and that interaction between sites increases with site size or population (Alden 1979: 170–71). Additionally, it assumes an isotropic topography, a frequent source of criticism, though less relevant in the context of the flat and alluvial Amuq Valley. Computationally, the degree of inter-action between sites, or their "gravity," is calculated with the equation $M_{ij} = A_i A_j / (d_{ij})^2$, where $A_i$ and $A_j$ are the areas of settlements $i$ and $j$ and $d_{ij}$ is the distance between them (Schacht 1987). Each site is therefore assigned an interaction index with every other site, and the first two degrees of proposed interaction are illustrated in Figure 5.1. From this procedure and its visual output, one can draw two important conclusions: that Tayinat is apparently overwhelmingly influential in the economy of the region, having close predicted ties with sites both large and small; and that the bulk of the plain is occupied by a settlement structure characterized by clusters, or nodes, of settlements, with tertiary villages connected primarily to secondary centers, and the secondary centers connected to Tell Tayinat. These secondary centers are precisely the same sites that occupy the second tier of the settlement hierarchy in terms of site size, and also those that have evidence for fortification as per Assyrian records. A tightly organized hierarchical model for the spatial organization of economic and political activity in Patina thus seems to emerge from combining these strands of evidence.

Yet there are cracks in this model that render it an imperfect, or at least incomplete, representation of the spatial distribution of Patina's political economy. First, a number of small settlements on the northwestern edge of the valley do not appear to fit comfortably within the three-tiered hierarchy indicated by gravity modeling. There is no second-tier settlement in their vicinity, and instead their nearest interaction neighbor is often predicted to be Tayinat, over two dozen kilometers away. Yet the general lack of settlements of all periods between this portion of the plain, the historical existence of a slightly later Lake of Antioch in precisely this location, and hydrological modeling that predicts accumulations of water in this region, suggests that direct access between these sites and Tayinat was not, in fact, possible, such that the gravity model's results are excessively strong in this case.

These villages thus seem to have existed outside of the Patina's settlement hierarchy. Second, the five Iron Age II sites in the Orontes delta seem to be completely outside of this system. One of these sites is Al Mina, the small but famous site excavated by Sir Leonard Woolley (1938a, 1938b) that has long been interpreted as an early Greek colony dating to the eighth century BCE (and later) on the basis of unusually high volumes of Greek pottery found there (Boardman 1959, 1990, 1999, 2002). Subsequent analysis of the many problems with the excavation and its history of interpretation (Saltz 1978),[5] the ongoing publication of locally produced ceramics, including Red Slipped Burnished Ware (Lehmann 2005), and the discovery of a possible reference to the settlement in the Iran Stele of Tiglath-pileser III that associates a coastal trading site named Aḫta with a "royal storehouse" in the vicinity (Tadmor and Yamada 2011: 85–86; Zadok 1996: 104–5), presumably Kunulua, all point toward Al Mina having served as Kunulua's port and entry point into Mediterranean trade networks (Luke 2003). Al Mina, in other words, was very much a part of Patina's political and economic life, despite being territorially removed from its geographical center.

Perhaps even more problematic to territorial homogeneity is a small monument known as the Antakya Stele, composed during the reign of the Neo-Assyrian ruler Adad-nirari III (811–783 BCE). Found during construction of a well halfway between the modern city of Antakya and the coast—well within Patina's ostensible territory—the stele consists of a boundary marker (Akk: *taḫūmu*) that records Adad-nirari negotiating between the Syro-Anatolian city-states of Hamath and Bit-Agusi, resulting in Hamath ceding the town of Naḫlasi and its associated fields to Bit-Agusi; they reportedly "divided the Orontes River between them." A boundary stele between two city-states located squarely within an area that should, by all reason, belong to neither of them is certainly unusual. One option to resolve the problem is to assume that the stele must have been sent down the Orontes from an original location to the south and east, where a Bit-Agusi/Hamath border would be more likely (Hawkins 1995b: 96; Younger 2000b: 272). But there is no particular reason why such a movement should have occurred, and indeed it is only offered to accord with contemporary cartographic sensibilities. If we accept its findspot as at or near its original place of installation, then we also have to accept the fact that settlements and territory between Kunulua and its port at Al Mina did not belong to Patina, at least not at all times. The practice of trading and purchasing settlements between individuals and political centers quite distant from one another has a strong local precedent in the second millennium, where tablets from Alalakh, Kunulua's Middle and Late Bronze Age predecessor as the regional capital city, demonstrate a highly similar practice of variable territorial affiliations caused by land and settlements changing hands (Casana 2009; Lauinger 2015).

Nor is Patina the only Syro-Anatolian city-state to have evidence for this uneven relationship between territory and political authority. The İncirli inscription, found in survey around the city of Kahramanmaraş, ancient Marash, capital of the Syro-Anatolian kingdom of Gurgum, was discussed in Chapter 2 in the context of its Phoenician-language inscription, one of three of the languages included in this trilingual text in addition to Akkadian and (possibly: cf. Swartz Dodd 2012: 214) Luwian. Here what is significant is its historical content: having stayed loyal to Assyria during a Syro-Anatolian rebellion led by Arpad, Awarikku, king of Que, is awarded territory previously belonging to Kummuḫ (Kaufman 2007: 9). Like the Amuq Valley, the forty-eight settlements occupied during the Iron Age II period in this region are also characterized by a tripartite settlement hierarchy, although apparently one without a single disproportionately large urban center (Swartz Dodd 2012: 218–26). And also like Patina, some of its territory appears to have transferred from one adjacent city-state to another, presumably for its material resources, agricultural productivity, and access to transportation corridors (2012: 225–29), this despite the fact that the Amanus Mountain range lies between Marash and Que.

A third example comes from the city-state of Bit-Agusi, in whose region an inscription concerning Kamani, king of Carchemish, was found in Cekke, north of Aleppo and 22 km east of 'Azaz (Barnett 1948; Figure 5.2). Lines 2–3 of the inscription on the stele's reverse describe Kamani as purchasing a settlement for the price of 600 mules (Giusfredi 2010: 254–55; Hawkins 2000: 143–51). In this case, unlike the Antakya and İncirli stelae, Assyria was completely uninvolved with the settlement transfer. Using the findspot of this and other isolated Iron Age stelae from the region, Brown and Smith (2016: 22–26 and Fig. 3.2) reconstruct Carchemish's territorial extent as waxing and waning as a result of historical forces like the presence or absence of Assyria, such that pieces like the Cekke stele are taken as indications of Carchemisean territorial control close to Aleppo up to the Qoueiq River, which formed a border for Carchemish's territory. But given the evidence presented earlier, as well as additional inscriptions from Carchemish such as KARKAMIŠ A4a and TÜNİP 1, which record the sale of estates and land for silver (Hawkins 2000: 151–56), it is more plausible that such texts are additional evidence for a different model of territoriality altogether. Although counterintuitive discoveries like four settlements on the west bank of the Euphrates being held by Ahuni of Bit-Adini "makes it sound as if the western hinterland of Karkamiš was entirely in the hands of Bit-Adini" (Hawkins 1995b: 91), for example, it is equally possible that these settlements had simply been sold and purchased.

In short, the archaeological and historical records converge on a complicated model of territorial sovereignty at the regional scale, one that is difficult to reconcile with the expectations of the nation-state. On the one hand, a stable, tell-based, three-tiered settlement hierarchy seems to have characterized the political

FIGURE 5.2
The Cekke stele, found in a field east of 'Azaz. (Barnett 1948: Pl. XIX)

economy, with a single urban center at the apex of an economic pyramid. However, archaeological indicators exist to complement this understanding with the recognition that settlements existed more or less outside of this hierarchy—such as the villages on the northwest edge of the Amuq Valley, or the Mediterranean-facing sites in the Orontes delta—even while both native and Assyrian historical sources point toward the easy transfer of land and territory between distant city-states. The only way to align these lines of evidence is to escape the territorial trap described earlier—the understanding of territorial sovereignty that equates political control with contiguous spatial distributions—and recognize instead a model of "malleable territoriality," a phenomenon that has also been identified within the Syro-Anatolian region of the mid second millennium (Lauinger 2015; Ristvet 2008). Authority was not evenly distributed across the landscape, nor contained within a fixed border, and contiguity of land and settlements was not a necessary requirement for political control. Although individual Syro-Anatolian city-states had core geographical regions in a broad sense, such as the Amuq Valley and its tributary valley systems for Patina, these political zones were permeated with territory or settlements that were technically not under Patina's domination. Instead, malleable territoriality implies that spatial control was patchy and highly variable through time in ways that will be difficult to track archaeologically—and also difficult to represent cartographically.

::::

## Syro-Anatolian Urbanism

### Syro-Anatolian Cities as "Strange Loops"

In his popular work on the nature of cognition, Douglas Hofstadter (1979) argued for the existence of "strange loops" in the human mind and the natural world. Such loops arise in hierarchical systems in which, when passing through the system from one level to the next, one nevertheless ends up at the same place where one started in an endless recursive discourse. The capital cities of SACC behave analogously to the strange loop insofar as they consist of hierarchical spatial systems that consistently reinforce the same ideological message of royal legitimacy at every stage of the hierarchy. But before looking at how the formal and symbolic properties of Syro-Anatolian urban centers combined in such meaningful ways, a combination that could only have been at least partially the result of a conscious strategy of urban planning, let us look briefly at the nature of the evidence available to us from over a century of exploration for Iron Age II urban layouts (as opposed to the modifications made to these layouts in the Assyrian period that were examined in the previous chapter).

The primary capital cities that have long been known and analyzed from earlier excavations, art historical, and philological enquiry, and which have already featured prominently in this volume in other contexts, are *Hamath*, where Danish excavations uncovered a large horizontal exposure in the upper city and extensive cremation burials in the lower city that are predominantly covered by modern occupation (Fugmann 1958; Riis 1948; Riis and Buhl 1990); *Tell Tayinat*, ancient Kunulua, where excavations old and new have contributed to our understanding of the upper city, and survey has provided preliminary indications of the nature of lower town settlement (Haines 1971; Osborne and Karacic 2017; Osborne et al. 2019); *Zincirli*, ancient Sam'al, where the upper city and fortification system were extensively explored in the late nineteenth and early twentieth century, and where renewed excavations have brought to light exciting remains from the previously unexcavated lower city (Herrmann 2017a; von Luschan 1893; von Luschan et al. 1898, 1902; von Luschan and Jacoby 1911; von Luschan and Andrae 1943); *Tell Rifaʿat*, ancient Arpad, only partially excavated in the mid-twentieth century (Seton-Williams 1961, 1967); *Tell Ahmar*, ancient Til-Barsip, major upper-city excavations in the early twentieth century and more recent renewed work in several sectors of the site in anticipation of dam-related flooding (Jamieson 2012; F. Thureau-Dangin and Dunand 1936); *Carchemish*, where British Museum excavations unearthed the monumental remains that have been the foundation of Syro-Anatolian studies since, and where a Turkish-Italian team has recently begun a renewed project for the first time in decades (Hogarth 1914; Marchetti 2014; Woolley 1921, 1952); *Tell Halaf*, ancient Gozan, where large-scale excavations uncovered much of the upper city and parts of the lower city, and whose results were refined by renewed work that was cut short by the civil war in Syria (Baghdo et al. 2009, 2012; Naumann 1950; Opitz and Moortgat 1955); and *Arslantepe*, ancient Melid, where deep alluvium may cover a potential lower city, but whose central tell has long been known for its Iron Age gate complex and associated architectural features (Delaporte 1940; Manuelli and Mori 2016). Capital cities that have *not* received substantial, or any, archaeological excavation include *Adana*, capital of Que[6]; *Amedi*, capital of Bit-Zamani; and *Marash*, capital of Gurgum; this is because their remains lie buried under modern cities. Another is *Samsat Höyük*, capital of Kummuḫ, now flooded by the Atatürk Dam.

Synthesizing the findings from these urban centers, several clear patterns emerge that indicate a shared conception of urban planning across the Syro-Anatolian region, on the principle that such standardization is unlikely to have occurred coincidentally (M. E. Smith 2007: 7–8). The most consistent of these is a tripartite spatial division in which the city is divided into three distinct zones marked by increasingly restrictive accessibility (Özyar 2013: 115).[7] Although the form of these cities is not identical in all instances—compare the circular layouts of Zincirli and Tell Rifaʿat with the angular outlines of Carchemish and Tell Halaf, for example—in all instances the cities are characterized by a fortification wall that encircles the lower town containing residences for commoners or nonroyal elites, another fortification surrounding the upper city containing public buildings and open spaces for large-scale performances and gatherings, and finally a fortified palace compound with additional open space (Figure 5.3). Furthermore, this spatial hierarchy is manifested not only in plan, but also in elevation, since each movement inward corresponds to an increase in elevation, such that palace compounds stood many meters above their cities' lower towns (Harmanşah 2013: 110; Mazzoni 1995: 184; M. Pucci 2008a). Only a handful of sites have their acropolis thoroughly excavated, but those that

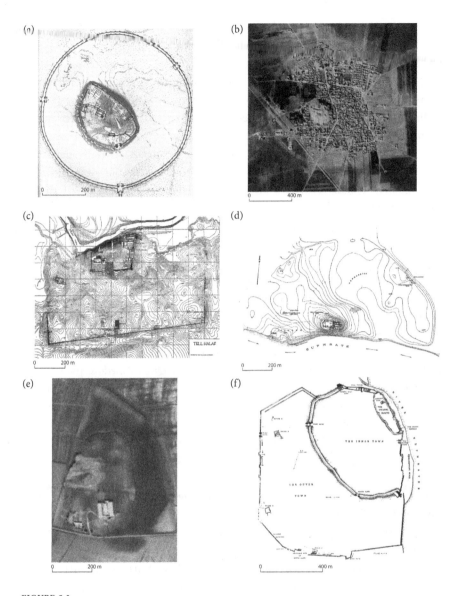

FIGURE 5.3
Comparative plan of Syro-Anatolian urban centers: (*a*) Zincirli; (*b*) Tell Rifa'at (Arpad); (*c*) Tell Halaf (Gozan); (*d*) Tell Ahmar (Til-Barsip); (*e*) Tell Tayinat (Kunulua); (*f*) Carchemish. Note the different scale used for the large sites of Tell Rifa'at and Carchemish.

do, including Zincirli, Hamath, Tell Halaf, and Tell Tayinat, show remarkable similarities in their layouts. At Tell Halaf, for example, two large palaces stood facing each other across a large open courtyard in an almost identical arrangement to that of Tell Tayinat; in both cases access to the inward-facing palace compound was gained by entering a gate and turning 180 degrees on a path connecting the gate to the palace portico (cf. Haines 1971: pl. 105; Naumann 1950: Plan 2). Such similarities between neighboring capitals lead to the inescapable conclusion that centralized planning was part of what led to their final urban morphologies.

While this shared spatial organization of urban planning within SACC has been identified before, less commonly recognized is the cumulative urban symbolism that was created by the coordination of ideologically charged inscriptions and monuments at significant spatial junctures throughout the city (Osborne 2014). One such juncture is the city gate that provided access into the hierarchical levels of the city, but also allowed for the regulation and control of traffic, and that scholars have long recognized as a significant ceremonial passageway (Mazzoni 1997). The Syro-Anatolian gate also carried significant political weight, however, especially since it was often used as a venue for royal inscriptions. These buildings can be understood as monuments that integrated visual, epigraphic, and architectural elements into a cohesive unit that communicated very specific meanings of political authority. The lengthiest and most famous of the gateway inscriptions from SACC is the late eighth-century Phoenician/Luwian bilingual from Karatepe, in which the author Azatiwada states that if anyone

effaces the name of Azatiwada from this gate and puts up his (own) name, or more than that, covets this city and pulls down this gate which Azatiwada made, and makes another gate for it and puts his (own) name on it, whether it is out of covetousness or whether it is out of hatred and malice that he pulls down this gate, —then let Ba'al-Shamem and El-Creator-of-Earth and Shamash-'olam and the whole generation of the sons of the god efface that kingdom and that king. (Röllig 1999: 54–55)

The direct association between the gate and royalty is explicit: an affront to the gate is simultaneously an affront to the king. And as the king and gate are connected, so the city and gate are related in a conceptual bundle, in that if one wants to take possession of the city, then replacing its gate served as the symbolic transfer of the city to its new suzerainty.[8] Passages like these are revealing of the expression of political authority in the urban context: royal power was closely associated with the city gate, which served as a synecdoche for the city, representing it *pars pro toto* (Mazzoni 1997: 332).

As if the association of royalty and city gate were not sufficiently evident in royal inscriptions, several Syro-Anatolian sites possessed huge royal statues that stood within these structures. Statues of a god or king in a remarkably homogeneous appearance (see later) have been found at Arslantepe (Delaporte 1940: 35–38, pls. XIV, XXVI–XXXI), Carchemish (Hogarth 1914: 28, pl. A4d; Woolley 1952: 192–99, pl. B 53–54), Çineköy (Tekoğlu et al. 2000), Ivriz (Dinçol 1994: Fig. 7-8), Karatepe (Çambel and Özyar 2003: Taf. 218–20), Marach (Messerschmidt 1906: 12–15), Tell Halaf (Opitz and Moortgat 1955: 114–17, pl. 130–35), Tell Tayinat (Gelb 1939: 39, pl. LXXIX; Harrison 2017: 286–88, Fig. 8), and Zincirli (von Luschan and Jacoby 1911: 288–89, 362–68) (Figure 5.4). Of these, the examples from Carchemish, Arslantepe, Karatepe, Tell Tayinat, and Zincirli were all found in gate complexes, while three others, Marash, Ivriz, and Çineköy, are from *ex situ* secondary contexts.

The tight conceptual nexus between gate and king in SACC is vividly attested at Carchemish's King's Gate, which marked the entrance from the Inner Town to the complex of monumental public structures at the foot of the acropolis (Harmanşah 2013: 134–52). Near this gate's inscribed western jamb was the statue of a seated figure wearing a horned helmet resting atop a double-lion base (Woolley 1921: pl. B.25). The brief Luwian inscription on the skirt of the statue itself, KARKAMIŠ A4d, labels the figure as "this god Atrisuhas" (Hawkins 2000: 101), whose name translates to "(image) soul of Suhis," meaning that we ought to see this statue as the deified version of this historically attested Carchemishean ruler (2000: 96, 101). The statue of a deified king in the King's Gate indicates an extremely close association between

FIGURE 5.4
Colossal statues from Syro-Anatolian sites: (*a*) Carchemish, King's Gate, the seated deified King Suha; (*b*) Tell Halaf, palace portico column, female; (*c*) Zincirli, Tor Q near Building J, buried; (*d*) Malatya, Lion Gate, buried (nose replaced by excavators); (*e*) profile of a man of height 1.75 m.

those structures and royal authority. The relationship is further cemented by the associated door jamb inscription KARKAMIŠ A11*a* in which, after describing the construction of the gate itself including the setting of its orthostats (see Chapter 3), Katuwas refers directly to the statue itself: "this god Atrisuhas I seated at these gates with goodness" (Hawkins 2000: 96). This seated statue was found by the excavators smashed on location into approximately sixty pieces (Woolley 1952: 199), a treatment of these statues that in fact occurs persistently throughout SACC (see later).

Equally common, however, is the deliberate burial of royal statues in or near the gates themselves. The most striking case is that of a colossal figure from the Lion's Gate at Arslantepe, ancient Melid, excavated by the French under Louis Delaporte during the 1930s. This immense object was found lying on its back before the two portal lions that stood in the door jambs of one of the gate chambers, entombed in a construction of stones placed around it (Delaporte 1940: 35–38, pl. XIV, XXV–XXVIII). This treatment might be taken as evidence of the animate status of the royal statue while it was standing in the gate prior to its final burial. A similar burial of a royal statue was reported at Zincirli by von Luschan, who associated the statue with a gate, Tor Q, 10 m away (von Luschan and Jacoby 1911: 363–65, taf. L). The 2.5 m statue was buried in a scenario almost identical with that from Arslantepe: lying on its back, the statue was deliberately encased in stones and earth. Because the statue lacks an inscription, the excavators interpreted it as the storm god Hadad based on the generally similar divine example they had excavated at Gerçin, but, like the statue from Arslantepe, Zincirli's figure lacks horns or any other divine attributes (1911, abb. 265–67). For this reason it is more plausibly understood as a royal figure (Orthmann 1971: 289, 545). Although the precise motives behind such burials are difficult to discern without further evidence (see later), the events reveal an understanding of royal statuary in which these statues were not merely depictions of kings but were themselves objects that demanded reverence (Elif Denel 2007; Ussishkin 1970). The presence of a royal statue in the gate was not dissimilar from the presence of the king himself, and we are again left with the conclusion that the gate was a critical space in Syro-Anatolian political discourse, emphasizing the breadth of royal authority in one of the urban center's most visible locations.

Symbolically tied to this phenomenon is the burial of five basalt portal lions in front of Zincirli's Inneres Burgthor, also known as the Thor der Quermauer (von Luschan et al. 1898: 127–31), whose original locations are not known (cf. reconstructions by Gilibert 2011: Fig. 38; von Luschan et al. 1898: abb. 37). Gauging from the large layer of burned reeds discovered above it, the burial event was concluded with a burning ceremony that took place over the pit after the burial was complete. The lions themselves are very large (see 1898, abb. 35–36), such that the burial can only have been a major undertaking. We thus have two linked phenomena that are both associated with the gate: the presence of royal or lion statues in these buildings, and the burial of royal or lion statues in or beside them. That this is not mere coincidence is demonstrated by the frequency with which Syro-Anatolian kings had their names inscribed in the section of an inscription that is placed directly onto the portal lions of the same gates where the royal statues are found. In the case of the Karatepe inscription, for example, the Phoenician signing of the portal lion in the North Gate (monument Phu/A IV) takes place at the conclusion of Azatiwada's lengthy text. The portion of the inscription actually written directly on the portal lion itself—and the only portion thus visually and physically separated from the bulk of the inscription located on flat orthostats behind the lion—"The name of Azatiwada only may last forever like the name of the sun and the moon!" (Röllig 1999: 53), a combined literary and visual enjambment that emphasized the king-lion association.[9] We see here the explicit identification of the portal lion with the ruler, and the direct association of king and gate, binding all three entities—king, gate, lion—into a single object that carried all three concepts simultaneously.

Besides Karatepe, there are royally signed portal lions at Arslan Tash (Galter 2004; Hawkins 2000: 246–48; Tadmor and Yamada 2011: 161–63), Carchemish, Marash (Hawkins 2000: 262), and Malatya (Hawkins 2000: 320–21) (Figure 5.5). The presence of these associations at multiple Syro-Anatolian cities is too consistent to be accidental. On the contrary, the portal lions were symbols of the king that were specifically designed to express his authority visually. By inscribing his name directly onto the portal lions the king was not only signing these statues in the sense of placing his name on them as one might sign a document; he was also *en*signing them in the sense of imbuing in these statues the ability to symbolize his own power, that is, rendering the statues signs themselves. It is logical, therefore, to find both royal statues and portal lions buried in Syro-Anatolian gateways: The burial of these objects bore the same meaning in both cases, for both were symbols of the king, indeed possibly the king himself.

## Palaces and Symbolism

A discussion of the form and meaning of urban layouts within SACC must perforce include their royal palaces, which in several Syro-Anatolian capitals consisted of the *bīt-ḫilāni* palace. The basic layout of this palace form and its influence on contemporary Assyrian architecture were described in the previous chapter; here I wish to draw attention to the ways in which this palace type reinforced the messaging that we have seen attested across Syro-Anatolian cities. Even more than other locations in the urban landscape, the importance of the *bīt-ḫilāni* as a cumulative

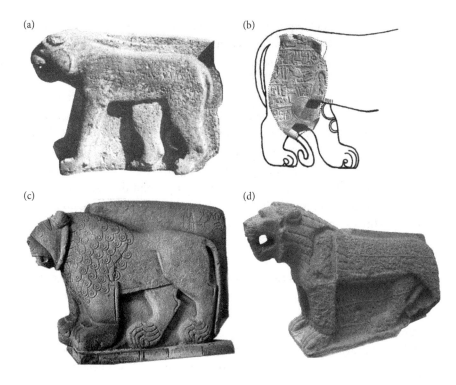

FIGURE 5.5
Royally signed portal lions: (*a*) Karatepe, North Gate; (*b*) Carchemish A14*b*, Great Staircase (Orthmann K/21); (*c*) Malatya 4 (Orthmann A/2); (*d*) Maraş 1. (Orthmann B/1)

symbol whose role was to communicate political power is manifest in texts and imagery, and also in the configuration of space within the palace itself (Osborne 2012). Beginning with written records, the textual material from the Syro-Anatolian city-states, whether in Luwian, Aramaic, or Phoenician, presents an explicit association of the king—or, rather, of kingship—with the physical object of the throne, and we thus have to consider the possibility that the connection of kingship and throne in the Iron Age was a relationship that depended on the existence of the material throne to be effective. In the sixteen-line inscription of Kulamuwa at Zincirli, for example, we read in line 9 that "I, Kulamuwa, the son of Hayya, sat upon my father's throne," and later a passage in lines 13–14 records " . . . Now, if any of my sons (14) who shall sit in my place does harm to this inscription . . . " (Gibson 1982: 35).[10] Kulamuwa is clearly referring to kingship when he refers to sitting on his father's throne and to his sons who will sit there after he is gone. If that is the case, then actually performing the role of kingship by definition involved being physically present on the throne. The physical location of the inscription in the portico entrance to Zluu irli's *bīt-hilāni* Building J, the space through which one passed en route to the throne room, would seem to reinforce this conclusion.

The words *sit, caused to sit, seated*,[11] and *throne* are ubiquitous throughout SACC.[12] In addition, the texts from the city-state of Kummuh referred to as BOYBEYPINARI 1 and 2 are quite clear that these statements are referring to physical objects and not simply metaphorical concepts. These two passages are two pairs of stone blocks which apparently served as podiums for the furniture described in the inscription. (See the illustration in Hawkins 2000: 335 for a reconstruction of how these pieces stood.) We learn from the first line of text on BOYBEYPINARI 1 that "This throne [THRONUS] and this table [MENSA] I Panamuwatis, the ruler Suppiluliumas's wife, dedicated" (Hawkins 2000: 336). Evidently, in this example and, by extrapolation, less explicit examples, when royal furniture like thrones are mentioned, actual objects are intended, even when those objects carry symbolic value. It appears that the material object of the throne and the metaphor of sitting in it as ruler were fused in a dialectical relationship of fact and symbol, in which the throne is at once a physical fact in space and a royal symbol in the texts, and sitting is both a metaphor and a physical action necessary for legitimate kingship.

Tell Tayinat provides material evidence to support these arguments. Inscription TELL TAYINAT 1, pieces of which were found in the courtyard before Tayinat's *bīt-hilāni* Building I (Haines 1971: 41),[13] includes two fragments that are portions of a large basalt piece of furniture, decorated with a substantial bas-relief inscription unfortunately too patchy to understand in detail. The iconography of the two fragments suggests that they derive from a monumental throne, including two throne legs and the beginning of the horizontal crossbar in Fragment 2, attached perpendicularly to what appears to be the back leg of the throne (Figure 5.6). This is not the actual throne that was used by the ruler of Patina, but rather a stone statue of a throne, not dissimilar to that found at the King's Gate at Carchemish (Woolley 1952: 199). Nevertheless, the statue indicates what the actual wooden throne may have looked like. The most interesting aspect of the fragments' iconography is that the back legs of the throne consist of architectural columns like the ones that would have decorated the portico of Tayinat's palace, Building I. This is evident especially in the "capital" that rests atop of the leg/column: this element is derived from the column bases that adorned the original entrance to Building I (Floor 3) (Haines 1971: pl. 75B), and that have nearly identical counterparts in palace K at Zincirli. The main difference in the throne fragment is that the column base has been turned upside down, as would befit a column base used as a capital, and that its middle and bottom registers are schematically presented without their guilloches, rosettes, and palmettes.

10 cm

FIGURE 5.6
Monumental throne fragment depicting the leg and crossbar of the throne along with
inscription TELL TAYINAT 1, fragment 2. Note the inverted column base being used as the
"capital" atop the "column" serving as the throne leg. (Photographs courtesy of the Oriental
Institute Museum)

Not only did the palace's accompanying furniture provide insight into architectural aspects of the palace that were otherwise unknown, including the likely
appearance of the *bīt-ḫilāni*'s columns, it also served as a powerful visual cue for
communicating the symbolic and political nature of the building. It is not coincidental that Tayinat's basalt throne, an object so heavily emphasized in Syro-
Anatolian texts, incorporated elements from the palace. In so doing, it became an
important component of the building's total effect, ultimately combining the palace,
the throne inside the palace, and the king on the throne in a nexus of symbolic
associations that rendered each of these three things at once representations of one
another. That the throne was destroyed, likely by the Assyrians in 738 BCE, is therefore hardly surprising. As a highly charged symbol of kingship that encapsulated
not just the king but also the king's palace, in addition to its own role of embodying

kingship in material form, it would have been an important piece for political rivals to destroy. Quite possibly, it *had* to be destroyed for the usurping power to claim legitimacy of its own.

These symbolic properties of the *bīt-ḫilāni* palace can be explored further through spatial analysis of the palace structure itself. One way to formally assess architectural configurations is with space syntax, developed by practicing architects in the late twentieth century (Hillier and Hanson 1984; Hillier 1996). Space syntax encompasses a series of graphical representations and quantitative analyses that describe a building's makeup with regard to the ease or difficulty with which individuals move through the building's constituent units; it is the relationships between those units, not the units themselves, which determines the nature of a building. Operating under a framework that examines buildings in terms of the configuration, or relationality, of spaces within them, it follows that there are certain social conclusions that can be made from a quantitative assessment of those relations. In general terms, spaces characterized by greater ease of accessibility tend to promote social interaction, while those that are relatively secluded tend to create greater social exclusion. Because the procedure is relatively easy to operationalize, and works well with ancient building plans—so long as conditions of preservation suffice to provide an accurate layout of rooms, including doorways (Cutting 2003)—space syntax has become a widely used tool of architectural analysis in archaeology.

Among the best preserved *bīt-ḫilāni* structures from SACC available for space syntax is the joint Building I/VI complex at Tell Tayinat (Figure 5.7). The east-west wing of the palace, Building I, measures 29 × 58 m, quite a substantial structure. The cobblestone and pebble porch, room E, was lined at the front with three large basalt column bases decorated with palmette patterns around the top and bottom, and a running guilloche and rosette pattern that encircled the middle torus. These are the column bases that are represented in the monumental throne of inscription TT 1. On the western side of the porch, one entered room D, a small vestibule that led to a stairway, of which the first four steps were preserved, up to the second story or roof. (The small rooms A and B are in the northern and western spaces of this staircase area, respectively; presumably they were underneath the staircase from room D, which was winding overhead.) From the porch, room E, one entered the largest room of the palace, room J.[14] Building I can be considered as comprising two main sections, a western and an eastern unit. The central feature of the western unit is clearly room J, the palace's largest room at 25.1 m × 7.1 m. From room J one could enter several surrounding rooms. Also from room J one passed into the eastern section of the building, a suite of rooms not dissimilar in shape from the square, or nearly square, Syro-Anatolian palaces like Zincirli's Hilanis II and III. Room K is the largest space in this unit at 18.9 × 6.9 m.

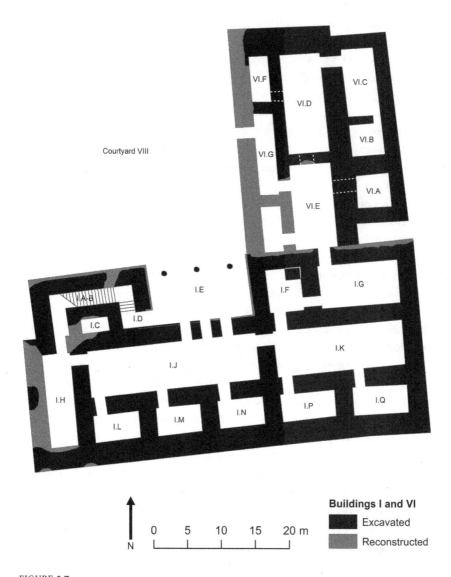

FIGURE 5.7
Plan of *bīt-ḥilāni* Building I/VI from Tell Tayinat, ancient Kunulua. (Modified from Haines 1971: Pl. 103)

From the room in the northeast corner of Building I, room G, one passed through a doorway into Building VI, the north-south wing of the palace. Due to subsequent building activity, the western edge of Building VI was not preserved at this level, and thus Haines reconstructed several rooms or portions of rooms in this part of the building (1971: pl. 103). Unfortunately, Haines offers little justification for the layout he provides, which is problematic since not only are several walls reconstructed, but several doorways between known walls also had to be added (from VI.E to VI.D, VI.E to VI.A, and VI.D to VI.F). The small proposed doorway from Courtyard VIII into Building VI is awkward, and perhaps the room would be more plausibly reconstructed as a portico, which would have the additional benefit of accounting for one or more of the three *ex situ* column bases found by the expedition (Haines 1971: pl. 113, 116–17).[15]

The first stage in conducting space syntax is reducing the complexity of a building plan to its constituent components of rooms, represented by circles, and relations of permeability between rooms (i.e., doorways) represented by lines. The exterior space outside of the building, referred to as the "carrier," or "root," is included in the graph as a circle and is usually kept visually distinct from the circles representing the interior rooms by some kind of label. Each room of a particular "depth" from the carrier—that is, the number of spaces one must pass through in order to get to the room in question from the carrier—is aligned on the same horizontal plane, such that the resulting graph is justified according to how "deep" each room in the building is. The final graph is thus referred to as a *j-graph*. The advantage of the *j-graph* is its ability to summarize and display the relative accessibility or segregation of a building in a visual format that can be immediately apprehended, even without any knowledge or appreciation of space syntax per se. The *j-graph* also is a powerful analytic device in that it is from this graph that a number of quantitative syntactical properties of a building can be calculated. Hillier and Hanson refer often to the properties of *symmetry* vs. *asymmetry* and *distributedness* vs. *nondistributedness*. In terms of these properties' social significance, Hillier and Hanson (1984: 96–97) note that *symmetry* in a building tends to promote social integration between social categories like inhabitants and visitors to a building, while *asymmetry* is correlated with segregation between social groups. Similarly, a greater degree of spatial *distributedness* across a building plan tends to be related to diffuse spatial control, or power, while greater *nondistributedness* is associated with unitary, superordinate spatial control.

Figure 5.8 shows the *j-graph* of Building I/VI from Tell Tayinat. Immediately apparent is the parallel architectural layout that characterizes both wings of the building: both Building I and Building VI have a single room at a depth of 1 (rooms I.E and VI.G, respectively) that leads into a further single room at a depth of 2 (rooms I.J and VI.E). This latter room serves as its building's control point from which the remainder of the building is accessed. Another feature to emerge from the *j-graph* in Figure 5.8 is the limited range of options available to the individual moving into the building from the courtyard. In almost every instance, each room in the entire complex can only be accessed via a single, specific route; there are practically no alternatives available. What this suggests is that the palace can be

Depth

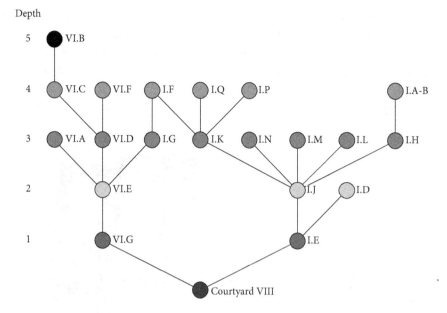

<figure>
FIGURE 5.8
Justified graph of Building I/VI according to the principles of space syntax.
</figure>

characterized as being *nondistributed* in the sense that in several—indeed, almost all—instances access between two rooms is controlled by another room, and there is generally only one way to access a specific room. At the same time, Figure 5.8 makes Building I/VI look fairly symmetrical. There is a significant exception to these generalizations, of course, and that is the link that exists between the two wings of the building in the passage between VI.E and I.G. This particular relationship of permeability has the effect of mitigating the quantitative variables that indicate integration/segregation, but as a single instance it does not counteract the overall impression of symmetry.

We can further consider the syntax property known as *control value*, which proposes a mathematical method to express the relative influence a room in a building exerts over its neighbors, based on the number of neighboring units with which they interact. The control value is determined in the following way: each room in a building is assigned a value of 1; this value is then divided equally among the rooms' immediate neighbors, such that a room with four neighbors gives one-quarter to each, for example; the values each room has received from its neighbors are then totaled, and a higher total indicates greater control (Hillier and Hanson 1984: 109). Because each room gives a certain amount of value to each neighbor but also receives a certain amount of value from each neighbor, rooms with control values less than 1 can be considered relatively weak control spaces; those with control values greater than 1 can be considered relatively controlling (Figure 5.9). The immediately striking feature of Figure 5.9 is the dominant presence of room I.J. At least according to the principle of the control value, I.J is, with a control value of 4.08, both alone in its category[16] and the only room to top a control value of 4. Room I.K is likewise alone in its class range, having a control value of 2.66. These

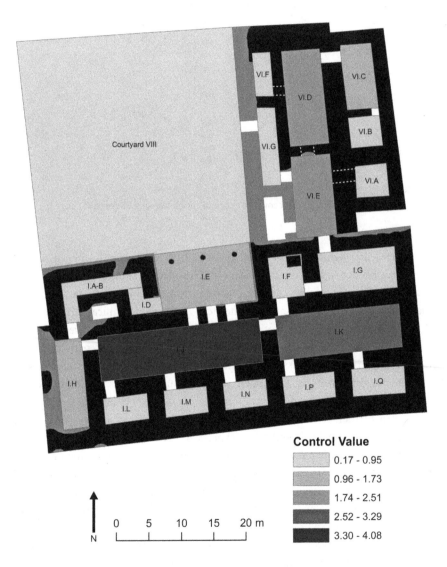

FIGURE 5.9
Plan of Building I/VI with rooms shaded according to their control value.

two rooms' high control values are a function of their having a high number of neighbors, neighbors that themselves have a low number of neighbors, such that I.J and I.K are giving small values to the rooms around them, but receiving high values from them.

Architectural parallels already lead us to believe that room I.J was a significant one, even the most significant one. Foremost among these is the known location of thrones in Iron Age palaces. Mostly these locations are determined from the stone throne bases or daises which are found in situ. Palace J and K from Zincirli, roughly contemporaneous with Building I/VI at Tayinat, both have hearth fixtures in the left side of their equivalent rooms, J.3 and K.2 respectively, and K.2 even has a throne base against the wall behind the hearth (Frankfort 1952: 122–24, von Luschan and Jacoby 1911: Abb. 175). Thrones are found in the equivalent locations in Assyrian throne room suites as well, beginning with room B of Ashurnasirpal II's Northwest Palace and continuing throughout subsequent Assyrian palaces at Khorsabad and Nineveh (Turner 1970: pl. XXXVIII). In light of these parallels, it would seem that room I.J is a very likely candidate for the palace complex's throne room, despite the absence of a throne base.

Combining these various threads of evidence to interpret the *bīt-ḫilāni* at Tell Tayinat, we see there was a consistent theme running throughout the corpora of works of art and historical inscriptions, both Syro-Anatolian and Assyrian. This motif was the importance of the royal throne and its nature as an object that fused the idea of legitimate kingship, the royal symbology of the palace, and the body of the king himself into a single object that communicated these messages to the viewer. This theme appeared in Luwian inscriptions that equate the establishment of the throne with acquiring rulership and, of course, the monumental throne fragments that were discovered in the courtyard before Tayinat's *bīt-ḫilāni* and whose formal properties demonstrate the visual equivalence of throne and palace. Space syntax then illustrated aspects of the actual performance of kingship in space. One of these was the unique significance of room I.J in Building I, a room that, if cultural and regional parallels are valid, can only have been the throne room of the palace. The palace was laid in such a way that encouraged interaction at the interface of visitor and king, but that nevertheless restricted visitors in their freedom of movement and contained them within this reception area. To demonstrate the meaningful relevance of this fact, consider that, once restricted to the reception area by the syntactical properties of the *bīt-ḫilāni*'s layout, the visitor to this building occupied an architectural space that was constructed out of symbols associated with kingship—columns, column bases, capitals, and the like—and shared that space with the throne, the unmistakable symbol of kingship, that was itself built out of architectural elements associated with the palace—columns, column bases, and volute capitals. These associations were present in writing and artistic display, just as they were present in physical space, to ensure the greatest possible efficacy of the *bīt-ḥilāni*'s message of political authority. The tightly bound nexus of symbols that the *bīt-ḥilāni* embodied communicated the message of authority to all who entered it, just as did the orientations of the walls themselves.

To conclude this section on SACC's urban layouts, the strange loop that these topographies, structures, and monuments created together is perhaps most easily grasped with a journey through a single Syro-Anatolian city. Tell Tayinat, ancient Kunulua, provides a strong case for how the meaningful properties of these buildings and sculptures were formally coordinated to achieve full symbolic effect because its history of excavation and survey has provided a reasonably thorough understanding of its Iron Age II layout, despite significant gaps in our spatial awareness of the city's plan (Figure 5.10).

An individual in Kunulua's lower town (perhaps having entered the city via Gateway XI on the eastern edge of the city) moved up into the upper city through Gateway VII and, while passing through that structure that itself conjured associations of both city and king, likewise encountered a monumental royal statue that may have not just represented, but embodied the king himself (Gelb 1939: LXXIX). From there one continued westward into the center of the upper city where one came upon Kunulua's sacred precinct marked by a pair of temples, Buildings II and XVI (Harrison and Osborne 2012; Osborne et al. 2019) that were situated at the center of the upper city, guaranteeing them maximum access (Osborne 2014: 204). Located in the vicinity, and possibly on a pedestal directly in front of Building XVI, was a lengthy Luwian inscription, TELL TAYINAT 2, boasting of the king's building accomplishments: Among other snippets in this highly fragmentary text we read " . . . I expelled . . . s from the land . . . ," " . . . I built . . . ," "and the latter wi[dened?] the roads . . . ," "I myself found them," "this statue . . . ," and so on. Although the evidence is exiguous, this appears to be the primary monument in Kunulua extolling the power of royal authority (Hawkins 2000: 367–75). Critically, renewed excavations in the space between these two temples have uncovered what appears to be another gateway, Building XVII, though its precise spatial relationship to its surroundings remains to be determined (Harrison and Denel 2017: 139–46). Basalt statues were found in association with it, including a beautifully carved life-size lion and the intact upper third of a colossal royal statue with a Luwian inscription on the back identifying him as Suppiluliuma II; the royal statue appears to have been buried face down in the passageway of the gate itself, while the lion was buried immediately beside the structure (2017: 146–51).[17] Once again, the pedestrian was barraged with royal symbolism in multiple forms: architecture, and human and animal statuary.

Only past these two symbolically rich locations did one continue on one's way toward Gate V and up into the palace compound that was itself the heart of royal

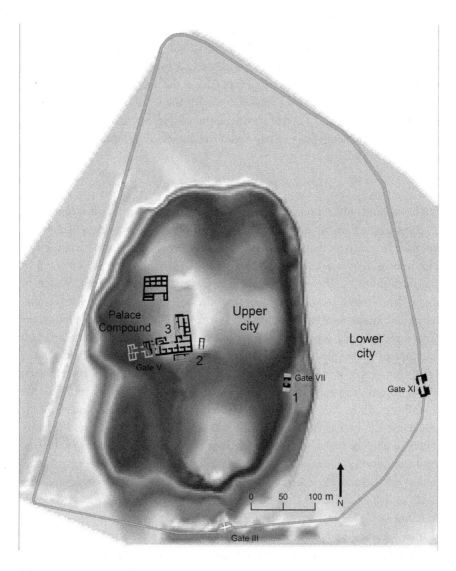

FIGURE 5.10
Site plan of Tell Tayinat, ancient Kunulua, according to present knowledge, with symbolic nodes marked: (1) Gateway VII, including destroyed colossal statue (McEwan 1937: Fig. 11); (2) Buildings II, XVI, and XVI, including colossal statue of Suppiluliuma II and accompanying Hieroglyphic Luwian inscription, destroyed inscription TELL TAYINAT 2, and life-size lion statue; (3) palace compound, including monumental basalt throne with the palace portico's "column base" and "columns" depicted as throne legs.

symbolism manifested in text, imagery, and the building itself. In this way the assemblage of meanings that was associated with Kunulua's monuments was continuously and inevitably reinforced by the relationship between city and pedestrian that the urban form imposed on its occupants. This is the definition of "strange loop" described earlier: no matter at what juncture in the urban hierarchy one found oneself, the same cluster of meanings was constantly present, such that escaping the symbolic-spatial hierarchy of a Syro-Anatolian city was all but impossible.

## Counter-monumentality and Urban Resistance

But lest this reconstruction of a monolithic urban symbology that confronted city dwellers in the Syro-Anatolian city-states with perpetual reminders of royal legitimacy be taken as the entirety of urban experience, it is worth recalling that this strange loop was a spatial hierarchy mostly designed and implemented by central authorities. The extent to which it was actually experienced as such by urban dwellers is a topic less frequently addressed than questions of urban planning and monumental art production. The reasons for this are clear enough: the large-scale building projects of the palace and the monumental stone arts that accompanied them are both well preserved and the disproportionate recipient of scholarly interest. Ironically, however, it is the very permanence of these objects that rendered them subject to protest, rendering them the sites where resistance to authority is, in fact, most visible (Osborne 2017a). Monuments are typically understood in archaeology (e.g., Van Dyke and Alcock 2003) as vehicles with which to analyze social memory in the sense of Maurice Halbwachs (1980) and Paul Connerton (1989). In the case of SACC, for example, monuments of royal figures lead naturally to interpretations of rulers being recast and reimagined after death as deified ancestors (Bonatz 2000, 2001: 68–70). Yet practices of counter-monumentality, or active and deliberate engagement with monuments in ways that are specifically counter to their original intent, reveals that the same process of materializing a specific celebrated message in a physical object (*sensu* DeMarrais et al. 1996: 18–19) simultaneously renders that message vulnerable to contestation and reinterpretation.

Earlier we saw how common it was in SACC for monumental statues to be placed in critical urban junctures like gateways. Because a number of statue fragments have been found in highly fragmentary condition, it is difficult to assess precisely how many have already been discovered. With one significant exception from Carchemish, these statues are standing figures, and all but one from Tell Halaf are males. Complete (or reconstructed) examples range from 2.5 to 3 m in height, which was increased even further by statue bases in the form of striding lions or bulls. At 3.8 m without a base, the royal monument from Malatya is the tallest in the corpus (Orthmann 1971: 522). Although each statue is unique, the iconography is consistent across the examples: a tall, robed figure standing or sitting atop a statue base comprised of lions or bulls grasps objects like a blade or a cup in hands kept close to his sides. He is dressed in a long gown and wears a curly beard with a shaved upper lip (Figure 5.4). As we have seen already, these statues were often found inscribed in one of the languages present in SACC.

Counter-monumental practices are attested across many of these objects, a phenomenon that complicates the traditional interpretation of the statues as representations of royal power. The seated Atrisuhas statue from Carchemish, for example, was found smashed into sixty pieces, its original appearance approximated by the reconstruction of the excavator (Woolley 1952: 199). There are three major aspects of the monuments' postinstallation treatment that reveal countermonumental activity toward the statues: one is complete destruction of the statue, another is the highly localized defacement of specific features of the individual's body, especially the nose, eyes, and hands, and a third is the deliberate burial of the statue. At least eleven of SACC's monumental statutes were discovered in various states of destruction, ranging from a few large chunks of statue to many dozen small fragments. The latter in particular would have required a sustained effort to accomplish, especially in the case of statues made of the extremely hard basalt, and signals an unusually extreme case of a counter-monumental practice. The usual culprit invoked for such unambiguous acts of destruction is the invading Assyrians at the time of their conquest (e.g., Ussishkin 1970: 128). They are a logical candidate, given their historically attested invasions of the region, and Assyrian destruction may have indeed been the case for many of these examples.

However, there is nothing directly connecting the Assyrians to any of the destruction events. The Syro-Anatolian city-states themselves were constantly at battle with one another over various disputes, and it is equally likely that they took turns destroying each other's symbols of royal authority during these conflicts. Even more intriguing is the presence of violent conflict within individual kingdoms. We learn from Shalmaneser III's Black Obelisk, for example, that the kingdom of Patina was convulsed by internal conflict surrounding a contested succession in 829 BCE (Grayson 1996: RIMA 3 A.0.102.14 146b–156a)[18]—precisely the time when Tayinat's two royal colossal statues were made, one of which was smashed to pieces. Likewise, we know that the city-state of Carchemish was home to two coeval dynasties during the tenth century BCE, the so-called Great Kings and Country Lords (Hawkins 1995c). Such internecine rivalries were endemic throughout the region. Equally as plausible as the Assyrians, then, is the likelihood that some of the broken monumental statues were destroyed by citizens of their own kingdoms.

More subtle, perhaps, is the minor defacing that some of the statues have received. Seven of the statues still with relatively complete bodies and heads nevertheless had their noses removed. This is too great a number to be an issue of preservation: these monuments must have been deliberately defaced. Also removed were eyes and eye inlays, though in this case it is more difficult to distinguish defacement from issues of preservation. This practice of nose removal has a Late Bronze Age Hittite precedent where it was conducted to remove the agency of the image, as indicated by contemporary texts and images (Goedegebuure 2012). This may also have continued to be the case for the Syro-Anatolian city-states, and it is possible that the removal of the nose, and sometimes eyes and hands, was intended to rob the ancestor of his or her sensory capabilities, such that it was no longer able to "smell," "see," or "touch." Either way, damaging the face of these statues was another clear act of resistance to the message of royal power associated with the memory of royal ancestors that was presented by the monuments. Particularly intriguing are the cases where both nose removal and total statue destruction are present, as is the case with two of the monuments from Carchemish, the statue from Gerçin, and two from Tell Halaf. Because there are statues that have had their noses removed but were not otherwise destroyed (Malatya, Zincirli), it follows that several of these statues were subjected to various episodes of counter-monumental practices as their reception moved back and forth between different communities of people over time.

Finally, the rare but significant treatment of the royal monuments described earlier bears mentioning: the burial of the statue either in a stone-lined pit, as at Zincirli, or in an above-ground tomb, as at Malatya. A third possible example is the newly discovered statue from Tell Tayinat, deposited in an unlined pit. These events indicate an almost reverential treatment of the statues, as one would bury a human. These burials, which would have involved considerable effort, were likely made by supporters of the royal establishment, the most unambiguous message in the archaeological record that the colossal royal figures were accepted as legitimate by at least a portion of the local population. Tell Tayinat even has examples of both statue treatments: fragments of a colossal statue were found in the 1930s excavations of Gateway VII, which controlled pedestrian traffic from the lower town into the acropolis, while a roughly contemporary and well-preserved example, bearing a Hieroglyphic Luwian inscription naming the figure as the king Suppiluliuma, was found face-down in a pit that cut through a stone surface before the city temple.

Quite unlike the common intent behind a monument's creation—to create and perpetually reproduce a specific message on the part of a particular individual or community as standard and universal—practices of counter-monumentality reveal that urban monuments were received by city dwellers in ways that were not necessarily compatible with the goal of the monuments to perpetuate royal legitimacy.

The historical record suggested a host of plausible culprits for these actions, ranging from disaffected local communities to conquering forces. That these events did not go unchallenged, however, is indicated by the postdefacing practice of ritual interment, a practice that is perhaps best understood as undertaken by someone sympathetic with the monument's original project. It will always be difficult to know the precise circumstances in which resistance to royal monuments was enacted. But it is clear that such circumstances arose quite frequently, and counter-monumentality in SACC is thus one of the best opportunities to discern tears in the tightly woven fabric of urban planning.

: : :

## Towns and Villages

Our knowledge of spatial dynamics outside of the largest Syro-Anatolian cities is slight. In addition, the excavations that have focused on secondary and tertiary settlements within the Syro-Anatolian city-states have rarely been of a sufficiently large horizontal scale to produce substantial town plans. Such is the case, for example, with the excavations at the roughly 5.5 ha Tell Abou Danné, located 25 km east of Aleppo, where horizontal exposure did not exceed 450 sq m (Lebeau 1983: 3, Figs. 3–5). Others have not produced significant architectural remains from the late second and early first millennium, such as the patchy, heavily pitted, and stratigraphically ambiguous architectural fragments from Level IIe-f at Kilise Tepe in the Göksu Valley (Bouthillier et al. 2014; Postgate 2007: 34; Postgate and Thomas 2007a: 152–63). Nevertheless, there are a small number of excavated sites whose horizontal exposures were sufficiently broad and well preserved to provide insight into the character of settlement layouts in nonurban centers.

One such site is Çatal Höyük in the Amuq Valley, 16 km northeast of Tell Tayinat. We saw earlier how gravity modeling predicted this site to be one of Patina's *ālāni dannūti*, or fortified cities, as labeled by the Assyrians, and its 10 ha size places it in the second tier of Patina's settlement hierarchy. (A possible lower town off the west side of the mound is faintly visible in satellite imagery, which would make the site approximately 15 ha in size; cf. Pucci 2019: pl. 191.) The mound was explored between 1933 and 1936 by the same Syrian-Hittite Expedition of the University of Chicago that excavated Tayinat, but overlapping with the Tayinat excavations for only one season (Haines 1971: 3). The primary goal of the excavation was to find monumental architecture from the capital of Patina, and although they were disappointed in this respect—hence the decision to remove to Tayinat—the result is a large amount of data from a secondary center within the kingdom. Like Tayinat, only the early periods were published in full (Braidwood and Braidwood 1960), although the late periods did have their architectural remains published

(Haines 1971), and a recent publication by Marina Pucci (2019) offers the final report. During the Iron II period, the site does not have discrete strata, but rather consists of continuously remodeled houses. The phases as presented by Haines and Pucci thus represent attempts to place this material into a coherent stratigraphic sequence, with choices made regarding what was considered contemporary during the creation of a compilation plan of the site during Amuq Phase O, the Iron Age II period (Figure 5.11).[19]

The site plan is clear that during the Iron Age II period the settlement was essentially covered with "crowded irregular complexes of private houses" (Haines 1971: 7). There do appear to be distinct streets through the city, some of which are even pebble laid. The two clearest of these pass north-south through the middle of Area I, and east-west in the southwest corner of the tell. But their irregularity nevertheless indicates that they were laid to accommodate where houses happened to have been built, and not the houses arranged according to the streets. Neither are the houses of a standard shape or size. In short, there is very little that is indicative of any overt political authority mandating the layout of the town's plan. On the contrary, the site is an excellent example of the Mediterranean style of settlement in which irregular lanes culminating in unpredictable cul-de-sacs and densely packed structures are highly evocative of a kinship-oriented social structure (Schloen 2001: 108–16, 127–33), suggesting that this town was largely under local autonomy, although the larger structure in Area IV may have served as some kind of elite residence.[20] In any event, Çatal Höyük appears not to have possessed any principles of restricted internal accessibility, monumentality, orthogonality, alignment, or geometric order during the Iron Age II.

One significant exception to this conclusion, of course, is the fortification wall that likely encircled the town, though it was only found preserved along the western edge (Haines 1971: 4–5). At 3 m in width, the wall was not enormous, but nevertheless represents a substantial defensive feature. The wall is therefore the likeliest indication for some kind of planning by a higher political authority, and it is the primary reason to consider it one of Patina's "fortified cities" mentioned earlier. Given the predominantly quotidian domestic character of the structures found throughout, it comes as some surprise that the settlement is walled at all. It is quite likely that the town had important economic functions that needed permanent protection, a likelihood that is supported by its location at the junction of the Amuq and Afrin transport corridors. It is also possible that, during times of military danger, people living in the nearby unprotected villages needed both a place to flee to and a fixed location in which to concentrate resistance, and for this purpose a protected site was created. If either or both of these were indeed roles played by the *ālāni dannūti* like Çatal Höyük, this would be modest evidence for involvement in the affairs of the town on the part of the political authority of Patina.

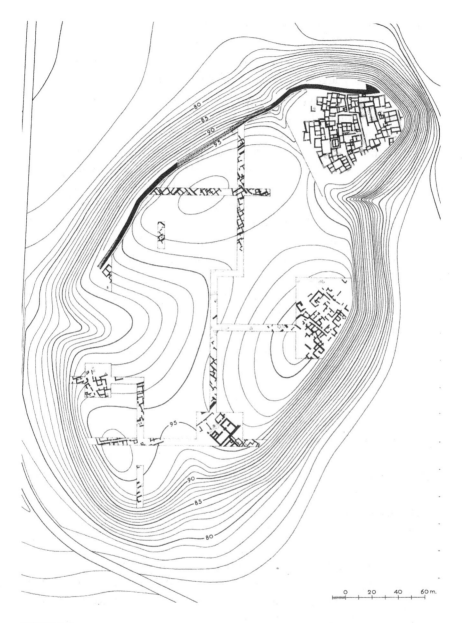

FIGURE 5.11
Plan of Çatal Höyük during the Iron Age II period, or Amuq Phase O. (Haines 1971: Pl. 20, courtesy of the Oriental Institute Museum)

In sum, its substantial areal extent notwithstanding, Çatal Höyük is not dissimilar from what one might expect from a village or hamlet in plan except for the fact that it had a fortification wall. It follows that the spatial expression of political power was far less marked at this tier of the settlement hierarchy than it was at the capital cities, where "strange loop" designs provided evidence of city planning that appears almost entirely missing here.

Another second-tier settlement that warrants mention is the site of 'Ain Dara, a 24 ha site in the Afrin Valley located roughly 18 km west of Tell Rifa'at, ancient Arpad. This site has unfortunately not yet received the same amount of horizontal exposure as Çatal Höyük, yet excavations in both the upper and lower city have revealed enough of its character to comprehend the nature of its planning. In the upper city, excavations unearthed a large temple with walls lined with orthostats whose dating has been subject to debate (Abu 'Assaf 1990); given the possibility that the orthostats are in secondary use and the lack of publication of any small finds, it is difficult to discern whether the temple's primary use phase belongs to the late second or early first millennium BCE (see Chapter 3). At 32 × 38 m in size, and replete with a variety of monumental sculpted basalt statuary, it is clear that this temple reflects the coordinated building effort of an authority higher than the regular citizens who lived at the site. The description provided by Elizabeth Stone and Paul Zimansky aptly indicate how political authority must have been involved in its construction:

> In both size and intricacy of workmanship it is virtually unparalleled: squared limestone and basalt blocks of enormous size pave the approach to it, reliefs of lions and sphinxes surround its exterior, rows of lions in protome standing more than two meters high once formed the faces of both the inner courtyard and the building itself, and four enormous footprints—each approximately one meter in length—carved into its threshold blocks give measure to the awesome majesty of the deity who resided there. (Stone and Zimansky 1999: 1)

Less clear is whether the acropolis was walled, although subsequent layers (Schicht I–VI) were fortified (Abu 'Assaf 1990: 1–10, Abb. 4, 6). The excavators of the large lower town plausibly speculated that the entire lower city was walled based on the morphology of the site, especially its steep sides and depressions where gates were likely situated (Stone and Zimansky 1999: 2). Yet excavations in two 10 × 10 m squares in the northeast quadrant of the site revealed a series of unimposing domestic structures belonging to the early first millennium BCE, or Iron Age II period (1999: 35–55). The excavators emphasize how mundane the material assemblage of this nonelite residential quarter is—"What strikes one most of all is how ordinary the place is" (1999: 139)—a remarkable finding given the extraordinary nature of the temple on the upper city. In the end, 'Ain Dara appears to have been a large settlement mostly occupied by common citizens that nevertheless saw significant intervention by authorities in the form of a monumental temple and fortification wall. This situation seems nearly identical to Tell Afis, ancient Hazrak, which likewise had a large-scale temple in its fortified upper city (Mazzoni 2014a).

By contrast, Sirkeli Höyük in the Cilician plain 40 km east of Adana is in many respects anomalous from the patterns displayed by other secondary centers. The site is perhaps best known as the setting of the Late Bronze Age relief of Muwatalli II (r. 1306–1282 BCE), the earliest known royal rock relief of the Hittite Empire (Ehringhaus 2005: 95–201), yet its Iron Age history is no less remarkable. The excavators tentatively associate it with Lawazantiya, birthplace of the famous Hittite queen Puduhepa, or the religious center Kummani (Kozal and Novák 2013: 230). Despite the fact that it was not a capital city, the settlement appears to have been as large as SACC's largest cities: the site has expanded in size with every season of fieldwork conducted by the ongoing research project there, which to date has discovered that the combined size of the upper mound and sprawling lower settlement at Sirkeli Höyük is at least 80 ha (Novák 2018: 263). Although the horizontal extent of excavations has remained limited, remote sensing has demonstrated this large lower town to possess not only dense occupation but also a double fortification wall. The size and site morphology of Sirkeli Höyük would thus place it among Syro-Anatolian capitals, yet its historical status within the city-state of Que correspond more with sites like Çatal Höyük and 'Ain Dara. Additional fieldwork at the site is necessary in order to clarify this apparent discrepancy.

At the bottom of the settlement hierarchy, the village—what the Assyrians referred to as the *ālāni ša limēti*, or "cities in the neighborhood—provides us with a view of the spatial order that characterized the majority of the Iron Age population of the Syro-Anatolian region. Here, too, there has been precious little Iron Age excavation across SACC with significant horizontal exposures, but a handful of excavation projects stand out for providing important details on rural architecture. One of these is Tell Mastuma, a site under 3 ha in size—and less at its surface—located 15 km west of Tell Afis, ancient Hazrak, and thus within the general area of the city-state of Hamath. Tell Mastuma was excavated by the Ancient Orient Museum of Tokyo from 1980 to 1995. Several preliminary articles appeared during those years in the *Bulletin of the Ancient Orient Museum* and elsewhere (Egami et al. 1988–89; Wada 1994; Wakita et al. 1995; Wakita et al. 2000), and a final excavation report was recently published (Iwasaki et al. 2009). This small, circular mound was excavated explicitly to provide a holistic picture of an Iron Age domestic site. The result was that roughly 40 percent of the Iron Age settlement was exposed, an unusually high proportion (2009: 3–7). Such an achievement was attainable because despite the site's long history of occupation, the Iron Age layer is close to the surface: the four phases (a–d) of uppermost Stratum I-2 belong to the ninth and eighth centuries (2009: 55–57).

Figure 5.12 shows the plan of the site and its residential blocks published by the excavators and reprinted in important syntheses (e.g., Akkermans and Schwartz 2003: Fig. 11.5). Using this plan, the excavators state that "the Iron Age settlement was laid out according to a well-organized plan" (Iwasaki et al. 2009: 91). At first this would appear to be a sound conclusion: the "central avenue" does seem remarkably straight (although roads do not necessarily have to be planned to be straight), and the "semicircular road" appears deliberately constructed as such. On closer inspection, however, the evidence for planning is lighter than it seems. For one thing, even the "central avenue" takes an unusual turn at the "north square," and the "semicircular road" is so constricted in the northwest corner of the exposed area "that a man could barely pass" (Iwasaki et al. 2009: 101). The curved passageway then becomes less a deliberate street and more an irregular path that happens to be curved in this area. Indeed, if one extrapolates the plan as it currently stands by two and a half times to occupy the full surface of the tell, it is entirely possible that the impression of regularity may only be an accident of the 40 percent surface exposure, high though that proportion may be. Even the houses on the edge of the site, which in Figure 5.12 the excavators have confidently restored as following the edge of the mound in a defensive manner, may prove to be far more irregular upon resumed excavation. If one were to expand the plan of the settlement to fill the entire surface of the mound, then it is much more likely that we would arrive at a settlement of irregular houses and streets resembling Çatal Höyük than we would the planned circular settlement of, for example, the roughly contemporary Tel Beer Sheba Stratum II in the southern Levant (Herzog 1997: 244–47).

Beyond the limitations of exposure, the excavators' interpretation of Tell Mastuma's Iron Age site plan is hampered by methodological decisions not noted on the plan itself. The plan provided in Figure 5.12 was created as follows:

> The northern half of the settlement is restored on the basis of the plan of Level a, while the southern part is restored on the basis of the plan of Level b, and the southernmost part is restored on the basis of the plans of Level c and Level d. Therefore, the restored settlement presented here is not a real plan of a specific architectural layout but a hypothetical archetype. (Iwasaki et al. 2009: 98)

Comparing the town's layout in the "archetype" and its actual remains, one realizes that the south gate was only there in the earliest of the four subphases; that the semicircular road was "interrupted or detoured" and block 1 not in use during subphase b; and that blocks 1 and 2 were both abandoned in subphase a (Iwasaki

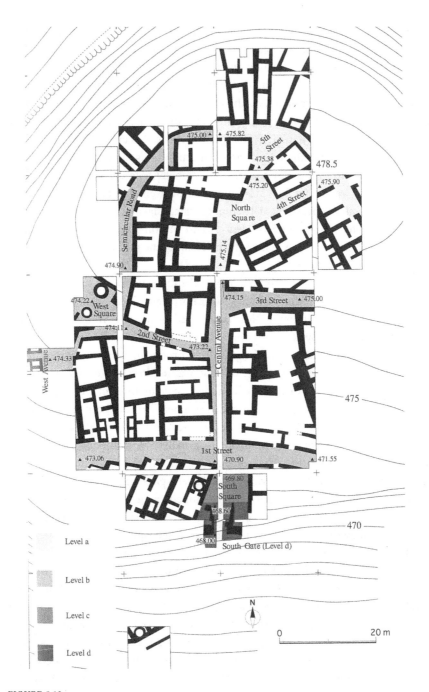

Level a

Level b

Level c

Level d

FIGURE 5.12
Plan of Tell Mastuma during the Iron Age II period, Stratum IIa–d. (Adapted from Iwasaki et al. 2009: Fig. 4.1)

et al. 2009; 98–102). By telescoping significant stratigraphical discrepancies into a single hypothetical occupation, the excavators have created a misleading final plan instead of accurate phase-by-phase illustrations. Combining the published plan with descriptions of the phases of Stratum IIa–d as excavated—which clearly render the village far less organized than the excavators' idealized reconstruction—it is apparent that there is no need to interpret the village as having been laid out according to a predetermined plan. On the contrary, it is even less likely that this village represents anything more than a collection of agglutinated structures like Çatal Höyük, and in this case we must additionally note the absence of any fortification wall, rendering Tell Mastuma without even that one degree of some kind of centralized oversight determining village layout. All of the structures were interpreted as domestic residences, and the differences between the four subphases of Stratum II are thus likely the result of the normal lifecycle of household demographics.[21]

Another village-level site to have received substantial horizontal exposure is Tille Höyük, located on the Euphrates River northeast of Samsat, and thus within the broad region of Kummuḫ. Now submerged in the reservoir created by the Atatürk Dam, Tille Höyük was excavated from 1978 to 1990 by the British Institute of Archaeology at Ankara as a salvage project, producing the most significant remains from its Iron Age levels (Blaylock 2009, 2016). Precise areal measurements are not available, partially because of a modern town on the southern slopes of the mound, but from the description provided it appears to have been approximately 1.5–2.0 ha in size during the Iron Age, with a lower terrace of roughly the same size, though of uncertain Iron Age occupation (Blaylock 2009: 3; 2016: 395). The site has been tentatively associated with Kulmadara, a town in the city-state of Kummuḫ named in two fragmentary inscriptions of Tiglath-pileser III (2009: 35–37).

Although Iron Age I remains were identified in limited soundings at Tille Höyük, nearly the entirety of the mound's surface was exposed in the Iron Age II period, dated by the excavators to the late tenth–late eighth century primarily on the basis of the appearance of Red Slipped Burnished Ware and Ribbed Ware at the period's outset and the 708 BCE conquest of Kummuḫ by Sargon II at its conclusion.[22] Levels IV–VII—with IV being the earliest—date to this period, although levels VI and VII were ephemeral and heavily pitted; even the earlier levels IV and V (Figure 5.13), though well preserved in plan, possessed extremely thin deposits (2009: 87–126, Table 2.4). Although level IV is spread across three small terraces whose orientations do not continue into the following phase, there is otherwise a great deal of continuity between levels IV and V. Structures of both phases have rectilinear plans with substantial private courtyards, rooms built side by side instead of sharing party walls, columned halls in the largest rooms, and posts that, where present, likely supported a second story. Likewise, the positioning of the streets is

FIGURE 5.13
Plan of Tille Höyük during the Iron Age II period: Level IV (*top*) and Level V (*bottom*).
(Blaylock 2009: Figs. 6.4 and 6.12, courtesy of the British Institute at Ankara)

similar enough that the excavators propose level V to have been a development of the same basic plan, rather than a separate replacement of level IV (2009: 110).

The most logical way to interpret these plans, which include the presence of querns and other domestic features as well as large brick- and stone-lined pits presumably used for grain storage, is as domestic residences whose sizes and room arrangements fluctuate over time with the expanding and contracting sizes of the households that occupy them.[23] Noting the same lack of broad exposures of early first-millennium nonpalatial sites that we saw earlier, the excavators parallel the architectural layout of Iron Age II Tille Höyük with the domestic residences of Çatal Höyük (2009: 124). Differences between them include the use of post bases at Tille and not Çatal, and the structural similarities are mostly generic, but it seems accurate that the dense distribution of irregularly laid, small houses divided by gravel-laid streets is indeed closely comparable.[24] Lacking the defensive wall and elite structure of Çatal, however, Tille Höyük in the early first millennium seems even closer to Tell Mastuma than to Çatal Höyük: an agglutinated village with no clear evidence for planning above the level of the household.

In sum, from what little we know about the built environments of multiple settlement types within the Syro-Anatolian city-states, it seems that the archaeological record displays a hierarchical order of royal investment in town planning: there is a significant degree of political authority on display at the capital city, but thereafter we see a distinct decrease of political authority in the townscape of secondary centers like Çatal Höyük and 'Ain Dara such that overt messages of power are only seen in the city wall and isolated elite structures. At the lowest scale of the settlement hierarchy we detect little to no evidence for anything beyond individual and family-based agency in the development of the village. This is, in fact, the driving force for the majority of the remains at Çatal Höyük, and, although we will not know until the area is more fully excavated, most likely the impetus behind the architecture of the lower town at 'Ain Dara as well. In this case, the archaeological evidence is quite compelling that political authority was most aggressively expressed at the urban capital city—though even here it did not go unchallenged, as we have seen—much less so in the fortified towns, and possibly not at all in the numerous villages. Clearly the capital city was the major focus of energy in terms of a royal effort to manipulate the built environment in such a way as to communicate his authority. If the nature of space is any indication, then beyond the capital city there is little evidence that the political authority of the rulers in Kunulua was felt at all, particularly in the villages.

::: 

## Conclusion

To the extent that our archaeological and historical evidence allows us to reconstruct notions of space and place in SACC, it is evident that the relationship of space and power was highly variable within individual Syro-Anatolian city-states. Depending on context, entirely different principles of spatial ordering may be in operation, such that definitive pictures of how space was envisioned and experienced are all but impossible to draw, and nearly every instance of spatial authority in the archaeological and historical record is rendered interpretively unstable by evidence for countervailing factors.

At the regional scale of analysis, territorial sovereignty is supported by contemporary Assyrian inscriptions that describe a three-tiered settlement hierarchy, one that is apparently confirmed by settlement pattern analysis that identifies a disproportionately large urban center and capital city, a handful of secondary settlements, and several dozen rural villages. But even while this model must reflect the operation of the political economy on some level, native textual sources from within SACC describe processes of trading settlements between kingdoms not even necessarily contiguous with one another, evidently continuing a Bronze Age practice in the region. Closer inspection of settlement patterns, too, reveals variable practices of territorial sovereignty, such as Al Mina's likely status as Kunulua's port despite being located several dozen kilometers away, or the existence of isolated villages apparently unconnected to settlement hierarchies. I therefore proposed that the Syro-Anatolian model of regional sovereignty be referred to as "malleable territoriality," a far cry from the container model of the nation-state.

Within the capital cities themselves, enough evidence for city planning exists that they seem to have been consciously designed as strange loops, recursive hierarchies where the same feature—in this case, a message of royal authority—appears and reappears regardless of what level one finds oneself in the hierarchy. City gates were symbolically associated with royal power in inscriptions, and royal statues were conspicuously placed in the physically elevated high-traffic gateways that funneled pedestrians deeper into the city to additional gateways lined with royal statuary, until one arrived at the royal palace, SACC's starkest and most successful combination of royal symbolism and spatial properties emphasizing control of access. This immensely effective coordination of formal urban design with symbolically laden text and imagery is testament to the ability of Syro-Anatolian city planners to shape urban morphology, and to the power of the king to communicate his message in the built environment. At the same time, however, materializing this message in physical form likewise rendered it vulnerable to challenge and contestation. Indeed, the majority of SACC's most recognizable pieces of monumental art are damaged in some way, whether outright destroyed or simply mutilated in specific locations, and several were found buried for motives that are difficult to discern. As challenging as specific instances of counter-monumentality may be to interpret historically, what is clear is that the message of royal authority displayed in Syro-Anatolian capital cities was under constant negotiation, and therefore one cannot assume analytically that the fact of a message's existence necessarily corresponds with its successful reception.

Finally, this chapter reached beyond the capital city and into the towns and villages of the Syro-Anatolian countryside to see what the built environments of secondary and tertiary settlements indicate regarding centralized intervention in settlement layouts. As noted by many scholars, the robust architectural evidence needed for this kind of investigation is lacking, but enough has been generated to formulate provisional conclusions. Unlike how even small-scale settlements tend to be interpreted by their excavators, the evidence for town planning is slim even in secondary centers, and nonexistent in rural villages. Large towns were apparently walled (e.g., Çatal Höyük, 'Ain Dara, Tell Afis), but either had little evidence for anything beyond small-scale domestic architecture (Çatal Höyük), or had a single sacred building that represented larger than household-scale energy investment ('Ain Dara, Tell Afis). This contrasts with the capital cities, where excavations and survey have begun to reveal evidence for elite activity even in lower towns (Herrmann 2017a; Osborne 2017b; Osborne and Karacic 2017). Villages and towns, meanwhile, seem to provide architectural evidence for nothing other than continuous cycles of household birth, growth, and decline, as one would expect in rural settings left to their own devices. To the extent that the major urban centers of SACC consist of "elites behind walls" (Novák 2018), therefore, it seems ever more likely that people living in nonurban centers did not experience their built environments conscious of centralized planning or messages of royal authority.

Insofar as space is implicated in the nation-state model, the discussion herein provides another reason to question the assumption of scholarship that these Iron Age polities can be understood in such terms. Quite unlike the nation-state, where the relationship of space and power is (allegedly) evenly applied throughout a contained territory, we have seen that Syro-Anatolian territories were not contained, but rather were malleable; that capital cities were tightly coordinated spatially and symbolically, but continually contested; and that the state's presence was barely felt in settlements beyond the capital. These findings are inconsistent with the expectations of the nation-state, and SACC's social logic of space provides further reasoning no longer to deploy it as our default model. The remarkable consistency of these findings across the Syro-Anatolian region, however, do point toward a justification for treating SACC as an analytical category, and this volume turns to this point in greater detail in the following concluding chapter.

## CHAPTER 6

# CONCLUSION
## *Defining the Syro-Anatolian Culture Complex*

THIS BOOK HAS SOUGHT TO reorient the way scholarship frames the Iron Age polities surrounding the northeast corner of the Mediterranean during the Iron Age. I have argued that, rather than stumble over the half-dozen various names that we deploy when discussing the region, we should instead recognize that the very existence of this terminological challenge is, in fact, the key to understanding this time and place. We have not been able to agree on an appropriate name because we have been using inappropriate conceptual tools to model these kingdoms politically and culturally. I have proposed "Syro-Anatolian Culture Complex," or SACC, as a terminological alternative, one that I believe is helpful precisely because it avoids anachronistic and ethnically predetermined assumptions about Iron Age states. But regardless of whether one approves of this specific label, which ultimately will remain a matter of personal preference and disciplinary affiliation, the more significant issue is the revised understanding of the Iron Age reality that lies beneath it. Rather than see the northeast corner of the Mediterranean Sea as blanketed by a quilt of discrete nations during the late second and early first millennium BCE, as most previous scholarship implicitly presents it, this volume has argued that the region was instead occupied by polities whose populations, identities and affiliations, and power structures were constantly in flux and thus difficult to characterize. At the same time, however, it is impossible to ignore the fact that the regionally shared sentiments and cultural expressions generated by physical and cultural mobility led to a relatively discrete cultural formation that can be recognized today.

The crux of the issue, then, is striking the right balance between, on the one hand, an essentialized reconstruction of the Iron Age in which real distinctions between city-states' demographic makeups, local historical trajectories, and region-specific

*The Syro-Anatolian City-States.* James F. Osborne, Oxford University Press (2021). © Oxford University Press.
DOI: 10.1093/oso/9780199315833.003.0006.

archaeological signatures are flattened by an excessively homogenized scholarly vision and, on the other, atomizing the Iron Age into its particular components and neglecting the considerable evidence for cultural practices held in common across a significant geographical expanse. Individual scholars will have their own sense of the most appropriate place to draw the line between these two opposing forces. This volume has attempted to take the best of both approaches by arguing that the messy and complicated nature of the data available to us is not a problem to be eradicated in our reconstructions, but rather a signpost toward the solution of how best to understand the Iron Age Syro-Anatolian social order: a variegated cultural and political world that nevertheless, through processes described in this book, partook in a cultural complex that is identifiable to the modern researcher. Before moving toward a preliminary effort to define SACC's parameters, let us briefly recapitulate what those processes were that this volume has outlined.

After outlining the volume's central problematic in Chapter 1, Chapter 2 explored the rise of SACC as a process of shared identity formation resulting out of population movements. Broadly speaking, SACC's demographic transformations across the Late Bronze–Iron Age transition can be divided into three regions. The first of these is northern Mesopotamia and southeastern Anatolia, where archaeological surveys and historical records indicate a widespread dispersal of small, rural communities usually interpreted as the settlement signature of the sedentarization of the Aramaeans, but likely also including a general process of ruralization. The second was the northeastern Mediterranean littoral. Here, increasingly copious historical indications point toward an Aegean or Cypriot connection not unlike the one long known from the southern Levant, supported by modest archaeological and art historical evidence—settlement pattern changes in the Amuq Valley, locally produced Late Helladic IIIC pottery in both the Amuq and Cilicia, and Aegean/Cypriot-inspired iconography in the reliefs from Karatepe in Cilicia—suggesting that at least a small-scale movement of people into this region from Cyprus or the Aegean took place. Finally, a movement of people into this region from the Anatolian plateau was posited based on a drop in settlement numbers in central Anatolia, the sudden burgeoning of Hieroglyphic Luwian inscriptions in southeastern Turkey and northern Syria, and the spread of cremation burials from Anatolia into the Syro-Anatolian region and beyond.

These population movements accelerated processes that were already in place in the Late Bronze Age, especially the limited presence of Luwian inscriptions and cremation burials in northern Syria, such that the point is less a series of sudden and large-scale immigrations that created an entirely new population in the region and more a gradual demographic shift that brought groups of nonlocal populations in contact with existing local inhabitants. The outcome was similar to what has been identified in a number of different parts of the world when population groups of multiple cultural origins are placed side by side: a single hybridized cultural formation that nevertheless accentuates different cultural traditions in different areas based on the unique demographic trajectories that occurred in each micro-region. For this reason, the long-standing debate about whether the Late Bronze–Iron Age transition was one characterized by change or continuity will now have to reckon with modifying the contours of that debate to suit the evidence brought to light in multiple different places.

Chapter 3 continued the thematic of mobility, but this time with respect to the role played by the movement of people, things, and ideas as implicated in culture and politics of the early first millennium BCE, or Iron Age II period. In each case we saw how mobility was not merely a byproduct of the sociopolitical organization of the Iron Age city-states, but a defining constitutive element of it. Most surprising of all, perhaps, is the evidence for mobility of the large stone orthostats that lined the base of walls at important junctures in the Syro-Anatolian city. While their appearance at the time of excavation presents their final order as a stage set built cumulatively over the decades as pieces got added to the scene, indications both direct (e.g., references to different original locations inscribed on the orthostats themselves, as per Tell Halaf and Carchemish) and indirect (e.g., different stylistic groups, as per Karatepe) suggest that the orthostats' final appearance was merely the latest in a series of recombinations that continuously shuffled the orthostats' spatial organization. Regardless of how precisely this phenomenon is to be interpreted in each instance, mobility is part of the very definition of an Iron Age orthostat in SACC.

The same is true of the portable luxury goods that traveled far and wide across SACC and beyond, like the famous ivories that have been so amply analyzed by art historians. In this case, a recent sea change in scholarship has disassociated style groups from having been produced necessarily in individual city-states. Yet this fact does not divorce the production and consumption of ivory products from the political. On the contrary, it remains highly likely that raw materials were procured by the palace, who also served as the primary consumer for the artists' final products. Although ivory carving is now seen to have been conducted in a highly mobile manner by communities of practice, the engine of that mobility remains the political sphere—demonstrated most vividly by many ivory pieces' final movement, their removal to Assyria at the hands of the Assyrian conquerors.

More controversial, perhaps, was the interpretation of Phoenician-language inscriptions in SACC as the manifestation of another example of cultural mobility implicated in politics. Contrary to prevailing views of these texts in the Syro-Anatolian city-states of Samal and Que as having been composed only for reasons of elite message signaling, I proposed that Phoenician was also chosen to facilitate economic relationships between the rulers of those Syro-Anatolian city-states with the mercantile network that was beginning to spread across the Mediterranean at precisely this time. In this scenario, the clustering of texts around the Amanus Mountains likely reflects this region's nature as a source of materials for trade across the Mediterranean, and the ninth- to eighth-century shift from Samal east of the Amanus to Que west of the mountain range reflects a shift in the political and economic affiliations that were forged by Phoenician-speaking traders at this time. If this is correct, then it is important for us to recall that SACC was populated not just its own inhabitants, but also by foreign merchants and other people moving about its landscape, of which Phoenician-speaking traders would be only one example.

Looming over any analysis of SACC is the Neo-Assyrian Empire, and Chapter 4 turned to examine the dynamics of the cultural relationships between the two entities. Although the military and political domination of Assyria over SACC is impossible to refute, it is also easy to misrepresent. Noting that the conquest and territorial assimilation of the Syro-Anatolian city-states by the Neo-Assyrian Empire was a process that took two hundred years to complete, we saw that this piecemeal imperial incorporation left plenty of time for cultural relationships between them to unfold in ways that do not align consistently with the undeniable political imbalance. Rather than reflecting a process in which political domination is manifested in cultural production as a process of Assyrianization, or acculturation into the cultural norms of the hegemonic power, we saw how Syro-Anatolian art and architecture never simply adopted or borrowed Assyrian patterns, but refashioned them into novel formulations that melded local tropes with Assyrian representations. Such could be seen in certain depictions of political rulers from Gozan (Hadd-yit'i) and Tabal (Hartapu), for example, both of whom blended highly local manners of royal self-styling with Assyrian visual rhetoric. But it could also be seen in the local urban and architectural continuity of Syro-Anatolian cities following the Assyrian conquests, or the Iron Age III period, when the majority of Syro-Anatolian upper cities saw their monumental buildings continue in use and symbolic means of expression like royally signed portal lions continue as a modified Assyrian practice. Despite political incorporation, therefore, Syro-Anatolian urban centers maintained a substantial degree of agency. At the same time, Assyrian cultural production itself incorporated Syro-Anatolian patterns including the motifs of the funerary banquet scene and the porticoed entryway of the bīt-ḥilāni into the internal arrangement of their much larger royal palaces. Ultimately, study of Assyrian and Syro-Anatolian cultural interaction on its own terms—as opposed to through the lens of military and political hegemony—leads to a greater appreciation of the significant influence SACC had on its more powerful neighbor.

The final thematic essay in this volume considered the relationship of space and power in the Syro-Anatolian built environment. Beginning at the largest spatial scale of territory and landscape, Chapter 5 documented archaeological and historical evidence for a three-tiered settlement hierarchy within the Syro-Anatolian city-state, yet simultaneously found a surprising amount of evidence for a malleable model of territoriality, one in which political sovereignty was not evenly distributed across the landscape. Urban centers, meanwhile, whose tight spatial coordination of royal symbolism leads them to appear like a "strange loop" of recursive symbolic hierarchy, saw frequent challenges to those very symbols by means of counter-monumental interventions and outright destructions. While spatial analysis of the *bīt-ḫilāni* palace leads us to consider the political message of authority as having been communicated successfully, the discovery of royal statues in various states of destruction leads us to realize that this message's reception was hardly uncontested. Continuing down the spatial hierarchy, second-order towns show some indications of centralized authority, like the temple at Tell Afis or the fortification wall of Çatal Höyük, but otherwise display precious little evidence for overt political control. By the time we reach rural settlements like Tille Höyük or Tell Mastuma, the appearance is one of villages almost entirely beyond the political ambit of the state. At all spatial scales of analysis, therefore, the relationship between space and power is highly variable, uneven, and under constant negotiation.

Each of the cases synthesized here was situated within a theoretical framework appropriate for the analysis that followed. The contributions made by the field of contemporary diaspora studies illuminated my reading of the social contacts and hybrid cultural formations wrought by population movements in antiquity. Likewise, insights drawn from cultural mobility and especially the new mobilities paradigm of sociology led me to envision the Iron Age polity less in terms of its stability and more by the ways in which it was able to marshal mobility as a political force. Once this relationship of power and movement, or kinopolitics, is brought to the fore, one sees mobility as a ubiquitous and defining aspect of Syro-Anatolian sociopolitical life. Scholarship in modern imperial history has used the metaphor of the middle ground to conceptualize the cultural hybridity that is created by the cultural impacts of political imperialism. Reading our archaeological and textual sources contrapuntally, we identified Assyrian-like cultural products in SACC not simply as the predictable acculturation of Assyrian influence inevitably enacted by political dominance, but as a creative and deliberate adaptation of both worlds to create new effects. Finally, theoretical literature on space and place enabled us to examine the expressions of power in the built environment in a more flexible light, seeing in them not straightforward expressions of authority but rather claims to power that rarely went untested. At the same time, this literature brought into high relief the variability of the expression of power across space.

None of these schools of thought could be applied in a direct sense to the case studies that followed; in each instance certain caveats and restrictions were necessary for us to be able to apply the insights they offer to the Iron Age material at hand. But adhering strictly to the original formulations of scholars writing in contexts far removed from the ancient Near East is not the point of such theoretical applications, which is rather to cast the evidence in a new light and to bring analysis of it into dialogue with scholarship from the broader humanities and social sciences. Although diaspora studies, mobility, hybridity and middle-ground studies, and space and place theory have separate origins and divergent intellectual trajectories, they cluster around a common set of assumptions. What these various traditions share is a destabilized subject, an awareness that sociopolitical formations past and present cannot be treated as monolithic and homogeneous entities. In certain cases, at least, social groups are more accurately understood as physically and symbolically mobile; spatially unmoored; culturally hybrid; and in a constant state of becoming. These have been the consistent arguments about SACC running through this volume.

If SACC is best characterized along these lines, then it follows that we should revise our models of these city-states accordingly. As I have argued at several points throughout this study, the nation-state model's association of ethnolinguistic communities with political formations is inapplicable. We cannot accurately understand these polities as being "Aramaean" or "Luwian" since they do not have a sufficiently fixed cultural origins or subsequent identity to warrant that assignation. By pulling apart the link between polity, ethnolinguistic groups, and territory that is the underpinning of the methodological nationalism frequently, if tacitly, deployed in Iron Age scholarship (Wimmer and Schiller 2002), and replacing it with a notion of hybrid cultural formations perpetually in flux, this volume has proposed a fundamental shift in how we conceive of the Syro-Anatolian city-states.

::: 

## Elements of the Syro-Anatolian Culture Complex: A First Attempt

If SACC is characterized above all by its fluidity and local variability, then it seems that trying to define its core elements is not an achievable objective. Yet for all the ambivalence described earlier, there remain shared cultural practices that scholars typically recognize as belonging to a genuine cultural sphere—hence the various unifying terminologies that have been debated here. To state outright what is intuitively obvious, there is no emic expression from SACC itself for the social group in which its constituent polities participated; any assessment of its cultural elements can only be an etic process of categorization. Furthermore, such a categorization has to begin with a clear acknowledgment of its limitations. Precisely because of the nature of SACC described earlier—its lack of ethnic fixity, its spatial unevenness, its diasporic origins—no fixed circle can ever be drawn around it, geographically or metaphorically. Any list of traits used to define SACC can only ever be a set of guiding principles, not a checklist for determining membership once a suitable threshold has been reached. There will always be individual places and kingdoms in which certain elements provided here are not present; likewise, the appearance of individual elements in specific regions does not necessarily indicate participation in SACC. Gauging membership in SACC will always be a matter for scholarly evaluation, and the following series of attributes, some more amply demonstrated than others, can serve as parameters for the debate.

First among these is a combination of foreign and local cultural antecedents that merged in the northeast corner of the Mediterranean Sea during the late second millennium BCE. Among the former are small-scale movements of people from the Anatolian plateau and the Aegean; among the latter are the demographic processes of sedentarization and ruralization witnessed in local settlement patterns. Together these traditions led to novel formulations of cultural tradition and innovation in a manner analogous to diasporic processes evident in other times and places.

This process of population movements and subsequent identity formation at the outset of the Iron Age led to a second characteristic of SACC: multiple language communities across the region and within individual city-states, attested most frequently by Luwian and Aramaic inscriptions, but also Phoenician, Samalian, and Akkadian. A significant degree of bi- and even trilingualism is to be expected among individuals, though not easy to document beyond explicit claims of multi-lingualism (e.g., Yariri, king of Carchemish).

By the time a relatively stable regional political system had taken shape at the start of the first millennium BCE, we find a third trait, a regional political structure characterized by small states that were dominated symbolically, and likely economically, by a single urban center. These city-states interacted with one another in a fashion analogous to the peer polity interaction model witnessed in societies of similar scale in other times and places.

Fourth, although these city-states occupied spatially recognizable broad spheres of influence, they nevertheless practiced a highly malleable territoriality, or a principle of regional sovereignty characterized by unstable borders, shifting political allegiances of settlements, and the absence of contiguity as a necessary or sufficient condition for political affiliation. At the same time, one recognizes in their settlement patterns a three-tiered settlement hierarchy, but one whose secondary and tertiary settlements were only partially integrated into the political economy of the state. Small rural sites in particular display little evidence for participation in the political sphere.

Another tripartite spatial organization is our fifth attribute of SACC, this time pertaining to capital cities comprised of outer towns, upper cities, and palace compounds, each with increasingly restricted accessibility maintained by gateways. In addition to this formal syntactical structure, capital cities were richly imbued with visual and verbal messages of royal authority, messages that were repeated at each stage of the urban spatial hierarchy, a phenomenon I have referred to as a "strange loop." The palace compounds of these capital cities were inward-facing and surrounded substantial open courtyards, designed to facilitate state-sponsored spectacles, evidenced not only by the courtyard space itself but also by the accoutrements of performance such as stone libation vessels and cup-marks. The palaces themselves, in many cases referred to as a *bīt-ḫilāni*, were typically free-standing and incorporated royal symbolism into their architectonic features. Their spatial properties were designed so as to encourage the interaction between visitors to and inhabitants of the palace, even while accessibility and movement within the palace itself could be tightly controlled. Likewise, freestanding temple buildings with small (i.e., one–three) numbers of rooms, were typically built according to the *in antis* plan. Although resembling one another in form, their size is highly variable, ranging from the modest Building XVI at Tell Tayinat to the huge temple of the Storm God at Aleppo. Reuse of these structures is frequently attested across the Iron Age.

Sixth, it is common across SACC to find orthostats decorated in low relief, portal lions, and adjacent freestanding monumental statues of kings and deities lining the walls of important high-trafficked portals such as gateways and porticoes. Only rarely was such monumental decoration applied to interior spaces (e.g., the Storm God temple at Aleppo). Despite their weight and size, orthostats in particular were involved in kinopolitics, or the politics of movement, and thus were highly mobile across the urban landscape, frequently being reused in later architectural projects for reasons that were diverse and circumstantial. Likewise, the archaeological con-text of many of the colossal statues is marked by burial, defacement, and destruc-tion, some of which was likely carried out during the Neo-Assyrian conquests, and others by rival Syro-Anatolian city-states or even internecine conflicts within the polity. Like the movement of orthostats mentioned earlier, this phenomenon of countermonumentality was culturally significant.

Closely related to this point is a seventh feature of SACC, the presence of elite monumental inscriptions proclaiming royal legitimacy in the same venues as the orthostats and statuary. Such texts were composed in multiple languages (Hieroglyphic Luwian, Aramaic, Samalian, Phoenician, Akkadian), including in languages different from that of the author's own name, and were occasionally bi- or trilingual. Generally brief and commemorative in nature, Syro-Anatolian texts are few compared with, for example, their Assyrian neighbors. Nonelite texts are generally missing, though a small number of ostraca and lead strips suggests that this may change with future discoveries and is not necessarily indicative of the an-cient reality.

An eighth aspect of SACC pertains to a region-wide suite of burial practices, the most conspicuous element of which is the practice of cremation. Differences between elite and nonelite burials are attested in the wealth of grave goods found with the burials, and in their locations: unlike the extramural cemeteries of nonelite citizens (Hamath, Yunus), the upper echelons of society were permitted to bury their cremations within the limits of the settlement. Cremation burials existed locally during the Bronze Age, but proliferated immensely during the Iron Age, including to sites and regions adjacent to SACC like Phoenicia. Closely related to this practice are the associated Syro-Anatolian funerary monuments depicting mortuary repasts for the deceased, most famously now the KTMW stele from Zincirli.

Some of these very monuments display material culture belonging to a ninth characteristic of SACC, the craft production of portable luxury goods that was not necessarily (or, not in every instance) organized by schools associated with individual city-states. Rather, this production is another example of cultural fluidity and mobility, with producers bonded by practice, not by polity. Organization of production is at present difficult to discern, but even while the acquisition of raw materials and the ultimate acquirer of the final products was likely the palace, the limited evidence available suggests that crafts were produced according to "individual specialization," that is, specialists who were independent, dispersed, small scale, and part-time. In broad terms, similar design motifs are attested across multiple media, including ivories, bronzes, and carved soft stone objects, as well as orthostats.

Tenth, despite regional fragmentation, the lack of political unification, and eventual conquest by the Assyrians, SACC possessed a geopolitical significance and cultural agency that impacted all of their neighbors, including the Neo-Assyrian Empire and Phoenicia, but also the Aegean, Phrygian, and Urartian worlds not discussed in this volume. Indeed, SACC provides an outstanding example of the efficacy of the middle ground and related heuristics like hybridity for the cultural agency of politically weaker parties in imperial dynamics.

To the extent that this preliminary list of SACC's cultural attributes is representative of an ancient culture group as defined by modern scholarship, a further question is evaluating which polities and regions can be identified as members of the group. In several cases the answer is difficult to determine, and scholars will disagree on what degree of shared traits is necessary to justify treating a particular city-state as being part of the same cultural phenomenon. In my opinion, mapping these traits according to our current knowledge of them presents a reasonably clear impression of group membership in three cardinal directions. To the east, Tell Halaf, ancient Gozan, capital of Bit-Baḫiani, makes the Khabur triangle the easternmost extent of SACC. With its burials, *bīt-ḫilāni* palace, and impressive orthostats and statuary, among other traits, Tell Halaf is a clear member of SACC; no such remains are yet known further to the east. To the north, the city-state of Melid with its capital based at Arslantepe marks an identifiable outer limit. The most northerly inscription with a named Country-Lord of Malatya is the ŞIRZI landscape monument (Hawkins 2000: 322–24), located roughly 60 km northwest of Arslantepe itself. The Hieroglyphic Luwian inscriptions and dynastic history, portal orthostats, and colossal statue in the Lion Gate have long placed this site within SACC, and continued work in its Iron Age levels has produced additional monumental arts as well as traditionally Syro-Anatolian luxury crafts such as carved ivory. To the south we can go at least as far as the city-state of Hama, whose material culture and architectural plan from Level E on the acropolis is in many respects similar to that of Tell Tayinat and Zincirli further north, and in whose territory both Hieroglyphic Luwian and Aramaic inscriptions have been found. It is possible that the historically attested Iron Age state based at Damascus will produce remains comparable to Hama and elsewhere when the city's Iron Age remains are discovered. Isolated orthostat fragments from Transjordan (Weber 2017) do not seem adequate to include the polities of Ammon, Moab, or Edom in SACC, belonging more appropriately in a southern Levantine cultural zone alongside their western neighbors Israel and Judah (who themselves also possess some of the traits listed here).

More challenging, however, is determining how far west we can extend our understanding of SACC. The Cilician Valley occupied by Que can be considered as a member, with its local Hittite legacy, decorated orthostats and monumental statuary, Aegean connections, lengthy inscriptions in Hieroglyphic Luwian and Phoenician imbued with typical Syro-Anatolian rhetoric and symbolism, and close political relations with eastern neighbors such as Samal. The capital city's remains have been exposed in limited excavations at Adana-Tepebağ, and this will eventually illuminate greatly our understanding of Que's regional setting. But what of Tabal further west, in the southeastern edge of the Anatolian plateau? For lack of evidence, here the record is more ambiguous. This volume has generally considered Tabal to be part of SACC—in the discussion of the Kızıldağ reliefs in Chapter 4, for example—but it must also be admitted that we know very little about the Iron Age archaeological record of southeastern Konya and Kayseri. The recent appreciation of a hitherto unknown Iron Age II capital city at Türkmen-Karahöyük ruled by Hartapu and surrounded by smaller sites indicates that this region was characterized by settlement patterns similar to regions further east. In addition, sculptural remains found at places like Göllüdağ, including portal lions, or the Ivriz rock relief depicting Warpalawa in Assyrian-like dress (with a nearby Hieroglyphic Luwian-Phoenician bilingual inscription), point to strong connections with SACC further east, and of course this area has furnished a great number of Hieroglyphic Luwian texts. It thus seems logical, barring future evidence to the contrary, to consider the region of Tabal as part of SACC, especially if at least some individuals from this region gradually moved east and south of the Taurus Mountains in the late second millennium BCE, as proposed in Chapter 2. Perhaps more than anywhere else within SACC, this region warrants greater archaeological elucidation.

The problem of how to categorize Tabal is evocative of the larger problematic of this volume: considering who belongs in SACC and who does not will, by definition, remain a perpetual challenge, depending as it does on a wide array of variables that were themselves continuously shifting. Likewise, group membership will always be determined by which variables are being examined, such that comparisons of palatial architecture will yield a slightly different configuration of regional cultural affiliations than, say, ivory carving. Furthermore, our considerations may change depending on the century—for example, whether one is examining the Iron Age I or II periods. But we can only work with the evidence at our disposal, and at present this volume has been able to make the case for a large and reasonably consistent, if highly variable internally, culture complex surrounding the northeast corner of the Mediterranean Sea during the Iron Age.

::::

## Conclusion: Moving Forward

In many respects the thematic chapters in this volume represent only an initial exploration of the Iron Age evidence from southeastern Anatolia and northern Syria, and there remains a significant amount of work to be conducted on SACC and its constituent polities. Archaeological excavations in the region continue apace, and it is to be expected that these will continue furnishing important data from household artifacts to inscribed monuments. Even at our current state of knowledge, however, much remains to be done.

One topic that did not receive adequate treatment here is political economy. How exactly did the Syro-Anatolian city-states generate wealth, and what were the social mechanisms by which that wealth was distributed? A variety of models for ancient economies have been used by historians and anthropologists, yet this literature has barely seen application in this time and place. Closely related to this issue is the nature of quotidian material culture. An oft-repeated archaeological lament is that scholarship has focused excessively on elite remains, a problem we have encountered at several places in this study. Although additional excavation at village-level settlements will have the obvious benefit of elucidating a sector of society that is to date only poorly understood, which will be inherently beneficial unto itself, there is the added fact that most of the evidence for the regional culture complex identified here exists primarily at the elite level. Further analysis in this vein will need to compare things like ceramic forms and manufacturing technology, tools used in textile production, domestic storage methods, and food processing implements like grinding stones in order to see how the materials of daily life and their spatial distributions align with the patterns attested in monumental arts and city planning. Recent fine-grained analyses of Iron Age I material culture and its regional connections from Tell Tayinat (Welton et al. 2019) and Arslantepe (Manuelli 2018) are exemplary of how this type of research can illuminate the subtleties of continuities and changes in nonelite assemblages.

Another aspect of SACC that did not receive sufficient attention in this volume is its diachronic evolution. Indeed, as outlined in the opening chapter, in order to demonstrate the existence of SACC in the first place, a synchronic stance had to be adopted. This decision had the benefit of allowing us to explore several themes that, although having their own independent significance, cumulatively point toward the recognition of the regional phenomenon I refer to as the Syro-Anatolian Culture Complex. But its shortcoming is that SACC's evolution through time has not been addressed systematically here, and that the rich particularities between the city-states have inevitably been dehistoricized. A logical next step in this project, therefore, will be to evaluate the composition of SACC as its characteristics fluctuated over time, as has recently begun to be analyzed with individual cultural elements such as urban histories (e.g., Herrmann 2017b) and monumental arts (e.g., Gilibert 2011).

A richer appreciation for the temporal element brings us to another topic that will have to be addressed elsewhere, and that is the disappearance of SACC from the historical and archaeological record of the ancient Near East. That the Neo-Assyrian Empire was responsible for the political demise of individual city-states is clear. Exactly how the conquest was implemented, how the Assyrians' program of forced deportations was enacted and what its archaeological signature looks like, and how and why Luwian apparently ceased to be spoken even while Aramaic became the regional lingua franca are all poorly understood. Scholarly attention on SACC tends to focus on the early first millennium BCE up until the moment of conquest and only slightly beyond; we need to extend this focus into the periods immediately following the Assyrian presence in the region to determine accurately how the imperial imposition permanently altered things like settlement patterns, urban trajectories, and general material culture. The Neo-Assyrian Empire operates as an unexamined deus ex machina for explaining the end of SACC, when in reality the end of political independence is separate from the termination of an entire suite of cultural behaviors. This cultural transformation was a process spanning several decades, and one whose contours have not yet been outlined.

If change over time is a subject that requires additional research, so, too, is SACC's relations with its cultural contemporaries and predecessors. This book has tried to refer consistently to the contemporary inhabitants of the central Levant, for example, as "Phoenician speakers," rather than "the Phoenicians," being reluctant to impose elsewhere the same methodological nationalism that this volume questions for SACC. But the question inevitably arises, whether the diasporic origins and cultural fluidity that we have found to characterize SACC are unique to it, or simply a characteristic of many, or even most, ancient Near Eastern cultures. Similar processes of cultural mobility are likely part of the Amorite narrative of the Middle Bronze Age, for example, just as the principles of malleable territoriality may complicate territorial reconstructions of ancient Israel and Judah and its southern Levantine neighbors in the early first millennium. If SACC is merely one example of diaspora and mobility among many, then a similar interpretive stance may need to be adopted in many different times and places.

Above all, current archaeological projects in the region are demonstrating the local flavor that characterizes each site and its surrounding micro-region. This volume has sought to assess larger interregional patterns even while staying faithful to the strong evidence for particularism on a site-by-site basis. At a methodological and theoretical level, therefore, it will be necessary for future findings to be slotted into region-wide patterns and for these larger narratives to incorporate site-based histories that only partially conform with neighboring areas. Perhaps the greatest challenge for scholarship in this area moving forward will be celebrating the high-resolution information offered by modern archaeological and historical analysis even while using that information to describe larger phenomena. Striking the right balance between the regional and the local will always be particularly imperative with a phenomenon like the Syro-Anatolian Culture Complex, in which variability is itself part of its very nature.

# NOTES

## CHAPTER 1

1. Chapter titles from Cohen (2009) are illustrative of this practice: "The Syro-Hittite scribes and officials, Hittite officials, and foreign scribes" and "The Syro-Hittite scholarly scribes and the Syro-Hittite tradition scholarly compositions."
2. Compare Josephine Quinn (2018: xix–xx), writing about the Phoenicians: "The fundamental difficulty with labels like "Phoenician" is that they offer answers to questions about historical explanation before they have even been asked. They assume an underlying commonality between the people they designate that cannot easily be demonstrated; they produce new identities where they did not to our knowledge exist; and they freeze in time particular identities that were in fact in a constant process of construction, from inside and out."
3. Another analog would be the Lapita Cultural Complex of the Pacific Ocean. See Specht et al. (2014) for summary and critique.
4. Indeed, not all classical Greek polities resembled the polis as reconstructed in contemporary scholarship (Brock and Hodkinson 2000).

## CHAPTER 2

1. See Harmanşah (2013: Table 1) for a summary of surveys conducted in southeastern Anatolian and northeastern Syria.
2. At the same time that they criticized pastoralism, paleobotanical evidence shows that the Assyrians were practicing a mixed agricultural-pastoral subsistence strategy themselves (Rosenzweig 2016).
3. Ussishkin concludes, contra Landsberger (1948: 35–37) who had argued that the state was first Neo-Hittite and later Aramaean, that in fact it was first Aramaean and only subsequently did it become Neo-Hittite (1971: 431).

4. The poorly preserved and challenging alphabetic inscription from Ördekburnu, 18 km south of Zincirli, might even represent "a mixed Luwian and Semitic code" (Gzella 2014: 75). This interpretation is far from certain, however, and others are confident the inscription is Samalian (Lemaire and Sass 2013).

5. In an unpublished conference paper, Frederico Giusfredi (2018) proposed that some of the features distinguishing Samalian from Aramaic were caused by linguistic influence from Luwian, which, if true, further helps the argument that both languages were being spoken in the region.

6. Late Bronze Age cremation burials are attested in the Troad, however, including Troy itself and the nearby site of Beşik-Tepe (e.g., Korfmann 1986).

7. Kreppner (2008: 268) raises, but rejects, the possibility that multiple burial types at the site can be explained on ethnic grounds. Nevertheless, it remains possible that the population of Dūr-Katlimmu was culturally, if not politically, diverse, or that the choice for some burials to be cremations was the outcome of proximity to local populations engaging in the practice.

8. See Altaweel and Squitieri (2018: Table 4.2) for a list of archaeological surveys conducted in central Anatolia.

9. Earlier surveys in this region by David French and James Mellaart do not have sufficient chronological resolution to be included here, nor do other seasons of survey published by Omura in his reports appearing regularly in *Anatolian Archaeological Studies*. More recent work by Douglas Baird is mostly unpublished for these periods. A number of new and ongoing surveys exist in Konya directed by Ömür Harmanşah, Yiğit Erbil, Çiğdem Maner, and Christoph Bachhuber and Michele Massa, among others, but likewise are so far only preliminarily published.

10. The translation of the term *nbš* as "soul" offered by Pardee (2009: 54) and its presence in the stele itself has recently been challenged by David Hawkins (2015) on analogy with Hieroglyphic Luwian *atri-*, a proposal that Virginia Herrmann (in press) convincingly rejects.

11. As Virginia Herrmann's (in press) recent study of the KTMW stele concludes, "we should not necessarily interpret this [mixture of features] as reflecting Luwian influence on the Semitic population of the northern Levant. Nor does the use of West Semitic mortuary terminology mean that comparison with Hittite and Luwian evidence is irrelevant . . . Rather, Anatolian Indo-European, Semitic, and (let us not forget!) Hurrian people had engaged in an intensive cultural interchange for many centuries in this region, resulting in a web of common practices that overlapped with other regional traditions and lacked any clear boundaries."

12. These numbers were derived from a maximalist reading of data kindly provided to me by Susanne Rutishauser, that is, accepting every possible marked site as a confirmed presence. I am deeply grateful to Dr. Rutishauser for sharing this information.

13. With respect to ceramics, Welton et al. (2019: 301) note: "The earliest forms demonstrate continuity with the Hittite Monochrome Ware (HMW) tradition of Late Bronze Age Anatolia, with parallels from highland central Anatolia and particularly from the terminal phases of the Hittite Empire Period."

14. This was previously read as *wa/i-ta₄-sà-ti-ni-za-*(REGIO), or the Wadasatinean (Hawkins 2000: 366). However, new readings of the *ta₄* and *ta₅* signs as *la/i* and *lá/í,* respectively (Rieken and Yakubovich 2010), combined with the recognition that *sà* is used before stops with the vowel not being read (Rieken 2010), led to the new reading of the place name as Walistin (and Palistin).

15. The Ahhiyawa-Hiyawa equation is not universally accepted. See Simon (2018: 315–16 and n. 13) for philological arguments against it.

## CHAPTER 3

1. All states are characterized by varying degrees of movement and stasis, but the point here is a shift in perspective where mobility, not stability, is the baseline against which social variables are measured, since mobility always exists to greater or lesser extents (much like temperature measures relative degrees of heat, not heat and cold).

2. Timothy Ingold (2013: 85–89) describes a world that is forever "worlding," referring to the ongoing changes that, at long enough time scales, are constantly taking place to features from archaeological sites to mountain ranges, whose appearance of stability is merely an artifice of our limited temporal perspectives.

3. The primary exception to this is the archaeological study of nomadism, inherently and deeply concerned with patterns of movement (e.g., Cribb 1991), even if that sense of mobility as an economic subsistence strategy is not what is intended here.

4. Although this reconstruction disagrees with Zsolt Simon (2018), who, like Yakubovich (2015), sees Greek speakers as the composers of the Phoenician inscriptions, it is consistent with his proposal (2018: 327–32) that the cultural and geographical origin of these texts lies in Cyprus, given Phoenician involvement on the island, and rich connections between Cilicia and Cyprus demonstrated ceramically (Lehmann 2008).

5. Hawkins (2000: 133) speculates that the name of the language in question (Luwian *sù+ra/i-*) is Urartian, though most scholars understand the term as Phoenician by virtue of its etymological relationship with the ancient name of Tyre (Ṣur) (see Simon 2012: 171 and references there).

6. To this list one might add the two small limestone plaques, or "amulets," from Arslan Taş, although their authenticity has been the subject of some debate (see Pardee 1998).

7. I do not have the space in this volume to fully consider the recent debates in Phoenician studies concerning the ancient ethnic identity—or lack thereof—of the Phoenicians. Suffice it to say here that recent arguments against an ancient Phoenician ethnicity (Martin 2017; Quinn 2018) are broadly consistent with the aims of this book, for example, my use of the ethnically neutral label SACC instead of the identity-laden Syro-Hittite. But whether or not Phoenician speakers who were present in Que identified as a recognizable social collective as such, the fact remains that the most felicitous interpretation of Phoenician-language inscriptions is the presence of Phoenician speakers, which leads us to ask what speakers of this language were doing in the region.

8. Following Brian Peckham (2001: 32), "The instruction, which is particularly in-teresting for its balanced and almost epic style, for its peculiarly Phoenician—perhaps specifically Byblian—ideology of kingship as a benefit to the people, and

for its traditional piety, confirms the age-old presence of articulate and educated Phoenicians in this part of Anatolia."

9. Aubet's rejection of this possibility is puzzling given her simultaneous acceptance of the notion that the funerary stelae found at Al-Bass must be related to the Syro-Anatolian mortuary monuments like the KTMW stele (Aubet 2013: 81).

10. Aslı Özyar (2013: 116–18) summarizes the setting thus: "located on the west bank of the Ceyhan/Pyramos, the stronghold once undoubtedly must have controlled and profited from the traffic in goods transported on the river and the old caravan road (Akyol/Ağyol/Kocayol) to its west, both connecting the Central Anatolian Plateau to the Mediterranean. It is conceivable that the inhabitants levied toll fees and provided in return safe passage of merchandise such as timber, including the prized cedar logs and a variety of metals, all available in the Taurus Mountain range."

11. Marta Luciani (2006: 410) has argued that rooms R and Y of Qatna's (Tell Mishrifeh) Late Bronze Age Lower City Palace represent secondary workshop locations for the final stage of production, that is, the fitting of finished carvings into their larger objects, noting that this finding implies the original carving itself took place elsewhere.

12. Barnett's (1982: pl. 2c) identification of tusks at Al Mina has been debunked based on their reassessment as cattle horn cores (Çakırlar and Ikram 2016: 170).

13. Collon's footnote reads as follows: "Professor Seton Lloyd has also informed me that elephants' tusks were found during the Oriental Institute Amuq excavations at Çatal Hüyük and Tell Tayinat." I have not been able to confirm this statement. Tusks from the Syrian-Hittite Expedition are not in the collections of the Oriental Institute Museum, but they may be in the storerooms of the Hatay Archaeology Museum in Antakya, Turkey.

14. A thorough reassessment of all evidence pertaining to elephants concludes decisively that elephant remains in Mesopotamia and the Levant come from a subspecies of the Asian elephant, a group that is conventionally referred to as the Syrian elephant, and that it was introduced in the region in the early second millennium BCE before becoming extinct around 700 BCE (Çakırlar and Ikram 2016, plus references therein).

15. Syrian elephant molars have also been found in this region, such as Iron Age I Kinet Höyük, although their use in the ivory trade is unclear given the molars' unsuitability for crafted items more elaborate than small objects such as buttons and pins (Çakırlar and Ikram 2016: 172–73).

16. This most recent movement of the orthostats in the context of colonial exploration of the Middle East will not be addressed here, despite constituting the most obvious example of kinopolitics of them all.

17. A single orthostat depicting a chariot riding over a fallen enemy soldier was found at the site in 1896 (Braidwood 1937: 33, Fig. 7). Its findspot is unknown, but its existence hints at a relief program at Tayinat that has not yet been excavated.

18. In an intriguing footnote in the final report, Woolley quotes Richard Barnett's disapproval of Woolley's conclusion that the reliefs of the Herald's Wall were strictly decorative and lacking in meaning: "Mr. Barnett objects to this: 'There is a meaning, but its interpretation is beyond us. These figures are magical, apotropaic in their object,

and we do not as yet possess the texts which would explain them. Hence they appear disconnected and without a plan'" (Woolley 1952: 186n1). Here Barnett anticipates the point I raised earlier, that we are unable to determine the extent to which our categorizations of ancient artistic products are the same groupings that people in the Iron Age would have recognized themselves.

19. See the closing "Plan der Zitadella 2004" in Gonnella et al. (2005) for a comparative sense of the scale of this building.

20. See Brown (2008: Appendix 1) for a description of each of the reliefs that have been found.

21. The relationship of the poorly preserved north wall and the pedestal wall is unclear in the photographs published in Kohlmeyer (2009), but it can be better understood by looking at Gonnella et al. (2005: Abb. 115, 128–29).

22. The excavators state that this relief is the depiction of the Storm God: "So wie der Block bestellt war, wurde er jedoch nicht weiter ausgearbeitet, sondern vielmehr auf die Seite gelegt und seine urspruengliche Hinterseite schliesslich mit dem Relief des Wettergottes versehen" (Gonnella et al. 2005: 111), but the scene with the Storm God and his chariot is in fact the next relief in the sequence to the east.

23. Winter (1979: 131), for example, does not attempt to explain why the inhabitants of Karatepe took orthostats from Domuztepe in her reconstruction, other than to say that it took place "for whatever reasons—economic or symbolic."

## CHAPTER 4

1. See papers in a special issue of *The William and Mary Quarterly*, 63(1), for critiques of the concept in the context of North American historical details specifically.

2. For an excellent summary of the Neo-Assyrian Empire and its vast scholarship, see Herrman and Tyson (2018), including references to textual and Assyriological sources.

3. Wicke (2015: 566) encourages a terminological distinction between "Assyrianized" and "Assyrianizing," the latter referring to the ongoing process of influence, and the latter referring to the result of such influence.

4. The most thorough analysis of Syro-Anatolian art's visual relationships with Neo-Assyrian art is Wicke (2015), part of an ongoing larger project by the author.

5. The correct spelling of the name, "Hartapu," was established by the discovery of the inscription TÜRKMEN-KARAHÖYÜK 1 in 2019, which eliminated the possibility that his name was Hartapus, as per the passages in Hawkins 2000 cited here. See Goedegebuure et al. 2020 for details.

6. In an earlier study David Hawkins (1992: 272) proposed that the relief and KIZILDAĞ 1 inscription were added together to the rest of the earlier group by the eighth-century Tablian ruler Wasusarma, speculating that perhaps this individual had expanded his territory to this region from the area of his own inscriptions further north near Kayseri. Under similar reasoning, Trevor Bryce (2012: 145) proposed that it was the eighth-century Tablian ruler Ambaris who was responsible for the relief.

7. See Oreshko (2017: 62–63) for a speculative attempt, unsuccessful in my view, to raise the date of the relief by several centuries.

8. Lorenzo d'Alfonso (2019) has recently argued based on paleographic and textual grounds that the TOPADA inscription dates to the late tenth or early ninth centuries, in which case the association of Wasusarmas and Uassurme no longer applies. A series of further historical consequences necessarily follow, including a new proposal for the ancient name of Phrygia. Although a detailed consideration of these suggestions in light of recent evidence will have to wait, the 2019 discoveries at Türkmen-Karahöyük, especially the new inscription TÜRKMEN-KARAHÖYÜK 1 described later in this text, render these proposals suspect.

9. The possibility is raised, but rejected, by Hawkins (2000: 439): "It could be argued that KIZILDAĞ-KARADAĞ shows a late but archaizing style in the same manner as TOPADA and that the inscriptions are simply not extensive enough to betray diagnostic late characteristics as TOPADA does. The clear links which it shows with Empire Period YALBURT and Late TOPADA certainly serve to place it between the two chronologically, as it is located geographically. But the links with YALBURT seems stronger, especially the remarkable parallels of content, and these in my opinion suggest an earlier rather than later date, probably to the period immediately following the fall of the Hittite Empire."

10. Weeden (2010: 47) notes the possibility that the winged disc did, in fact, originally cap the opening cartouche of TOPADA, even though it is not present today.

11. TISP is directed by the author under the umbrella of the larger Konya Regional Archaeological Survey Project (KRASP), a landscape project co-directed by Michele Massa and Christoph Bachhuber that is devoted to understanding the history of human occupation across the Konya Plain (Massa et al. 2020).

12. The name and title appear twice in TÜRKMEN-KARAHÖYÜK 1, first as Kartapu and second as Hartapu.

13. For a proposal that Türkmen-Karahöyük might also have been the famously lost Hittite capital city of Tarḫuntašša, see Massa et al. (2020: 65–66). Its Iron Age name—that is, its name during the reign of Hartapu—remains unknown.

14. Strictly speaking, the possibility that multiple rulers named Hartapu composed inscriptions on this sacred outcrop cannot be excluded and would be supported most effectively be the early paleography of KIZILDAĞ 4. However, that text may simply be yet another example of archaizing, and until further evidence appears the simplest authorship scenario is that all the texts by Hartapu, son of Mursili, located on the Kızıldağ outcrop and environs were composed by the same individual.

15. Brown (2008: 343) notes a very convincing parallel with a glazed brick panel from Fort Shalmaneser at Nimrud.

16. Younger (2000) provides references to different readings and interpretations, but the fundamental scenario remains the same in all.

17. The Karatepe excavators present an array of parallels to items represented in this relief, including the vessels, the chair, and the table, most of which situate the scene squarely within SACC (Çambel and Özyar 2003: 100–104). The proposed parallel between the table and the wooden table from Gordion's Tumulus MM is less convincing.

18. The structural similarity I reconstruct here between Ashurbanipal's garden scene and Syro-Anatolian funerary monuments is true regardless of whether one accepts the

identification of specific items in the scene as having a non-Assyrian origin but displayed in Assyrian court style, or prefers to see them as proper Assyrian products (cf. Albenda 1977; Feldman 2014: 100–101; Fischer and Wicke 2016).

19. The date of the structure from Tille Höyük level VIII with the pebble courtyard is right on the cusp of Assyria's 708 BCE conquest of Kummuḫ (cf. Blaylock 2009: 162; Bunnens 2016: 66).

20. Although Bunnens (2016: 68) dismisses the possibility, it is difficult to see how the mosaic floor of Megaron 2 from the Early Phrygian level of Gordion, destroyed ca. 800 BCE, and containing patches of checkboard patterning among its many motifs, is not related to the roughly contemporary checkerboard pattern attested in SACC.

21. These material indicators complement the many linguistic and administrative indicators of Aramaean influence on Assyrian culture, including the lexical impact of Aramaic on Akkadian (Tadmor 1982).

22. This location of the text compromises Galter's (2004: 451–56) interpretation that a trilingual was used so as to ensure a successful reading regardless of whoever gained power in the region after the inscription was set.

23. A similar archaeological signature has been identified at Tel Dan in the southern Levant, although here the hybrid local-Assyrian structures and material culture are interpreted as the result of the Assyrians actively choosing to be flexible due to ecological conditions (Thareani 2016).

24. Also highly significant, although not examined here, are the ramifications that Assyrian presence had on the internal sociopolitical dynamics in individual Syro-Anatolian kingdoms, whose rulers were led to create their own court cultures to be emulated by their own officials and vassals (Herrmann 2018).

## CHAPTER 5

1. Clifford Geertz (1979), the champion of interpretive anthropology, noted the methodological inevitability that interpretation of foreign (or, in our case, ancient) cultures involved not just "experience-near" concepts, or those concepts by which the culture in question understands its own actions and beliefs, but also "experience-distant" concepts, those that render a culture's symbols and patterns of thought and behavior intelligible to others.

2. Data remain lacking for the narrow river valley connecting the Amuq Valley with the Orontes delta, partially because of the urban sprawl of the modern city of Antakya and surrounding suburbs, and partially because of deep colluvium from the mountain sides that have buried archaeological sites along this thin stretch of the Orontes Valley.

3. A three-tiered settlement hierarchy may also be indicated in the mid-eighth-century Samalian-language inscription by Panamuwa I. Gibson (1975: 67) translates the pertinent phrase as "In my days command was given . . . to establish cities and establish towns; and to the inhabitants of the villages my authority extended." Unfortunately, the translation of the terms used for the settlements is highly uncertain, and Younger (2000b: 156) prefers to leave them untranslated: "In my days it was commanded throughout all my land to reconstruct ṬYRT and to reconstruct ZRRY and to build the villages of the dominion."

4. Depictions of settlements on the bronze panels placed on the wooden gateway doors at the Assyrian site of Balawat also illustrate fortified cities in Patina surrounded by water (e.g., King 1915: pls. XXV, XXVII).

5. Without going into detail about the many problems inherent in the data from Al Mina, which has been presented exhaustively elsewhere, it is always necessary to keep in mind that the site was excavated poorly even by the standards of the day, the material was not collected in any systematic fashion, the recording system was inadequate and inconsistently applied, material thought to be Greek imports was disproportionately kept while local ceramics were almost entirely uncollected, the publication record is thin and focuses exclusively on Greek material culture, and post excavation the material was scattered in institutions around the world. Under these conditions it is challenging to make sense of the cultural nature and political affiliation of the early levels of Al Mina on archaeological grounds, and the site awaits renewed excavation.

6. The remains of Iron Age Adana have recently begun to be brought to light in the Tepebağ district of the modern city.

7. For a related classification of Syro-Anatolian cities into four components relating to performance—a walled city center; the segmentation of the city center into ceremonial and residential quarters; the presence of open space like streets and plazas; and an isolated central building, or palace—see Gilibert (2013: 37–40).

8. Other evocative inscriptions along these lines include KARKAMIŠ A11a, an orthostat set as a jamb on the western side of that site's King's Gate. The inscription by the ruler Katuwas mentions that "these gates (of) my grandfathers passed down to me" (Hawkins 2000: 95), implying that the gate was an inalienable possession of the king. See Harmanşah (2013: 148–52) for additional interpretation of the inscriptions in the King's Gate.

9. The South Gate's parallel inscription similarly begins on a portal lion. Though this monument (Pho/B I) is broken at the opening of the text, it presumably also began with "I am Azatiwada," making it another example at the site of a portal lion being signed with the king's name (Röllig 1999: 55).

10. That Younger felt compelled to add the gloss "(reign)" following the word "sit" in line 14 is indicative of today's predilection to consider royal "sitting" as a metaphor for "ruling" (2000: 148).

11. These words and phrases are generally represented by the logogram SOLIUM, only occasionally accompanied by phonetic complements. The accompanying grammatical ambiguity often makes it difficult to determine which translation is best, and in particular, whether or not the phrase in question is using the logogram as a transitive or intransitive verb.

12. Passages include the Karatepe bilingual (where it is present in both the Phoenician and the Luwian exemplars) (Hawkins 2000: 50), twice in isolated stelae from Hamath (2000: 405–7), in the Karahöyük and Izgin stelae of Malatya (2000: 288–92, 314–15), in KARKAMIŠ A21+ from the Great Staircase and Yararis's inscription A6 of the Royal Buttress (2000: 123–26, 158–60), on the *ex situ* colossal statue from Marash (2000: 255–57), and on the two pairs of podium blocks known as BOYBEYPINARI 1 and 2 from Kummuh (2000: 334–36).

13. Ignace Gelb (1939: 39) appears to have misunderstood the excavation records of the Syrian Hittite Expedition, placing both the inscription fragments and pieces of a colossal statue in Gateway VII, the gate on the east side of the acropolis between the acropolis and the lower city (also Hawkins 2000: 365–66, 2009: 167). In fact, although the colossal statue fragments that were thought to be associated with the inscription fragments *do* come from that gate, the inscriptional material appears to have been scattered around the acropolis (Harrison 2009a: 174; see illustration in 2009b: 179; cf. Ussishkin 1989: 488).

14. The threshold between these two rooms had been removed by later phases of the palace and thus was reconstructed by Haines on the basis of later phases (Haines 1971: 46–47).

15. One space that Haines does not label is the room whose entire existence is hypothetical, that is, the only space with none of its four walls identified. This is the small space south of VI.G, west of VI.E, and north of I.F. For the sake of consistency with published accounts, I have kept this room in the building plan but will not be incorporating it in the following space syntax analysis. The same is true for room I.C, the "staircase interior" of Building I.

16. These value ranges were determined in ArcMAP 10 using the "Equal Values" classification symbology, not the default classification method of "Natural Breaks (Jenks)." Data classification methods, including the several options offered by ArcMAP, have slightly different values depending on what one wants to emphasize or what statistical properties of values one considers most relevant to the question at hand. I have decided that dividing the total range into equal parts, here a range of 0.77/0.78, was the most representative treatment of the data.

17. The precise context of the lion statue is unfortunately difficult to reconstruct: although burial in a pit that cut a layer of sherds appears to be the most plausible interpretation of its findspot, the possibility that it was deliberately placed on its side with mudbricks then built up around it cannot be eliminated (Harrison and Denel 2017: 146).

18. Intriguingly, this same passage refers to Shalmaneser III's field marshal, Daiiān-Aššur, installing a statue of Shalmaneser in Kunulua's temple. This statue has never been found (if it were ever actually erected), although fragments of an Assyrian stele apparently to be dated to the reign of Sargon II have appeared at the site (Lauinger and Batiuk 2015).

19. Pucci (2019: 191–95) dates the start of Phase O, marked by the appearance of Red Slipped Burnished Ware, to 850 BCE at the earliest primarily on the basis of imported pottery at the site, especially Black-on-Red Ware from Cyprus (Schreiber 2003) and Cypro-Geometric pottery (Gjerstad 1948). This Cypriot pottery is itself dated on the basis of its Levantine contexts, however, and recent radiocarbon dates from stratified contexts at the nearby site of Tell Tayinat indicate that Red Slipped Burnished Ware began in the third quarter of the tenth century (Welton et al. 2019: 322–23). I therefore treat the town plan of Pucci's Phase O "middle" as belonging to roughly 850–750 BCE, not 750–600 BCE (cf. Pucci 2019: pls. 194–96).

20. In my opinion, it is an exaggeration to say that "in this level a single structure dominates the whole sector" (Pucci 2019: 126), and parallels with the *bīt-ḫilāni* palace are similarly unwarranted (Pucci 2019: 127, Fig. 32, Haines 1971: 19).

21. A reassessment of House b4–1 in the southeastern portion of the excavation area proposes that this structure was, in fact, a poorly preserved *in antis* temple whose plan was obscured by subsequent occupation, and whose construction might be associated with the temples claimed to have been built by Zakkur (Nishiyama 2012). This is an intriguing proposal, though possibly contradicted by the lack of cultic objects in the building itself, which "mainly relate to daily use" (2012: 109).

22. Earlier dates for the appearance of Ribbed Ware in the Iron Age I period have been proposed elsewhere, for example, Müller (2003), who suggests redating the stratigraphic sequence of Tille Höyük to align it with the results of the site of Lidar Höyük, 33 km further downstream on the Euphrates. This proposal is soundly rejected by Blaylock (2016: 19–20) due to Tille's relative sequence, its larger horizontal Iron Age exposures, and its use of whole pots in the ceramic sequence.

23. This seems more plausible, for example, than the excavators' tentative suggestion that the slightly more robust and more consistently aligned buildings of level V (as compared with level IV) represent "a hint of overall planning and monumentality" (Blaylock 2009: 108).

24. The rectangular buildings with column bases, in fact, resemble a contemporary building recently discovered adjacent to the Lion's Gate at Arslantepe (Blaylock 2016: xxi), interpreted there as a guard house and subsequently a reception hall (Manuelli 2010: 75; Frangipane and Liverani 2013: 354–56).

# BIBLIOGRAPHY

Abou Assaf, A., Bordreuil, P., and Millard, A. (1982), *La Statue de Tell Fekherye et son Inscription Bilingue Assyro-Araméenne* (Paris: Editions Recherche sur les Civilisations).

Abu 'Assaf, 'Ali (1990), *Der Tempel von 'Ain Dara* (Damaszener Forschungen Band 3; Mainz am Rhein: Philipp von Zabern).

Adams, William Y., Gerven, Dennis P. Van, and Levy, Richard S. (1978), "The Retreat from Migrationism," *Annual Review of Anthropology*, 7, 483–532.

Affanni, Giorgio (2009), "Ivory Sphinxes of North Syrian Tradition: the Flame and Frond School," in Serena M. Cecchini, Stefania Mazzoni, and Elena Scigliuzzo (eds.), *Syrian and Phoenician Ivories of the Early First Millennium BCE: Chronology, Regional Styles and Iconographic Repertories, Patterns or Inter-regional Distributions. Acts of the International Workshop, Pisa, December 9th–11th 2004* (Pisa: Edizioni ETS), 171–85.

Agnew, John (1994), "The Territorial Trap: The Geographical Assumptions of International Relations Theory," *Review of International Political Economy*, 1, 53–80.

Agnew, John (2009), *Globalization and Sovereignty* (Lanham, MD: Rowman & Littlefield).

Ahrens, Alexander, Kozal, Ekin, and Novák, Mirko (2010), "Sirkeli Höyük in Smooth Cilicia: A General Overview from the 4th to the 1st Millennium BC," in Paolo Matthiae et al. (eds.), *Proceedings of the 6th International Congress on the Archaeology of the Ancient Near East* (2; Wiesbaden: Harrassowitz Verlag), 55–74.

Akçay A. (2016), "Hartapu: Kimin Kralı?," in Sedat Erkut S and Özlem Sir Gavaz (eds.), *ANTAHŠUM^SAR "ÇİĞDEM": Eski Anadolu Araştırmalarına ve Hititlere Adanmış Bir Hayat. Ahmet Ünal Armağanı* (Istanbul: Arkeoloji ve Sanat Yayınları), 9–24.

Akkermans, Peter M. M. G. and Schwartz, Glenn M. (2003), *The Archaeology of Syria: From Complex Hunter-Gatherers to Early Urban Societies (ca. 16,000–300 B.C.)* (Cambridge: Cambridge University Press).

Akurgal, Ekrem (1949), *Späthethitische Bildkunst* (Ankara Üniversitesi Dil ve Tarih-Coğrafya Fakültesi Yayınları; Ankara: Archaeologisches Inst. der Univ.).

al-Bahloul, Khozama, Barro, Andrea, and d'Alfonso, Lorenzo (2005), "Area H: The Iron Age Cremation Cemetery," in Luc Bachelot and Frederick Mario Fales (eds.), *Tell Shiukh Fawqani: 1994–1998* (History of the Ancient Near East; Padua: S.A.R.G.O.N Editrice e libreria), 997–1048.

Albenda, Pauline (1977), "Landscape Bas-Reliefs in the *Bīt Ḫilāni* of Ashurbanipal," *Bulletin of the American Schools of Oriental Research*, 225, 29–48.

Albenda, Pauline (1988), "The Gateway and Portal Stone Reliefs from Arslan Tash," *Bulletin of the American Schools of Oriental Research*, 271, 5–30.

Albright, William Foxwell (1942), "A Votive Stele Erected by Ben-Hadad I of Damascus to the God Melcarth," *Bulletin of the American Schools of Oriental Research*, 87, 23–29.

Albright, William Foxwell (1975), "Syria, the Philistines, and Phoenicia," in I. E. S. Edwards et al. (eds.), *The Cambridge Ancient History, Vol. II, Part 2: History of the Middle East and Aegean Region c. 1380–1000 B.C.* (Cambridge: Cambridge University Press), 507–36.

Alden, John (1979), "A Reconstruction of Toltec Period Political Units in the Valley of Mexico," in K. Cooke and C. Renfrew (eds.), *Transformations: Mathematical Approaches to Culture Change* (New York: Academic Press), 169–200.

Altaweel, Mark and Squitieri, Andrea (2018), *Revolutionizing a World: From Small States to Universalism in the Pre-Islamic Near East* (London: UCL Press).

Alvaro, Corrado (2012), "The Topography and Architecture at Arslantepe during the Second and First Millennia BC: Reconsidering More Than 100 Years of Researches," *Origini*, XXXIV, 345–60.

Anderson, Bendeict R. (1983), *Imagined Communities: Reflections on the Origin and Spread of Nationalism* (London: Verso).

Ando, Clifford (2017), "Introduction: States and State Power in Antiquity," in Clifford Ando and Seth Richardson (eds.), *Ancient States and Infrastructural Power: Europe, Asia, and America* (Philadelphia: University of Philadelphia Press), 1–16.

Andrae, Walter (1924), *Hethitische Inschriften auf Bleistreifen aus Assur* (Wissenschaftliche Veröffentlichungen der Deutschen Orientgesellschaft; Osnabrück).

Anthony, David W. (1990), "Migration in Archaeology: The Baby and the Bathwater," *American Anthropologist*, 92 (4), 895–914.

Anthony, David W. (1992), "The Bath Refilled: Migration in Archeology," *American Anthropologist*, 94 (1), 174–76.

Antonaccio, Carla M. (2013), "Networking the Middle Ground? The Greek Diaspora, Tenth to Fifth Century BC," *Archaeological Review from Cambridge*, 28 (1), 237–51.

Appadurai, Arjun (1996), *Modernity at Large: Cultural Dimensions of Globalizations* (Minneapolis: University of Minnesota Press).

Aro, Sanna (2003), "Art and Architecture," in H. Craig Melchert (ed.), *The Luwians* (Leiden: Brill), 281–337.

Aro, Sanna (2010), "Luwians in Aleppo?," in Itamar Singer (ed.), *ipamati kistamati pari tumatimis: Luwian and Hittite Studies Presented to J. David Hawkins on the Occasion of His 70th Birthday* (Tel Aviv: Institute of Archaeology, Tel Aviv University), 1–9.

Aro, Sanna (2013), "Carchemish Before and After 1200 BC," in Alice Mouton, Ian Rutherford, and Ilya Yakubovich (eds.), *Luwian Identities: Culture, Language and Religion between Anatolia and the Aegean* (Leiden, Boston: Brill), 233–76.

Ataç, Mehmet-Ali (2012), "'The Charms of Tyranny': Conceptions of Power in the 'Garden Scene' of Ashurbanipal Reconsidered," in Gernot Wilhelm (ed.), *Organization, Representation, and Symbols of Power in the Ancient Near East: Proceedings of the 54th Rencontre Assyriologique Internationale at Würzburg 20–25 July 2008.* (Winona Lake, IN: Eisenbrauns), 411–27.

Atici, Levent, et al. (eds.) (2014), *Current Research at Kültepe-Kanesh: An Interdisciplinary and Integrative Approach to Trade Networks, Internationalism, and Identity* (Lockwood Press on behalf of the American Schools of Oriental Research).

Aubet, Maria Eugenia (2008), "Political and Economic Implications of the New Phoenician Chronologies," in Claudia Sagona (ed.), *Beyond the Homland: Markers in Phoenician Chronology* (Leuven: Peeters), 179–91.

Aubet, Maria Eugenia (2010), "The Phoenician Cemetery of Tyre," *Near Eastern Archaeology*, 73 (2–3), 144–55.

Aubet, Maria Eugenia (2013), "Cremation and social memory in Iron Age Phoenicia," in Oswald Loretz et al. (eds.), *Ritual, Religion and Reason: Studies in the Ancient World in Honour of Paolo Xella* (Münster: Ugarit-Verlag), 77–87.

Bagg, Ariel (2013), "Palestine under Assyrian Rule: A New Look at the Assyrian Imperial Policy in the West," *Journal of the American Oriental Society*, 133 (1), 119–44.

Baghdo, A. M. H., et al. (eds.) (2009), *Ausgrabungen auf dem Tell Halaf in Nordost-Syrien, Teil 1. Vorbericht über die erste und zweite syrisch-deutsche Grabungskampagne auf dem Tell Halaf* (Wiesbaden: Harrassowitz).

Baghdo, A. M. H., et al. (eds.) (2012), *Ausgrabungen auf dem Tell Halaf, Teil II, Vorbericht über die dritte bis fünfte syrisch-deutsche Grabungskampagne auf dem Tell Halaf* (Wiesbaden: Harrassowitz).

Barnett, Richard D. (1935), "The Nimrud Ivories and the Art of the Phoenicians," *Iraq*, 2 (2), 179–210.

Barnett, Richard D. (1948), "Hittite Hieroglyphic Texts at Aleppo," *Iraq*, 10 (2), 122–39.

Barnett, Richard D. (1957), *A Catalogue of the Nimrud Ivories: With Other Examples of Ancient Near Eastern Ivories in the British Museum* (London: Trustees of the British Museum).

Barnett, Richard D. (1976), *Sculptures from the North Palace of Ashurbanipal at Nineveh (668–627 B.C.)* (London: British Museum Publications).

Barnett, Richard D. (1982), *Ancient Ivories in the Middle East* (Qedem; Jerusalem: Israel Exploration Society).

Barth, Fredrik (ed.) (1969), *Ethnic Groups and Boundaries: The Social Organization of Culture Difference* (Bergen: Universitetsforlaget).

Beaudry, Mary C. and Parno, Travis G. (2013a), "Introduction: Mobilities in Contemporary and Historical Archaeology," in Mary C. Beaudry and Travis G. Parno (eds.), *Archaeologies of Mobility and Movement* (New York: Springer), 1–14.

Beaudry, Mary C. and Parno, Travis G. (eds.) (2013b), *Archaeologies of Mobility and Movement* (Contributions to Global Historical Archaeology, New York: Springer).

Beyer, Dominique (2001), *Emar IV: Les Sceaux* (Fribourg: Éditions Universitaires/ Vandenhoeck & Ruprecht).

Bhabha, Homi (1990), "DissemiNation: Time, Narrative, and the Margins of the Modern Nation," in Homi K. Bhabha (ed.), *Nation and Narration* (London: Routledge), 291–322.

Bhabha, Homi (1994), *The Location of Culture* (London: Routledge).

Bienkowski, Piotr (1982), "Some Remarks on the Practice of Cremation in the Levant," *Levant*, 14, 80–89.

Binford, Lewis R. (1965), "Archaeological Systematics and the Study of Culture Process," *American Antiquity*, 31, 203–10.

Birney, Kathleen (2008), "Tracking the Cooking Pot à la Steatite: Signs of Cyprus in Iron Age Syria," *American Journal of Archaeology*, 112, 565–80.

Bittel, Kurt (1976), *Die Hethiter: Die Kunst Anatoliens vom Ende des 3. bis zum Anfang des 1. Jahrtausends vor Christus* (Munich: C. H. Beck).

Bittel, Kurt, et al. (1958), *Die hethitischen Grabfunde von Osmankayası* (Boğazköy-Hattuša: Verlag Gebr. Mann).

Blaylock, Stuart (2009), *Tille Höyük 3.1: The Iron Age: Introduction, Stratification and Architecture* (Ankara: British Institute at Ankara).

Blaylock, Stuart (2016), *Tille Höyük 3.2: The Iron Age: Pottery, Objects and Conclusions* (Ankara: British Institute at Ankara).

Boardman, John (1959), "Greek Potters at Al Mina?," *Anatolian Studies*, 9, 163–69.

Boardman, John (1990), "Al Mina and History," *Oxford Journal of Archaeology*, 9, 169–90.

Boardman, John (1999), "The Excavated History of Al Mina," in Gocha Tsetskhladze (ed.), *Ancient Greeks West and East* (Leiden: Brill), 135–62.

Boardman, John (2002), "Al Mina: The Study of a Site," *Ancient West & East*, 2, 315–31.

Bonatz, Dominik (2000), *Das syro-hethitische Grabdenkmal: Untersuchungen zur Entstehung einer neuen Bildgattung in der Eisenzeit im nordsyrisch-südostanatolischen Raum* (Mainz: P. von Zabern Verlag).

Bonatz, Dominik (2001), "Mnemohistory in Syro-Hittite Iconography," in Tzvi Abusch (ed.), *Historiography in the Cuneiform World: Proceedings of the 45th Rencontre Assyriologique Internationale* (Bethesda, MD: CDL), 65–77.

Bonatz, Dominik (2004), "Objekte der Kleinkunst als Ideenträger zwischen dem syro-anatolischen und dem assyrischen Raum: Das Problem der Elfenbeine," in Mirko Novák, Friedhelm Prayon, and Anne-Maria Wittke (eds.), *Die Aussenwirkung des Spathethitischen Kulturraumes: Güteraustausch-Kulturkontakt-Kulturtransfer* (Münster: Ugarit-Verlag), 387–404.

Bonatz, Dominik (2014), "Katumuwa's Banquet Scene," in Virginia Rimmer Herrmann and J. David Schloen (eds.), *In Remembrance of Me: Feasting with the Dead in the Ancient Middle East* (Oriental Institute Museum Publications; Chicago: The Oriental Institute of the University of Chicago), 39–44.

Bonomo, Antonio and Zaina, Federico (2016), "Karkemish. Report on the 2011 and 2012 Excavations in Area F," *Gaziantep Regional Project Occasional Paper*, 2016 (1), 1–24.

Bossert, Eva-Maria (2014), "Keramik," in Halet Çambel (ed.), *Karatepe-Aslantaş Azatiwataya. Band 2* (Wiesbaden: Reichert Verlag), 111–53.

Bourdieu, Pierre (1977), *Outline of a Theory of Practice* (Cambridge Studies in Social Anthropology; Cambridge: Cambridge University Press).

Bouthillier, Christina, et al. (2014), "Further Work at Kilise Tepe, 2007–2011: Refining the Bronze to Iron Age Transition," *Anatolian Studies*, 64, 95–161.

Brah, Avtar (1996), *Cartographies of Diaspora: Contesting Identities* (London: Routledge).

Braidwood, Robert J. (1937), *Mounds in the Plain of Antioch: An Archeological Survey* (Chicago: University of Chicago Press).

Braidwood, Robert J. and Braidwood, Linda S. (1960), *Excavations in the Plain of Antioch I: The Earlier Assemblages, Phases A-J* (OIP 61; Chicago: University of Chicago Press).

Bridgland, D. R., et al. (2003), "A Long Quaternary Terrace Sequence in the Orontes River Valley, Syria: A Record of Uplift and of Human Occupation," *Current Science*, 84, 1080–89.

Brock, Roger and Hodkinson, Stephen (eds.) (2000), *Alternatives to Athens: Varities of Political Organization and Community in Ancient Greece* (Oxford: Oxford University Press).

Brown, Brian (2008a), "The Kilamuwa Relief: Ethnicity, Class and Power in Iron Age North Syria," in Joaquin M. Córdoba et al. (eds.), *Proceedings of the 5th International Congress on the Archaeology of the Ancient Near East* (Madrid: Centro Superior de Estudios sobre el Oriente Próximo y Egipto), 339–55.

Brown, Brian (2008b), "Monumentalizing Identities: North Syrian Urbanism, 1200–800 BCE," unpublished PhD thesis (University of California, Berkeley).

Brown, Michael and Smith, Stefan L. (2016), "The Land of Carchemish and its Neighbours during the Neo-Hittite Period (c. 1190–717 BC)," in Tony J. Wilkinson, Edgar Peltenburg, and Eleanor Barbanes Wilkinson (eds.), *Carchemish in Context: The Land of Carchemish Project, 2006–2010* (Oxford: Oxbow Books), 22–37.

Brubaker, Rogers (2005), "The 'Diaspora' Diaspora," *Ethnic and Racial Studies*, 28 (1), 1–19.

Bryce, Trevor (2003), "History," in H. Craig Melchert (ed.), *The Luwians* (Leiden: Brill), 27–127.

Bryce, Trevor (2012), *The World of the Neo-Hittite Kingdoms: A Political and Military History* (Oxford: Oxford University Press).

Bryce, Trevor (2016), "The Land of Hiyawa (Que) Revisited," *Anatolian Studies*, 66.

Bunnens, Guy (1995), "Hittites and Aramaeans at Til Barsib: A Reappraisal," in K. v. Lerberghe and A. Schoors (eds.), *Immigration and Emigration within the Ancient Near East. Festschrift E. Lipinski* (Orientalia Lovaniensa Analecta; Leuven: Uitgeverij Peeters en Departement Oriëntalistiek), 19–27.

Bunnens, Guy (1997), "Carved Ivories from Til Barsip," *American Journal of Archaeology*, 101, 435–50.

Bunnens, Guy (2000a), "Syria in the Iron Age: Problems of Definition," in Guy Bunnens (ed.), *Essays on Syria in the Iron Age* (Louvain: Peeters Press), 3–19.

Bunnens, Guy (ed.) (2000b), *Essays on Syria in the Iron Age* (ANES Supplement, Louvain: Peeters Press).

Bunnens, Guy (2005), "From Carchemish to Nimrud: Between Visual Writing and Textual Illustration," in Ph. Talon and V. Van der Stede (eds.), *Si un Homme ... Texts Offerts en Hommage à André Finet* (Subartu XVI; Brussels: Brepols), 21–24.

Bunnens, Guy (2009), "Assyrian Empire Building and Aramization of Culture as Seen from Tell Ahmar/Til Barsib," *Syria*, 86, 67–82.

Bunnens, Guy (2016), "Neo-Assyrian Pebble Mosaics in their Architectural Context," in John MacGinnis, Dirk Wicke, and Tina Greenfield (eds.), *The Provincial Archaeology of the Assyrian Empire* (Cambridge: McDonald Institute for Archaeological Research), 59–70.

Burmeister, Stefan (2000), "Archaeology and Migration: Approaches to an Archaeological Proof of Migration," *Current Anthropology*, 41 (4), 119–67

Çakırlar, Canan and Ikram, Salima (2016), "'When Elephants Battle, the Grass Suffers.' Power, Ivory and the Syrian Elephant," *Levant*, 48 (2), 167–83.

Çambel, Halet (1999), *Corpus of Hieroglyphic Luwian Inscriptions vol. II: Karatepe-Arslantaş* (Berlin: Walter de Gruyter).

Çambel, Halet (ed.) (2014), *Karatepe-Aslantaş, Azatiwataya. Band 2* (Wiesbaden: Reichert Verlag).

Çambel, Halet and Özyar, Aslı (2003), *Karatepe-Aslantaş, Azatiwataya. Die Bildwerke* (Mainz: von Zabern).

Cameron, Catherine M. (2013), "How People Moved among Ancient Societies: Broadening the View," *American Anthropologist*, 115 (2), 218–31.

Casana, Jesse (2009), "Alalakh and the Archaeological Landscape of Mukish: The Political Geography and Population of a Late Bronze Age Kingdom," *Bulletin of the American Schools of Oriental Research*, 353, 7–37.

Casana, Jesse (2013), "Radial Route Systems and Agro-Pastoral Strategies in the Fertile Crescent: New Discoveries from Western Syria and Southwestern Iran," *Journal of Anthropological Archaeology*, 32, 257–73.

Casana, Jesse and Herrmann, Jason T. (2010), "Settlement History and Urban Planning at Zincirli Höyük, Southern Turkey," *Journal of Mediterranean Archaeology*, 23 (1), 55–80.

Casana, Jesse J. and Wilkinson, Tony J. (2005), "Gazetteer of Sites," in Kutlu Aslihan Yener (ed.), *The Amuq Valley Regional Projects, Volume 1* (Chicago: The Oriental Institute of the University of Chicago Press), 203–80.

Caubet, Annie (2013), "Working Ivory in Syria and Anatolia during the Late Bronze–Iron Age," in K. Aslıhan Yener (ed.), *Across the Border: Late Bronze-Iron Age Relations between Syria and Anatolia* (Ancient Near Eastern Studies Supplement Series; Leuven: Peeters), 449–63.

Cecchini, Serena Maria (2000), "The Textile Industry in Northern Syria during the Iron Age according to the Evidence from the Tell Afis Excavations," in G. Bunnens (ed.), *Essays on Syria in the Iron Age* (Louvain: Peeters Press), 211–34.

Cecchini, Serena Maria (2009), "Les Ivoires de Arslan Tash," in Serena Maria Cecchini, Stefania Mazzoni, and Elena Scigliuzzo (eds.), *Syrian and Phoenician Ivories of the Early First Millennium BCE: Chronology, Regional Styles and Iconographic Repertories, Patterns of Inter-regional Distribution* (Pisa: Edizioni ETS), 87–105.

Cecchini, Serena Maria (2014), "Tell Afis in the Iron Age: The Official Buildings on the Eastern Acropolis," *Near Eastern Archaeology*, 77 (1), 58–63.

Cecchini, S. M. and Mazzoni, S. (eds.) (1998), *Tell Afis (Siria): scavi sull'acropoli 1988–1992 = the 1988–1992 Excavations on the Acropolis* (Pisa: Ediziones ETS).

Certeau, Michel de (1984), *The Practice of Everyday Life*, trans. Steven Rendall (Berkeley: University of California Press).

Charlton, Thomas H. and Nichols, Deborah L. (1997), "The City-State Concept: Development and Applications," in Deborah L. Nichols and Thomas H. Charlton (eds.), *The Archaeology of City-States: Cross-Cultural Approaches* (Washington, DC: Smithsonian Institution Press), 1–14.

Childe, V. Gordon (1925), *The Dawn of European Civilization* (New York: A.A. Knopf).

Childe, V. Gordon (1950a), *Prehistoric Migrations in Europe* (Oslo: Aschehoug).

Childe, V. Gordon (1950b), "The Urban Revolution," *The Town Planning Review*, 21 (1), 3–17.

Cholidis, Nadja and Martin, Lutz (eds.) (2010), *Tell Halaf V. Im Krieg zerstörte Denkmäler und ihre Restaurierung* (Berlin: De Gruyter).

Chorowicz, Jean, et al. (1994), "The Maras Triple Junction (southern Turkey) Based on Digital Elevation Model and Satellite Imagery Interpretation," *Journal of Geophysical Research*, 99 (B10), 20,225–20,42.

Cinquatti, Arianna (2015), "Question of Style: The Use of Qualitative and Quantitative Methods to Assess the Significance of First Millennium BCE Ivory Carving Traditions," *Altorientalische Forschungen*, 42 (1), 46–58.

Clifford, James (1994), "Diasporas," *Cultural Anthropology*, 9 (3), 302–38.

Clifford, James (1997), *Routes: Travel and Translation in the Late Twentieth Century* (Cambridge, MA: Harvard University Press).

Clifford, James and Marcus, George E. (eds.) (1986), *Writing Culture: The Poetics and Politics of Ethnography* (Berkeley: University of California Press).

Cline, Eric H. (2014), *1177 B.C. The Year Civilization Collapsed* (Princeton, NJ: Princeton University Press).

Cohen, Robin (2008), *Global Diasporas: An Introduction* (London: Routledge).

Cohen, Yoram (2009), *The Scribes and Scholars of the City of Emar in the Late Bronze Age* (Winona Lake, IN: Eisenbrauns).

Collingwood, Robin George (1946), "Preliminary Analysis: The Idea of a Philosophy of Something, and in Particular, of a Philosophy of History," *The Idea of History* (Oxford: Oxford University Press), 335–58.

Collins, Billie Jean (2007), *The Hittites and Their World* (Atlanta, GA: Society of Biblical Literature).

Collins, T. (1971), "The Kilamuwa Inscription—A Phoenician Poem," *Welt des Orients*, 6, 183–88.

Collon, Dominique (1977), "Ivory," *Iraq*, 39 (2), 219–22.

Connerton, Paul (1989), *How Societies Remember* (Cambridge: Cambridge University Press).

Cooper, Lisa (2006), *Early Urbanism on the Syrian Euphrates* (New York: Routledge).

Costin, Cathy L. (1991), "Craft Specialization: Issues in Defining, Documenting, and Explaining the Organization of Production," in Michael Schiffer (ed.), *Archaeological Method and Theory, Volume 3* (Tucson: University of Arizona Press), 1–56.

Courbin, Paul (1993), *Fouilles de Bassit: Tombes du Fer* (Paris: Éditions Recherche sur les Civilisations).

Cowgill, George L. (2004), "Origins and Development of Urbanism: Archaeological Perspectives," *Annual Review of Anthropology*, 33, 525–49.

Cresswell, Tim (2010), "Towards a Politics of Mobility," *Environment and Planning D: Society and Space*, 28, 17–31.

Cribb, Paul (1991), *Nomads in Archaeology* (Cambridge: Cambridge University Press).

Curtis, John (2014), "Assyria: Establishing the Imagery of Empire," in Joan Aruz, Sarah B. Graff, and Yelena Rakic (eds.), *Assyria to Iberia at the Dawn of the Classical Age* (New York: The Metropolitan Museum of Art), 52–74.

Cutting, Marion (2003), "The Use of Spatial Analysis to Study Prehistoric Settlement Architecture," *Oxford Journal of Archaeology*, 22 (1), 1–21.

d'Alfonso, Lorenzo (2014), "The Kingdom of Tarhuntassa: A Reassessment of its Timeline and Political Significance," in P. Taracha (ed.), *Proceedings of the Eighth International Congress of Hittitology: Warsaw, 5–9 September 2011* (Warsaw: Wydawnictwo Agade), 221–39.

d'Alfonso, Lorenzo (2019), "War in Anatolia in the Post-Hittite Period: The Anatolian Hieroglyphic Inscription of TOPADA Revised," *Journal of Cuneiform Studies*, 71, 133–52.

D'Altroy, Terence N. (1992), *Provincial Power in the Inka Empire* (Washington, DC: Smithsonian Institution Press).

Dalley, Stephanie (2000), "Shamshi-ilu, Language and Power in the Western Assyrian Empire," in Guy Bunnens (ed.), *Essays on Syria in the Iron Age* (ANES Supplement; Louvain: Peeters Press), 79–88.

Delaporte, Louis (1934), "Céramique du Hittite Recent," *Review Hittites et Asian*, II (15), 257–85.

Delaporte, Louis (1940), *Malatya-Arslantepe I: La Porte des Lions* (Paris: E. de Boccard).

DeMarrais, Elizabeth, Castillo, Luis Jaime, and Earle, Timothy (1996), "Ideology, Materialization, and Power Strategies," *Current Anthropology*, 37 (1), 15–31.

Denel, Elif (2006), "Development of Elite Cultures and Sociopolitical Complexity in Early Iron Age Kingdoms of Northern Syria and Southeastern Anatolia," Unpublished PhD dissertation, Bryn Mawr College.

Denel, Elif (2007), "Ceremony and Kingship at Carchemish," in Jack Cheng and Marian H. Feldman (eds.), *Ancient Near Eastern Art in Context: Studies in Honor of Irene J. Winter* (Leiden: Brill), 179–204.

di Paolo, Silvana (2009), "What Production Model Can Be Deduced for First-Millennium BC Syro-Phoenician Ivories?," in Serena M. Cecchini, Stefania Mazzoni, and Elena Scigliuzzo (eds.), *Syrian and Phoenician Ivories of the Early First Millennium BCE: Chronology, Regional Styles and Iconographic Repertories, Patterns or Inter-regional Distributions* (Pisa: Edizioni ETS), 133–53.

Dietler, Michael (2005), "The Archaeology of Colonization and the Colonization of Archaeology: Theoretical Challenges from an Ancient Mediterranean Colonial Encounter," in G. J. Stein (ed.), *The Archaeology of Colonial Encounters* (Santa Fe, NM: School of American Research Press), 33–68.

Dietler, M. and Herbich, I. (1998), "Habitus, Techniques and Style: An Integrated Approach to the Social Understanding of Material Culture and Boundaries," in M. Stark (ed.), *The Archaeology of Social Boundaries* (Washington, DC: Smithsonian Institution).

Dinçol, Belkıs (1994), "New Archaeological and Epigraphical Finds from Ivriz: A Preliminary Report," *Tel Aviv*, 21, 117–28.

Dinçol, Belkıs, et al. (2015), "Two New Inscribed Storm-God Stelae from Arsuz (İskenderun): ARSUZ 1 and 2," *Anatolian Studies*, 65, 59–77.

Dion, Paul-Eugène (1997), *Les Araméens à l'âge du Fer: Histoire Politiques et Structures Sociales* (Paris: Librairie Lecoffre).

Dommelen, Peter van (2005), "Colonial Interactions and Hyrbid Practices: Phoenician and Carthaginian Settlement in the Ancient Mediterranean," in G. J. Stein (ed.), *The Archaeology of Colonial Encounters* (Santa Fe, NM: School of American Research Press), 109–41.

Dommelen, Peter van (2014), "Moving On: Archaeological Perspectives on Mobility and Migration," *World Archaeology*, 46 (4), 477–83.

Donner, Herbert and Röllig, W. (1966), *Kanaanäische und Aramäische Inschriften*, 3 vols. (2nd ed.; Wiesbaden: Harrassowitz).

Dornemann, Rudolph H. (2003), "Seven Seasons of ASOR Excavations at Tell Qarqur, Syria, 1993–1999," *Annual of the American Schools of Oriental Research*, 56.

Dothan, Trude (1981), *The Philistines and their Material Culture* (New Haven, CT: Yale University Press, Israel Exploration Society).

Drüppel, K., et al. (2011), "Aramaic Basalt Statues from Tell Halaf, Syria: Locating the Ancient Quarries," *Archaeometry*, 53 (3), 441–68.

Dufoix, Stéphane (2008), *Diasporas*, trans. William Rodarmor (Berkeley: University of California Press).

Dupont-Sommer, André (1950), "Deux Nouvelles Inscriptions Sémitiques Trouvée en Cilicie," *Jahrbuch für Kleinasiatische Forschungen*, 1, 43–47.

Dupré, Sylvestre (1983), *Porsuk I: la céramique de l'âge du bronze et de l'âge du fer* (Paris: Editions Recherche sur les Civilisations).

Düring, Bleda S., Visser, Eva, and Akkermans, Peter M. M. G. (2015), "Skeletons in the Fortress: The Late Bronze Age Burials of Tell Sabi Abyad, Syria," *Levant*, 47 (1), 30–50.

Eckardt, Hella (ed.) (2010), *Roman Diasporas: Archaeological Approaches to Mobility and Diversity in the Roman Empire* (Journal of Roman Archaeology Supplementary Series, Portsmouth, RI: Journal of Roman Archaeology, LLC).

Egami, Namio, Wakita, Shigeo, and Ishida, Keiko (1988–89), "Excavations at Tell Mastuma, Syria, 1988," *Bulletin of the Ancient Orient Museum*, X, 47–75.

Ehringhaus, Horst (2005), *Götter, Herrscher, Inschriften: Die Felsreliefs der Hethitischen Grossreichszeit in der Türkei* (Mainz am Rhein: Philipp von Zabern).

Eisenstadt, Shmuel N. (1963), *The Political Systems of Empires* (New Brunswick, NJ: Transaction).

Elayi, Josette (2018), *The History of Phoenicia*, trans. Andrew Plummer (Atlanta, GA: Lockwood Press).

Emanuel, Jeffrey P. (2015), "King Taita and His 'Palistin': Philistine State or Neo-Hittite Kingdom," *Antiguo Oriente*, 13, 11–40.

Engels, Friedrich (1902), *The Origin of the Family, Private Property and the State*, trans. Ernest Untermann (Chicago: C.H. Kerr and Company).

Epperson, Terrence W. (2004), "Critical Race Theory and the Archaeology of the African Diaspora," *Historical Archaeology*, 38 (1), 101–08.

Ezzo, Joseph A. and Price, T. Douglas (2002), "Migration, Regional Reorganization, and Spatial Group Composition at Grasshoper Pueblo, Arizona," *Journal of Archaeological Science*, 29, 499–520.

Fabian, Johannes (1983), *Time and the Other: How Anthropology Makes Its Object* (New York: Columbia University Press).

Feinman, Gary M. and Marcus, Joyce (1998), "Introduction," in Gary M. Feinman and Joyce Marcus (eds.), *Archaic States* (Santa Fe, NM: School of American Research Press), 3–13.

Feldman, Marian H. (2014), *Communities of Style: Portable Luxury Arts, Identity and Collective Memory in the Iron Age Levant* (Chicago: University of Chicago Press).

Feldman, Marian H. (2015), "Houses of Ivory: The Consumption of Ivories in the Iron Age Levant," *Altorientalische Forschungen*, 42 (1), 97–111.

Finley, Moses (1981), "The Ancient City: From Fustel de Coulanges to Max Weber and Beyond," *Economy and Society in Ancient Greece* (London: Chatto and Windus), 3–23.

Finley, Moses (1987/89), "The City," *Opus*, 6 (8), 303–13.

Fischer, Erika (2007), *Ägyptische und ägyptisierende Elfenbeine aus Megiddo und Lachisch: Inschriftenfunde, Flaschen, Löffel* (Alter Orient und Altes Testament; Münster: Ugarit-Verlag).

Fischer, Erika and Wicke, Dirk (2016), "Review of *Communities of Style: Portable Luxury Arts, Identity, and Collective Memory in the Iron Age Levant*, by Marian H. Feldman," *American Journal of Archaeology*, 120 (4), doi:10.3764/ajaonline1204.FischerWicke.

Ford, James A. and Steward, Julian H. (1954), "On the Concept of Types," *American Anthropologist*, 56 (1), 42–57.

Foucault, Michel (1984), "Space, Knowledge, and Power," in Paul Rabinow (ed.), *The Foucault Reader* (New York: Pantheon Books), 239–56.

Fowler, William Warde (1893), *The City-State of the Greeks and Romans: A Survey Introductory to the Study of Ancient History* (London: Macmillan).

Frangipane, Marcella (2018), "Different Trajectories in State Formation in Greater Mesopotamia: A View from Arslantepe," *Journal of Archaeological Research*, 26, 3–63.

Frangipane, Marcella and Liverani, Mario (2013), "Neo-Hittite Melid: Continuity or Discontinuity?," in K. Aslıhan Yener (ed.), *Across the Border: Late Bronze–Iron Age Relations between Syria and Anatolia* (Leuven: Peeters), 349–71.

Frankenstein, Susan (1979), "The Phoenicians in the Far West: A Function of Neo-Assyrian Imperialism," in Mogens Trolle Larsen (ed.), *Power and Propaganda: A Symposium on Ancient Empires* (Copenhagen Studies in Assyriology; Copenhagen: Akademisk Forlag), 263–94.

Frankfort, Henri (1952), "The Origin of the Bit Hilani," *Iraq* 14 (2), 120–31.

Frankfort, Henri (1996), *The Art and Architecture of the Ancient Orient* (New Haven, CT: Yale University Press).

Fried, M. H. (1967), *The Evolution of Political Society: An Essay in Political Anthropology* (New York: Random House).

Fuchs, Andreas (1994), *Die Inschriften Sargons II. aus Khorsabad* (Göttingen: Cuvillier Verlag).

Fugmann, Ejnar (1958), *Hama: Fouilles et recherches de la Fondation Carlsberg, 1931–1938: L'architecture, des périodes pre-Hellénistiques* (Copenhague Nationalmuseet).

Galil, Gershon (2014), "A Concise History of Palistin/Patin/Unqi/'mq in the 11th–9th Centuries BC," *Semitica*, 56, 75–104.

Galil, Gershon, et al. (eds.) (2012), *The Ancient Near East in the 12th–10th Centuries BCE: Culture and History. Proceedings of the International Conference Held at the University of Haifa, 2–5 May, 2010* (Alter Orient und Altes Testament, Münster: Ugarit-Verlag).

Galter, Hannes D. (2004), "Militärgrenze und Euphrathandel. Der sozio-ökonomische Hintergrund der Trilinguen von Arslan Tash," in Robert Rollinger and Christoph Ulf (eds.), *Commerce and Monetary Systems in the Ancient World. Means of Transmission and Cultural Interaction. Proceedings of the Fifth Annual Symposium of the Assyrian and Babylonian Intellectual Heritage Project* (Stuttgart: Franz Steiner Verlag), 444–60.

Garstang, John (1908), "Excavations at Sakje-Geuzi in North Syria, Preliminary Report for 1908," *Annals of Anthropology and Archaeology*, 1, 97–117.

Gates, Marie-Henriette (2004), "The 2002 Season at Kinet Höyük (Yeşil-Dörtyol, Hatay)," *Kazı Sonuçları Toplantısı*, 25 (1), 405–16.

Gates, Marie-Henriette (2008), "2007 Season at Kinet Höyük (Yeşil-Dörtyol, Hatay)," *Kazı Sonuçları Toplantısı*, 30 (2), 351–68.

Geertz, Clifford (1979), "From the Native's Point of View: On the Nature of Anthropological Understanding," in P. Rabinow and W. M. Sullivan (eds.), *Interpretive Social Science: A Reader* (Berkeley: University of California Press), 225–42.

Gelb, Ignace (1939), *Hittite Hieroglyphic Monuments* (Oriental Institute Publications 45; Chicago: University of Chicago Press).

Genge, Heinz (1979), *Nordsyrisch-Südanatolische Reliefs: Eine Archäologisch-Historische Untersuchung: Datierung und Bestimmung* (København: Det Kongelige Danske Videnskabernes Selskab; kommissionær, Munksgaards Boghandel).

Genz, Hermann (2011), "The Iron Age in Central Anatolia," in Gocha R. Tsetskhladze (ed.), *The Black Sea, Greece, Anatolia and Europe in the First Millennium BC* (Leuven: Peeters), 331–68.

Gevirtz, Stanley (1967), "A Spindle Whorl with Phoenician Inscription," *Journal of Near Eastern Studies*, 26 (1), 13–16.

Giacosa, Gabriele (2016), "The Iron I and II Pottery Assemblages at Karkemish," *Karkemish-Tayinat Workshop* (Bologna).

Gibson, John C. L. (1975), *Textbook of Syrian Semitic Inscriptions, Volume II: Aramaic Inscriptions Including Inscriptions in the Dialect of Zenjirli* (Oxford: Clarendon Press).

Gibson, John C. L. (1982), *Textbook of Syrian Semitic Inscriptions, Volume III: Phoenician Inscriptions Including the Mixed Dialect of Arslan Tash* (Oxford: Clarendon Press).

Gilibert, Alessandra (2004), "Jenseits von Stil und Ikonographie: Späthethitischen Einflüsse auf has assyrische Wandrelief," in Mirko Novák, Friedhelm Prayon, and Anne-Maria Wittke (eds.), *Die Aussenwirkung des Späthethitischen Kulturraumes: Güteraustausch-Kulturkontakt-Kulturtransfer* (Münster: Ugarit-Verlag), 373–385.

Gilibert, Alessandra (2011), *Syro-Hittite Monumental Art and the Archaeology of Performance: The Stone Reliefs at Carchemish and Zincirli in the Earlier First Millennium BCE* (Topoi: Berlin Studies of the Ancient World; Berlin: De Gruyter).

Gilibert, Alessandra (2013), "Death, Amusement and the City: Civic Spectacles and the Theatre Palace of Kapara, King of Gūzanā," *KASKAL*, 10, 35–68.

Gilroy, Paul (1993), *The Black Atlantic: Modernity and Double Consciousness* (London: Verso).

Giusfredi, Frederico (2010), *Sources for a Socio-Economic History of the Neo-Hittite States* (Texte der Hethiter; Heidelberg: Universitätsverlag Winter).

Giusfredi, Frederico (2018), "Cultural Contact and Language Contact in Iron Age Syria and Anatolia: A Preliminary Assessment," *Beyond All Boundaries: Anatolia in the 1st Millennium B.C.*, unpublished conference paper (Ascona, Switzerland).

Gjerstad, Einar (1948), *The Swedish Cyprus Expedition Vol. IV Part 2. The Cypro-Geometric, Cypro-Archaic, und Cypro-Classical Periods* (Stockholm: The Swedish Cyprus Expedition).

Glatz, Claudia and Casana, Jesse (2016), "Of Highland-Lowland Borderlands: Local Societies and Foreign Power in the Zagros-Mesopotamian Interface," *Journal of Anthropological Archaeology*, 44, 127–47.

Goedegebuure, Petra M. (2012), "Hittite Iconoclasm: Disconnecting the Icon, Disempowering the Referent," in Natalie May (ed.), *Iconoclasm and Text Destruction in the Ancient Near East and Beyond* (Chicago: The Oriental Institute of the University of Chicago), 407–52.

Goedegebuure P., van den Hout, T., Osborne, J. F., et al. (2020), "TÜRKMEN-KARAHÖYÜK 1: A New Hieroglyphic Luwian Inscription from Great King Hartapu, Son of Mursili, Conqueror of Phrygia," *Anatolian Studies*, 70, 29–43.

Goldmann, Hetty (ed.) (1963), *Excavations at Gözlü Kule, Tarsus, Volume III: The Iron Age* (Princeton, NJ: Princeton University Press).

Gonnella, J., Khayyata, W., and Kohlmeyer, K. (2005), *Die Zitadelle von Aleppo und der Tempel des Wettergottes* (Münster: Rhema).

Grayson, A. Kirk (1991), *The Royal Inscriptions of Mesopotamia, Assyrian Periods. Volume 2. Assyrian Rulers of the Early First Millennium BC I (1114–859 BC)* (Toronto: University of Toronto Press).

Grayson, A. Kirk (1996), *The Royal Inscriptions of Mesopotamia, Assyrian Periods. Volume 3. Assyrian Rulers of the Early First Millennium BC II (858–745BC)* (Toronto: University of Toronto Press).

Grayson, A. Kirk and Novotny, Jamie R. (2011), *Royal Inscriptions of the Neo-Assyrian Period, Volume 3: Royal Inscriptions of Sennacherib, King of Assyria (704–681 BC)* (Winona Lake, IN: Eisenbrauns).

Greenblatt, Stephen (2010), "Cultural Mobility: An Introduction," in Stephen Greenblatt (ed.), *Cultural Mobility: A Manifesto* (Cambridge: Cambridge University Press), 1–23.

Greenfield, Jonas C. and Shaffer, Aaron (1983), "Notes on the Akkadian-Aramaic Bilingual Statue from Tell Fekherye," *Iraq*, 45 (1), 109–16.

Griffeth, Robert and Thomas, Carol G. (eds.) (1981), *The City-State in Five Cultures* (Santa Barbara, CA: ABC-Clio).

Gunter, Ann C. (2009), *Greek Art and the Orient* (Cambridge: Cambridge University Press).

Güterbock, H. G. (1954), "Carchemish," *Journal of Near Eastern Studies*, 13 (2), 102–14.

Gzella, Holger (2014), "Language and Script," in Herbert Niehr (ed.), *The Aramaeans in Ancient Syria* (Leiden: Brill), 71–107.

Haines, Richard C. (1971), *Excavations in the Plain of Antioch II: The Structural Remains of the Later Phases. Chatal Hüyük, Tell al-Judaidah, and Tell Ta'yinat* (OIP 95; Chicago: University of Chicago Press).

Hakenbeck, Susanne, et al. (2010), "Diet and Mobility in Early Medieval Bavaria: A Study of Carbon and Nitrogen Stable Isotopes," *American Journal of Physical Anthropology*, 143, 235–49.

Halbwachs, Maurice (1980), *The Collective Memory*, trans. Francis J. Ditter and Vida Yazdi Ditter (New York: Harper & Row).

Hall, Stuart (1990), "Cultural Identity and Diaspora," in Jonathan Rutherford (ed.), *Identity: Community, Culture, Difference* (London: Lawrence & Wishart), 222–37.

Hallo, W.W. and Younger, K. L. (eds.) (2003), *The Context of Scripture, Volume 2. Monumental Inscriptions from the Biblical World* (Leiden: Brill).

Hansen, Mogens Herman (2000a), "The Concepts of City-State and City-State Culture," in Mogens Herman Hansen (ed.), *A Comparative Study of Thirty City-State Cultures: An Investigation Conducted by the Copenhagen Polis Center* (Copenhagen: The Royal Danish Academy of Sciences and Letters), 11–34.

Hansen, Mogens Herman (ed.) (2000b), *A Comparative Study of Thirty City-State Cultures: An Investigation Conducted by the Copenhagen Polis Center* (Copenhagen: The Royal Danish Academy of Sciences and Letters).

Harmanşah, Ömür (2007), "Upright Stones and Building Narratives: Formation of a Shared Architectural Practice in the Ancient Near East," in Jack Cheng and Marian H. Feldman (eds.), *Ancient Near Eastern Art in Context: Studies in Honor of Irene J. Winter by Her Students* (Leiden: Brill), 69–99.

Harmanşah, Ömür (2013), *Cities and the Shaping of Memory in the Ancient Near East* (Cambridge: Cambridge University Press).

Harmanşah, Ömür (2018), "Encounters, Interactions, and a Shared Cultural Sphere: The Assyrian Empire and the Syro-Hittite States of the Iron Age," in Kemalettin Köroğlu and Selim Ferruh Adalı (eds.), *The Assyrians: Kingdom of the God Aššur from Tigris to Taurus* (Istanbul: Tupraş—Yapı Kredi Yaınları), 256–75.

Harrison, Timothy P. (2001), "Tell Ta'yinat and the Kingdom of Unqi," in P. M. Michèle Daviau, John W. Wevers, and Michael Weigl (eds.), *The World of the Aramaeans* (2; Sheffield: Sheffield Academic Press), 115–32.

Harrison, Timothy P. (2009a), "Review of Karatepe-Aslantaş: Azatiwataya: Die Bildwerke," *Journal of Near Eastern Studies*, 68 (1), 47–50.

Harrison, Timothy P. (2009b), "Lifting the Veil on a 'Dark Age': Ta'yinat and the North Orontes Valley during the Early Iron Age," in J. David Schloen (ed.), *Exploring the Longue Durée: Essays in Honor of Lawrence E. Stager* (Winona Lake, IN: Eisenbrauns), 171–84.

Harrison, Timothy P. (2009c), "Neo-Hittites in the 'Land of Palistin': Renewed Investigations at Tell Ta'yinat on the Plain of Antioch," *Near Eastern Archaeology*, 72 (4), 174–89.

Harrison, Timothy P. (2017), "Royal Self-Representation and the Legitimation of Authority at Tayinat (Ancient Kunulua)," in Christoph Levin and Reinhard Müller (eds.), *Herrschaftslegitimation in vorderorientalischen Reichen der Eisenzeit* (Tübingen: Mohr Siebeck), 277–99.

Harrison, Timothy P. and Osborne, James F. (2012), "Building XVI and the Neo-Assyrian Sacred Precinct at Tell Tayinat," *Journal of Cuneiform Studies*, 64, 125–43.

Harrison, Timothy P. and Denel, Elif (2017), "The Neo-Hittite Citadel Gate at Tayinat (Ancient Kunulua)," in Sharon Steadman and Gregory McMahon (eds.),

*The Archaeology of Anatolian· Recent Discoveries (2015–2016), Vol.* 2 (Newcastle, UK: Cambridge Scholars), 137–55.

Hausleiter, A. and Reiche, A. (eds.) (1999), *Iron Age Pottery in Northern Mesopotamia, Northern Syria and South-East Anatolia. Papers Presented at the Meetings of the International "Table Ronde" at Heidelberg (1995) and Niebrow (1997)* (Münster: Ugarit-Verlag).

Hawkins, J. David (1982), "The Neo-Hittite States in Syria and Anatolia," *Cambridge Ancient History* (III/1; Cambridge: Cambridge University Press), 372–441.

Hawkins, J. David (1984), "The Syro-Hittite States," in John Boardman (ed.), *The Cambridge Ancient History, Plates to Volume III* (Cambridge: Cambridge University Press), 65–92.

Hawkins, J. David (1987), "The Kululu Lead Strips: Economic Documents in Hieroglyphic Luwian," *Anatolian Studies*, 37, 135–62.

Hawkins, J. David (1988), "Kuzi-Tešub and the 'Great Kings' of Karkamiš," *Anatolian Studies*, 38, 99–108.

Hawkins, J. David (1992), "The Inscriptions of Kızıldağ and the Karadağ in the Light of the Yalburt Inscription," in Heinrich Otten et al. (eds.), *Hittite and Other Anatolian and Near Eastern Studies in Honour of Sedat Alp* (Ankara: Türk Tarih Kurumu Basımevi), 259–74.

Hawkins, J. David (1995a), "Karkamish and Karatepe: Neo-Hittite City-States in North Syria," in Jack M. Sasson (ed.), *Civilizations of the Ancient Near East* (Farmington Hills, MI: Hendrickson), 1295–307.

Hawkins, J. David (1995b), "The Political Geography of North Syrian and South-East Anatolia in the Neo-Assyrian Period," in Mario Liverani (ed.), *Neo-Assyrian Geography* (Quaderni di Geografia Storica; Rome: University of Rome), 87–102.

Hawkins, J. David (1995c), "Great Kings and Country Lords at Malatya and Karkamis," in Theo P. J. van den Hout and Johan de Roos (eds.), *Studio Historiae Ardens: Ancient Near Eastern Studies Presented to Philo H. J. Houwink ten Cate* (Istanbul: Nederlands Historisch-Archaeologisch Instituut te Istanbul), 75–86.

Hawkins, J. David (2000), *Corpus of Hieroglyphic Luwian Inscriptions vol. 1: Inscriptions of the Iron Age* (Berlin: Walter de Gruyter).

Hawkins, J. David (2003), "Scripts and Texts," in H. Craig Melchert (ed.), *The Luwians* (Leiden: Brill), 128–69.

Hawkins, J. David (2009), "Cilicia, The Amuq, and Aleppo," *Near Eastern Archaeology*, 72 (4), 164–73.

Hawkins, J. David (2011), "The Inscriptions of the Aleppo Temple," *Anatolian Studies*, 61, 35–54.

Hawkins, J. David (2015), "The Soul in the Stele?," in Alfonso Archi (ed.), *Tradition and Innovation in the Ancient Near East. Proceedings of the 57th Rencontre Assyriologique Internationale at Rome, 4–8 July 2011* (Winona Lake, IN: Eisenbrauns), 49–58.

Hayes, Katherine H. (2015), "Indigeneity and Diaspora: Colonialism and the Classification of Displacement," in Craig N. Cipolla and Katherine Howlett Hayes (eds.), *Rethinking Colonialism: Comparative Archaeological Approaches* (Gainesville: University Press of Florida), 54–75.

Heffron, Yağmur (2017), "Testing the Middle Ground in Assyro-Anatolian Marriages of the Kārum Period," *Iraq*, 79, 71–83.

Heltzer, Michael (1995), "Phoenician Trade and Phoenicians in Hamath," in K. Van Lerberghe and A. Schoors (eds.), *Immigration and Emigration within the Ancient Near East. Festschrift E. Lipinski* (Leuven: Peeters), 101–105.

Herrmann, Georgina (1986), *Ivories from Room SW 37, Fort Shalmaneser* (London: British School of Archaeology in Iraq).

Herrmann, Georgina (1989), "The Nimrud Ivories, 1: the Flame and Frond School," *Iraq*, 51, 85–109.

Herrmann, Georgina (1997), "The Nimrud Ivories, 3: The Assyrian Tradition," in Hartmut Waetzold and Harold Hauptmann (eds.), *Assyrien im Wandel der Zeiten, XXXIXe Rencontre Assyriologique Internationale, Heidelberg 6–10 Juli 1992* (Heidelberg: Heidelberger Orientverlag), 285–90.

Herrmann, Georgina and Laidlaw, Stuart (2009), *Ivories from the North West Palace (1845–1992)* (London: British Institute for the Study of Iraq).

Herrmann, Georgina and Laidlaw, Stuart (2013), *Ivories from Nimrud (1949–1963) VII: Ivories from Rooms SW11/12 and T10, Fort Shalmaneser* (London: The British Institute for the Study of Iraq).

Herrmann, Georgina, Coffey, Helena, and Laidlaw, Stuart (2004), *The Published Ivories from Fort Shalmaneser, Nimrud: A Scanned Archive of Photographs* (London: Institute of Archaeology, University College London and the British School of Archaeology in Iraq).

Herrmann, Virginia R. (2014), "The Katumuwa Stele in Archaeological Context," in Virginia Rimmer Herrmann and J. David Schloen (eds.), *In Remembrance of Me: Feasting with the Dead in the Ancient Middle East* (Oriental Institute Museum Publications; Chicago: The Oriental Intitute of the University of Chicago), 49–56.

Herrmann, Virginia R. (2017a), "Urban Organization Under Empire: Iron Age Sam'al (Zincirli, Turkey) from Royal to Provincial Capital," *Levant*, 49 (3), 284–311.

Herrmann, Virginia R. (2017b), "Appropriation and Emulation in the Earliest Sculptures from Zincirli (Iron Age Sam'al)," *American Journal of Archaeology*, 121 (2), 237–74.

Herrmann, Virginia R. (2018), "Cosmopolitan Politics in the Neo-Assyrian Empire: Local Elite Identity at Zincirli-Sam'al," *Semitica*, 60, 493–535.

Herrmann, Virginia R. (In press), "Only an Image? *nbš, atri-* and the Katumuwa Inscription," in Petra Goedegebuure and Joost Hazenbos (eds.), *Festschrift for Theo van den Hout* (Chicago: Oriental Institute of the University of Chicago).

Herrmann, Virginia and Schloen, David (2016), "Assyrian Impact on the Kingdom of Sam'al: The View from Zincirli," in J. MacGinnis and D. Wicke (eds.), *The Provincial Archaeology of the Assyrian Empire* (Cambridge: McDonald Institute for Archaeological Research), 265–74.

Herrmann, Virginia R. and Tyson, Craig T. (2018), "Introduction: The Construction of the Imperial Periphery in Neo-Assyrian Studies," in Craig W. Tyson (ed.), *Imperial Peripheries in the Neo-Assyrian Period* (Chicago: University Press of Chicago), 3–40.

Herrmann, Virginia R., Hout, Theo van den, and Beyazlar, Ahmet (2016), "A New Hieroglyphic Luwian Inscription from Pancarlı Höyük: Language and Power in Early Iron Age Sam'al-Y'DY," *Journal of Near Eastern Studies*, 75 (1), 53–70.

Herskovits, Melville J. (1938), *Acculturation: The Study of Culture Contact* (New York: J. J. Augustin).

Herzog, Ze'ev (1997), *Archaeology of the City: Urban Planning in Ancient Israel and its Social Implications* (Tel Aviv: Emery and Claire Yass Archaeology Press).

Highcock, Nancy, et al. (2015), "Kınık Höyük: A New Archaeological Project in Southern Cappadocia," in Sharon Steadman and Gregory McMahon (eds.), *The Archaeology of Anatolia: Recent Discoveries (2011–2014)* (Newcastle: Cambridge Scholars Press), 98–127.

Hillier, Bill (1996), *Space Is the Machine: A Configurational Theory of Architecture* (Cambridge: Cambridge University Press).

Hillier, Bill and Hanson, Julienne (1984), *The Social Logic of Space* (New York: Cambridge University Press).

Hodos, Tamar, Knappett, Carl, and Kilikoglu, Vassilis (2005), "Middle and Late Iron Age Painted Ceramics from Kinet Höyük: Macro, Micro and Elemental Analyses," *Anatolian Studies,* 55, 61–87.

Hofstadter, Douglas R. (1979), *Gödel, Escher, Bach: An Eternal Golden Braid* (New York: Vintage Books).

Hogarth, D. G. (1914), *Carchemish: Report on the Excavations at Jerablus on Behalf of the British Museum. Part I. Introductory* (Oxford: University Press).

Hrouda, Barthel (1962), *Tell Halaf, vierter Band: Die Kleinfunde aus historischer Zeit* (Berlin: Walter de Gruyter & Co.).

Hruby, Zachary X. and Flad, Rowan K. (eds.) (2007), *Rethinking Craft Specialization in Complex Societies: Archaeological Analyses of the Social Meaning of Production* (Archeological Papers of the American Anthropological Association, Arlington, VA: American Anthropological Association).

Huehnergard, John (1995), "What Is Aramaic?," *Aram,* 7, 261–82.

Ikeda, Y. (1979), "Royal Cities and Fortified Cities," *Iraq,* 41, 75–87.

Ingold, Tim (2013), *Making: Anthropology, Archaeology, Art, and Architecture* (Abingdon: Routledge).

Iwasaki, Takuya, et al. (eds.) (2009), *Tell Mastuma: An Iron Age Settlement in Northwest Syria* (Memoirs of the Ancient Orient Museum, vol. III, Tokyo: Ancient Orient Museum).

Jamieson, Andrew (2012), *Tell Ahmar III: Neo-Assyrian Pottery from Area C* (Ancient Near Eastern Studies; Leuven: Peeters).

Janeway, Brian (2006–2007), "The Nature and Extent of Aegean Contact at Tell Ta'yinat and Vicinity in the Early Iron Age: Evidence of the Sea Peoples?," in Timothy P. Harrison (ed.), *Cyprus, The Sea Peoples and the Eastern Mediterranean: Regional Perspectives of Continuity and Change* (Toronto: Canadian Institute for Mediterranean Studies), 123–46.

Janeway, Brian (2017), *Sea Peoples of the Northern Levant? Aegean-Style Pottery from Early Iron Age Tell Tayinat* (Winona Lake, IN: Eisenbrauns).

Joffe, Alexander H. (2002), "The Rise of Secondary States in the Iron Age Levant," *Journal of the Economic and Social History of the Orient,* 45 (4), 425–67.

Jones, Sian (1997), *The Archaeology of Ethnicity: Constructing Identities in the Past and Present* (London: Routledge).

Kaufman, Stephen A. (1982), "Reflections on the Assyrian-Aramaic Bilingual from Tell-Fakhariyeh," *Maarav*, 3, 137–75.

Kaufman, Stephen A. (2007), "The Phoenician Inscription of the Incirli Trilingual: A Tentative Reconstruction and Translation," *Maarav*, 14 (2), 7–26.

Kertai, David (2017), "Embellishing the Interior Spaces of Assyria's Royal Palaces: The Bēt-Ḥilāni Reconsidered," *Iraq*, 79, 85–104.

Kertai, David (2019), "Architectural Assemblages: The Northwest Complex at Zincirli," *Cambridge Archaeological Journal*, 29 (1), 81–101.

Khoury, Philip S. and Kostiner, Joseph (eds.) (1990), *Tribe and State Formation in the Middle East* (Berkeley: University of California Press).

King, L. W. (1915), *Bronze Reliefs from the Gates of Shalmaneser, King of Assyria B.C. 860–825* (London: Printed by Order of the Trustees).

Kinnier Wilson, J. V. (1962), "The Kurba'il Statue of Shalmaneser III," *Iraq*, 24 (2), 90–115.

Kintigh, Keith W. (1994), "Contending with Contemporaneity in Settlement-Pattern Studies," *American Antiquity*, 59 (1), 143–48.

Klengel, Horst (2000), "The 'Crisis Years' and the New Political System in Early Iron Age Syria: Some Introductory Remakrs," in Guy Bunnens (ed.), *Essays on Syria in the Iron Age* (Louvain: Peeters), 21–30.

Kluckhohn, Clyde (1936), "Some Reflections on the Method and Theory of the Kulturkreislehre," *American Anthropologist*, 38, 157–96.

Knapp, A. Bernard and Manning, Sturt W. (2016), "Crisis in Context: The End of the Late Bronze Age in the Eastern Mediterranean," *American Journal of Archaeology*, 120 (1), 99–149.

Knight, Vernon James, Brown, James A., and Lankford, George E. (2001), "On the Subject Matter of Southeastern Ceremonial Complex Art," *Southeastern Archaeology*, 20 (2), 129–41.

Kohlmeyer, Kay (2000), *Der Tempel des Wettergottes von Aleppo* (Münster: Rhema-Verlag).

Kohlmeyer, Kay (2008), "Zur Datierung der Skupturen von 'Ain Dara," in D. Bonatz, R. M. Czichon, and F. J. Kreppner (eds.), *Fundstellen: Gesammelte Schriften zur Archäologie und Geschichte Altvorderasiens ad honorem Hartmut Kühne* (Wiesbaden: Harrassowitz), 119–30.

Kohlmeyer, Kay (2009), "The Temple of the Storm God in Aleppo During the Late Bronze and Early Iron Ages," *Near Eastern Archaeology*, 72 (4), 190–202.

Kohlmeyer, Kay (2012), "Der Tempel des Wettergottes von Aleppo: Baugeschichte und Bautyp, räumliche Bezüg, Inventar und bildliche Ausstattung," in J. Kamlah (ed.), *Temple Building and Temple Cult: Architecture and Cultic Paraphernalia of Temples in the Levant (2.-1. Mill. B.C.E.)* (Wiesbaden: Harrassowitz), 55–78.

Korfmann, Manfred (1986), "Beşik-Tepe: Vorbericht über die Ergebnisse der Grabungen von 1984: Grabungen am Beşik-Yassıtepe, Beşik-Sivritepe und im Beşik-Gräberfeld," *Archäologischer Anzeiger*, 303–29.

Košak, S. (1981), "Western Neighbors of the Hittites," in Benjamin Mazar (ed.), *Eretz-Israel 15: Y. Aharoni Memorial Volume* (Jerusalem: The Israel Exploration Society; The Institute of Archaeology), 12*–16*.

Kozal, Ekin and Novák, Mirko (2013), "Sirkeli Höyük: A Bronze and Iron Age Urban Settlement in Plain Cilicia," in Ünsal Yalçın (ed,), Anatolian Metal VI (Bochum: Deutschen Bergbau-Museum).

Kraeling, Emil (1918), Aram and Israel; or, The Aramaeans in Syria and Mesopotamia (New York: Columbia University Press).

Krebernik, Manfred and Seidl, Ursula (1997), "Ein Schildbeschlag mit Bukranion und alphabetischer Inschrift," Zeitschrift für Assyriologie, 87 (1), 101–11.

Kreppner, Florian Janoscha (2008), "Eine Aussergewöhnlicke Brandbestattungsitte in Dūr-Katlimmu während der ersten Hälfte des ersten Jt. v. Chr.," in Dominik Bonatz, Rainer M. Czichon, and F. Janoscha Kreppner (eds.), Fundstellen: Gesammelte Schriften zur Archäologie und Geschichte Altvorderasiens ad honorem Hartmut Kühne (Wiesbaden: Harrassowitz), 263–76.

Kühn, Dagmar (2014), "Society, Institutions, Law, and Economy," in Herbert Niehr (ed.), The Aramaeans in Ancient Syria (Leiden: Brill), 37–70.

Laessøe, Jørgen (1959), "A Statue of Shalmaneser III, from Nimrud," Iraq, 21 (2), 147–57.

Landsberger, B. (1948), Sam'al (Ankara: Drückerei der Türkischen Historischen Gesellschaft).

Lanfranchi, Giovanni-Battista (2007), "The Luwian-Phoenician Bilinguals of Çineköy and Karatepe: An Ideological Dialogue," in R. Rollinger, A. Luther, and J. Wieshöfer (eds.), Getrennte Wege? Kommunikation, Raum und Wahrnehmung in der alten Welt (Mainz: Verlag Antike), 179–217.

Langenegger, Felix (1950), "Die Bauten und Schichten des Burghügels," in Rudolf Naumann (ed.), Tell Halaf, vol. II. Die Bauwerke (Berlin: Walter de Gruyter), 3–324.

Larsen, Mogens T. (1996), The Conquest of Assyria: Excavations in an Antique Land, 1840–1860 (London: Routledge).

Larsen, Mogens Trolle and Lassen, Agnete Wisti (2014), "Cultural Exchange at Kültepe," in Michael Kozuh (ed.), Extraction and Control: Studies in Honor of Matthew W. Stolper (Chicago: The Oriental Institute of the University of Chicago), 171–88.

Lauinger, Jacob (2012), "Esarhaddon's Succession Treaty at Tell Tayinat: Text and Commentary," Journal of Cuneiform Studies, 64, 87–123.

Lauinger, Jacob (2013), "The Neo-Assyrian adê: Treaty, Oath, or Something Else?," Zeitschrift für Altorientalische und Biblische Rechtsgeschichte, 19, 99–115.

Lauinger, Jacob (2015), Following the Man of Yamhad: Settlement and Territory at Old Babylonian Alalah (Leiden: Brill).

Lauinger, Jacob and Batiuk, Stephen (2015), "A Stele of Sargon II at Tell Tayinat," Zeitschrift für Assyriologie, 105 (1), 54–68.

Lawrence, Dan and Ricci, Andrea (2016), "Long-Term Settlement Trends in the Birecik-Carchemish Sector," in Tony J. Wilkinson, Edgar Peltenburg, and Eleanor Barbanes Wilkinson (eds.), Carchemish in Context: The Land of Carchemish Project, 2006–2010 (Oxford: Oxbow Books), 38–67.

Layard, Austen H. (1853), Discoveries in the Ruins of Nineveh and Babylon; with Travels in Armenia, Kurdistan and the Desert: Being the Result of a Second Expedition Undertaken for the Trustees of the British Museum (London: J. Murray).

Lebeau, M. (1983), *La Céramique de l'âge du Fer II-III: à Tell Abou Danné et ses Rapports avec la Céramique Contemporaine en Syrie* (Paris: Éditions Recherche sur les Civilisations).

Lefebvre, Henri (1991), *The Production of Space*, trans. Donald Nicholson-Smith (Oxford, UK: Blackwell).

Lehmann, Gunnar (2005), "Al Mina and the East: A Report on Research in Progress," in Alexandra Villing (ed.), *The Greeks in the East* (London: British Museum), 61–92.

Lehmann, Gunnar (2007), "Decorated Pottery Styles in the Northern Levant during the Early Iron Age and their Relationship with Cyprus and the Aegean," *Ugarit-Forschungen*, 39, 487–550.

Lehmann, Gunnar (2008), "North Syria and Cilicia, c.1200–330 BCE," in Claudia Sagona (ed.), *Beyond the Homeland: Markers in Phoenician Chronology* (Ancient Near Eastern Studies Supplement Series; Leuven: Peeters), 205–46.

Lehmann, Gunnar (2017), "The Late Bronze—Iron Age Transition and the Problem of the Sea Peoples Phenomenon in Cilicia," in Peter M. Fischer and Teresa Bürge (eds.), *"Sea Peoples" Up-to-Date: New Research on Transformations in the Eastern Mediterranean in the 13th–11th Centuries BCE* (Vienna: Verlag der Österreichischen Akademie der Wissenschaften), 229–55.

Lehmann, Gunnar and Killebrew, Ann E. (2010), "Palace 6000 at Megiddo in Context: Iron Age Central Hall Tetra-Partite Residencies and the *Bīt-Ḫilāni* Building Tradition in the Levant," *Bulletin of the American Schools of Oriental Research*, 359, 13–33.

Lemaire, André (1983), "L'Inscription Phénicienne de Hassan-Beyli Reconsiderée," *Rivista di Studi Fenici*, 11, 9–19.

Lemaire, André (2001), "Les langues du royaume de Sam'al aux IXe -VIIIe s. av. J.-C. et leurs relations avec le royaume de Qué," in Éric Jean, Ali M. Dinçol, and Serra Durugönül (eds.), *La Cilicie: Espaces et pouvoirs locaux (2e millénaire av. J.-C.—4e siècle ap. J.-C.). Actes de la Table Ronde Internationale d'Istanbul, 2–5 Novembre 1999* (Paris: De Boccard), 185–93.

Lemaire, André and Sass, Benjamin (2013), "The Mortuary Stele with Sam'alian Inscription from Ördekburnu near Zincirli," *Bulletin of the American Schools of Oriental Research*, 369, 57–136.

Liebmann, Matthew (2013), "Parsing Hybridity: Archaeologies of Amalgamation in Seventeenth-Century New Mexico," in Jeb J. Card (ed.), *The Archaeology of Hybrid Material Culture* (Carbondale: Southern Illinois University Press), 25–49.

Lilley, Ian (2004), "Diaspora and Identity in Archaeology: Moving Beyond the Black Atlantic," in Lynn Meskell and Robert W. Preucel (eds.), *A Companion to Social Archaeology* (Malden, MA: Blackwell), 287–312.

Lilley, Ian (2006), "Archaeology, Diaspora and Decolonization," *Journal of Social Archaeology*, 6 (1), 28–47.

Lipiński, Edward (1994), *Studies in Aramaic Inscriptions and Onomastics II* (Leuven: Peeters).

Lipiński, Edward (2000), *The Aramaeans: Their Ancient History, Culture, Religion* (Leuven: Peeters).

Lipiński, Edward (2004), *Itineraria Phoenicia* (Leuven: Peeters).

Lipovitch, David R. (2006–2007), "Modeling a Mycenaean Menu: Can Aegean Populations be Defined in Near Eastern Contexts Based on Their Diet?," in T.P. Harrison (ed.), *Cyprus, the Sea Peoples and the Eastern Mediterranean. Regional Perspectives of Continuity and Change* (Toronto: Canadian Institute for Mediterranean Studies), 14/ 59.

Liverani, Mario (1988), "The Growth of the Assyrian Empire in the Habur/Middle Euphrates Area: A New Paradigm," *State Archives of Assyria Bulletin*, II (2), 81–98.

Liverani, Mario (1992), *Studies on the Annals of Ashurnasirpal II. 2: Topographical Analysis* (Quaderni di Geografica Storica; Roma: Centro Stampa d'Atenio).

Liverani, Mario (2014), *The Ancient Near East: History, Society, and Economy*, trans. Soraia Tabatabai (London: Routledge/Taylor & Francis Group).

Loon, Maurits N. Van (1991), *Anatolia in the Earlier First Millennium B.C.* (Leiden: Brill).

Loud, Gordon and Altman, Charles B. (1938), *Khorsabad, Part II: The Citadel and the Town* (Oriental Institute Publications; Chicago: University of Chicago Press).

Luciani, Marta (2006), "Palatial Workshops at Qatna?," *Baghdader Mitteilungen*, 37, 403–26.

Luke, Joanna (2003), *Ports of Trade, Al Mina and Geometric Greek Pottery in the Levant* (BAR International Series 1100; Oxford: Archaeopress).

Lumsden, Stephen (2008), "Material Culture and the Middle Ground in the Old Assyrian Colony Period," in Cécile Michel (ed.), *Old Assyrian Studies in Memory of Paul Garelli* (Leiden: Nederlands Instituut voor het Nabije Oosten), 21–43.

Luttwak, Edward N. (1976), *The Grand Strategy of the Roman Empire* (Baltimore: Johns Hopkins University Press).

Lyman, R. Lee and O'Brien, Michael J. (2004), "A History of Normative Theory in Americanist Archaeology," *Journal of Archaeological Method and Theory*, 11 (4), 369–96.

Malamat, A. (1973), "The Aramaeans," in D. J. Wiseman (ed.), *Peoples of Old Testament Times* (Oxford: Clarendon Press), 134–55.

Malkin, Irad (1998), "The Middle Ground: Philoktetes in Italy," *Kernos*, 11, 131–41.

Malkin, Irad (2002), "A Colonial Middle Ground: Greek, Etruscan, and Local Elites in the Bay of Naples," in Claire L. Lyons and John K. Papadopoulos (eds.), *The Archaeology of Colonialism* (Los Angeles, CA: Getty Research Institute), 151–81.

Mallory, J. P. (1991), *In Search of the Indo-Europeans: Language, Archaeology, and Myth* (London: Thames & Hudson).

Mann, Michael (1986), *The Sources of Social Power, V. 1. A History of Power from the Beginning to A.D. 1760* (Cambridge: Cambridge University Press).

Manning, Sturt, Lorentzen, Brita, and Kearns, Catherine (2014), "Chronology Building in the Orontes Watershed: From Samples and Archaeology to Bayesian Chronological Modeling and Climate," *Annual Meeting of the American Schools of Oriental Research*, unpublished conference paper (San Diego, CA).

Manuelli, Federico (2010), "Foreign Influences and Local Tradition in the Iron Age Pottery Production from Arslantepe. Evidence from the New Excavations of the Neo-Hittite Levels," *Mesopotamia*, XLV, 71–84.

Manuelli, Federico (2011), "Malatya-Melid between the Late Bronze and the Iron Age. Continuity and Change at Arslantepe: Preliminary Observations on the Pottery

Assemblages," in K. Strobel (ed.), *Empires after the Empire. Anatolia, Syria and Assyria after Šuppiluliuma II* (Firenze: LoGisma), 61–86.

Manuelli, Federico (2018), "Drifting Southward? Tracing Aspects of Cultural Continuity and Change in the Late 2nd Millennium BC Syro-Anatolian Region," *Studia Ebaitica*, 4, 139–86.

Manuelli, Federico and Mori, Lucia (2016), "'The King at the Gate.' Monumental Fortifications and the Rise of Local Elites at Arslantepe at the End of the 2nd Millennium BCE," *Origini*, XXXIX, 209–41.

Manuelli, Federico and Pittman, Holly (2018), "A 'Flame and Frond' Ivory Plaque from the Neo-Hittite Excavations at Arslantepe/Melid: Regionalisms and Communities in Iron Age Anatolia," *Origini*, XLI, 139–69.

Marchetti, Nicolò (2012), "Karkemish on the Euphrates: Excavating a City's History," *Near Eastern Archaeology*, 75 (3), 132–47.

Marchetti, Nicolò (2015), "The 2014 Joint Turco-Italian Excavations at Karkemish," *Kazı Sonuçları Toplantısı*, 37, 363–80.

Marchetti, Nicolò (ed.) (2014), *Karkemish: An Ancient Capital on the Euphrates* (Researches on the Archaeology of the Ancient Near East, Bologna: Ante Quem).

Marcus, Joyce and Sabloff, Jeremy A. (2008), "Introduction," in Joyce Marcus and Jeremy A. Sabloff (eds.), *The Ancient City: New Perspectives on Urbanism in the Old and New World* (Santa Fe, NM: School for Advanced Research Press), 3–26.

Markoe, Glenn E. (2000), *Phoenicians* (Peoples of the Past; Berkeley: University of California Press).

Martin, S. Rebecca (2017), *The Art of Contact: Comparative Approaches to Greek and Phoenician Art* (Philadelphia: University of Pennsylvania Press).

Massa, Michele, Bachhuber, Christoph, Şahin, Fatma, Erpehlivan, Hüsyin, Osborne, James F., and Lauricella, Anthony J. (2020), "Urbanisation and State Formation in the Central Anatolian Bronze and Iron Ages: A Regional Perspective from the Konya and Karaman Plains," *Anatolian Studies*, 70, 45–75.

Massa, Michele, and Osborne, James F. (In prep), "Iron Age Peak Sanctuaries in Southern Anatolia: Kızıldağ and Karadağ Revisited."

Matessi, Alvise, Tomassini, Pieri, and Bianca, Maria (2018), "South-Central: Archaeology," in Mark Weeden and Lee Ullmann (eds.), *Hittite Landscape and Geography* (Leiden, Boston: Brill), 89–105.

Matney, Timothy (2010), "Material Culture and Identity: Assyrians, Aramaeans, and the Indigenous Peoples of Iron Age Southeastern Anatolia," in Sharon R. Steadman and Jennifer C. Ross (eds.), *Agency and Identity in the Ancient Near East: New Paths Forward* (London: Equinox), 129–47.

Matthers, J. (ed.) (1981), *The River Qoueiq, North Syria, and Its Catchment: Studies Arising from the Tell Rifa'at Survey 1977–1979* (Oxford: British Archaeological Reports).

Mazzoni, Stefania (1994), "Aramaean and Luwian New Foundations," in Stefania Mazzoni (ed.), *Nuove Fondazioni nel Vicino Oriente Antico: Realtà e Ideologia* (Pisa: Giardini Editori E Stampatori), 319–40.

Mazzoni, Stefania (1995), "Settlement Pattern and New Urbanization in Syria at the Time of the Assyrian Conquest," in Mario Liverani (ed.), *Neo-Assyrian Geography* (Rome: University of Rome), 181–91.

Mazzoni, Stefania (1997), "The Gate and the City: Change and Continuity in Syro-Hittite Urban Ideology," in G. Wilhelm (ed.), *Die Orientalische Stadt: Kontinuität, Wandel, Bruch* (Saarbrücken: Saarbrücker Druckerei und Verlag), 307–38.

Mazzoni, Stefania (1998), *The Italian Excavations of Tell Afis (Syria): From Chiefdom to an Aramaean State* (Pisa: Ediz-iones ETS).

Mazzoni, Stefania (2000a), "Syria and the Periodization of the Iron Age: A Cross-Cultural Perspective," in Guy Bunnens (ed.), *Essays on Syria in the Iron Age* (Louvain: Peeters), 31–59.

Mazzoni, Stefania (2000b), "Syria and the Chronology of the Iron Age," *Isimu*, 3, 121–38.

Mazzoni, Stefania (2000c), "Crisis and Change: The Beginning of the Iron Age in Syria," in P. Matthiae, et al. (eds.), *Proceedings of the First International Congress on the Art and Archaeology of the Ancient Near East: Rome, May 18th–23rd, 1998* (Rome: Università degli Studi di Roma "La Sapienza"), 1043–60.

Mazzoni, Stefania (2001), "Syro-Hittite Pyxides: Between Major and Minor Art," in J.-W. Meyer, M. Novák, and A. Pruss (eds.), *Beiträge zur vorderasiatischen Archäologie: Winfried Orthmann gewidmet* (Frankfourt am Main: Johann Wolfgang Goethe-Universität), 292–309.

Mazzoni, Stefania (2008), "Review of Karatepe-Aslantaş: Die Bildwerke," *American Journal of Archaeology*, 112 (4), doi:10.3764/ajaonline1124.Mazzoni.

Mazzoni, Stefania (2009), "Ivories and Art Traditions in the Hama Region," in Serena M. Cecchini, Stefania Mazzoni, and Elena Scigliuzzo (eds.), *Syrian and Phoenician Ivories of the Early First Millennium BCE: Chronology, Regional Styles and Iconographic Repertories, Patterns or Inter-regional Distributions* (Pisa: Edizioni ETS), 107–32.

Mazzoni, Stefania (2010), "Syro-Hittite Temples and the Traditional *in antis* Plan," in J. Becker, R. Hempelmann, and E. Rehm (eds.), *Kulturlandschaft Syrien: Zentrum und Peripherie; Festschrift für Jan-Waalke Meyer* (Münster: Ugarit-Verlag), 359–76.

Mazzoni, Stefania (2013), "Arts and Cross-Cultural Communication in the Early 1st Millennium: The Syro-Anatolian Contact," in K. Aslıhan Yener (ed.), *Across the Border: Late Bronze-Iron Age Relations between Syria and Anatolia. Proceedings of a Symposium held at the Research Center of Anatolian Studies, Koç University, Istanbul, May 31–June 1, 2010* (Ancient Near Eastern Studies Supplement; Leuven: Peeters), 465–92.

Mazzoni, Stefania (2014a), "Tell Afis in the Iron Age: The Temple on the Acropolis," *Near Eastern Archaeology*, 77 (1), 44–52.

Mazzoni, Stefania (2014b), "The Aramean States during the Iron Age II-III Periods," in Margreet L. Steiner and Ann E. Killebrew (eds.), *The Oxford Handbook of the Archaeology of the Levant c. 8000–332 BCE* (Oxford: Oxford University Press), 683–705.

McEwan, C. W. (1937), "The Syrian Expedition of the Oriental Institute of the University of Chicago," *American Journal of Archaeology*, 41 (1), 8–16.

Mee, C. (1978), "Aegean Trade and Settlement in Anatolia in the Second Millennium B.C.," *Anatolian Studies*, 28, 121–56.

Melchert, H. Craig (2010), "Remarks on the Kuttamuwa Inscription," *Kubaba*, 1, 4–11.

Melchert, H. G. (ed.) (2003), *The Luwians* (Leiden: Brill).

Mellink, Machteld J. (1956), *A Hittite Cemetery at Gordion* (Philadelphia: The University Museum of the University of Pennsylvania).

Mellink, Machteld J. (1958), "Review of Tell Halaf III: Die Bildwerke by Dietrich Opitz and Anton Moortgat," *American Journal of Archaeology*, 62 (4), 438–40.

Merriman, Peter (2012), *Mobility, Space, and Culture* (London: Routledge).

Messerschmidt, L. (1906), "Corpus Inscriptionum Hettiticarum, Zweiter Nachtrag," *Mitteilungen der Vorderasiatischen Gesellschaft*, XI (5).

Miller, Robert (1986), "Elephants, Ivory, and Charcoal: An Ecological Perspective," *Bulletin of the American Schools of Oriental Research*, 264, 29–43.

Moorey, Peter Roger Stuart (1980), *Cemeteries of the First Millennium B.C. at Deve Hüyük, Near Carchemish, Salvaged by T.E. Lawrence and C.L. Woolley in 1913* (BAR International Series; Oxford: BAR).

Morandi Bonacossi, Daniele (2000), "The Syrian Jaziereh in the Late Assyrian Period: A View from the Countryside," in Guy Bunnens (ed.), *Essays on Syria in the Iron Age* (Leuvens: Peeters), 349–96.

Morgan, Lewis Henry (1877), *Ancient Society* (New York: H. Holt).

Morrison, Kathleen D. (2001), "Sources, Approaches, Definitions," in Susan E. Alcock, et al. (eds.), *Empires: Perspectives from Archaeology and History* (Cambridge: Cambridge University Press), 1–9.

Mosca, Paul G. and Russell, James (1987), "A Phoenician Inscription from Cebel Ires Dağı in Rough Cilicia," *Epigraphica Anatolica*, 9, 1–27.

Müller, Uwe (2003), "A Change to Continuity: Bronze Age Traditions in Early Iron Age," in B. Fischer et al. (eds.), *Identifying Changes: The Transition from Bronze to Iron Ages in Anatolia and its Neighbouring Regions* (Istanbul: Türk Eskiçağ Bilimleri Enstitüsü), 137–50.

Myhre, Bente Magnus and Myhre, Bjørn (1972), "The Concept 'Immigration' in Archaeological Contexts Illustrated by Examples from West Norwegian North Norwegian Early Iron Age," *Norwegian Archaological Review*, 5 (1), 45–70.

Nail, Thomas (2015), *The Figure of the Migrant* (Stanford, CA: Stanford University Press).

Naumann, R. (ed.) (1950), *Tell Halaf, vol. II. Die Bauwerke* (Berlin: Walter de Gruyter).

Nichols, D. L. and Charlton, T. H. (eds.) (1997), *The Archaeology of City-States: Cross-Cultural Approaches* (Washington, DC: Smithsonian Institution Press).

Niehr, Herbert (2016), "The Power of Language: Language Situation and Language Policy in Sam'al," in Omer Sergi, Manfred Oeming, and Izaak de Hulster (eds.), *In Search for Israel and Aram: Politics, Culture, and Identity* (Tübingen: Mohr Siebeck), 305–32.

Niemeyer, Hans Georg (2004), "The Phoenicians and the Birth of a Multinational Mediterranean Society," in Robert Rollinger and Christoph Ulf (eds.), *Commerce and Monetary Systems in the Ancient World: Means of Transmission and Cultural Interaction; Proceedings of the Fifth Annual Symposium of the Assyrian and Babylonian Intellectual Heritage Project Held in Innsbruck, Austria, October 3rd–8th, 2002* (Melammu Symposia; Stuttgart: Franz Steiner Verlag), 245–56.

Nishiyama, Shin'ichi (2012), "A Local Temple in the Iron Age Village? Reassessing a Building Complex at Tell Mastuma in the Northern Levant," *Orient*, 47, 91–124.

Novák, Mirko (2005), "Arameans and Luwians—Processes of an Acculturation," in W.H. Van Soldt (ed.), *Ethnicity in Ancient Mesopotamia. Papers Read at the 48th Rencontre Assyiologique Internationale, Leiden, 1–4 July 2002* (Publications de L'Institut Historique-Archéologique Néerlandais de Stamboul; Leiden: Nederlands Instituut voor Het Nabije Oosten), 252–66.

Novák, Mirko (2012), "The Temple of 'Ain Dāra in the Context of Imperial and Neo-Hittite Architecture and Art," in Jens Kamlah (ed.), *Temple Building and Temple Cult: Architecture and Cultic Paraphernalia of Temples in the Levant (2.-1. Mill. B.C.E.)* (Wiesbaden: Harrassowitz), 41–54.

Novák, Mirko (2013), "Gōzān and Gūzāna: Anatolians, Aramaeans, and Assyrians in Tell Halaf," in Dominik Bonatz and Lutz Martin (eds.), *100 Jahre archäologische Feldforschungen in Nordost-Syrien—eine Bilanz* (Wiesbaden: Harrassowitz Verlag), 259–80.

Novák, Mirko (2018), "Elites behind Walls: Citadels and the Segregation of Elites in Anatolia, the Levant and Mesopotamia," in Ünsal Yalçın (ed.), *Anatolian Metal VIII: Eliten—Handwerk—Prestigegüter* (Bochum: Deutschen Bergbau-Museum), 255–68.

Novák, Mirko (2019), "Histoire des principautés néo-hittites (louvito-araméennes)," in Vincent Blanchard (ed.), *Royaumes oubliés: De l'empire Hittite aux Araméens* (Paris: Louvre éditions, Lienart), 105–13.

Novák M., D'Agata A. L., Caneva, I., et al. (2017), "A Comparative Stratigraphy of Cilicia: Results of the First Three Cilician Chronology Workshops," *Altorientalische Forschungen* 44: 150–86.

Novák, M., and Schmid, J. (2019), "The Palaces of Gōzāna (Tall Ḫalaf)," in D. Wicke (ed.), *Der Palast im antiken und islamischen Orient* (Wiesbaden: Harrassowitz), 215–34.

O'Connor, M. (1977), "The Rhetoric of the Kilamuwa Inscription," *Bulletin of the American Schools of Oriental Research*, 226, 15–29.

Omura, Sachihiro (2000), "Preliminary Report of the General Survey in Central Anatolia (1999)," *Anatolian Archaeological Studies*, IX, 37–76.

Omura, Sachihiro (2001), "Preliminary Report of the General Survey in Central Anatolia (2000)," *Anatolian Archaeological Studies*, X, 37–78.

Opitz, Dietrich (1927), "Die Lage von Waššuganni," *Zeitschrift für Assyriologie*, 37, 299–301.

Opitz, Dietrich and Moortgat, Anton (1955), *Tell Halaf, vol. III: Die Bildwerke* (Berlin: Walter de Gruyter).

Oppenheim, A. Leo (1964), *Ancient Mesopotamia: Portrait of a Dead Civilization* (Chicago: University of Chicago Press).

Oreshko, Rotislav (2017), "Hartapu and the Land of Maša: A New Look at the KIZILDAĞ-KARADAĞ Group," *Altorientalische Forschungen*, 44 (1), 47–67.

Orser, C. E. Jr. (1998), "The Archaeology of the African Diaspora," *Annual Review of Anthropology*, 27, 63–82.

Orthmann, W. (1971), *Untersuchungen zur späthethitischen Kunst* (Bonn: R.Habelt).

Orthmann, W. (2002), "Die Bildkunst im Übergang von der Großreichszeit zur Späthethitischen Periode," in E. A. Braun-Holzinger and H. Matthäus (eds.), *Die Nahöstlichen Kulturen und Griechenland an der Wende vom 2. zum 1. Jahrtausend v. Chr.: Kontinuität und Wandel von Strukturen und Mechanismen Kultureller Interaktion* (Möhnesee: Bibliopolis), 153–59.

Orthmann, Winfried (1967), *Das Gräberfeld bei Ilıca* (Wiesbaden: Franz Steiner Verlag).

Orthmann, Winfried (1993), "Zur Datierung des Istar-Reliefs aus Tell 'Ain Dārā," *Istanbul Mitteilungen*, 43, 245–51.

Orthmann, Winfried (2009), "Untersuchungen am 'Kultraum,'" in A. M. H. Baghdo et al. (eds.), *Ausgrabungen auf dem Tell Halaf in Nordost-Syrien, Teil 1. Vorbericht über die erste und zweite syrisch-deutsche Grabungskampagne auf dem Tell Halaf* (Wiesbaden: Harrassowitz), 61–64.

Orthmann, Winfried (2013), "Stone Sculpture of the Iron Age in Northern Syria," in Winfried Orthmann, Michel al-Maqdissi, and Paolo Matthiae (eds.), *Archéologie et Histoire de la Syrie Volume 1: La Syrie de l'époque néolithique à l'âge du fer* (Schriften zur Vorderasiatischen Archäologie; Wiesbaden: Harrasowitz), 525–42.

Orthmann, Winfried, Sollee, Alexander, and Wartke, Ralf-B. (2012), "Ausgrabungen in der Unterstadt des Tell Halaf," in A. M. H. Baghdo et al. (eds.), *Ausgrabungen auf dem Tell Halaf, Teil II, Vorbericht über die dritte bis fünfte syrisch-deutsche Grabungskampagne auf dem Tell Halaf* (Wiesbaden: Harrassowitz), 109–32.

Osborne, James F. (2012), "Communicating Power in the Bīt Ḫilāni Palace," *Bulletin of the American Schools of Oriental Research*, 368, 29–66.

Osborne, James F. (2013), "Sovereignty and Territoriality in the City-State: A Case Study from the Amuq Valley, Turkey," *Journal of Anthropological Archaeology*, 32, 774–90.

Osborne, James F. (2014), "Settlement Planning and Urban Symbology in Syro-Anatolian Cities," *Cambridge Archaeological Journal*, 24 (2), 195–214.

Osborne, James F. (2015), "Ancient Cities and Power: The Archaeology of Urbanism in the Iron Age Capitals of Northern Mesopotamia," *International Journal of Urban Sciences*, 19 (1), 7–19.

Osborne, James F. (2017a), "Counter-Monumentality and the Vulnerability of Memory," *Journa of Social Archaeology*, 17 (2), 163–87.

Osborne, James F. (2017b), "Exploring the Lower Settlements of Iron Age Capitals in Anatolia and Syria," *Antiquity*, 91 (355), 90–107.

Osborne, James F. and Karacic, Steven (2017), "Urbanism beyond the Acropolis: The Tayinat Lower Town Project Surface Survey, 2014–2015," *Anatolica*, 43, 37–70.

Osborne, James F., et al. (2019), "Urban Built Environments of the Early First Millennium BCE: Results of the Tayinat Archaeological Project, 2004–2012," *Bulletin of the American Schools of Oriental Research*, 382, 261–312.

Osborne, James F., Massa M, Şahin F, et al. (2020), "The City of Hartapu: Results of the Türkmen-Karahöyük Intensive Survey Project," *Anatolian Studies*, 70, 1–27.

Özyar, Aslı (1991), "Architectural Relief Sculpture at Karkamish, Malatya, and Tell Halaf: A Technical and Iconographic Study," unpublished PhD thesis (Bryn Mawr College).

Özyar, Aslı (1998), "The Use and Abuse of Re-use at Karkamish," in G. Arsebük, M. J. Mellink, and W. Schirmer (eds.), *Light on Top of the Black Hill: Studies Presented to Halet Çambel* (Istanbul: Ege Yayınları), 633–40.

Özyar, Aslı (2003), "Architectural Reliefs in Anatolia through Time: Contextualizing the Gate Sculptures of Karatepe-Aslantaş/Azitawataya," in B. Fischer (ed.), *Identifying*

*Çhungoaı The Transition from Bronze to Iron Ages in Anatolia and Its Neighbouring Regions: Proceedings of the International Workshop Istanbul, November 8–9, 2002* (Istanbul: Türk Eskiçağ Bilimleri Enstitüsü), 107–15.

Özyar, Aslı (2013), "The Writing on the Wall: Reviewing Sculpture and Inscription on the Gates of the Iron Age Citadel of Azatiwataya (Karatepe-Aslantaş)," in Scott Redford and Nine Ergin (eds.), *Cities and Citadels in Turkey: From the Iron Age to the Seljuks* (Leuven: Peeters), 115–35.

Özyar, Aslı (2014), "Phoenicians and Greeks in Cilicia? Coining Elite Identity in Iron Age Anatolia," in Joan Aruz, Sarah B. Graff, and Yelena Rakic (eds.), *Assyria to Iberia at the Dawn of the Classical Age* (New York: The Metropolitan Museum of Art), 136–46.

Pamir, Hatice (2005), "The Orontes Delta Survey," in K. A. Yener (ed.), *The Amuq Valley Regional Projects, Volume 1: Surveys in the Plain of Antioch and Orontes Delta, Turkey, 1995–2002* (Chicago: The Oriental Institute of the University of Chicago), 67–98.

Paolo, Silvana di (2015), "Beyond Design and Style: Enhancing the Material Dimensions of Artefacts through Technological Complexity," *Altorientalische Forschungen*, 42 (1), 71–79.

Pardee, Dennis (1998), "Les document d'Arslan Tash: authentiques ou faux?," *Syria*, 75, 15–54.

Pardee, Dennis (2009), "A New Aramaic Inscription from Zincirli," *Bulletin of the American Schools of Oriental Research*, 356, 51–71.

Pardee, Dennis (2014), "The Katumuwa Inscription," in Virginia Rimmer Herrmann and J. David Schloen (eds.), *In Remembrance of Me: Feasting with the Dead in the Ancient Near East* (Oriental Institute Museum Publications; Chicago: The Oriental Institute of the University of Chicago), 45–48.

Parker, Bradley J. (2001), *The Mechanics of Empire: The Northern Frontier of Assyria as a Case Study in Imperial Dynamics* (Helsinki: Neo-Assyrian Text Corpus Project).

Parker, Bradley J. (2013), "Geographies of Power: Territoriality and Empire during the Mesopotamian Iron Age," in James F. Osborne and Parker VanValkenburgh (eds.), *Territoriality in Archaeology* (Archeological Papers of the American Anthropological Association; Arlington, VA: American Anthropological Association), 126–44.

Parpola, Simo (2004), "National and Ethnic Identity in the Neo-Assyrian Empire and Assyrian Identity in Post-Empire Times," *Journal of Assyrian Academic Studies*, 18 (2), 5–22.

Payne, Annick (2006), "Multilingual Inscriptions and their Audiences: Cilicia and Lycia," in Seth Sanders (ed.), *Margins of Writing, Origins of Cultures* (Chicago: Oriental Institute of the University of Chicago), 121–36.

Peckham, Brian (2001), "Phoenicians and Aramaeans: The Literary and Epigraphic Evidence," in Michèle Daviau, John William Wevers, and Michael Weigl (eds.), *The World of the Aramaeans II: Studies in Honour of Paul Eugène Dion* (Sheffield: Sheffield Academic Press), 33–44.

Pfälzner, Peter (2013), "The Elephant Hunters of Bronze Age Syria," in Joan Aruz, Sarah B. Graff, and Yelena Rakic (eds.), *Cultures in Contact: From Mesopotamia to the Mediterranean in the Second Millennium B.C.* (New York: The Metropolitan Museum of Art, New York), 112–31.

Pfälzner, Peter (2016), "The Elephants of the Orontes," in Dominique Parayre (ed.), *Le fleuve rebelle: Géographie historique du moyen Oronte d'Ebla à l'époque médiévale* (Syria Supplément IV; Beyrouth: Presses de l'Ifpo), 159–82.

Pitard, Wayne T. (1988), "The Identity of the Bir-Hadad of the Melqart Stela," *Bulletin of the American Schools of Oriental Research*, 272, 3–21.

Pizzimenti, Sara and Zaina, Federico (2016), "The Iron Age at Karkemish between Tradition and Innovation: The Case Study of the Pottery Assemblage from Area C," in Oskar Kaelin and Hans-Peter Mathys (eds.), *Proceedings of the 9th International Congress on the Archaeology of the Ancient Near East Volume 3* (Wiesbaden: Harrassowitz Verlag), 361–76.

Porter, B. N. (2000), "Assyrian Propaganda for the West: Esarhaddon's Stelae from Til Barsip and Sam'al," in G. Bunnens (ed.), *Essays on Syria in the Iron Age* (Louvain: Peeters Press), 143–76.

Postgate, Nicholas (1974), "Some Remarks on Conditions in the Assyrian Countryside," *Journal of the Economic and Social History of the Orient*, 17, 225–43.

Postgate, Nicholas (1992), "The Land of Assur and the Yoke of Assur," *World Archaeology*, 23 (3), 247–63.

Postgate, Nicholas (2007), "The Excavations and Their Results," in Nicholas Postgate and David Thomas (eds.), *Excavations at Kilise Tepe 1994–1998: From Bronze Age to Byzantine in Western Cilicia. Volume 1: Text* (London: British Institute at Ankara; McDonald Institute for Archaeological Research), 31–42.

Postgate, Nicholas and Thomas, David (2007a), "Level II: the End of the Bronze Age and the Iron Age," in Nicholas Postgate and David Thomas (eds.), *Excavations at Kilise Tepe, 1994–1998: From Bronze Age to Byzantine in Western Cilicia, Volume 1: Text* (London: British Institute at Ankar; McDonald Institute for Archaeological Research), 121–70.

Postgate, Nicholas and Thomas, David (eds.) (2007b), *Excavations at Kilise Tepe 1994–1998: From Bronze Age to Byzantine in Western Cilicia. Volume 1: Text* (London, Cambridge: British Institute at Ankara, McDonald Institute for Archaeological Research).

Poulsen, Frederik (1912), *Der Orient und die frühgriechsche Kunst* (Leipzig, Berlin: Druck, Verlag von B. G. Teubner).

Pucci, Marina (2006), "Enclosing Open Spaces: The Organisation of External Areas in Syro-Hittite Architecture," in Joseph Maran (ed.), *Constructing Power: Architecture, Ideology and Social Practice* (Hamburg: LIT Verlag), 1–12.

Pucci, Marina (2008a), *Functional Analysis of Space in Syro-Hittite Architecture* (Oxford: British Archaeological Reports).

Pucci, Marina (2008b), "The King's Gate Complex at Karkamiš: Analysis of Space," in Dominik Bonatz, Rainer M. Czichon, and F. Janoscha Kreppner (eds.), *Fundstellen: Gesammelte Schriften zur Archäologie und Geschichte Altvorderasiens ad honorem Hartmut Kühne* (Wiesbaden: Harrassowitz), 215–24.

Pucci, Marina (2015), "Founding and Planning a New Town: The Southern Town Gate at Zincirli," in Paola Ciafardoni and Deborah Giannessi (eds.), *From the Treasures of Syria: Essays on Art and Archaeology in Honour of Stefania Mazzoni* (Leiden: Nederlands Instituut voor Het Nabije Oosten), 35–74.

Pucci, Marina (2017), "Searching for the Hittites in South Eastern Anatolia: Zincirli and the Hittite Material Culture," in Müller, Doğan-Alparslan, Andreas Schachner, and Metin Alparslan (eds.), *The Discovery of an Anatolian Empire / Bir Anadolu İmparatorluğunun Keşfi* (Istanbul: Türk Eskiçağ Bilimleri Enstitüsü), 239–48.

Pucci, Marina (2019), *Excavations in the Plain of Antioch III: Stratigraphy, Pottery, and Small Finds from Chatal Höyük in the Amuq Plain* (Oriental Institute Publications; Chicago: The Oriental Institute of the University of Chicago).

Quinn, Josephine Crawley (2018), *In Search of the Phoenicians* (Princeton, NJ: Princeton University Press).

Radner, Karen (2006), "Provinz. C. Assyrien," in Dietz Otto and Michael P. Streck (eds.), *Reallexikon der Assyriologie und Vorderasiatischen Archäologie 11.1/2: Prinz, Prinzessin— Qattara* (Berlin: de Gruyter), 42–68.

Ramsay, William Mitchell and Bell, Gertrude L. (1909), *The Thousand and One Churches* (London: Hodder and Stoughton).

Renfrew, Colin (1987), *Archaeology and Language: The Puzzle of Indo-European Origins* (New York: Cambridge University Press).

Renfrew, Colin and Cherry, John F. (eds.) (1986), *Peer Polity Interaction and Socio-political Change* (Cambridge: Cambridge University Press).

Renger, J. and Hrouda, B. (1972–1975), "Ḫilāni, bīt. A. Nach Neuassyrischen Inschriftlichen Zeugnissen. B. Archäologischen," in D. O. Edzard (ed.), *Reallexikon der Assyriologie und Vorderasiatischen Archäologie 4* (Berlin: de Gruyter), 405–409.

Rieken, Elisabeth (2010), "Das Zeichen <sà> im Hieroglyphen-Luwischen," in Aygül Süel (ed.), *Acts of the VIIth International Congress of Hittitology, Çorum, August 25–31, 2008* (Ankara: T. C. Çorum Valiliği), 651–60.

Rieken, Elisabeth and Yakubovich, Ilya (2010), "The New Values of Luwian Signs L 319 and L 172," in Itamar Singer (ed.), *Luwian and Hittite Studies Presented to J. David Hawkins on the Occasion of His 70th Birthday* (Tel Aviv: Insitute of Archaeology, Tel Aviv University), 199–219.

Riis, P. J. (1948), *Hama, Fouilles et Recherches 1931–1938, Vol. II-3: Les Cimetières à Crémation* (Copenhagen: Fondation Carlsberg).

Riis, P. J. and Buhl, Marie-Louise (1990), *Hama: Fouilles et Recherches de la Fondation Carlsberg, 1931–1938, II/2: Les Objets de la Période dite Syro-Hittite (Âge du Fer)* (Copenhague: Nationalmuseets Skrifter).

Rimmer Herrmann, Virginia (2011), "Society and Economy under Empire at Iron Age Sam'al (Zincirli Höyük, Turkey)," Unpublished PhD dissertation, University of Chicago.

Ristvet, Lauren (2008), "Legal and Archaeological Territories of the Second Millennium BC in Northern Mesopotamia," *Antiquity*, 82, 585–99.

Rojas, Felipe and Sergueenkova, Valeria (2014), "Traces of Tarhuntas: Greek, Roman, and Byzantine Interaction with Hittite Monuments," *Journal of Mediterranean Archaeology*, 27 (2), 135–60.

Röllig, Wolfgang (1999), "Appendix I. The Phoenician Inscriptions," in Halet Çambel (ed.), *Corpus of Hieroglyphic Luwian Inscriptions vol. II: Karatepe-Arslantaş* (Berlin: Walter de Gruyter), 50–81.

Rosenzweig, Melissa S. (2016), "Cultivating Subjects in the Neo-Assyrian Empire," *Journal of Social Archaeology*, 16 (3), 307–34.

Rosenzweig, Melissa S. and Marston, John M. (2018), "Archaeologies of Empire and Environment," *Journal of Anthropological Archaeology* 52: 87–102.

Routledge, Bruce (2014), *Archaeology and State Theory: Subjects and Objects of Power* (New York: Bloomsbury).

Rutishauser, Susanne (2016), "Settlement System Cilicia. Reconstruction of the Historical Geography based on Remote Sensing, Archaeology and Texts," Unpublished PhD dissertation, University of Bern.

Rutishauser, Susanne (2017), "Siedlungskammer Kilikien," *Altorientalische Forschungen*, 44 (2), 121–49.

Sader, Hélène (1987), *Les états Araméens de Syrie depuis leur Foundation jusqu'à leur Transformation en Provinces Assyriennes* (Beirut: Franz Steiner Verlag).

Sader, Hélène (1992), "The 12th Century B.C. in Syria; The Problem of the Rise of the Aramaeans," in W. A. Ward and M. Joukowsky (eds.), *The Crisis Years: The Twelfth Century B.C. from Beyond the Danube to the Tigris* (Iowa: Kendall/Hunt), 157–64.

Sader, Hélène (2000), "The Aramaean Kingdoms of Syria: Origin and Formation Processes," in Guy Bunnens (ed.), *Essays on Syria in the Iron Age* (Louvain: Peeters), 61–76.

Sader, Hélène (2014), "History," in Herbert Niehr (ed.), *The Aramaeans in Ancient Syria* (Leiden: Brill), 11–36.

Safran, William (1991), "Diasporas in Modern Societies: Myths of Homeland and Return," *Diaspora*, 1 (1), 83–99.

Sagona, Antonia and Zimansky, Paul (2009), *Ancient Turkey* (Abingdon: Routledge).

Said, Edward (1993), *Culture and Imperialism* (New York: Vintage Books).

Salazar, Noel B. and Smart, Alan (2011), "Introduction: Anthropological Takes on (Im) Mobility," *Identities: Global Studies in Culture and Power*, 18, i–ix.

Saltz, Diane L. (1978), "Greek Geometric Pottery in the East: The Chronological Implications," unpublished PhD thesis (Harvard University).

Schachner, Andreas (2007), *Bilder Eines Weltreichs: Kunst- und kulturgeschichtliche Untersuchungen zu den Verzierungen eines Tores aus Balawat (Imgur-Enlil) aus der Zeit von Salmanassar III, König von Assyrien* (Turnhout: Brepols).

Schachner, Gregson (2010), *Population Circulation and the Transformation of Ancient Zuni Communities* (Tucson: University of Arizona Press).

Schacht, Robert (1987), "Early Historic Cultures," in Frank Hole (ed.), *The Archaeology of Western Iran* (Smithsonian Series in Archaeological Inquiry; Washington, DC: Smithsonian Institution Press), 171–203.

Schirmer, Wulf (1993), "Die Bauanlagen auf dem Göllüdağ in Kappadokien," *Architectura*, 23, 121–31.

Schirmer, Wulf (1999), "Eine richtige Bergstadt? Die Bauanlagen auf dem Göllüdağ und ihre historischen Zugangswege," in E. L. Schwandner and K. Rheidt (eds.), *Stadt und Umland: Neue Ergebnisse der archäologischen Bau- und Siedlungsforschung* (Mainze am Rhein: Verlag Philipp von Zabern), 129–42.

Schloen, J. David (2001), *The House of the Father as Fact and Symbol: Patrimonialism in Ugarit and the Ancient Near East* (Winona Lake, IL: Eisenbrauns)

Schloen, J. David (2014), "The City of Katumuwa: The Iron Age Kingdom of Sam'al and the Excavation of Zincirli," in Virginia Rimmer Herrmann and J. David Schloen (eds.), *In Remembrance of Me: Feasting with the Dead in the Ancient Middle East* (Oriental Institute Museum Publications; Chicago: The Oriental Institute of the University of Chicago), 27–38.

Schloen, J. David and Fink, Amir S. (2009a), "Searching for Ancient Sam'al: New Excavations at Zincirli in Turkey," *Near Eastern Archaeology*, 72 (4), 203–19.

Schloen, J. David and Fink, Amir S. (2009b), "New Excavations at Zincirli Höyük in Turkey (Ancient Sam'al) and the Discovery of an Inscribed Mortuary Stele," *Bulletin of the American Schools of Oriental Research*, 356, 1–13.

Schreiber, Nicola (2003), *The Cypro-Phoenician Pottery of the Iron Age* (Leiden: Brill).

Schwartz, Glenn M. (1989), "The Origins of the Aramaeans in Syria and Northern Mesopotamia: Research Problems and Potential Strategies," in O. M. C. Haex, H. H. Curvers, and P. M. M. G. Akkermans (eds.), *To the Euphrates and Beyond: Archaeological Studies in Honour of Maurits N. van Loon* (Rotterdam: A. A. Balkema), 275–91.

Schwemer, Daniel (2001), *Die Wettergottgestalten Mesopotamiens und Nordsyriens im Zeitalter der Keilschriftkulturen: Materialien und Studien nach den schriftlichen Quellen* (Wiesbaden: Harrassowitz).

Seeher, Jürgen (1993), "Körperbestattung und Kremation—ein Gegensatz?," *Istanbuler Mitteilungen*, 43, 219–26.

Seeher, Jürgen (2011), "The Plateau: The Hittites," in Sharon R. Steadman and Gregory McMahaon (eds.), *The Oxford Handbook of Ancient Anatolia* (Oxford: Oxford University Press), 376–92.

Service, E. R. (1962), *Primitive Social Organization* (New York: Random House).

Seton-Williams, M. V. (1954), "Cilician Survey," *Anatolian Studies*, 4, 121–54.

Seton-Williams, M. V. (1961), "Preliminary Report on the Excavations at Tell Rifa'at," *Iraq* (23), 68–87.

Seton-Williams, M. V. (1967), "The Excavations at Tell Rifa'at, 1964: Second Preliminary Report," *Iraq*, 29, 16–33.

Sewell, William H. Jr. (1997), "Geertz, Cultural Systems, and History: From Synchrony to Transformation," *Representations*, 58, 33–55.

Sewell, William H. Jr. (1999), "The Concept(s) of Culture," in Victoria E. Bonnell and Lynn Hunt (eds.), *Beyond the Cultural Turn: New Directions in the Study of Society and Culture* (Berkeley: University of California Press), 35–61.

Sewell, William H. Jr. (2005), *Logics of History: Society, Theory and Social Transformation* (Chicago: University of Chicago Press).

Sheller, Mimi (2017), "From Spatial Turn to Mobilities Turn," *Current Sociology*, 65 (4), 623–39.

Sheller, Mimi and Urry, John (2006), "The New Mobilities Paradigm," *Environment and Planning A*, 38, 207–26.

Shennan, Stephen (1989), "Introduction: Archaeological Approaches to Cultural Identity," in Stephen Shennan (ed.), *Archaeological Approaches to Cultural Identity* (London: Routledge), 1–32.

Sherratt, Susan (1998), "'Sea Peoples' and the Economic Structure of the Late Second Millennium in the Eastern Mediterranean," in S. Gitin, A. Mazar, and E. Stern (eds.), *Mediterranean Peoples in Transition: Thirteenth to Early Tenth Centuries BCE* (Jerusalem: Israel Exploration Society), 292–313.

Sicker-Akman, Martina (2014), "Die Bauwerke," in Halet Çambel (ed.), *Karatepe-Aslantaş Azatiwataya. Band 2* (Wiesbaden: Reichert Verlag), 13–109.

Simon, Zsolt (2012), "Where is the Land of Sura of the Hieroglyphic Luwian Inscriptions KARKAMIŠ A4b and Why Were Cappadocians Called Syrians by Greeks?," *Altorientalische Forschungen*, 39 (1), 167–80.

Simon, Zsolt (2014), "Awarikus und Warikas: Zwei Könige von Hiyawa," *Zeitschrift für Assyriologie*, 104 (1), 91–103.

Simon, Zsolt (2017), "Der luwische Name *Awarikus*," *Beiträge zur Namenforschung*, 52 (2), 115–22.

Simon, Zsolt (2018a), "Die Griechen und das Phönizische im späthethitischen Staat Hiyawa," in Peter-Arnold Mumm (ed.), *Sprachen, Völker und Phantome: Sprach- und kulturwissenschaftliche Studien zur Ethnizität* (Berlin: de Gruyter), 313–38.

Simon, Zsolt (2018b), "Sapaziti, Sapalulme und die Suppiluliumas von W/Pal(a)stin(a/i)," *Altorientalische Forschungen*, 45 (1), 122–32.

Singer, Itamar (1975), "Hittite *ḫilammar* and Hierglyphic Luwian *\*ḫilana*," *Zeitschrift für Assyriologie und Vorderasiatische Archäologie*, 65, 69–103.

Singer, Itamar (1996), "Great Kings of Tarḫuntašša," *Studi Micenei ed Egeo-Anatolici*, 38, 63–71.

Singer, Itamar (2005), "On Luwians and Hittites (review of Melchert 2003)," *Bibliotheca Orientalis*, 62 (5–6), 430–52.

Singer, Itamar (2009), "'In Hattuša the Royal House Declined': Royal Mortuary Cult in 13th Century Hatti," in Franca Pecchilio Daddi, Giulia Torri, and Carlo Corti (eds.), *Central-North Anatolia in the Hittite Period: New Perspectives in Light of Recent Research* (Roma: Herder), 169–91.

Singer, Itamar (2012), "The Philistines in the North and the Kingdom of Taita," in Gershon Galil et al. (eds.), *The Ancient Near East in the 12th–10th Centuries BCE: Culture and History. Proceedings of the International Conference Held at the University of Haifa, 2–5 May, 2010* (Alter Orient und Altes Testament; Münster: Ugarit-Verlag), 451–71.

Sinopoli, Carla M. (1994), "The Archaeology of Empires," *Annual Review of Anthropology*, 23, 159–80.

Slatkin, Montgomery and Racimo, Fernando (2016), "Ancient DNA and Human History," *Proceedings of the National Academy of Sciences*, 113 (23), 6380–87.

Smith, Adam T. (2003), *The Political Landscape: Constellations of Authority in Early Complex Polities* (Berkeley: University of California Press).

Smith, Adam T. (2011), "Archaeologies of Sovereignty," *Annual Review of Anthropology*, 40, 415–32.

Smith, Anthony D. (1987), *The Ethnic Origins of Nations* (Oxford: Blackwell).

Smith, Anthony D. (1995), *Nations and Nationalism in a Global Era* (Cambridge, MA: Polity Press).

Smith, Michael E. (2007), "Form and Meaning in the Earliest Cities: A New Approach to Ancient Urban Planning," *Journal of Planning History*, 6 (1), 3–47.

Smith, Michael E. (2008), *Aztec City-State Capitals* (Gainesville: University Press of Florida).

Smith, Monica L. (2005), "Networks, Territories, and the Cartography of Ancient States," *Annals of the Assocation of American Geographers*, 95, 832–49.

Smith, Monica L. (2007), "Territories, Corridors, and Networks: A Biological Model for the Premodern State," *Complexity*, 12 (4), 28–35.

Soja, Edward W. (1989), *Postmodern Geographies: The Reassertion of Space in Critical Social Theory* (London: Verso).

Spaulding, Albert C. (1953), "Statistical Techniques for the Discovery of Artifact Types," *American Antiquity*, 18 (4), 305–13.

Specht, Jim, Denham, Tim, Goff, James, and Terrell, John Edward (2014), "Deconstructing the Lapita Cultural Complex in the Bismarck Archipelago," *Journal of Archaeological Research*, 22 (2), 89–140.

Stager, Lawrence E. (1995), "The Impact of the Sea Peoples in Canaan (1185–1050 BCE)," in T. E. Levy (ed.), *The Archaeology of Society in the Holy Land* (London: Leicester University Press).

Stager, Lawrence E. (1998), "Forging an Identity: The Emergence of Ancient Israel," in Michael D. Coogan (ed.), *The Oxford History of the Biblical World* (Oxford: Oxford University Press), 90–131.

Stein, Gil J. (1999), *Rethinking World-Systems: Diasporas, Colonies, and Interaction in Uruk Mesopotamia* (Tucson: University of Arizona Press).

Stein, Gil J. (2008), "A Theoretical Model for Political Economy and Social Identity in the Old Assyrian Colonies of Anatolia," *TÜBA-AR*, 11, 25–37.

Stockhammer, Philipp W. (2013), "From Hybridity to Entanglement, From Essentialism to Practice," *Archaeological Review from Cambridge*, 28 (1), 11–28.

Stoler, Ann Laura and McGranahan, Carole (2007), "Introduction: Refiguring Imperial Terrains," in Ann Laura Stoler, Carole McGranahan, and Peter C. Perdue (eds.), *Imerial Formations* (Santa Fe, NM: School for Advanced Research Press), 3–42.

Stone, E. C. and Zimansky, P. E. (1999), *The Iron Age Settlement at 'Ain Dara, Syria* (Oxford: British Archaeological Reports).

Stone, Elizabeth (1997), "City-States and Their Centers: The Mesopotamian Example," in Deborah L. Nichols and Thomas H. Charlton (eds.), *The Archaeology of City-States: Cross-Cultural Approaches* (Washington, DC: Smithsonian Institution Press), 15–26.

Struble, Eudora J. and Herrmann, Virginia Rimmer (2009), "An Eternal Feast at Sam'al: The New Iron Age Mortuary Stele from Zincirli in Context," *Bulletin of the American Schools of Oriental Research*, 356, 15–49.

Summers, Geoffrey (2017), "After the Collapse, Continuities and Discontinuities in the Early Iron Age of Central Anatolia," in Andreas Schachner (ed.), *Innovation versus*

*Beharrung: Was macht den Unterschied des Hethitischen Reichs im Anatolien des 2. Jahrtausends v. Chr.?* (Istanbul: Deutschen Archäologischen Instituts Istanbul), 257–74.

Sürenhagen, Dietrich (1986), "Ein Königssiegel aus Kargamis," *Mitteilungen der Deutschen Orient-Gesellschaft*, 118, 183–90.

Sürenhagen, Dietrich (2008), "Hartapus—Ein Sohn Mursili II.?," *Studi Micenei ed Egeo-Anatolici*, 50.

Suriano, Matthew J. (2014), "Historical Geography of the Ancient Levant," in Margaret L. Steiner and Ann E. Killebrew (eds.), *The Oxford Handbook of the Archaeology of the Levant c. 8000–332 BCE* (Oxford: Oxford University Press), 9–23.

Suter, Claudia E. (2010), "Luxury Goods in Ancient Israel: Questions of Consumption and Production," in Paolo Matthiae et al. (eds.), *Proceedings of the 6th International Congress of the Archaeology of the Ancient Near East, 5 May–10 May 2009, "Sapienza," Universita di Roma: Volume 1* (Wiesbaden: Harrassowitz), 993–1002.

Suter, Claudia E. (2015), "Classifying Iron Age Levantine Ivories: Impracticalities and a New Approach," *Altorientalische Forschungen*, 42 (1), 31–45.

Swartz Dodd, Lynn (2012), "Squeezing Blood from a Stone: The Archaeological Context of the Incirli Inscription," in Marilyn J. Lundberg, Steven Fine, and Wayne T. Pitard (eds.), *Puzzling Out the Past: Studies in Northwest Semitic Languages and Literatures in Honor of Bruce Zuckerman* (Leiden, Boston: Brill), 213–33.

Swift, Gustavus (1958), "The Pottery of the 'Amuq Phases K to O and Its Historical Relationships," unpublished PhD thesis (University of Chicago).

Szuchman, Jeffrey Justin (2007), "Prelude to Empire: Middle Assyrian Hanigalbat and the Rise of the Aramaeans," unpublished PhD thesis (University of California, Los Angeles).

Tadmor, Hayim (1982), "The Aramaization of Assyria: Aspects of Western Impact," in H.-J. Nissen and J. Renger (eds.), *Mesopotamien und seine Nachbarn. 25. Rencontre Assyriologique Internationale* (Berlin: Dietrich Reimer Verlag), 449–70.

Tadmor, Hayim and Yamada, Shigeo (2011), *The Royal Inscriptions of Tiglath-pileser III (744–727 BC) and Shalmaneser V (726–722 BC), Kings of Assyria* (The Royal Inscriptions of the Neo-Assyrian Period, 1; Winona Lake, IN: Eisenbrauns).

Tamur, Erhan (2017), "Style, Ethnicity and the Archaeology of the Aramaeans: The Problem of Ethnic Markers in the Art of the Syro-Anatolian Region in the Iron Age," *Forum Kritische Archäologie*, 6, 1–72.

Taylor, J. du Plat, Williams, M. V. Seton, and Waechter, J. (1950), "The Excavations at Sakce Gözü," *Iraq*, 12 (2), 53–138.

Tekoğlu, Recai, et al. (2000), "La Bilingue Royale Louvito-Phénicienne de Çineköy," *Comptes Rendus de l'Académie des Inscriptions et Belles-Lettres*, 2000 (3), 961–1006.

Tenu, Aline (2009), "Assyrians and Aramaeans in the Euphrates Valley Viewed from the Cemetery of Tell Shiukh Fawqani (Syria)," *Syria*, 86, 83–96.

Thareani, Yifat (2016), "Imperializing the Province: A Residence of a Neo-Assyrian City Governor at Tel Dan," *Levant*, 48 (3), 254–83.

Thuesen, Ingolf (2002), "The Neo-Hittite City-State," in Mogens Herman Hansen (ed.), *A Comparative Study of Six City-State Cultures: An Investigation Conducted by the*

Copenhagen Polis Centre (Copenhagen: The Royal Danish Academy of Sciences and Letters), 43–55.

Thureau-Dangin, F. and Dunand, M. (1936), *Til-Barsib* (Paris: Librairie Orientaliste Paul Geuther).

Thureau-Dangin, François, et al. (1931), *Arslan-Tash* (Paris: P. Geuthner).

Tölölyan, Khachig (2007), "The Contemporary Discourse of Diaspora Studies," *Comparative Studies of South Asia, Africa and the Middle East*, 27 (3), 647–55.

Trigger, Bruce (1968), *Beyond History: The Methods of Prehistory* (New York: Holt, Rinehart and Winston).

Trigger, Bruce (2003), *Understanding Early Civilizations: A Comparative Study* (Cambridge: Cambridge University Press).

Tropper, J. (1993), *Inschriften von Zincirli: Neue Edition und Vergleichende Grammatik des Phönizischen, Sam'alischen und Aramäischen Textkorpus* (Abhandlungen zur Literatur Alt-Syrien-Palästinas; Münster: Ugarit-Verlag).

Tuan, Yi-Fu (1974), *Topophilia: A Study of Environmental Perception, Attitudes, and Values* (Englewood Cliffs, NJ: Prentice-Hall).

Tuan, Yi-Fu (1977), *Space and Place: The Perspective of Experience* (Minneapolis: University of Minnesota Press).

Turner, Geoffrey (1970), "The State Apartments of Late Assyrian Palaces," *Iraq*, 32 (2), 177–213.

Tylor, Edward Burnett (1881), *Anthropology: An Introduction to the Study of Man and Civilization* (London: Macmillan).

Ur, Jason (2003), "CORONA Satellite Photography and Ancient Road Networks: A Northern Mesopotamian Case Study," *Antiquity*, 77, 102–15.

Urry, John (2007), *Mobilities* (Cambridge, UK; Malden, MA: Polity Press).

Ussishkin, David (1969), "The Date of the Neo-Hittite Enclosure in Karatepe," *Anatolian Studies*, 19, 121–37.

Ussishkin, David (1970), "The Syro-Hittite Ritual Burial of Monuments," *Journal of Near Eastern Studies*, 29, 124–28.

Ussishkin, David (1971), "Was Bit-Adini a Neo-Hittite or Aramaean State?," *Orientalia*, 40, 431–37.

Ussishkin, David (1989), "The Erection of Royal Monuments in City-Gates," in K. Emre et al. (eds.), *Anatolia and the Ancient Near East: Studies in Honor of Tahsin Özgüç* (Ankara: Türk Tarih Kurumu Basımevi), 485–96.

van den Hout, Theo P. J. (1994), "Death as a Privilege: The Hittite Royal Funerary Ritual," in J. M. Bremmer and Th. P. J. van den Hout (eds.), *Hidden Futures: Death and Immortality in Ancient Egypt, Anatolia, the Classical, Biblical and Arabic-Islamic World* (Amsterdam: Amsterdam University Press), 37–75.

Van Dyke, Ruth M. and Alcock, Susan E. (eds.) (2003), *Archaeologies of Memory* (Malden, MA: Blackwell).

VanValkenburgh, Nathaniel P. and Osborne, James F. (2013), "Home Turf: Archaeology, Territoriality, and Politics," in James F. Osborne and Nathaniel P. VanValkenburgh (eds.), *Territoriality in Archaeology* (Archeological Papers of the American Anthropological Association; Arlington, VA: American Anthropological Association), 1–27.

VanValkenburgh, Parker (2013), "Hybridity, Creolization, Mestizaje: A Comment," *Archaeological Review from Cambridge*, 28 (1), 301–22.

Van Zeist, W. and Bottema, S. (1991), *Late Quaternary Vegetation of the Near East* (TübingerAtlas des Vorderen Orients A 18; Wiesbaden: L. Reichert).

Venturi, Fabrizio (2000), "Le premier âge du Fer a Tell Afis et en Syrie septentrionale," in Guy Bunnens (ed.), *Essays on Syria in the Iron Age* (Louvian: Peeters Press), 505–57.

Venturi, Fabrizio (2007), *La Siria nell'età delle trasformazioni (13–10 sec. a. C.): Nuovi contributi dallo scavo di Tell Afis* (Studi e Testi Orientali; Bologna: Clueb).

von Dassow, Eva (2012), "Temporality and Periodization in Ancient Near Eastern History," *Social Science History*, 37 (1), 113–43.

von Luschan, F. (1893), *Ausgrabungen in Sendschirli, Bd. I: Einleitung und Inschriften, Mittelingen aus den Orientalischen Sammlungen der Königlichen Museen zu Berlin 11* (Berlin: G. Reimer).

von Luschan, F. (1902), *Ausgrabungen in Sendschirli, Bd. III: Die Thorsculpturen* (Mittelingen aus den Orientalischen Sammlungen der Königlichen Museen zu Berlin Berlin: G. Reimer).

von Luschan, F. and Jacoby, Gustav (1911), *Ausgrabungen in Sendschirli, Bd. IV* (Mittelingen aus den Orientalischen Sammlungen der Königlichen Museen zu Berlin; Berlin: G. Reimer).

von Luschan, F. and Andrae, W. (1943), *Ausgrabungen in Sendschirli, Bd. V: Die Kleinfunde von Sendschirli* (Mittelingen aus den Orientalischen Sammlungen der Königlichen Museen zu Berlin; Berlin: de Gruyter).

von Luschan, F., Humann, Carl, and Koldewey, Robert (1898), *Ausgrabungen in Sendschirli, Bd. II: Ausgrabungsbericht und Architectur* (Mittelingen aus den Orientalischen Sammlungen der Königlichen Museen zu Berlin; Berlin: Spemann).

Wada, Hisahiko (1994), "Pottery Vessels in the Iron Age II in the Southern Area of Tell Mastuma in 1993 Season," *Bulletin of the Ancient Orient Museum*, XV, 51–76.

Wakita, Shigeo, Wada, Hisahiko, and Nishiyama, Shin'ichi (2000), "Tell Mastuma: Change in Settlement Plans and Historical Context during the First Quarter of the First Millennium B.C.," in Guy Bunnens (ed.), *Essays on Syria in the Iron Age* (Ancient Near Eastern Studies Supplement; Louvain: Peeters Press), 537–57.

Wakita, Shigeo, et al. (1995), "Tell Mastuma: A Preliminary Report of the Excavations at Idlib, Syria, in 1994 and 1995," *Bulletin of the Ancient Orient Museum*, XVI, 1–73.

Ward, William A. and Joukowsky, Martha Sharp (eds.) (1992), *The Crisis Years: The 12th Century B.C.: From Beyond the Danube to the Tigris* (Dubuque, IA: Kendall/Hunt).

Warf, Barney and Arias, Santa (eds.) (2009), *The Spatial Turn: Interdisciplinary Perspectives* (London: Routledge).

Waring, Antonio J. and Holder, Preston (1945), "A Prehistoric Ceremonial Complex in the Southeastern United States," *American Anthropologist*, 47, 1–34.

Weber, Martin (2017), "Two (?) Lion Reliefs from Iron Age Moab: Further Evidence for an Architectural and Intellectual *Koiné* in the Levant?," *Bulletin of the American Schools of Oriental Research*, 377, 85–106.

Weber, Max (1965), *Politics as a Vocation*, trans. H.H. Gerth and C. Wright Mills (Philadelphia: Fortress Press).

Weeden, Mark (2010), "Tuwati and Wasusarma: Imitating the Behaviour of Assyria," *Iraq*, 72, 39–61.

Weeden, Mark (2013), "After the Hittites: The Kingdoms of Karkamish and Palistin in Northern Syria," *Bulletin of the Institute of Classical Studies*, 56 (2), 1–20.

Welton, Lynn, Batiuk, Stephen, and Harrison, Timothy P. (2011), "Tell Tayinat in the Late Third Millennium. Recent Investigations of the Tayinat Archaeological Project, 2008–2010," *Anatolica*, 37, 147–85.

Welton, Lynn, et al. (2019), "Shifting Networks and Community Identity at Tell Tayinat in the Iron I (ca. 12th to Mid 10th Century B.C.E.)," *American Journal of Archaeology*, 123 (2), 291–333.

Wheatley, Paul (1971), *The Pivot of the Four Quarters: A Preliminary Enquiry Into the Origins and Character of the Ancient Chinese City* (Chicago: Aldine).

White, Richard (1991), *The Middle Ground: Indians, Empires, and Republics in the Great Lakes Region, 1650–1815* (New York: Cambridge University Press).

White, Richard (2006), "Creative Misunderstandings and New Understandings," *The William and Mary Quarterly*, 63 (1), 9–14.

Wicke, Dirk (2005), "'Roundcheeked and Ringletted': gibt es einen nordwestsyrischen Regionalstil in der altorientalischen Elfenbeinschnitzerei?," in Claudia E. Suter and Christoph Uehlinger (eds.), *Crafts and Images in Contact: Studies on Eastern Mediterranean Art of the First Millennium BCE* (Friburg: Academic Press and Vandenhoeck & Ruprecht), 23–42.

Wicke, Dirk (2008), *Vorderasiatische Pyxiden der Spätbronzezeit under der Früheisenzeit* (Alter Orient und Altes Testament; Münster: Ugarit-Verlag).

Wicke, Dirk (2009), "'Intermediate Tradition'—dreifach Problematisch," in Serena Maria Checchini, Stefania Mazzoni, and Elena Scigliuzzo (eds.), *Syrian and Phoenician Ivories of the Early First Millennium BCE: Chronology, Regional Styles and Iconographic Repertories, Patterns or Inter-regional Distribution* (Pisa: Edizioni ETS), 239–84.

Wicke, Dirk (2015), "Assyrian or Assyrianized: Reflections on the Impact of Assyrian Art in Southern Anatolia," in Robert Rollinger and Erik van Dongen (eds.), *Mesopotamia in the Ancient World: Impact, Continuities, Parallels. Proceedings of the Seventh Symposium of the Melammu Project Held in Obergurgl, Austria, November 4–8, 2013* (Münster: Ugarit-Verlag), 561–601.

Wicke, Dirk (2016), "Connecting Seals—Seals Connecting: the 'FSV' Group of iron Age Knobbed Stamp-Seals," in John MacGinnis, Dirk Wicke, and Tina Greenfield (eds.), *The Provincial Archaeology of the Assyrian Empire* (Cambridge: McDonald Institute for Archaeological Research), 85–93.

Wilkinson, Tony J. (1994), "The Structure and Dynamics of Dry-Farming States in Upper Mesopotamia," *Current Anthropology*, 35 (5), 483–520.

Wilkinson, Tony J. (2003), *Archaeological Landscapes of the Near East* (Tuscon: University of Arizona Press).

Wilkinson, Tony J. (2016), "The Landscapes of Carchemish," in Tony J. Wilkinson, Edgar Peltenburg, and Eleanor Barbanes Wilkinson (eds.), *Carchemish in Context: The Land of Carchemish Project, 2006–2010* (Oxford: Oxbow Books), 68–105.

Wilkinson, Tony J. and Barbanes, Eleanor (2000), "Settlement Patterns in the Syrian Jazira During the Iron Age," in Guy Bunnens (ed.), *Essays on Syria in the Iron Age* (Louvain: Peeters Press), 397–422.

Wimmer, Andreas and Schiller, Nina Glick (2002), "Methodological Nationalism and Beyond: Nation-State Building, Migration, and the Social Sciences," *Global Networks*, 2, 301–34.

Winter, Irene J. (1973), "North Syria in the Early First Millennium B.C., with Special Reference to Ivory Carving," unpublished PhD dissertation (Columbia University).

Winter, Irene J. (1976a), "Phoenician and North Syrian Ivory Carving in Historical Context: Questions of Style and Distribution," *Iraq*, 38 (1), 1–22.

Winter, Irene J. (1976b), "Carved Ivory Furniture Panels from Nimrud: A Coherent Subgroup of the North Syrian Style," *Metropolitan Museum Journal*, 11, 25–54.

Winter, Irene J. (1979), "On the Problems of Karatepe: The Reliefs and Their Context," *Anatolian Studies*, 29, 115–51.

Winter, Irene J. (1981), "Is There a South Syrian Style of Ivory Carving in the Early First Millennium B.C.?," *Iraq*, 43 (2), 101–30.

Winter, Irene J. (1982), "Art as Evidence for Interaction: Relations between the Assyrian Empire and North Syria," in H. J. Nissen and J. Renger (eds.), *Mesopotamien und seine Nachbarn* (Berlin: Rheimer), 355–82.

Winter, Irene J. (1983), "Carchemish ša kišad puratti," *Anatolian Studies*, 33, 177–97.

Winter, Irene J. (1988), "North Syria as a Bronzeworking Centre in the Early First Millennium B.C.: Luxury Commodities at Home and Abroad," in J. E. Curtis (ed.), *Bronze-Working Centres of Western Asia c. 1000–539 B.C.* (London: Kegan Paul International in association with the British Museum), 193–225.

Winter, Irene J. (1989), "North Syrian Ivories and Tell Halaf Reliefs: The Impact of Luxory Goods upon 'Major' Arts," in A. Leonard Jr. and B. B. Williams (eds.), *Essays in Ancient Civilization Presented to Helene J. Kantor* (Chicago: University of Chicago Press), 321–37.

Winter, Irene J. (2005), "Establishing Group Boundaries: Toward Methodological Refinement in the Determination of Sets as a Prior Condition to the Analysis of Cultural Contact and/or Innovation in First Millennium BCE Ivory Carving," in Claudia E. Suter and Christoph Uehlinger (eds.), *Crafts and Images in Contact: Studies on Eastern Mediterranean Art of the First Millennium BCE* (Fribuourg: Academic Press), 23–42.

Wiseman, D. J. (1958), "The Vassal-Treaties of Esarhaddon," *Iraq*, 20 (1), i–ii, 1–99.

Wolf, Eric R. (1982), *Europe and the People without History* (Berkeley: University of California Press).

Woolley, C. Leonard (1921), *Carchemish II. The Town Defenses* (London: Printed by Order of the Trustees of the British Museum).

Woolley, C. Leonard (1938a), "Excavations at al Mina, Sueidia. I. The Archaeological Report," *The Journal of Hellenic Studies*, 58 (1), 1–30.

Woolley, C. Leonard (1938b), "Excavations at al Mina, Sueidia. II," *The Journal of Hellenic Studies*, 58 (2), 133–70.

Woolley, C. Leonard (1939–1940), "The Iron-Age Graves of Carchemish," *Liverpool Annals of Archaeology and Anthropology*, 26, 11–37.

Woolley, C. Leonard (1952), *Carchemish III: The Excavations in the Inner Town* (London: Printed by order of the Trustees of the British Museum).

Woolley, C. Leonard (1955), *Alalakh. An Account of the Excavations at Tell Atchana in the Hatay, 1937–1949* (Oxford: Society of Antiquaries).

Woudhuizen, Frederik C. (2007), "Great King Wasusarma's Victory Memorial at Topada," *Ancient West & East*, 6, 23–41.

Yakubovich, Ilya (2010), *Sociolinguistics of the Luvian Language* (Leiden: Brill).

Yakubovich, Ilya (2011), "Luwian and the Luwians," in Sharon Steadman and Gregory McMahon (eds.), *The Oxford Handbook of Ancient Anatolia 10,000–323 B.C.E.* (Oxford: Oxford University Press), 534–47.

Yakubovich, Ilya (2015), "Phoenician and Luwian in Early Iron Age Cilicia," *Anatolian Studies*, 65, 35–53.

Yasur-Landau, Assaf (2010), *The Philistines and Aegean Migration at the End of the Late Bronze Age* (New York: Cambridge University Press).

Yener, Aslıhan (ed.) (2013), *Across the Border: Late Bronze-Iron Age Relations between Syria and Anatolia: Proceedings of a Symposium Held at the Research Center of Anatolian Studies, Koç University, Istanbul, May 31–June 1, 2010* (Ancient Near Eastern Studies Supplement, Leuven: Peeters).

Yener, K. Aslıhan, Dinçol, Belkis, and Peker, Hasan (2014), "Prince Tuthaliya and Princess Ašnuhepa," *N.A.B.U.*, 4, 136–38.

Yener, Kutlu Aslıhan, et al. (2000), "The Amuq Valley Regional Project, 1995–1998," *American Journal of Archaeology*, 104 (2), 163–220.

Yener, Kutlu Aslıhan (ed.) (2005), *The Amuq Valley Regional Projects Volume 1: Surveys in the Plain of Antioch and Orontes Delta, Turkey, 1995–2002* (Chicago: Oriental Institute of the University of Chicago).

Yoffee, Norman (2005), *Myths of the Archaic State: Evolution of the Earliest Cities, States, and Civilizations* (Cambridge: Cambridge University Press).

Young, Ian (2002), "The Languages of Ancient Sam'al," *Maarav*, 9, 93–105.

Younger, K. Lawson (2000a), "The Hadad Inscription," in William W. Hallo and K. Lawson Younger Jr. (eds.), *The Context of Scripture, Volume II: Monumental Inscriptions from the Biblical World* (Leiden: Brill), 156–58.

Younger, K. Lawson (2000b), "Antakya Stela," in William W. Hallo and K. Lawson Younger Jr. (eds.), *The Context of Scripture, Volume II: Monumental Inscriptions from the Biblical World* (Leiden: Brill), 272.

Younger, K. Lawson (2000c), "The Kulamuwa Inscription," in William W. Hallo and K. Lawson Younger Jr. (eds.), *The Context of Scripture, Volume II: Monumental Inscriptions from the Biblical World* (Leiden: Brill), 147–48.

Younger, K. Lawson (2016), *A Political History of the Arameans: From Their Origins to the End of their Polities* (Atlanta, GA: SBL Press).

Yukich, Sarah T. K. (2013), "Spatial Dimensions of Social Complexity: Environment, Economy, and Settlement in the Jabbul Plain, 3000–550 BC," Unpublished PhD dissertation, Johns Hopkins University.

Zadok, Ran (1996), "Geographical and Onomastic Remarks," *Nouvelles Assyriologiques Brèves et Utilitaires*, 1, 11–13.

# INDEX

*For the benefit of digital users, indexed terms that span two pages (e.g., 52–53) may, on occasion, appear on only one of those pages.*

*Note: words in all caps are the names of Hieroglyphic Luwian inscriptions as per Hawkins 2000.*